STOP!

This is the back of the book.
You wouldn't want to spoil a great ending!

This book is printed "manga-style," in the authentic Japanese right-to-left format. Since none of the artwork has been flipped or altered, readers get to experience the story just as the creator intended. You've been asking for it, so TOKYOPOP® delivered: authentic, hot-off-the-press, and far more fun!

...IT'S A MOCKERY OF LOVE. MOM AND DAD ARE BOTH HAVING AFFAIRS, BUT THEY REFUSE TO GET DIVORCED.
MOM THINKS ABOUT HER FINANCES, AND DAD'S JUST CONCERNED WITH APPEARANCES.
WHAT ABOUT ME?!
DON'T THEY UNDERSTAND HOW DAMAGING IT IS TO WATCH YOUR PARENTS IN SUCH A HOLLOW, SPITEFUL MARRIAGE?
I'M...
I'M NEVER GETTING MARRIED.
MEIKO...
IS THAT WHY YOU NEVER GO OUT ON DATES?
Even though you're popular.
GLEAM
OH, NO! DON'T GET ME WRONG. I JUST HAVEN'T MET ANYONE WHO'S MY TYPE.
I STILL LIKE BOYS. I JUST DON'T WANT TO MARRY THEM.
UH-OH. I'VE GOTTA GO.
WHAT'S GOING ON?
MY FAMILY'S HAVING DINNER WITH THE MATSUURAS.
I HAVE TO TALK THE FOUR OF THEM OUT OF THIS NONSENSE, NO MATTER WHAT!

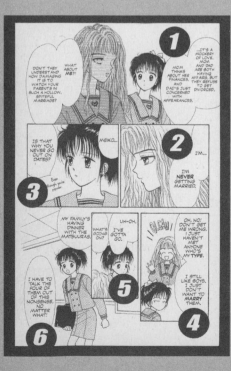

DIRECTIONS:

If this is your first time reading manga-style, here's a quick guide to help you understand how it works.

It's easy...just start in the top right panel and follow the numbers. Have fun, and look for more 100% authentic manga from TOKYOPOP®!

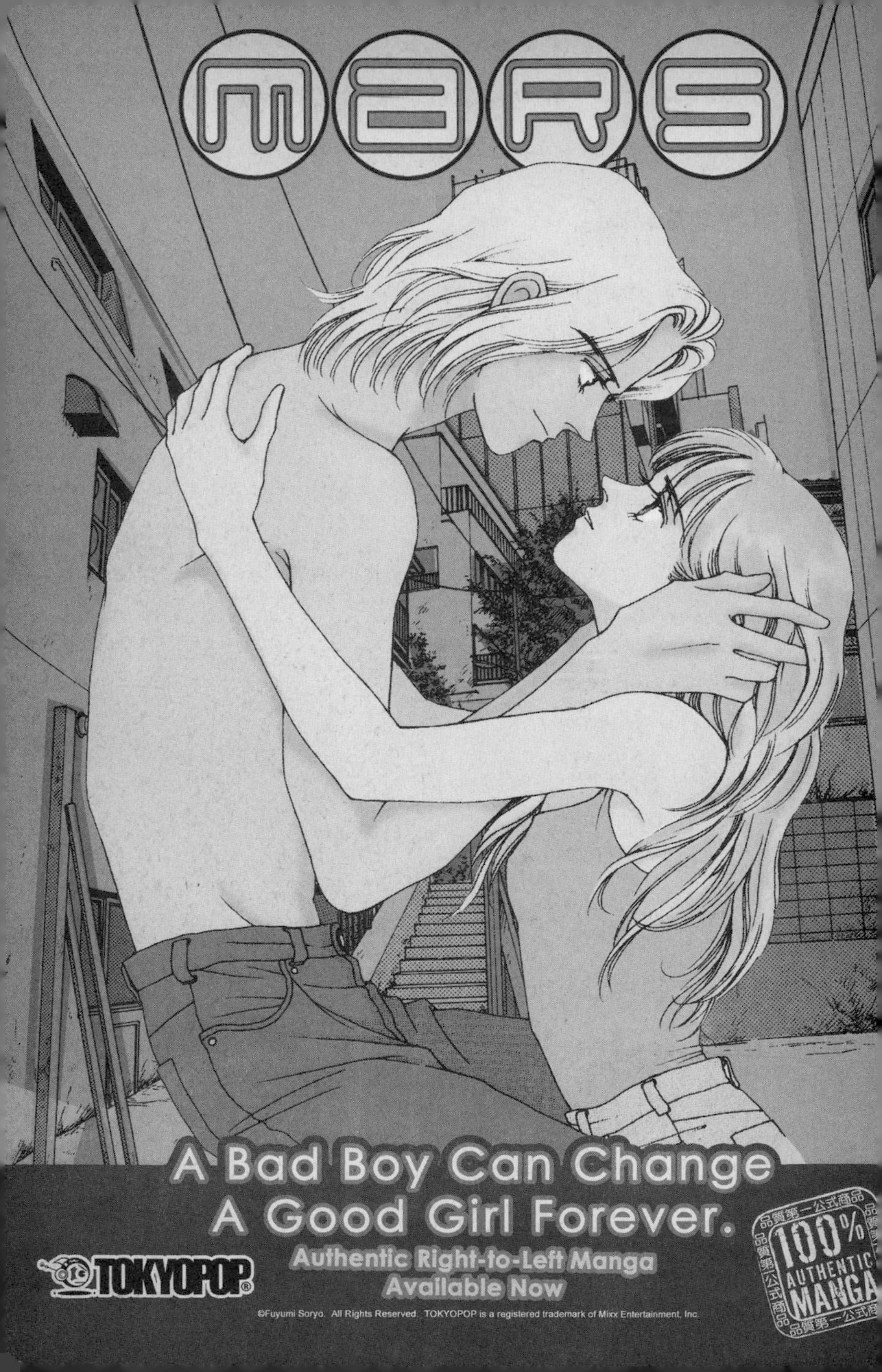
MARS
A Bad Boy Can Change
A Good Girl Forever.
TOKYOPOP®
Authentic Right-to-Left Manga
Available Now
©Fuyumi Soryo. All Rights Reserved. TOKYOPOP is a registered trademark of Mixx Entertainment, Inc.
100% AUTHENTIC MANGA
品質第一公式商品

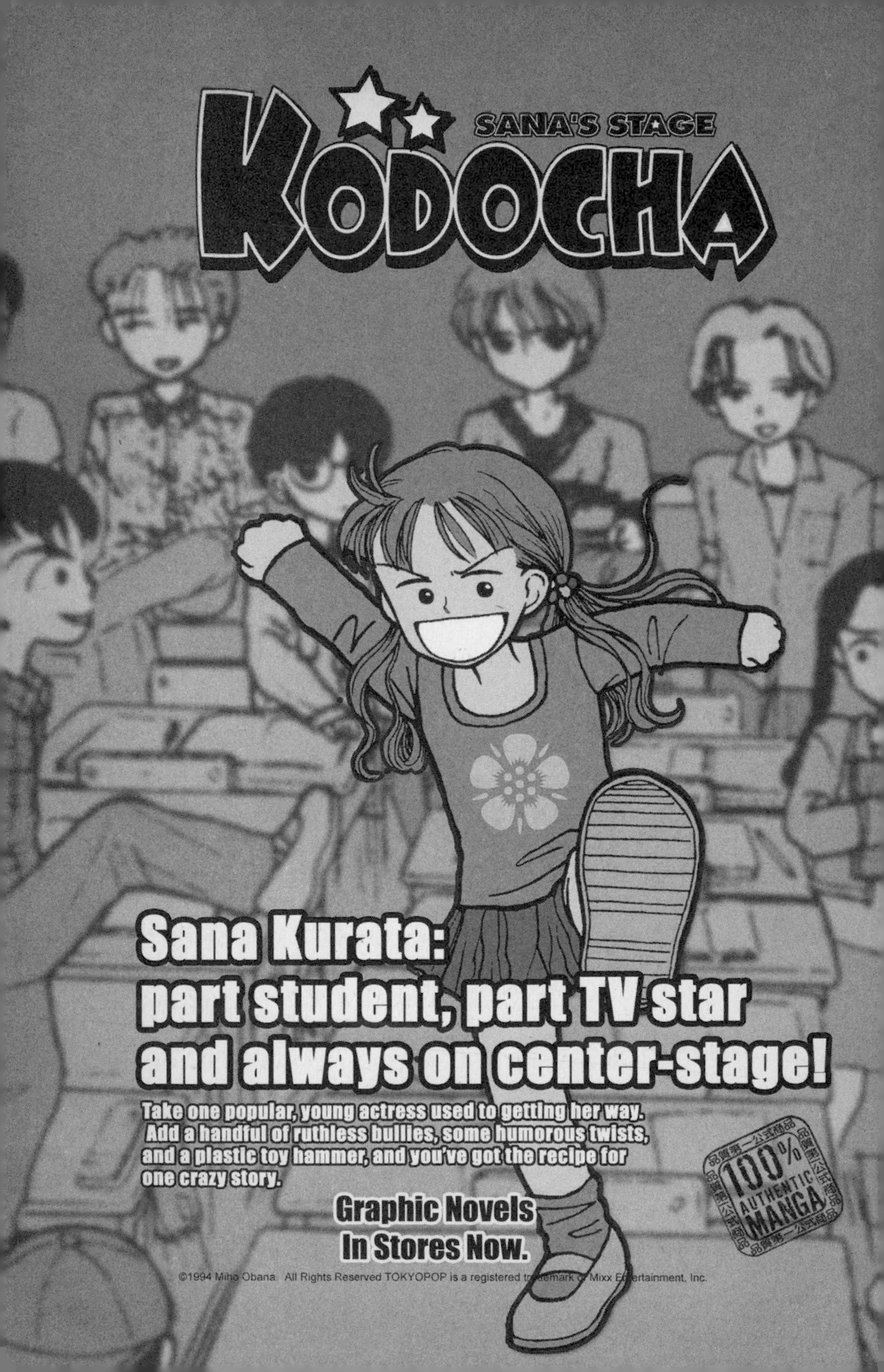
KODOCHA
SANA'S STAGE
Sana Kurata:
part student, part TV star
and always on center-stage!
Take one popular, young actress used to getting her way.
Add a handful of ruthless bullies, some humorous twists,
and a plastic toy hammer, and you've got the recipe for
one crazy story.
Graphic Novels
In Stores Now.
100% AUTHENTIC MANGA
©1994 Miho Obana. All Rights Reserved TOKYOPOP is a registered trademark of Mixx Entertainment, Inc.

Marmalade Boy

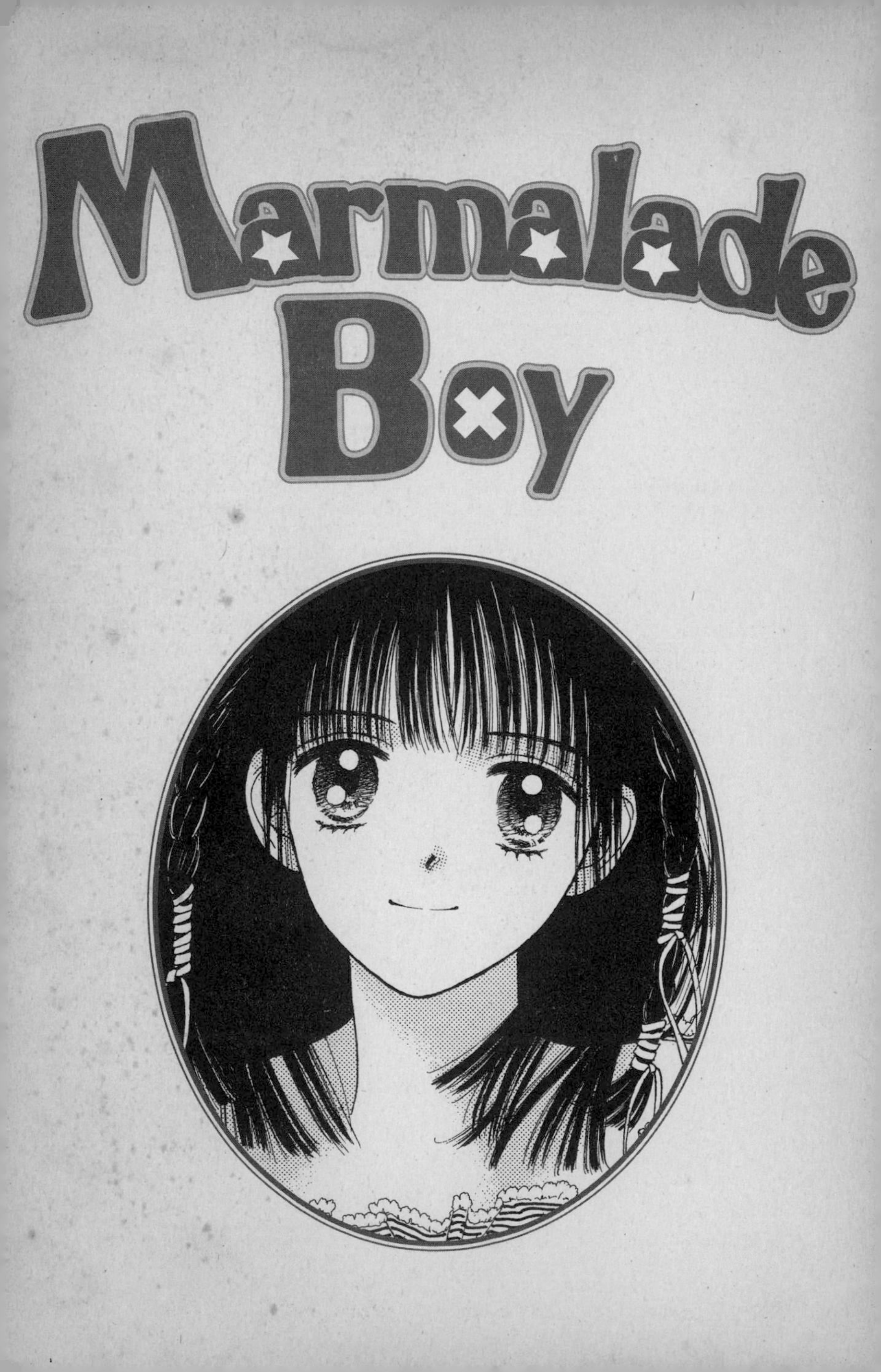

Other 100% Authentic Manga Available from TOKYOPOP®:

COWBOY BEBOP
All-new adventures of interstellar bounty hunting, based on the hit anime seen on Cartoon Network.

MARMALADE BOY
A tangled teen romance for the new millennium.

REAL BOUT HIGH SCHOOL
At Daimon High, teachers don't break up fights...they grade them.

MARS
Biker Rei and artist Kira are as different as night and day, but fate binds them in this angst-filled romance.

GTO
Biker gang member Onizuka is going back to school...as a teacher!

CHOBITS
In the future, boys will be boys and girls will be...robots? The newest hit series from CLAMP!

SKULL MAN
They took his family. They took his face. They took his soul. Now, he's going to take his revenge.

DRAGON KNIGHTS
Part dragon, part knight, ALL glam. The most inept knights on the block are out to kick some demon butt.

INITIAL D
Delivery boy Tak has a gift for driving, but can he compete in the high-stakes world of street racing?

PARADISE KISS
High fashion and deep passion collide in this hot new shojo series!

KODOCHA: Sana's Stage
There's a rumble in the jungle gym when child star Sana Kurata and bully Akito Hayama collide.

ANGELIC LAYER
In the future, the most popular game is Angelic Layer, where hand-raised robots battle for supremacy.

LOVE HINA
Can Keitaro handle living in a dorm with five cute girls...and still make it through school?

Also Available from TOKYOPOP®:

PRIEST
The quick and the undead in one macabre manga.

RAGNAROK
In the final battle between gods and men, only a small band of heroes stand in the way of total annihilation.

Marmalade Boy

Vol. 4

By

Wataru Yoshizumi

TOKYOPOP®

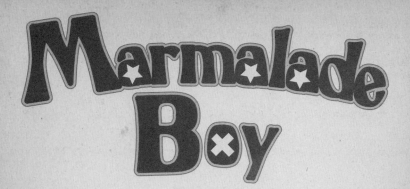

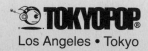

Los Angeles • Tokyo

Story and Art — Wataru Yoshizumi

Translator — Jack Niida
English Adaptation — Deb Baer
Retouch and Lettering — Yoffy
Graphic Designer — Anna Kernbaum
Senior Editor — Julie Taylor

Production Managers — Mario Rodriguez and Jennifer Wagner
Art Director — Matthew Alford
Brand Manager — Joel Baral
VP of Production — Ron Klamert
Publisher — Stuart Levy

Email: editor@tokyopop.com
Come visit us online at www.TOKYOPOP.com

A TOKYOPOP® MANGA
TOKYOPOP® is an imprint of Mixx Entertainment, Inc.
5900 Wilshire Blvd. Ste 2000, Los Angeles, CA 90036

ISBN: 1-931514-57-7
First TOKYOPOP® printing: November 2002
10 9 8 7 6 5 4 3 2 1
Printed in Canada

Main Characters

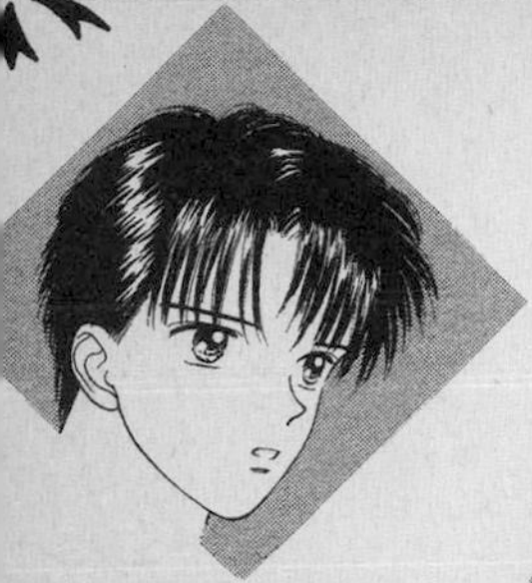

GINTA SUOU: MIKI'S CLASSMATE WHO PROFESSED HIS UNDYING LOVE FOR HER—BUT WANTS HER TO FORGET ABOUT YUU ONCE AND FOR ALL.

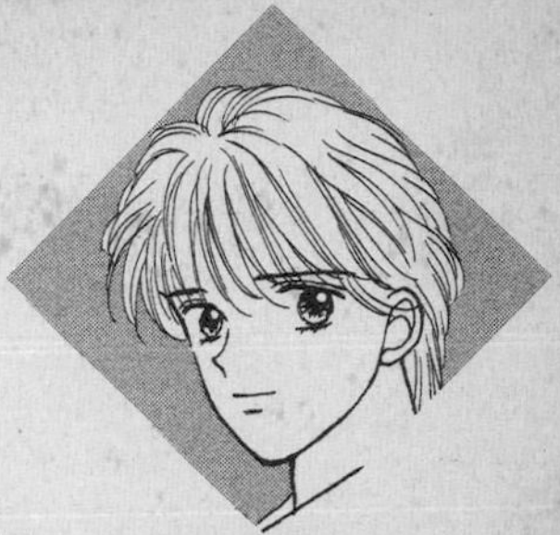

YUU MATSUURA: MIKI'S STEPBROTHER...KINDA. HE'S COOL, BUT KINDA MEAN TO HER...WHICH MAKES HER LIKE HIM EVEN MORE.

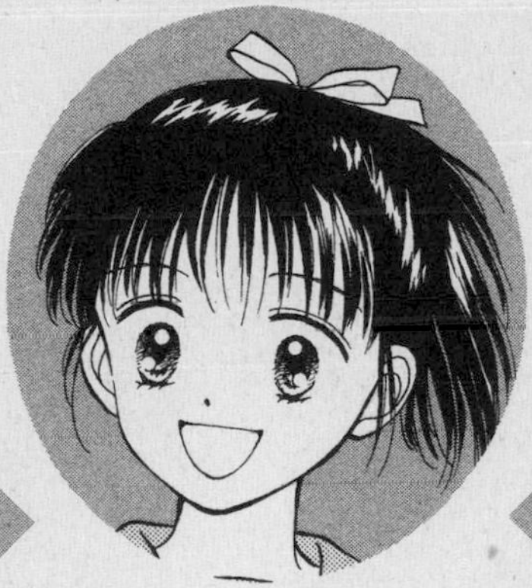

MIKI KOISHIKAWA: ALWAYS CHEERFUL, BUT SLOW ON THE UPTAKE. IS HAVING A HARD TIME DECIDING WHO SHE LOVES MORE—YUU OR GINTA.

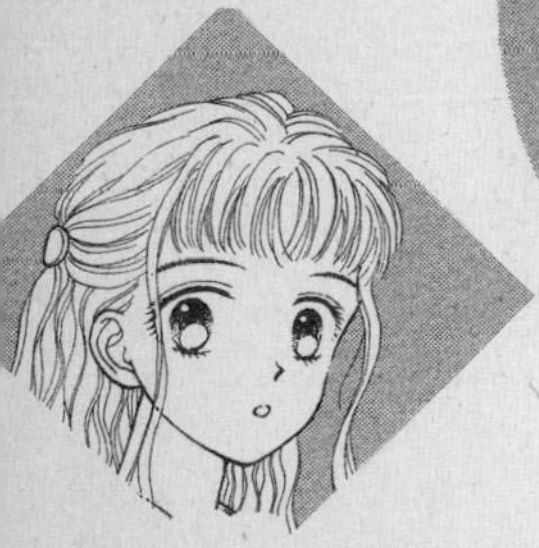

MEIKO AKIZUKI: MIKI'S BEST FRIEND. HAD A SCANDALOUS AFFAIR WITH A TEACHER WHO LEFT TOWN TO WORK FOR HIS FAMILY BUSINESS.

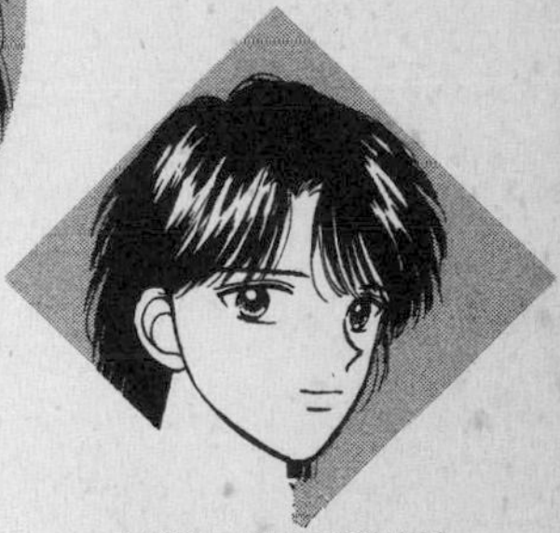

SATOSHI MIWA: DEBONAIRE STUDENT COUNCIL LEADER WHO IS AFTER YUU—AND NOT JUST FOR HIS VOTE!

THE STORY SO FAR...

DURING BREAKFAST ONE DAY, MIKI'S PARENTS BREAK IT TO HER THAT THEY'RE GETTING DIVORCED AND SWAPPING SPOUSES WITH ANOTHER COUPLE! NOW MIKI HAS FOUR PARENTS AND A NEW STEPBROTHER, YUU, WHO KEEPS TEASING HER. YUU'S SWEET ON THE OUTSIDE, BUT HE'S GOT A BITTER STREAK - HE'S A MARMALADE BOY! AS MIKI GETS TO KNOW YUU, SHE STARTS TO FORM A CRUSH ON HIM.

THINGS GET COMPLICATED WHEN MIKI'S OLD CRUSH, THE TENNIS CHAMP, GINTA, CONFESSES HIS LOVE FOR HER. AND THINGS GET EVEN MORE CONFUSING WHEN YUU'S EX-GIRLFRIEND, ARMINI, TRANSFERS TO MIKI'S SCHOOL AND TRIES TO WIN YUU BACK. DRAMA-RAMA!

WITH MAJOR CRUSHES ON BOTH GINTA AND YUU, MIKI FINDS HERSELF WAGING AN INNER BATTLE SHE KNOWS SHE CAN NEVER TRULY WIN. AND JUST WHEN MIKI'S WORLD CAN'T GET ANY MORE CONFUSING, HER BEST FRIEND CONFESSES SHE'S BEEN HAVING AN AFFAIR WITH NACHAN, THEIR TEACHER, AND NEEDS MIKI'S HELP—PRONTO! DESPITE HER WHIRLWIND SOAP OPERA OF ROMANTIC TRAUMA, MIKI IS DETERMINED TO GET THE GUY OF HER DREAMS...IF ONLY SHE CAN FIGURE OUT WHICH ONE HE IS.

THEN ALL HELL BREAKS LOOSE WHEN A CUTE DUDE NAMED MIWA ENTERS THE PICTURE AND DEVELOPS AN UNUSUAL OBSESSION WITH YUU. WHAT EXACTLY ARE HIS INTENTIONS...?!

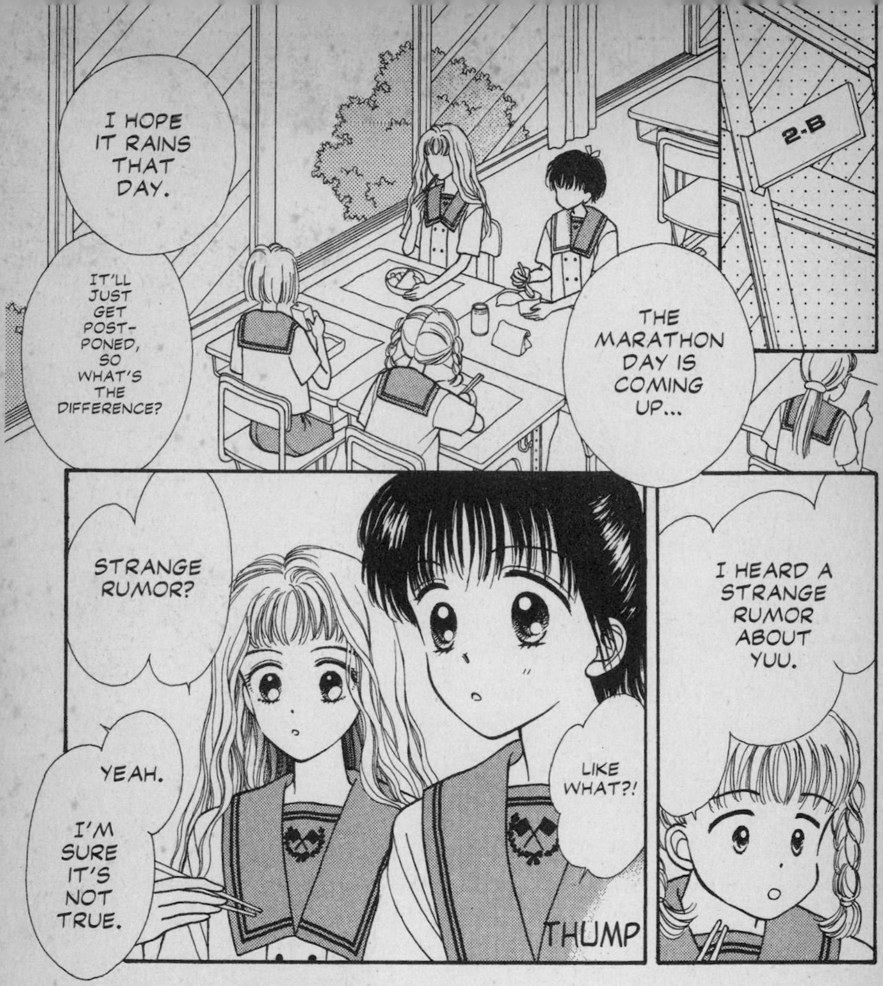
2-B
THE MARATHON DAY IS COMING UP...
I HOPE IT RAINS THAT DAY.
IT'LL JUST GET POST-PONED, SO WHAT'S THE DIFFERENCE?
I HEARD A STRANGE RUMOR ABOUT YUU.
STRANGE RUMOR?
LIKE WHAT?!
YEAH.
I'M SURE IT'S NOT TRUE.
THUMP

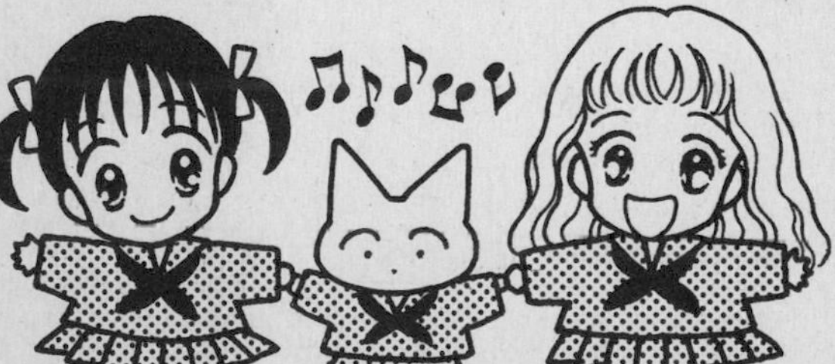

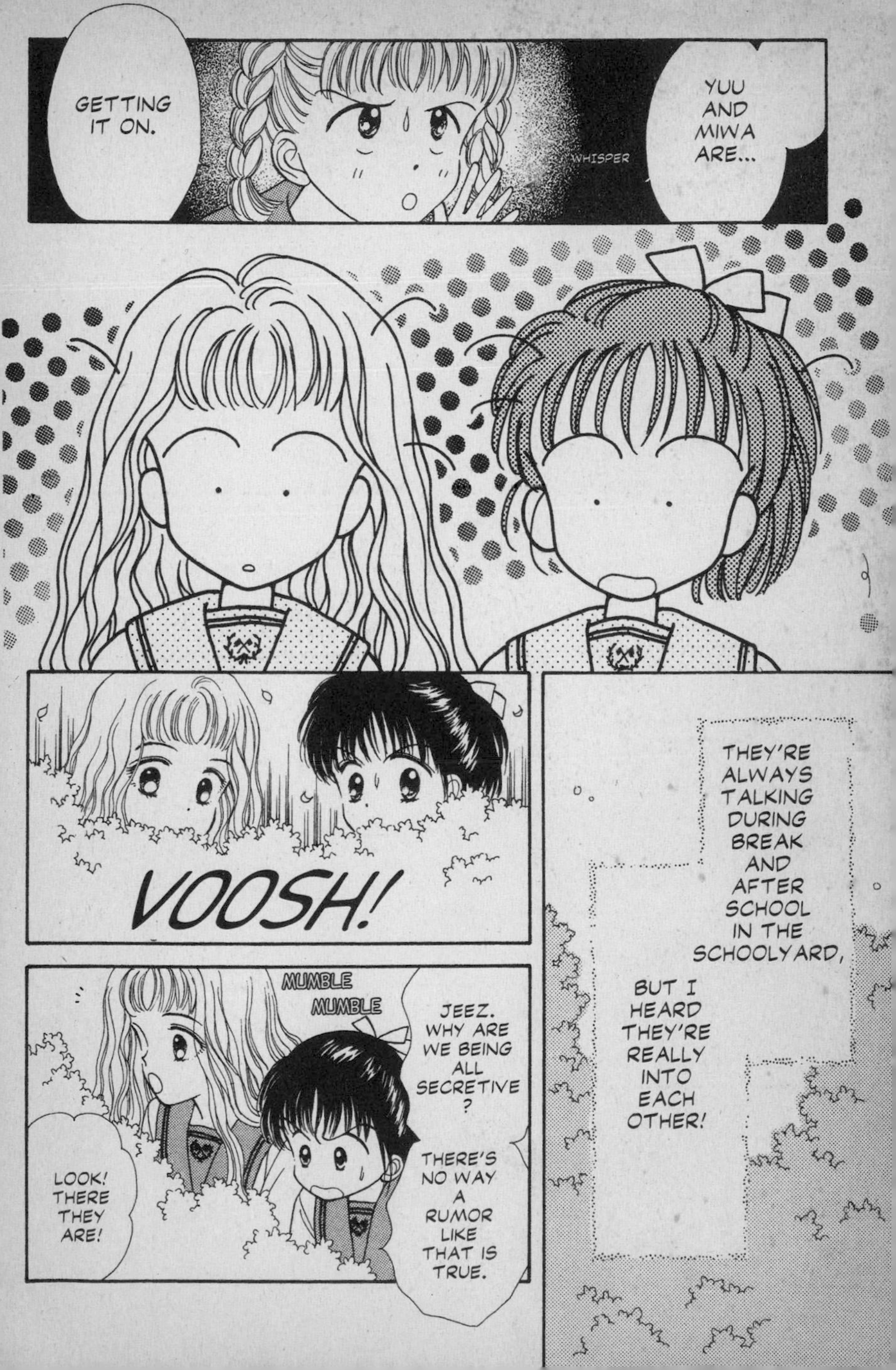
YUU AND MIWA ARE...
WHISPER
GETTING IT ON.
THEY'RE ALWAYS TALKING DURING BREAK AND AFTER SCHOOL IN THE SCHOOLYARD,
BUT I HEARD THEY'RE REALLY INTO EACH OTHER!
VOOSH!
MUMBLE MUMBLE
JEEZ. WHY ARE WE BEING ALL SECRETIVE?
THERE'S NO WAY A RUMOR LIKE THAT IS TRUE.
LOOK! THERE THEY ARE!

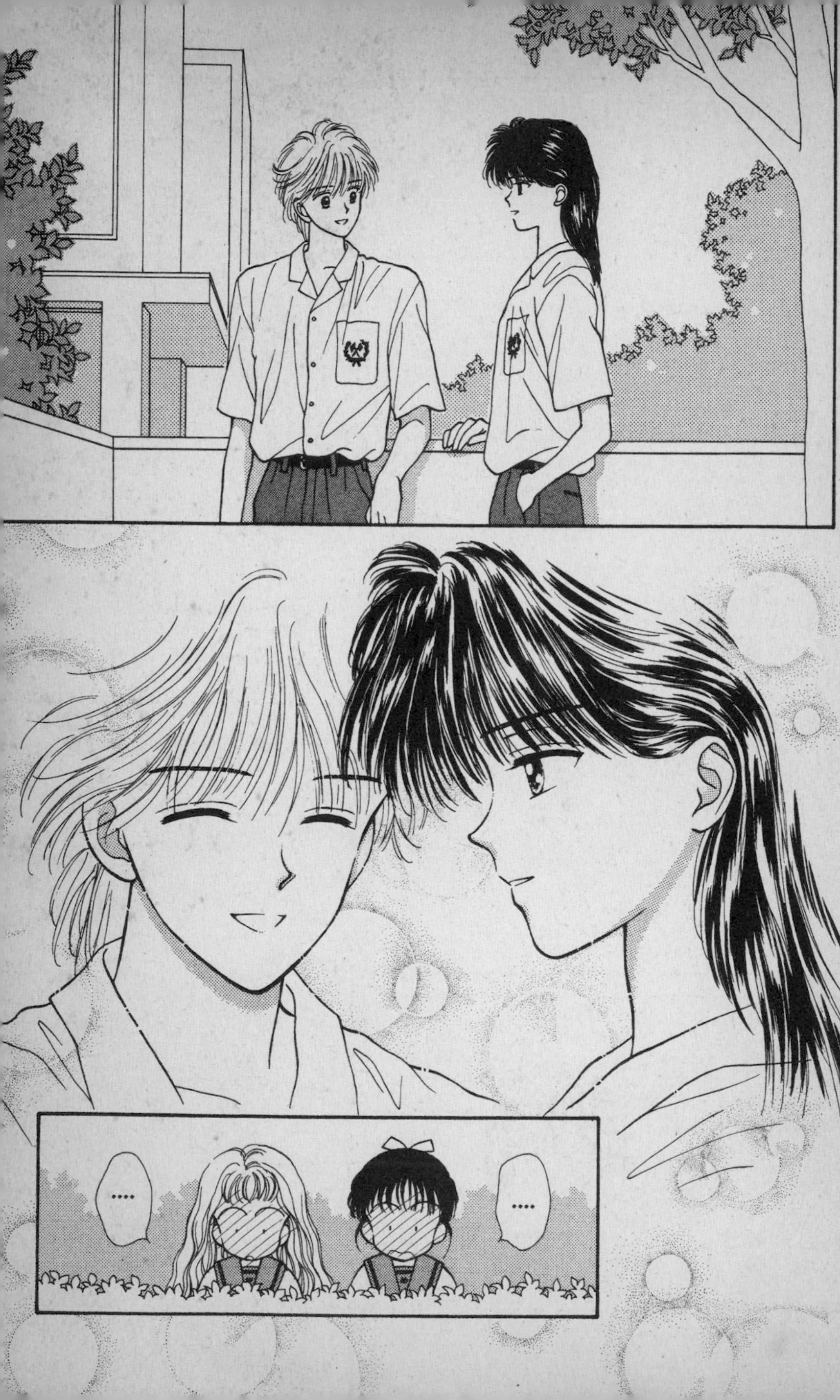
....
....

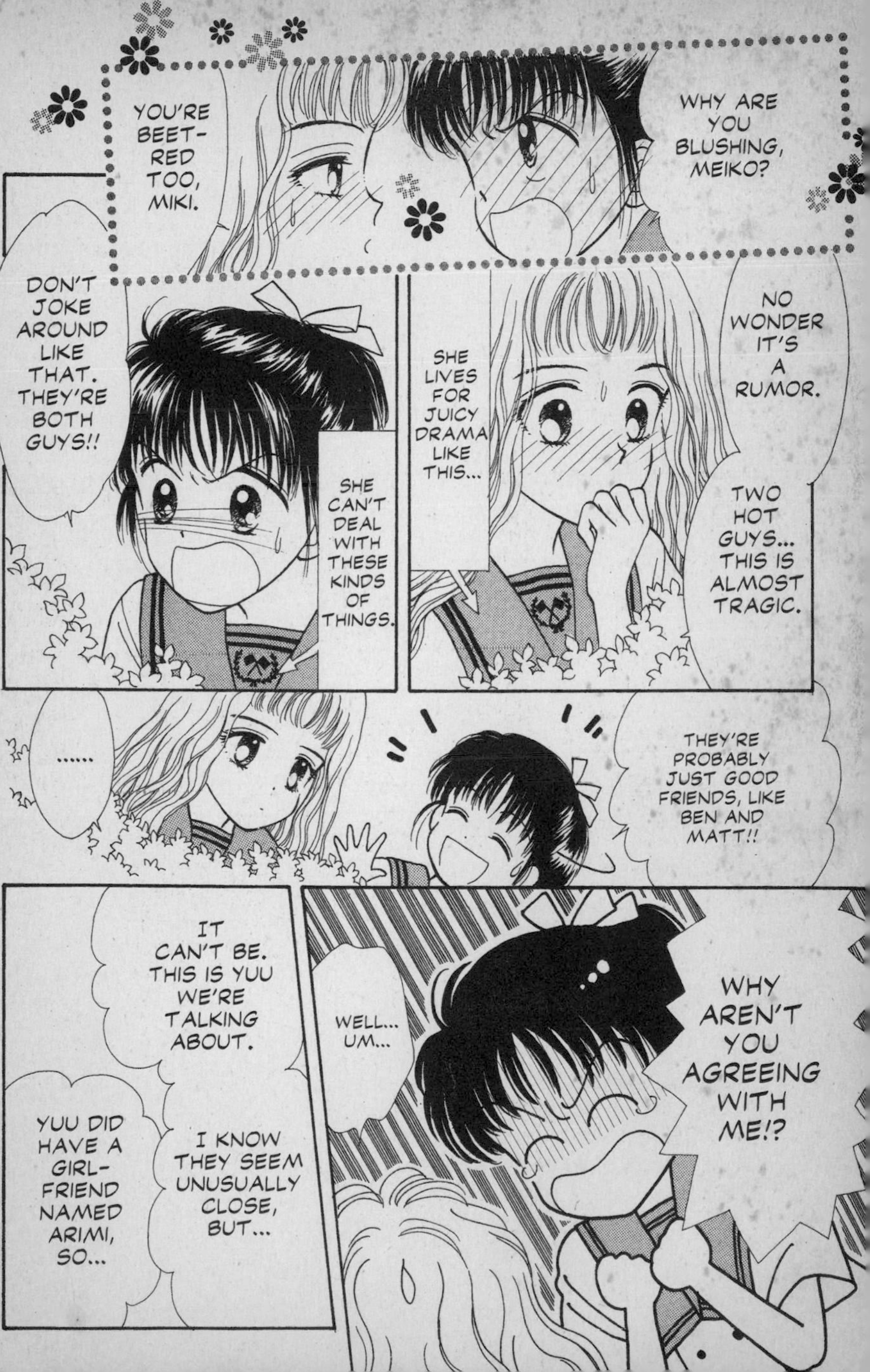
WHY ARE YOU BLUSHING, MEIKO?
YOU'RE BEET-RED TOO, MIKI.
NO WONDER IT'S A RUMOR.
SHE LIVES FOR JUICY DRAMA LIKE THIS...
TWO HOT GUYS... THIS IS ALMOST TRAGIC.
DON'T JOKE AROUND LIKE THAT. THEY'RE BOTH GUYS!!
SHE CAN'T DEAL WITH THESE KINDS OF THINGS.
THEY'RE PROBABLY JUST GOOD FRIENDS, LIKE BEN AND MATT!!
......
WHY AREN'T YOU AGREEING WITH ME!?
WELL... UM...
IT CAN'T BE. THIS IS YUU WE'RE TALKING ABOUT.
I KNOW THEY SEEM UNUSUALLY CLOSE, BUT...
YUU DID HAVE A GIRLFRIEND NAMED ARIMI, SO...

FREE TALK ①

Hi, this is Yoshizumi. It's been almost half a year since the release of Marmalade Boy #3. Today is February 27, 1994 and by the time this volume is released, the TV series should be starting, too. It was around August when my director told me Marmalade Boy might become a TV animation series. I was given the okay to tell people that the TV series was going to start in December and the animation starts on March 13. Time sure goes by fast. It seems like yesterday when my director told me about the animation release. I hope everyone gets to see it!

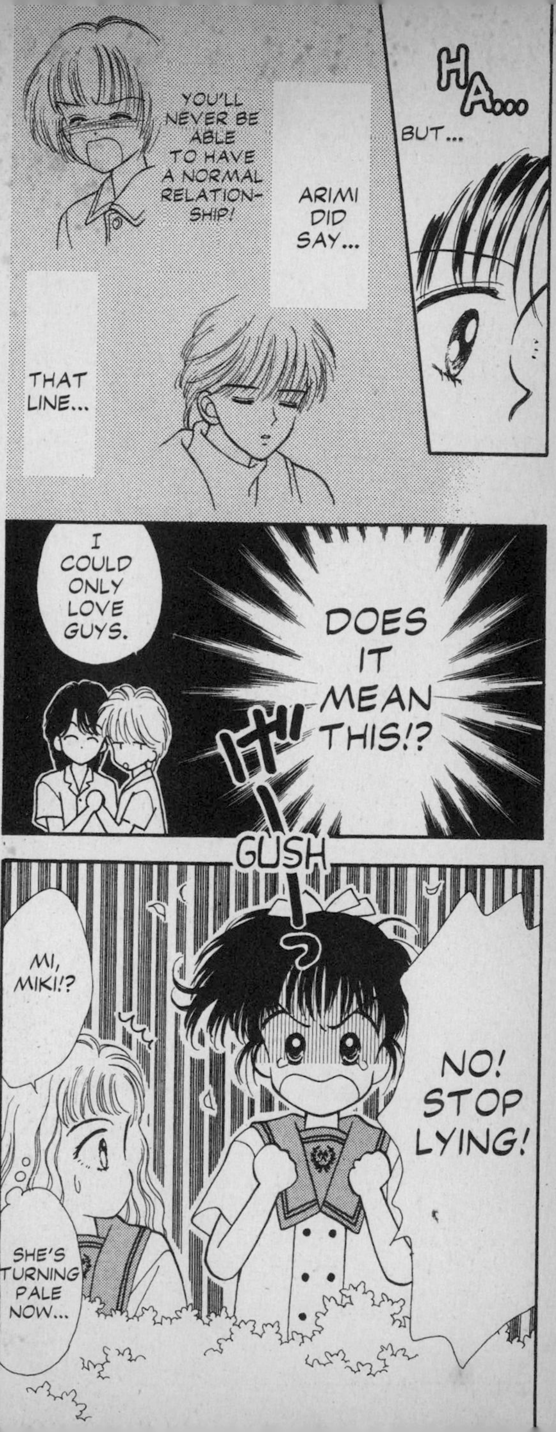
HA...
BUT...
ARIMI DID SAY...
YOU'LL NEVER BE ABLE TO HAVE A NORMAL RELATION-SHIP!
THAT LINE...
DOES IT MEAN THIS!?
I COULD ONLY LOVE GUYS.
GUSH
NO! STOP LYING!
MI, MIKI!?
SHE'S TURNING PALE NOW...

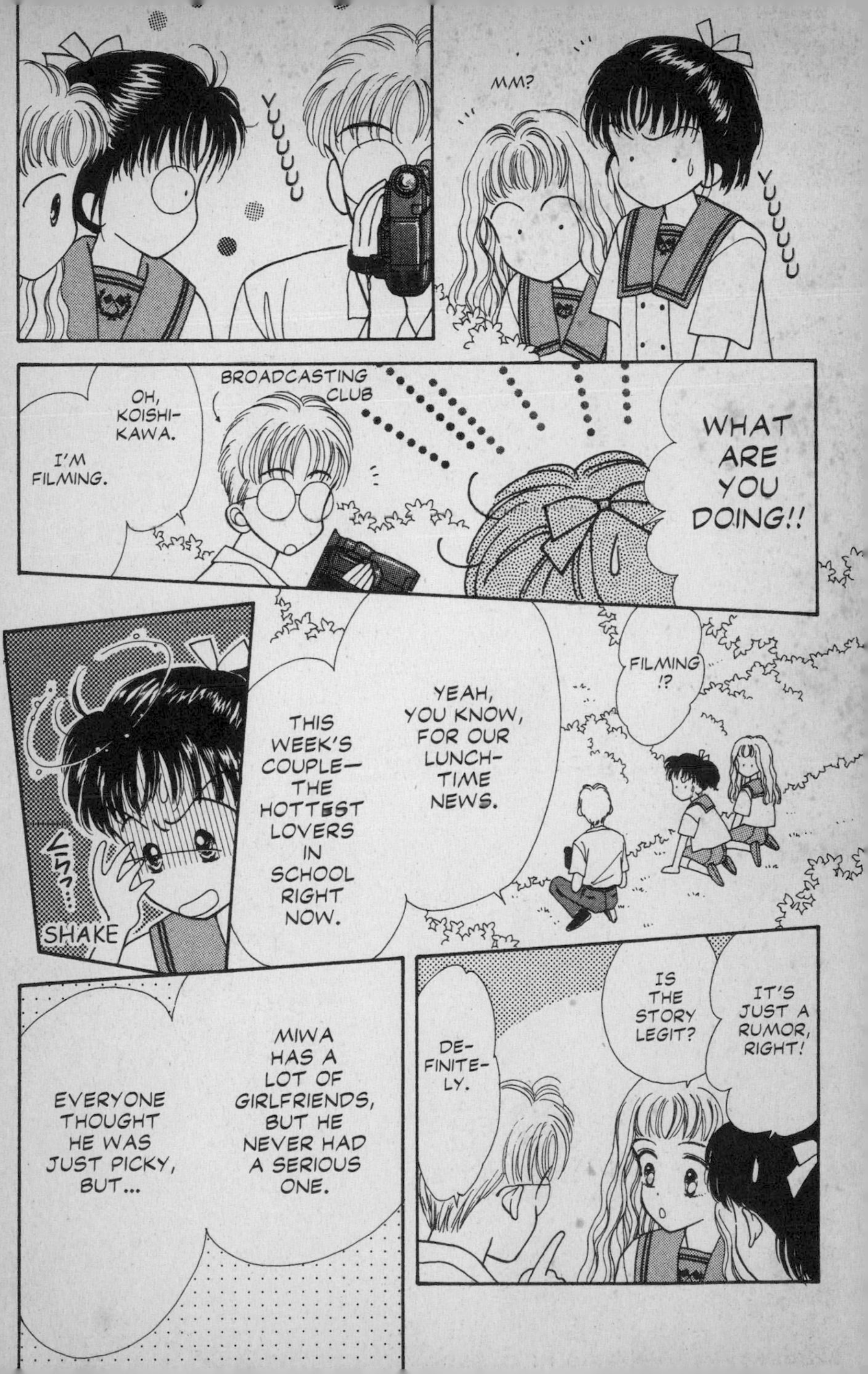
MM?
YUUUUUU
YUUUUUU
WHAT ARE YOU DOING!!
BROADCASTING CLUB
OH, KOISHI-KAWA.
I'M FILMING.
FILMING!?
YEAH, YOU KNOW, FOR OUR LUNCH-TIME NEWS.
THIS WEEK'S COUPLE— THE HOTTEST LOVERS IN SCHOOL RIGHT NOW.
SHAKE
IT'S JUST A RUMOR, RIGHT!
IS THE STORY LEGIT?
DE-FINITE-LY.
MIWA HAS A LOT OF GIRLFRIENDS, BUT HE NEVER HAD A SERIOUS ONE.
EVERYONE THOUGHT HE WAS JUST PICKY, BUT...

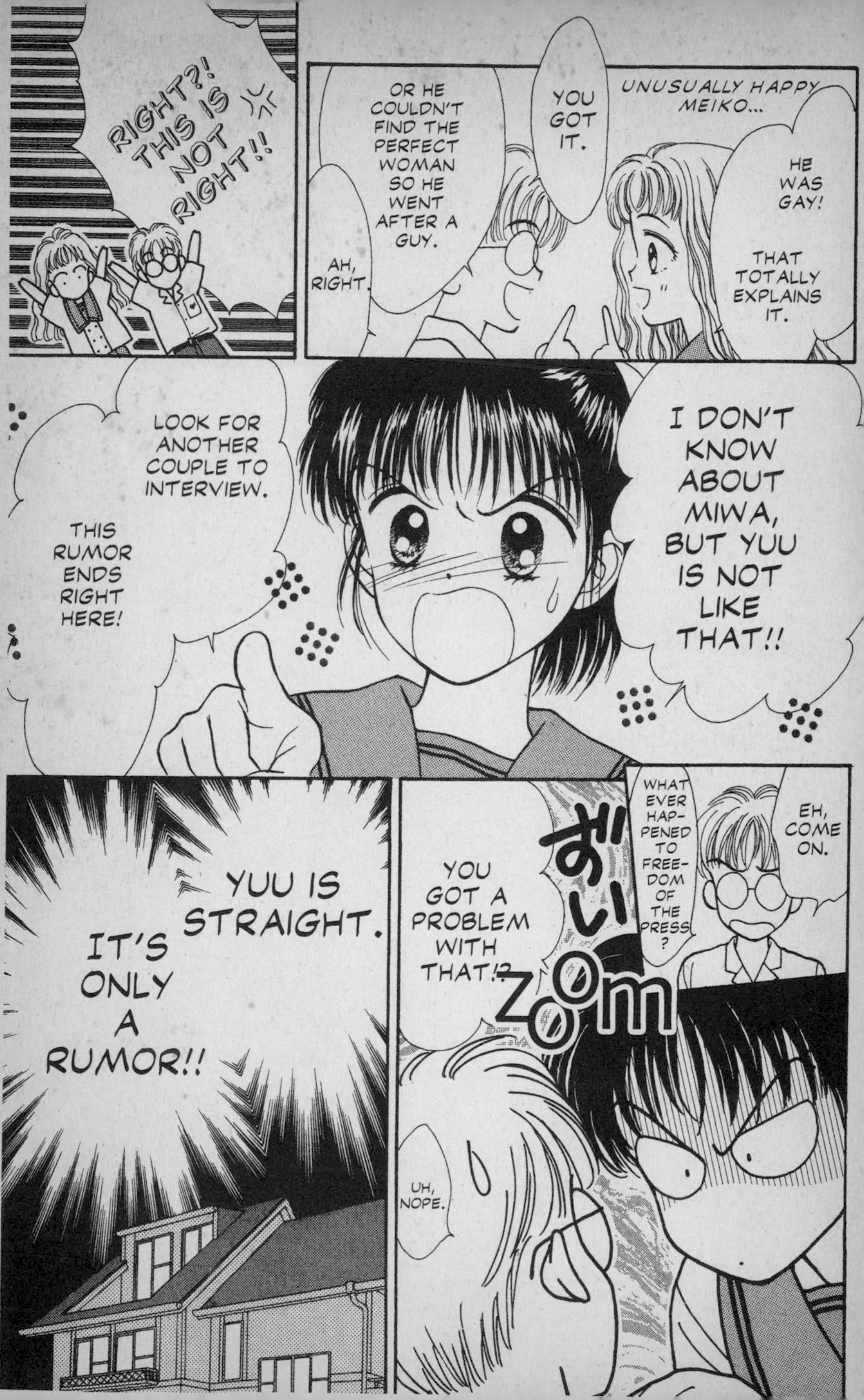
UNUSUALLY HAPPY MEIKO...
HE WAS GAY!
THAT TOTALLY EXPLAINS IT.
YOU GOT IT.
OR HE COULDN'T FIND THE PERFECT WOMAN SO HE WENT AFTER A GUY.
AH, RIGHT.
RIGHT?! THIS IS NOT RIGHT!!
I DON'T KNOW ABOUT MIWA, BUT YUU IS NOT LIKE THAT!!
LOOK FOR ANOTHER COUPLE TO INTERVIEW.
THIS RUMOR ENDS RIGHT HERE!
EH, COME ON.
WHATEVER HAPPENED TO FREEDOM OF THE PRESS?
おい
YOU GOT A PROBLEM WITH THAT!?
ZOOM
UH, NOPE.
YUU IS STRAIGHT.
IT'S ONLY A RUMOR!!

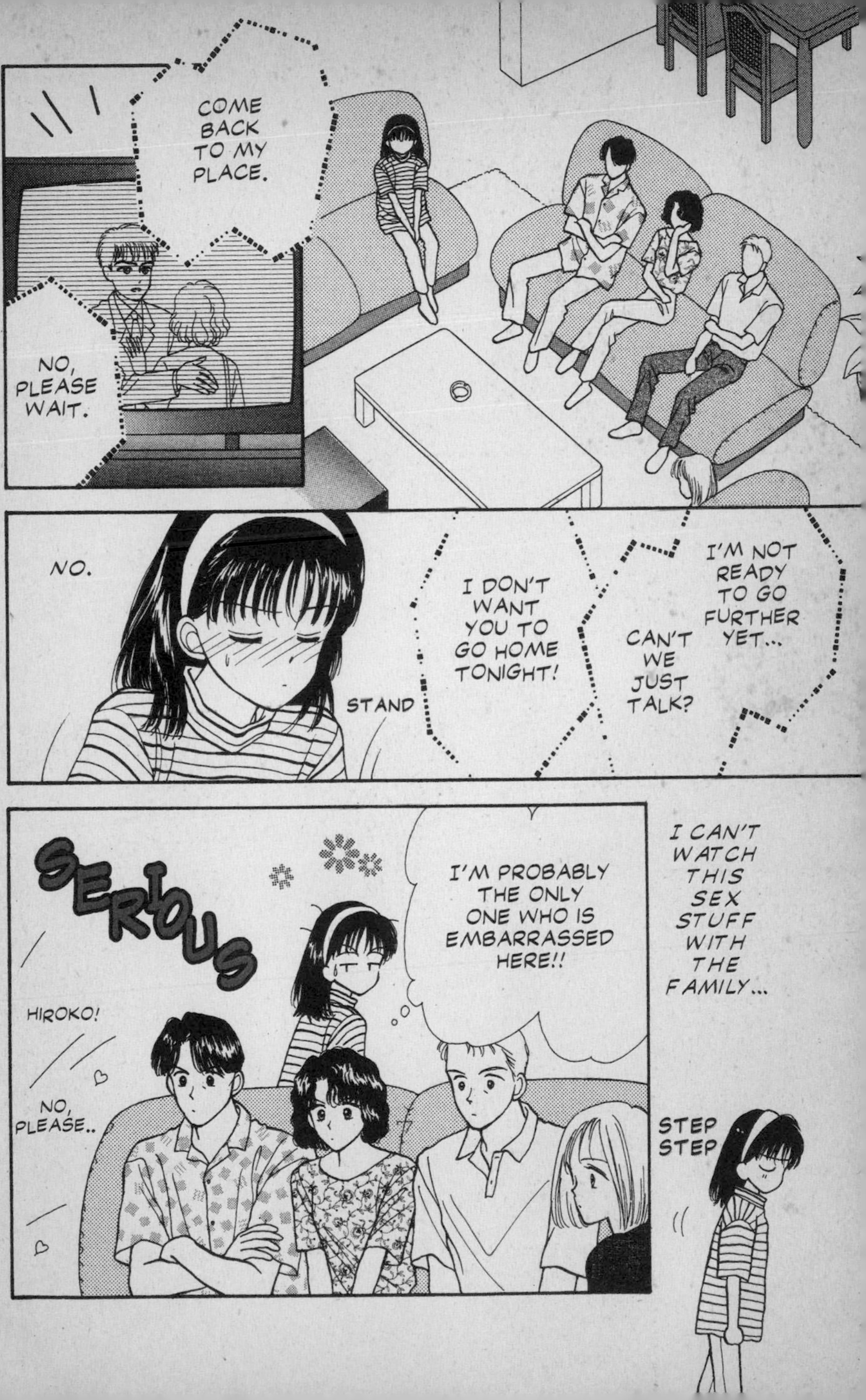
COME BACK TO MY PLACE.
NO, PLEASE WAIT.
I'M NOT READY TO GO FURTHER YET...
CAN'T WE JUST TALK?
I DON'T WANT YOU TO GO HOME TONIGHT!
STAND
NO.
I CAN'T WATCH THIS SEX STUFF WITH THE FAMILY...
STEP STEP
I'M PROBABLY THE ONLY ONE WHO IS EMBARRASSED HERE!!
SERIOUS
HIROKO!
NO, PLEASE..

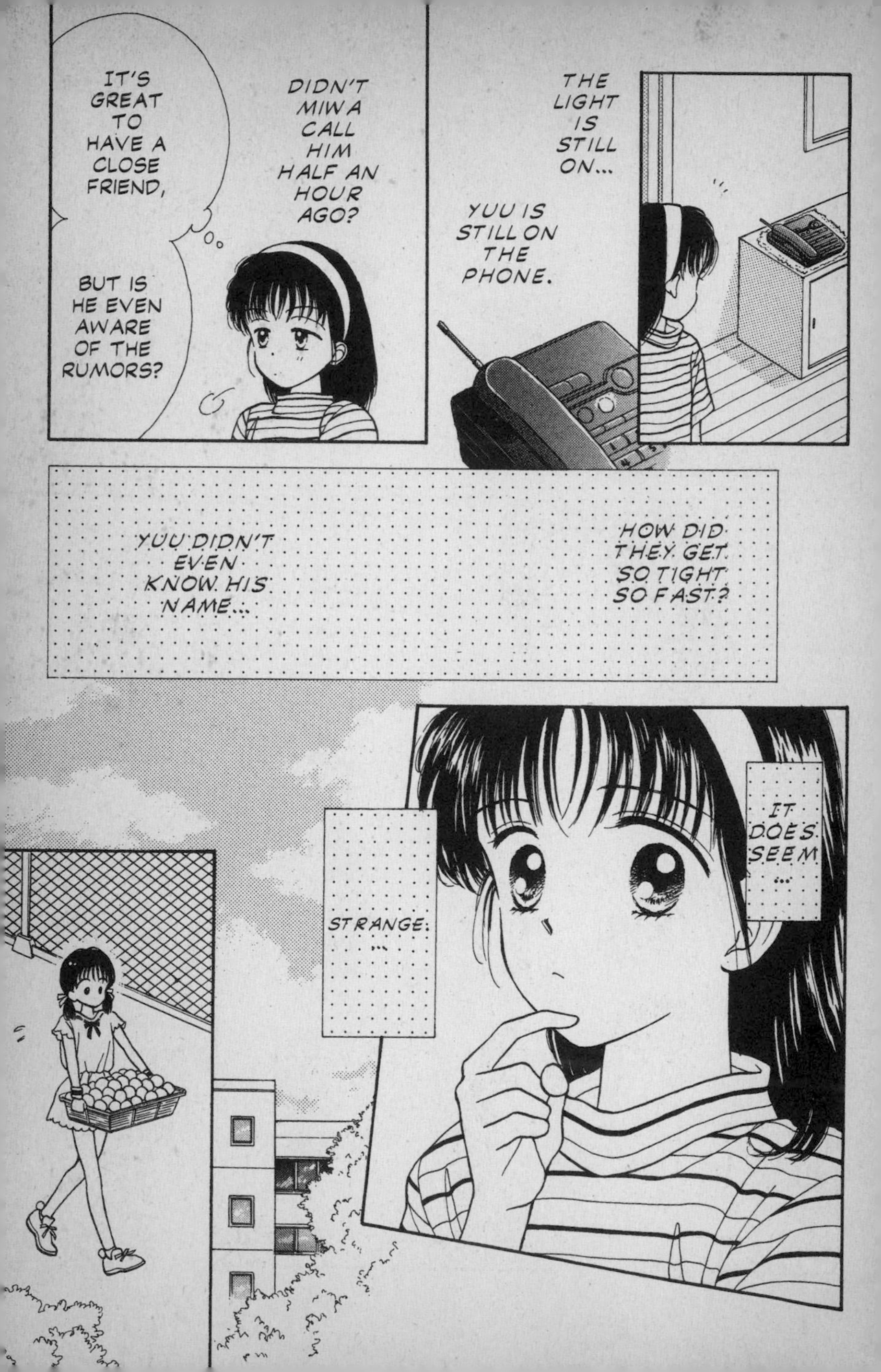
THE LIGHT IS STILL ON...
YUU IS STILL ON THE PHONE.
DIDN'T MIWA CALL HIM HALF AN HOUR AGO?
IT'S GREAT TO HAVE A CLOSE FRIEND,
BUT IS HE EVEN AWARE OF THE RUMORS?
HOW DID THEY GET SO TIGHT SO FAST?
YUU DIDN'T EVEN KNOW HIS NAME...
IT DOES SEEM...
STRANGE...

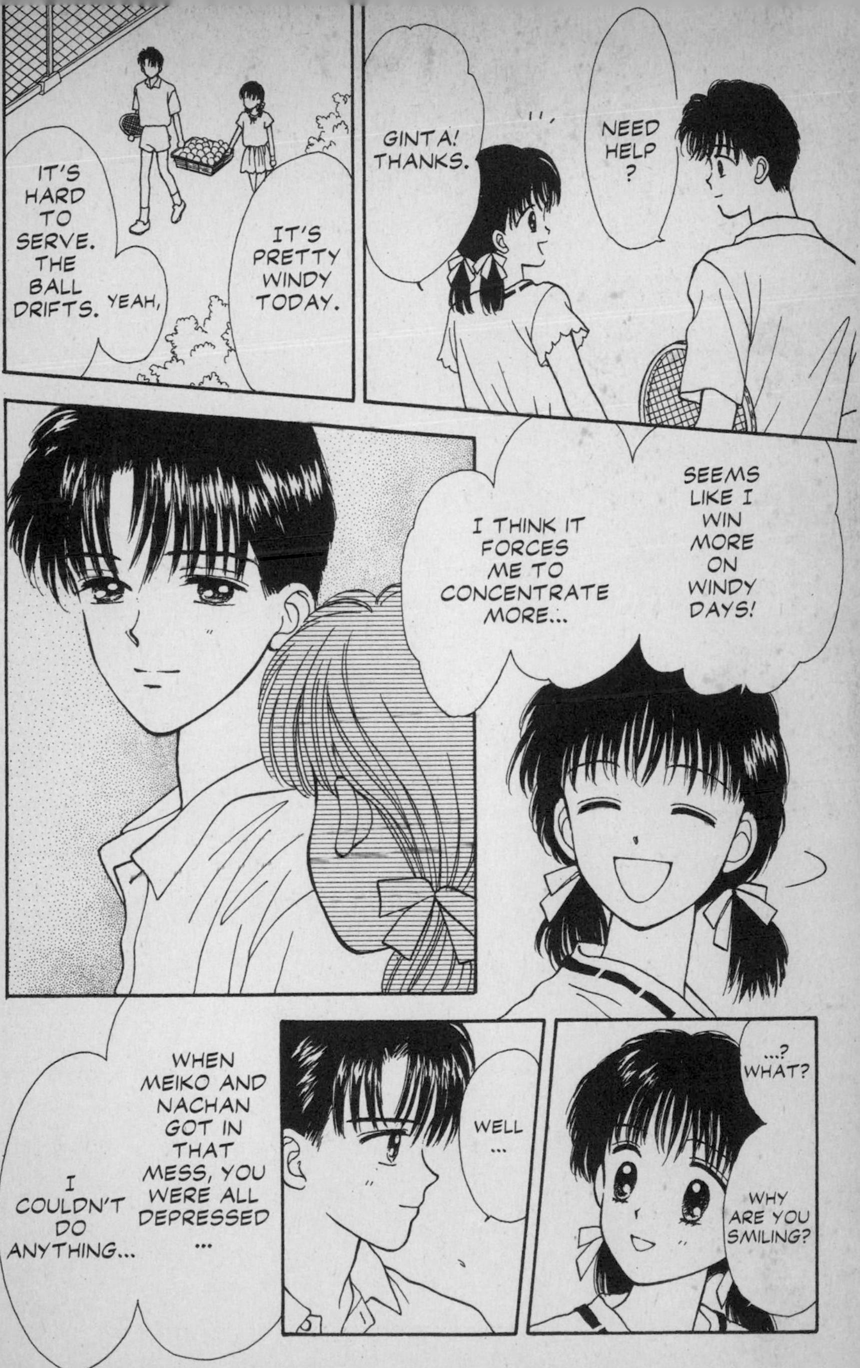
NEED HELP?
GINTA! THANKS.
IT'S PRETTY WINDY TODAY.
YEAH,
IT'S HARD TO SERVE. THE BALL DRIFTS.
SEEMS LIKE I WIN MORE ON WINDY DAYS!
I THINK IT FORCES ME TO CONCENTRATE MORE...
...? WHAT?
WHY ARE YOU SMILING?
WELL ...
WHEN MEIKO AND NACHAN GOT IN THAT MESS, YOU WERE ALL DEPRESSED ...
I COULDN'T DO ANYTHING...

FREE TALK ②

When the Marmalade Boy animation series was being created, I thought the animation staff would do absolutely everything. Fortunately, the producer told me they wanted to keep it close to the comic, so I was given the chance to give some pointers and advice. I was very excited to be part of the creation!

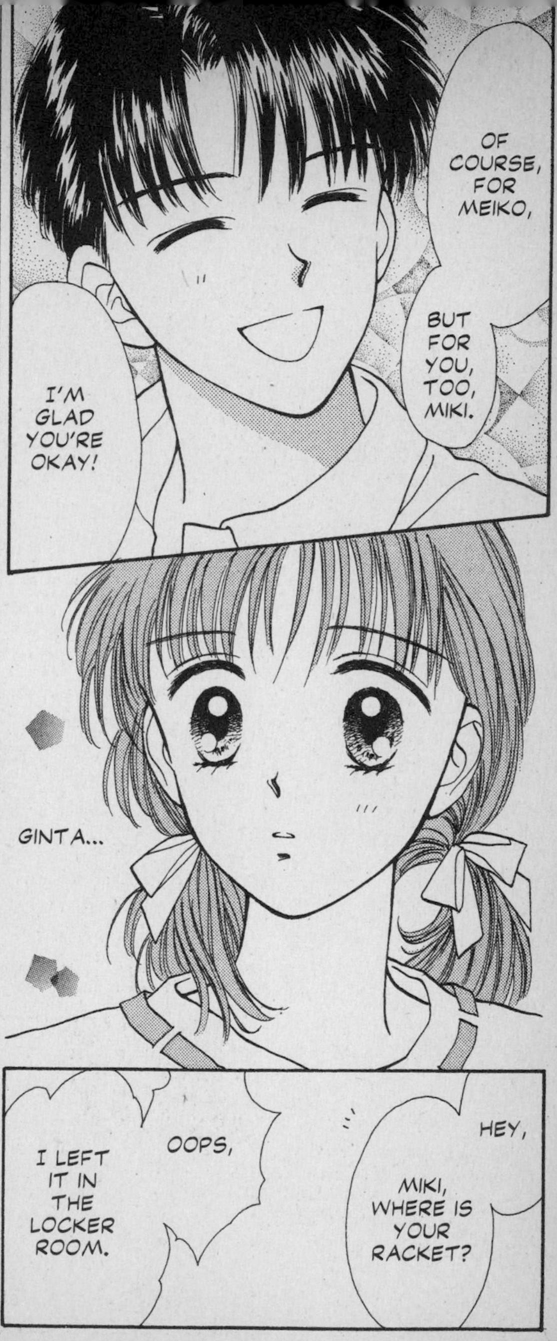
OF COURSE, FOR MEIKO,
BUT FOR YOU, TOO, MIKI.
I'M GLAD YOU'RE OKAY!
GINTA...
HEY,
MIKI, WHERE IS YOUR RACKET?
OOPS,
I LEFT IT IN THE LOCKER ROOM.

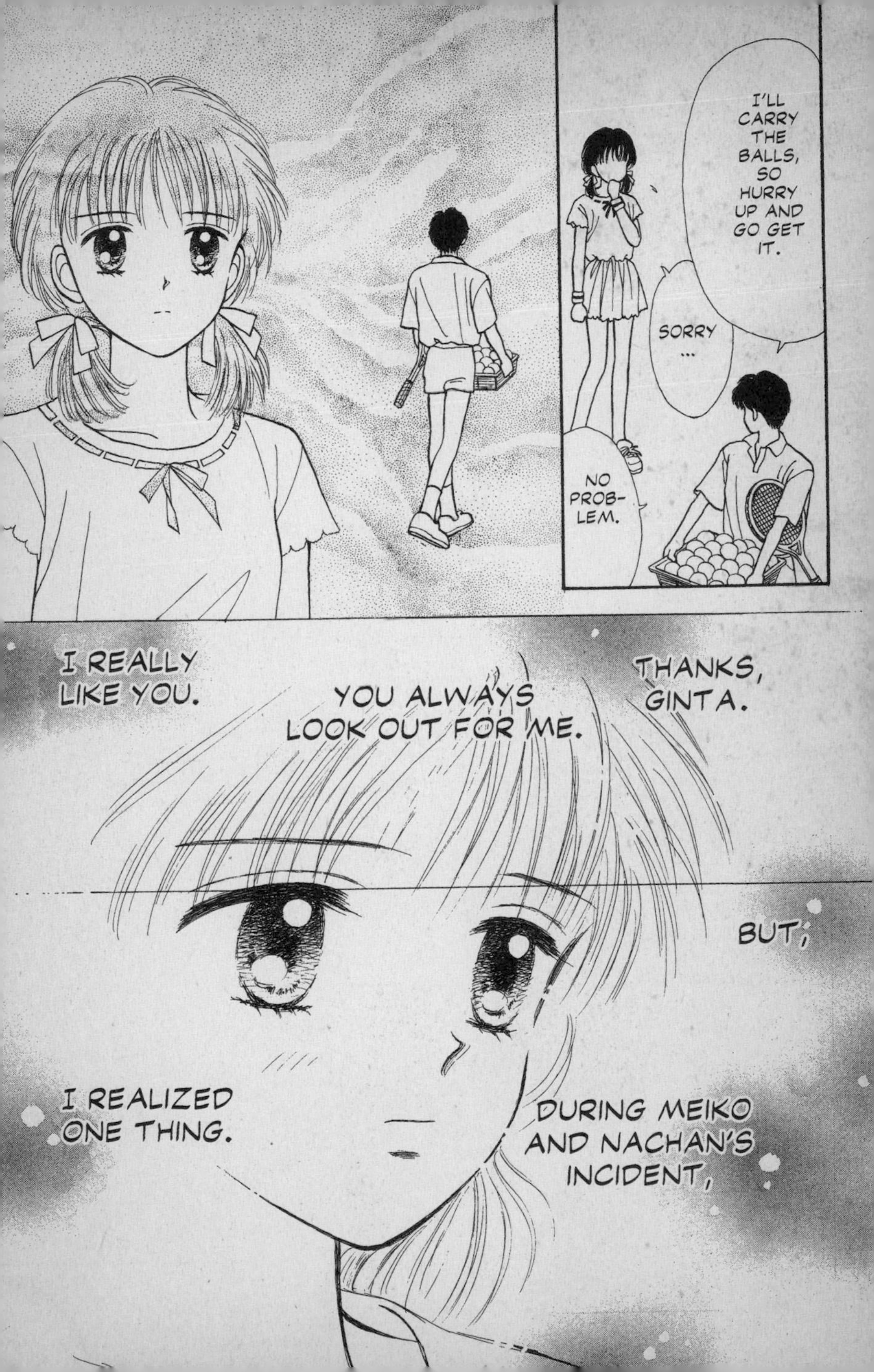
I'LL CARRY THE BALLS, SO HURRY UP AND GO GET IT.
SORRY ...
NO PROBLEM.
THANKS, GINTA.
YOU ALWAYS LOOK OUT FOR ME.
I REALLY LIKE YOU.
BUT,
DURING MEIKO AND NACHAN'S INCIDENT,
I REALIZED ONE THING.

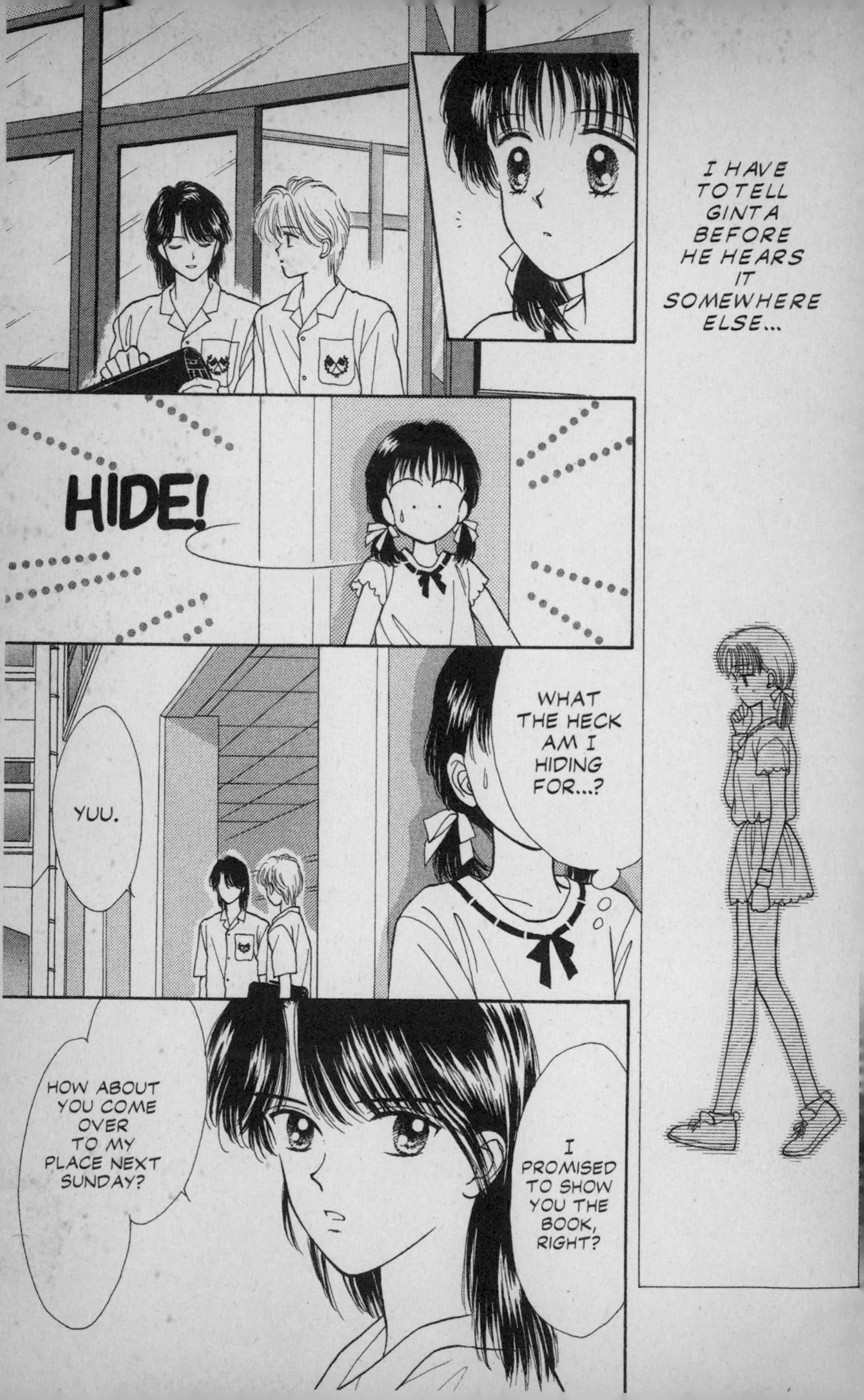
I HAVE TO TELL GINTA BEFORE HE HEARS IT SOMEWHERE ELSE...
HIDE!
WHAT THE HECK AM I HIDING FOR...?
YUU.
I PROMISED TO SHOW YOU THE BOOK, RIGHT?
HOW ABOUT YOU COME OVER TO MY PLACE NEXT SUNDAY?

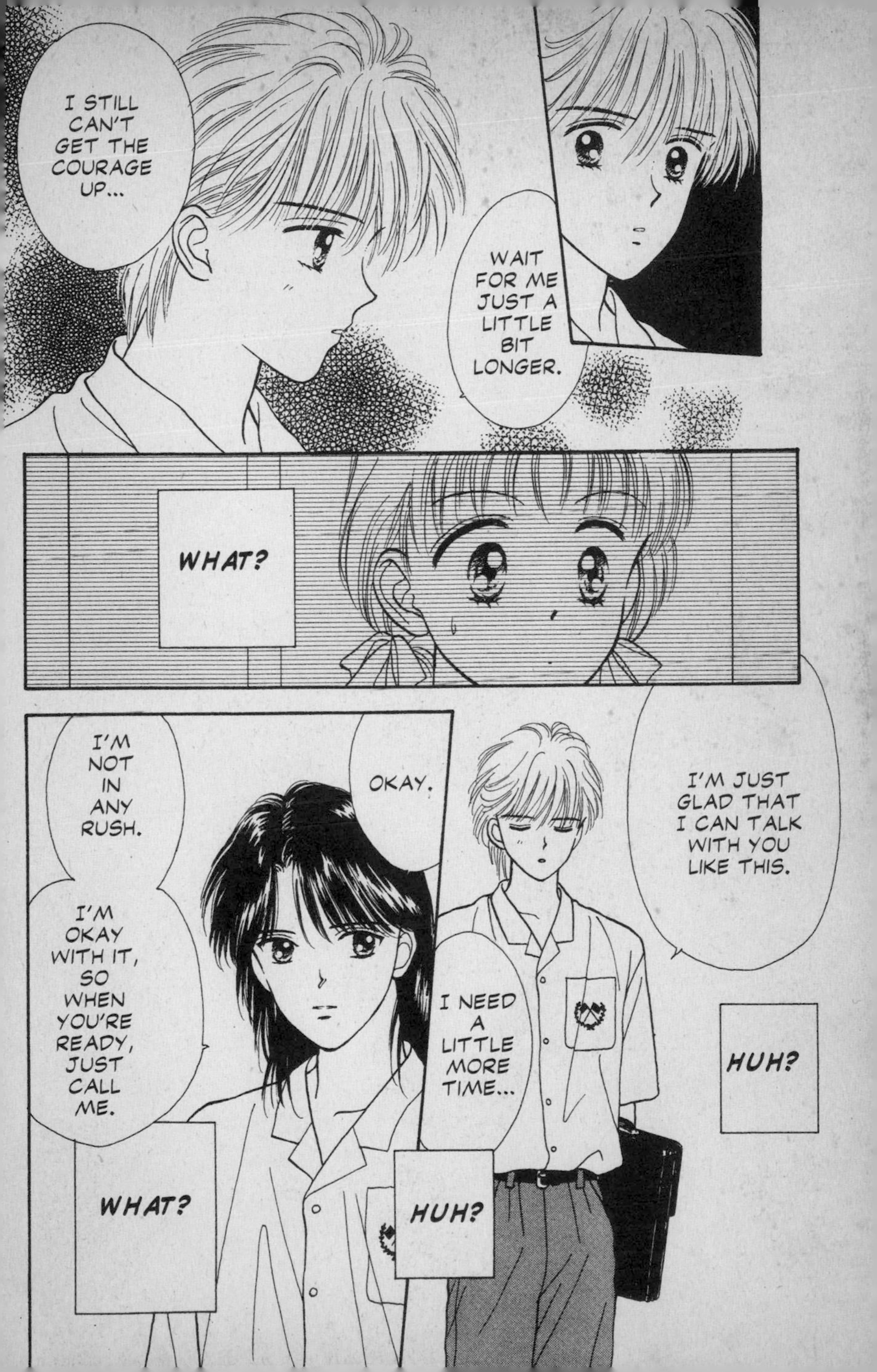

I STILL CAN'T GET THE COURAGE UP...
WAIT FOR ME JUST A LITTLE BIT LONGER.
WHAT?
I'M JUST GLAD THAT I CAN TALK WITH YOU LIKE THIS.
HUH?
I NEED A LITTLE MORE TIME...
HUH?
OKAY.
I'M NOT IN ANY RUSH.
I'M OKAY WITH IT, SO WHEN YOU'RE READY, JUST CALL ME.
WHAT?

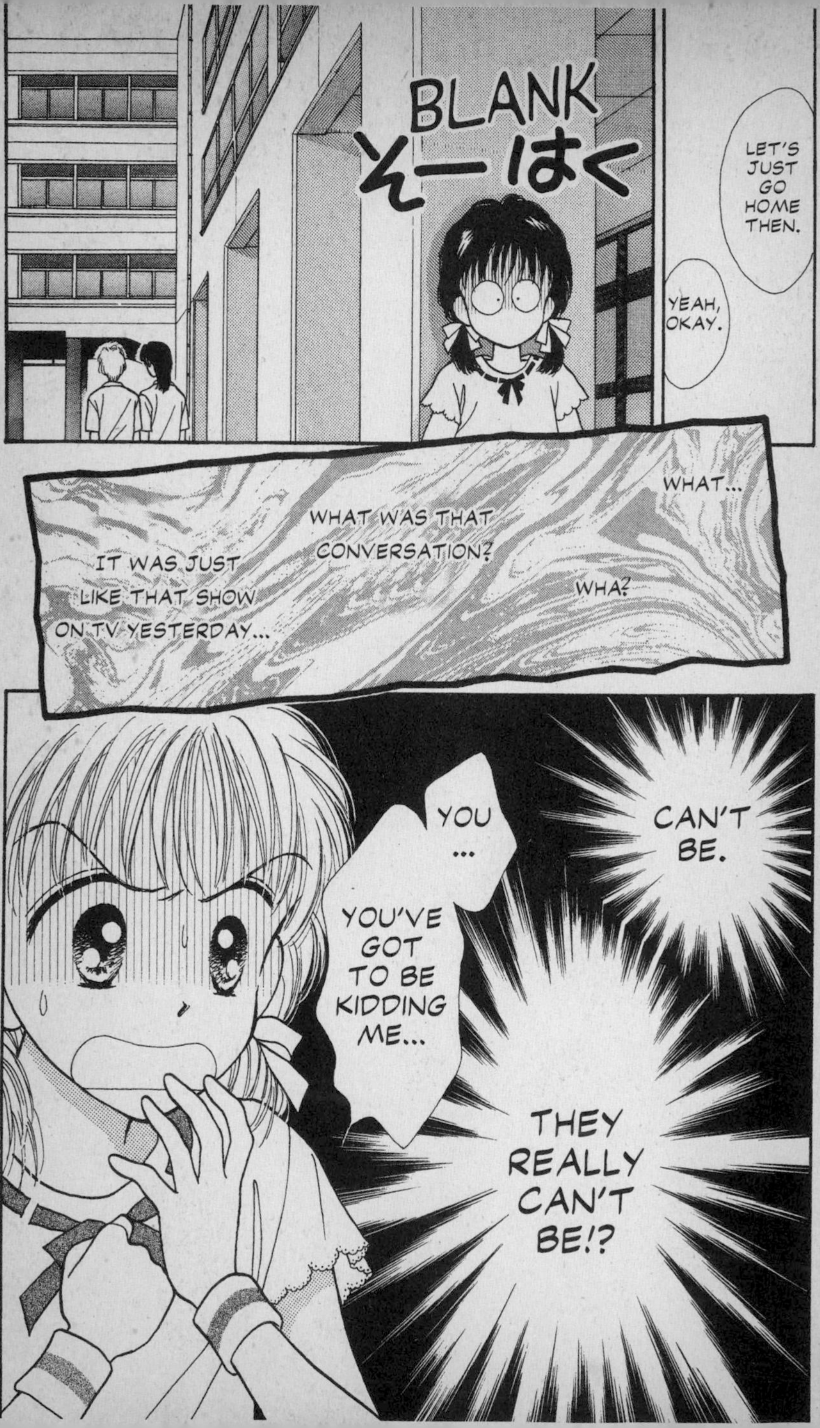
LET'S JUST GO HOME THEN.
YEAH, OKAY.
BLANK
そーはく
WHAT...
WHA?
WHAT WAS THAT CONVERSATION?
IT WAS JUST LIKE THAT SHOW ON TV YESTERDAY...
CAN'T BE.
YOU ...
YOU'VE GOT TO BE KIDDING ME...
THEY REALLY CAN'T BE!?

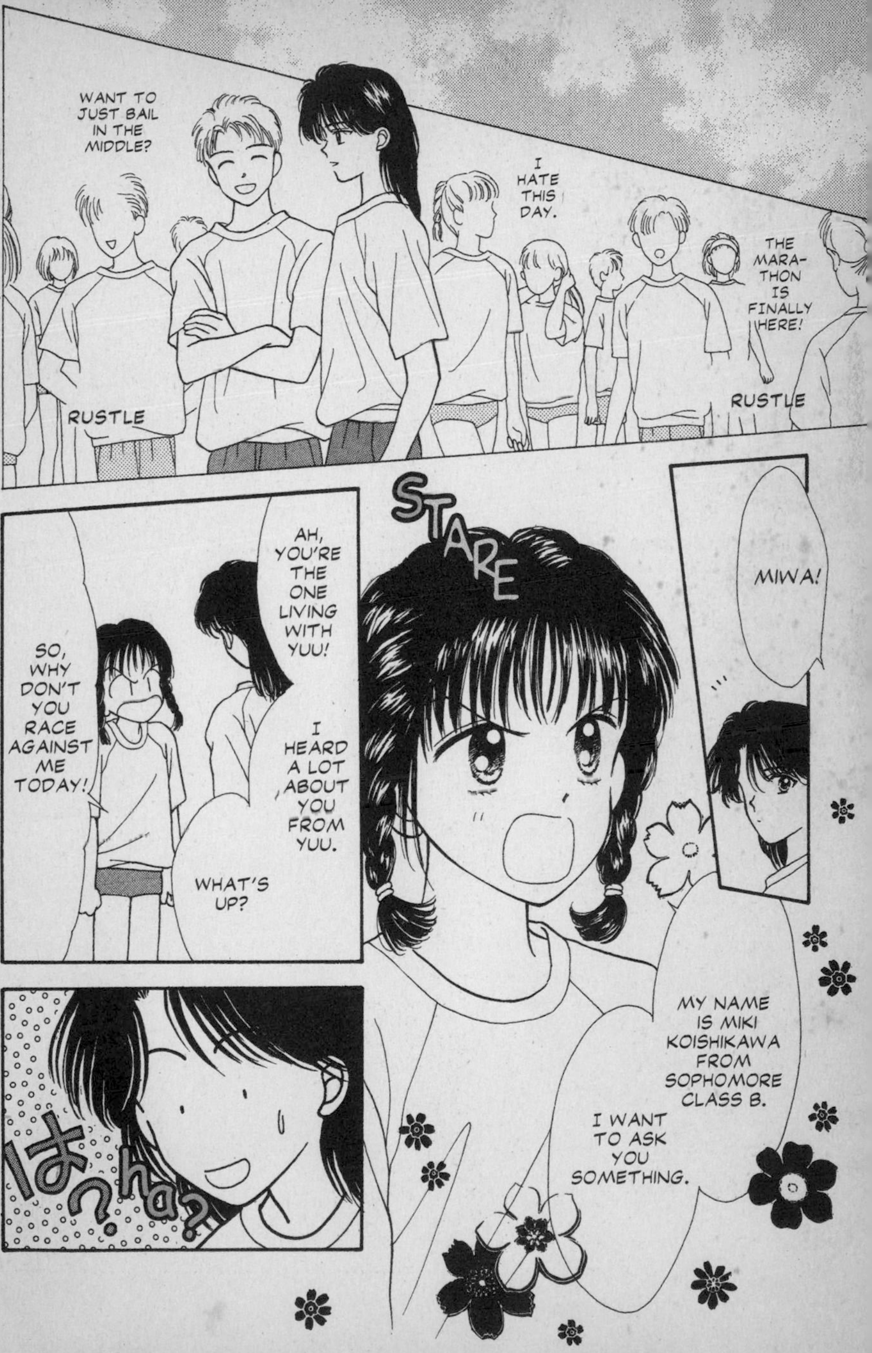
THE MARATHON IS FINALLY HERE!
RUSTLE
I HATE THIS DAY.
WANT TO JUST BAIL IN THE MIDDLE?
RUSTLE
MIWA!
...
STARE
MY NAME IS MIKI KOISHIKAWA FROM SOPHOMORE CLASS B.
I WANT TO ASK YOU SOMETHING.
AH, YOU'RE THE ONE LIVING WITH YUU!
I HEARD A LOT ABOUT YOU FROM YUU.
WHAT'S UP?
SO, WHY DON'T YOU RACE AGAINST ME TODAY!
は? ha?

FREE TALK ③

I thought the character design for the animation will be different from the original, but I was wrong. The director was doing everything he could to make it look close to the original as possible. Also the backgrounds look very nice. Chida, the graphic designer, is really working hard on this.

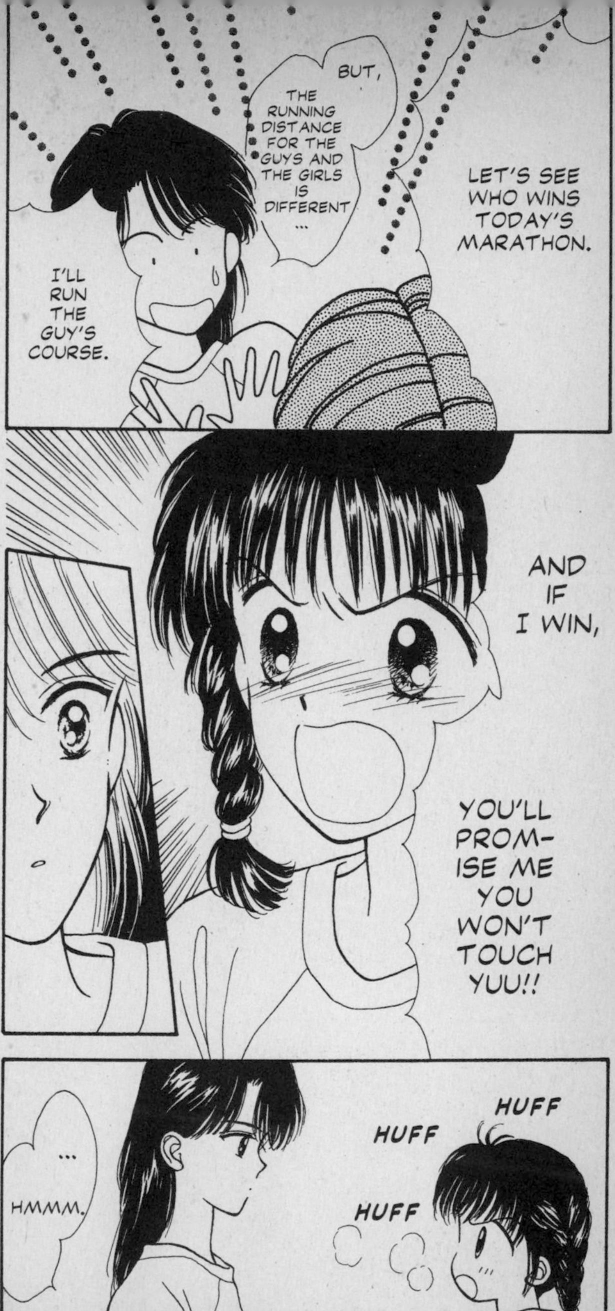
LET'S SEE WHO WINS TODAY'S MARATHON.
BUT, THE RUNNING DISTANCE FOR THE GUYS AND THE GIRLS IS DIFFERENT ...
I'LL RUN THE GUY'S COURSE.
AND IF I WIN,
YOU'LL PROMISE ME YOU WON'T TOUCH YUU!!
HUFF
HUFF
HUFF
...
HMMM.

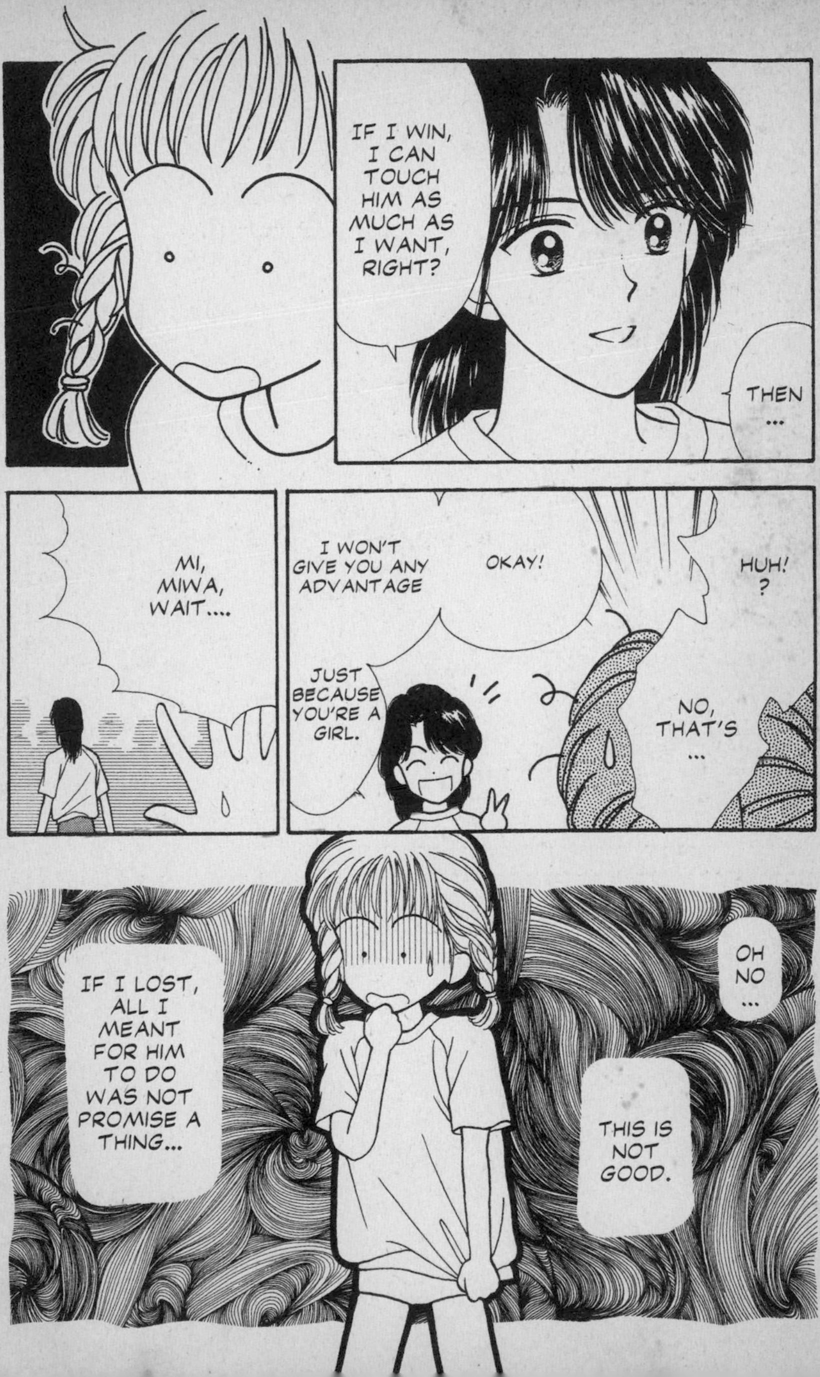
THEN ...
IF I WIN, I CAN TOUCH HIM AS MUCH AS I WANT, RIGHT?
HUH! ?
NO, THAT'S ...
OKAY!
I WON'T GIVE YOU ANY ADVANTAGE
JUST BECAUSE YOU'RE A GIRL.
MI, MIWA, WAIT....
OH NO ...
THIS IS NOT GOOD.
IF I LOST, ALL I MEANT FOR HIM TO DO WAS NOT PROMISE A THING...

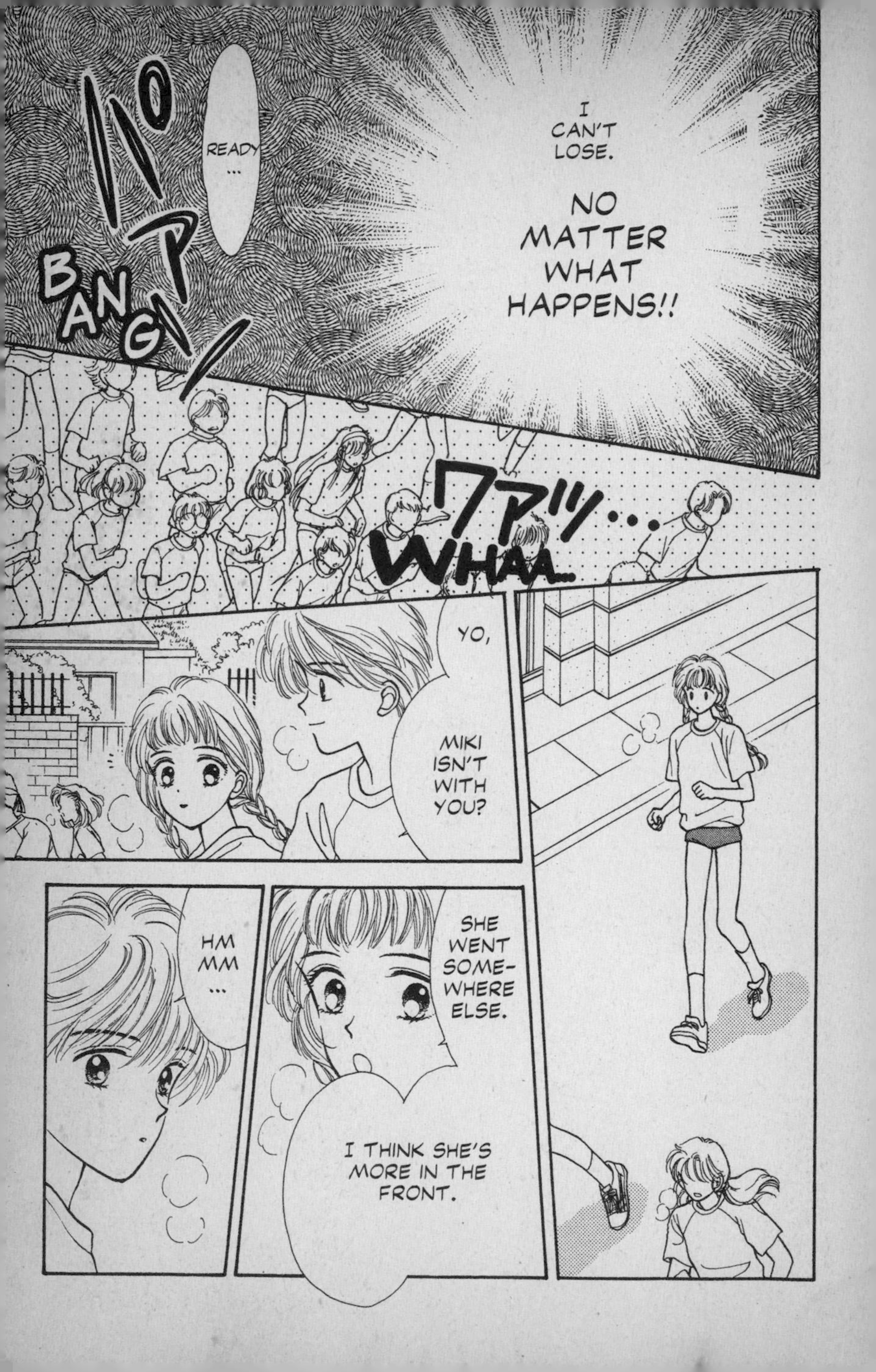
I CAN'T LOSE.
NO MATTER WHAT HAPPENS!!
READY...
BANG!
ワアッ…
WHAA...
YO,
MIKI ISN'T WITH YOU?
SHE WENT SOME-WHERE ELSE.
I THINK SHE'S MORE IN THE FRONT.
HM MM ...

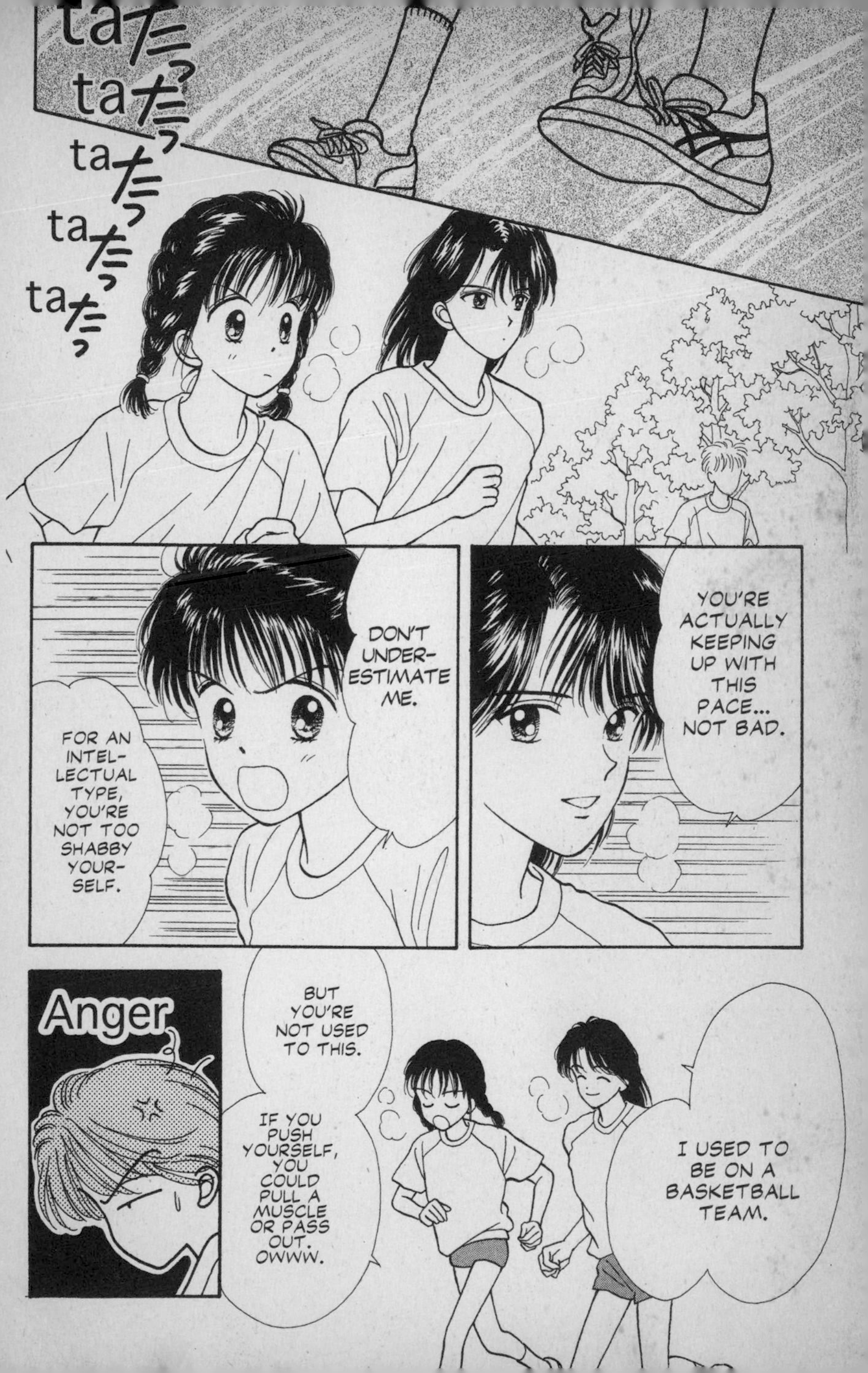
ta たっ
ta たっ
ta たっ
ta たっ
ta たっ
YOU'RE ACTUALLY KEEPING UP WITH THIS PACE... NOT BAD.
DON'T UNDER-ESTIMATE ME.
FOR AN INTEL-LECTUAL TYPE, YOU'RE NOT TOO SHABBY YOUR-SELF.
I USED TO BE ON A BASKETBALL TEAM.
BUT YOU'RE NOT USED TO THIS.
IF YOU PUSH YOURSELF, YOU COULD PULL A MUSCLE OR PASS OUT. OWWW.
Anger

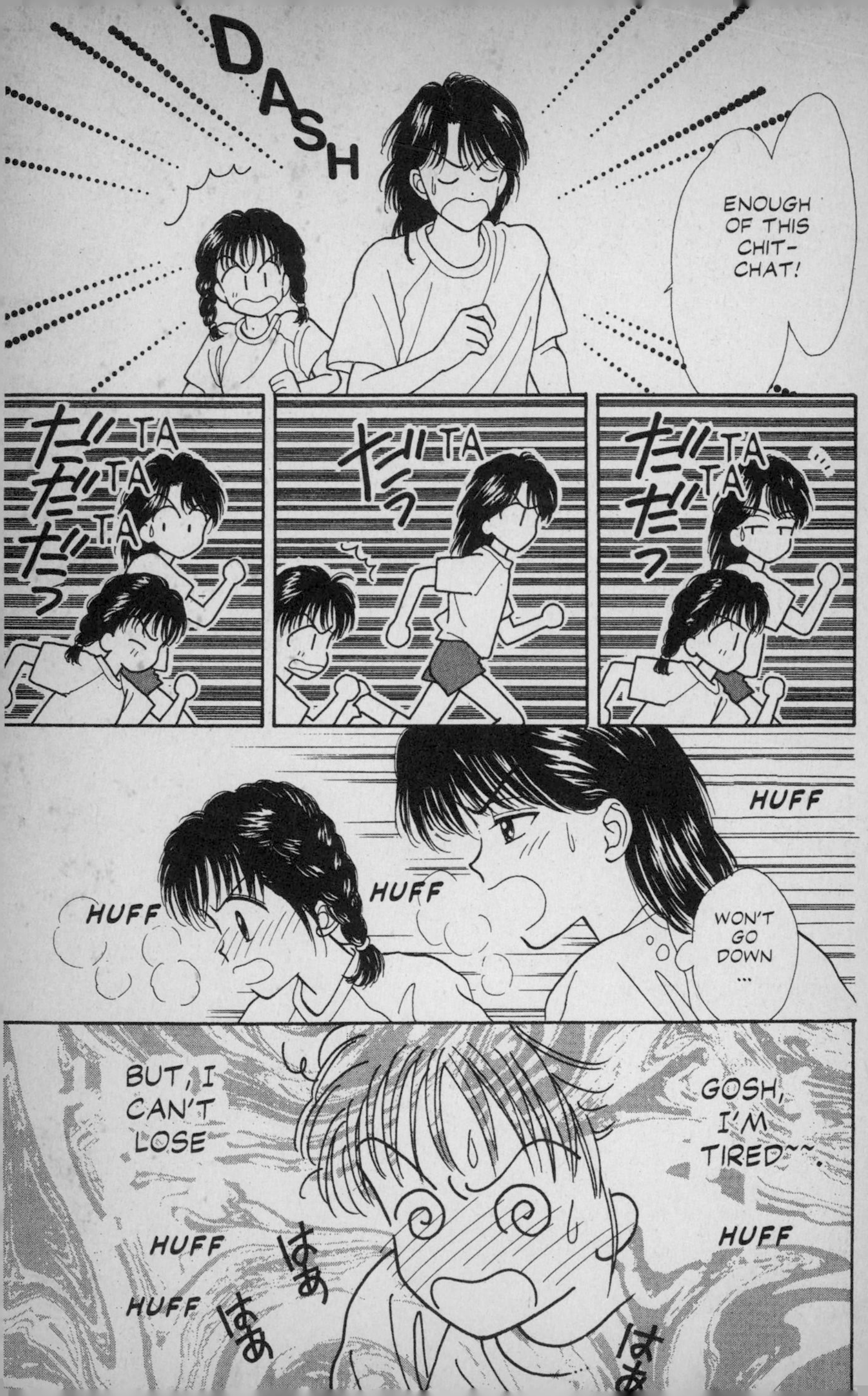
ENOUGH OF THIS CHIT-CHAT!
DASH
TA TA
TA
TA TA TA
HUFF
WON'T GO DOWN ...
HUFF
HUFF
GOSH, I'M TIRED~~.
HUFF
はあ
BUT, I CAN'T LOSE
はあ
HUFF
はあ
HUFF

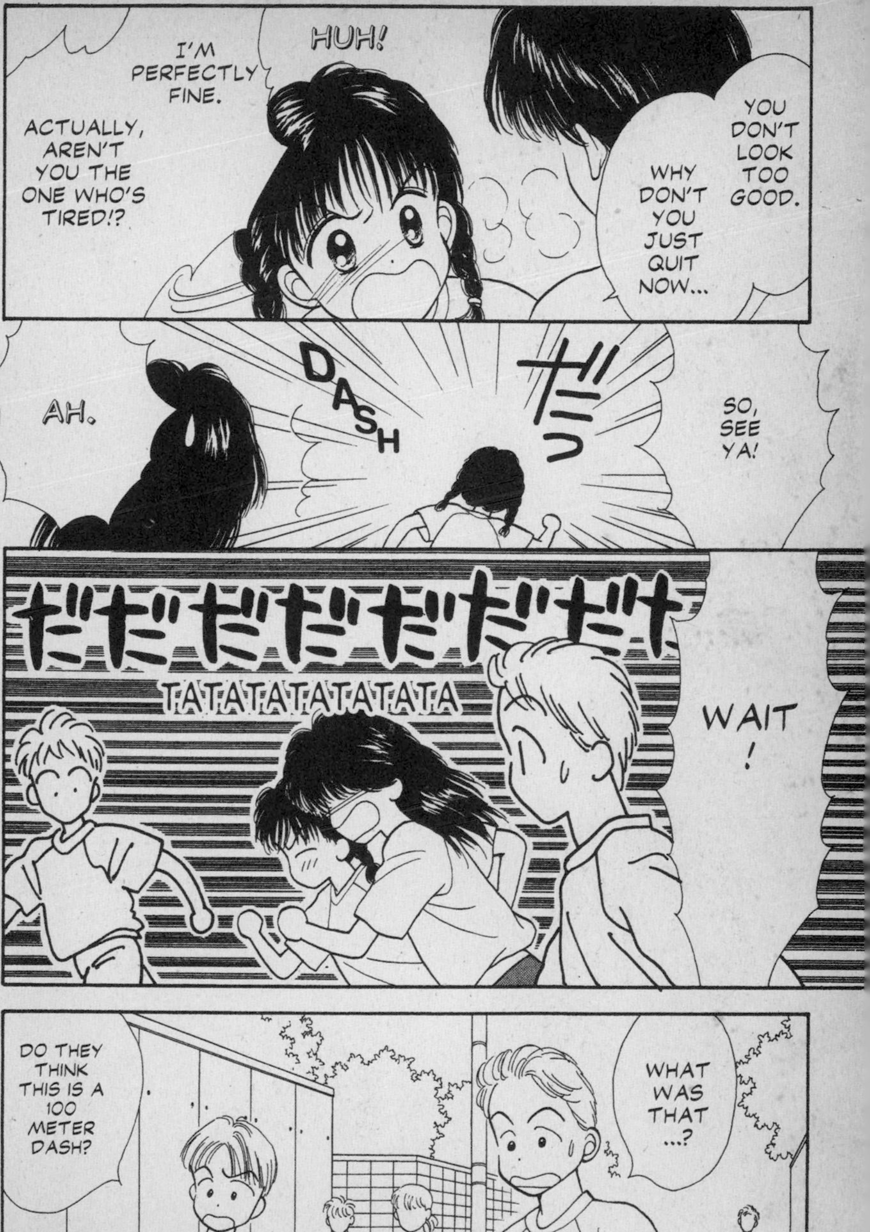
YOU DON'T LOOK TOO GOOD.
WHY DON'T YOU JUST QUIT NOW...
HUH!
I'M PERFECTLY FINE.
ACTUALLY, AREN'T YOU THE ONE WHO'S TIRED!?
SO, SEE YA!
ダッ
DASH
AH.
WAIT!
だだだだだだだ
TATATATATATATATA
WHAT WAS THAT ...?
DO THEY THINK THIS IS A 100 METER DASH?

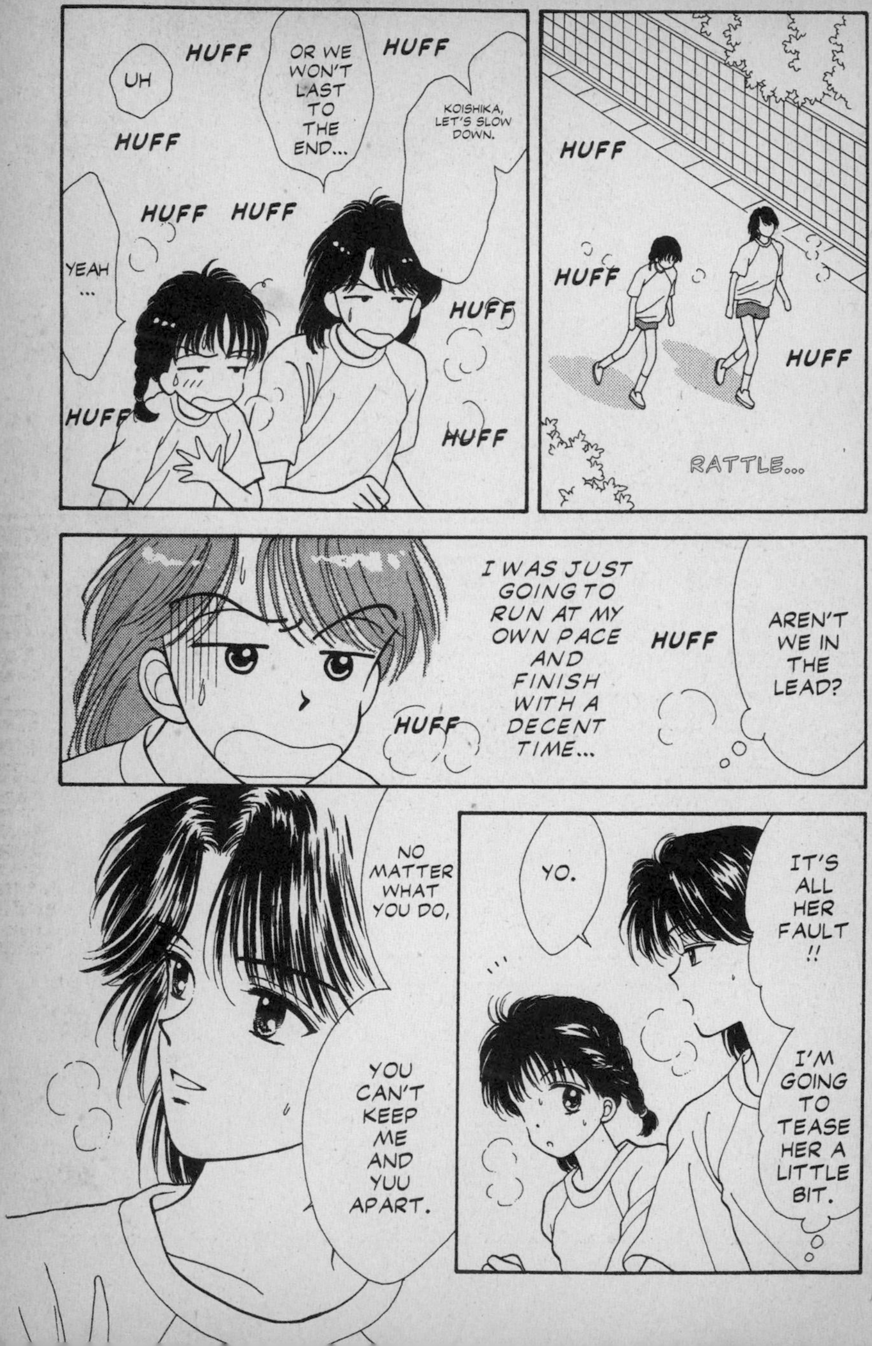
HUFF
HUFF
RATTLE...
KOISHIKA, LET'S SLOW DOWN.
HUFF
OR WE WON'T LAST TO THE END...
HUFF
UH
HUFF
HUFF HUFF
HUFF
YEAH ...
HUFF
HUFF
HUFF
AREN'T WE IN THE LEAD?
HUFF
I WAS JUST GOING TO RUN AT MY OWN PACE AND FINISH WITH A DECENT TIME...
HUFF
IT'S ALL HER FAULT !!
I'M GOING TO TEASE HER A LITTLE BIT.
YO.
NO MATTER WHAT YOU DO,
YOU CAN'T KEEP ME AND YUU APART.

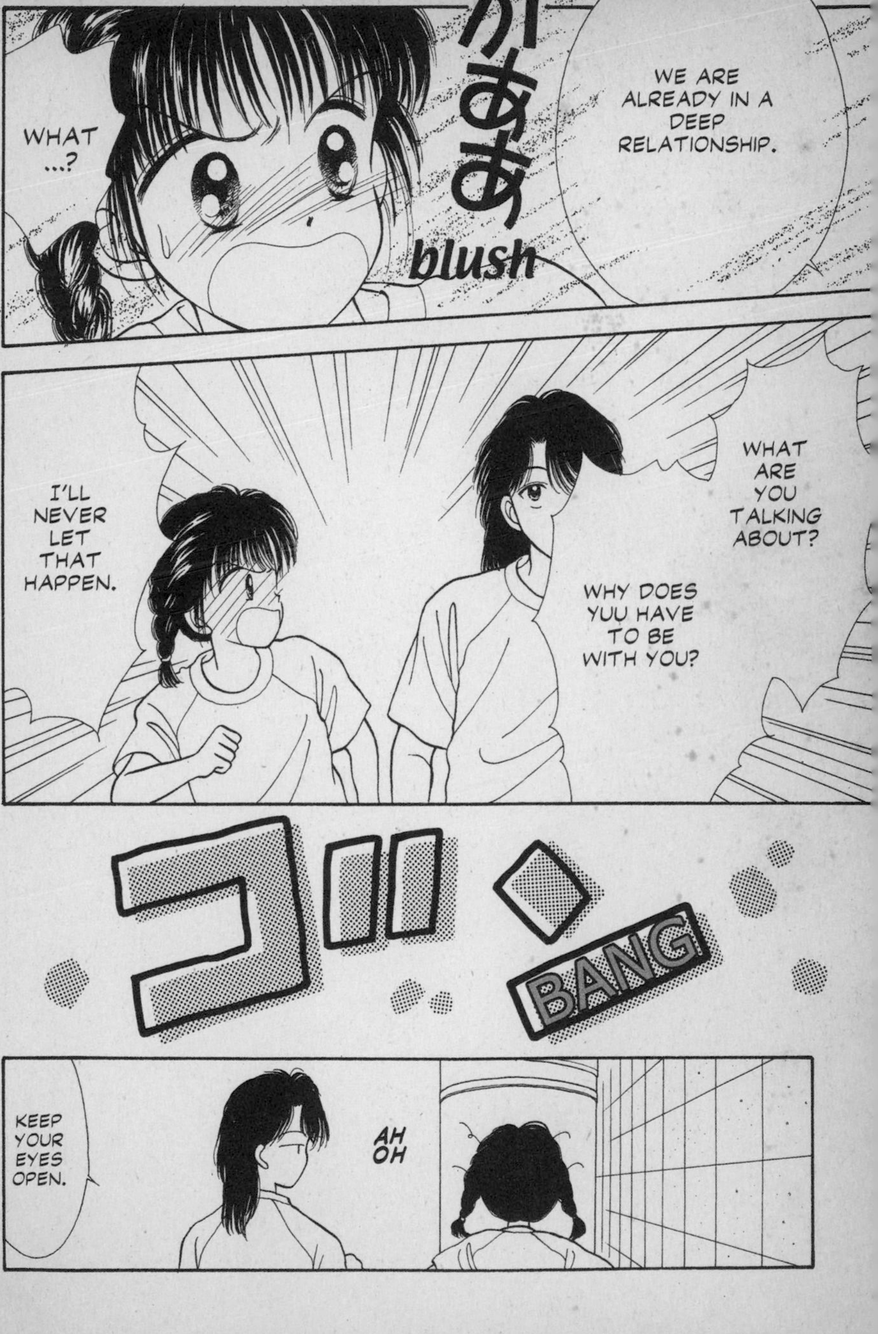
WE ARE ALREADY IN A DEEP RELATIONSHIP.
かあぁ
blush
WHAT ...?
WHAT ARE YOU TALKING ABOUT?
WHY DOES YUU HAVE TO BE WITH YOU?
I'LL NEVER LET THAT HAPPEN.
ゴッ
BANG
AH OH
KEEP YOUR EYES OPEN.

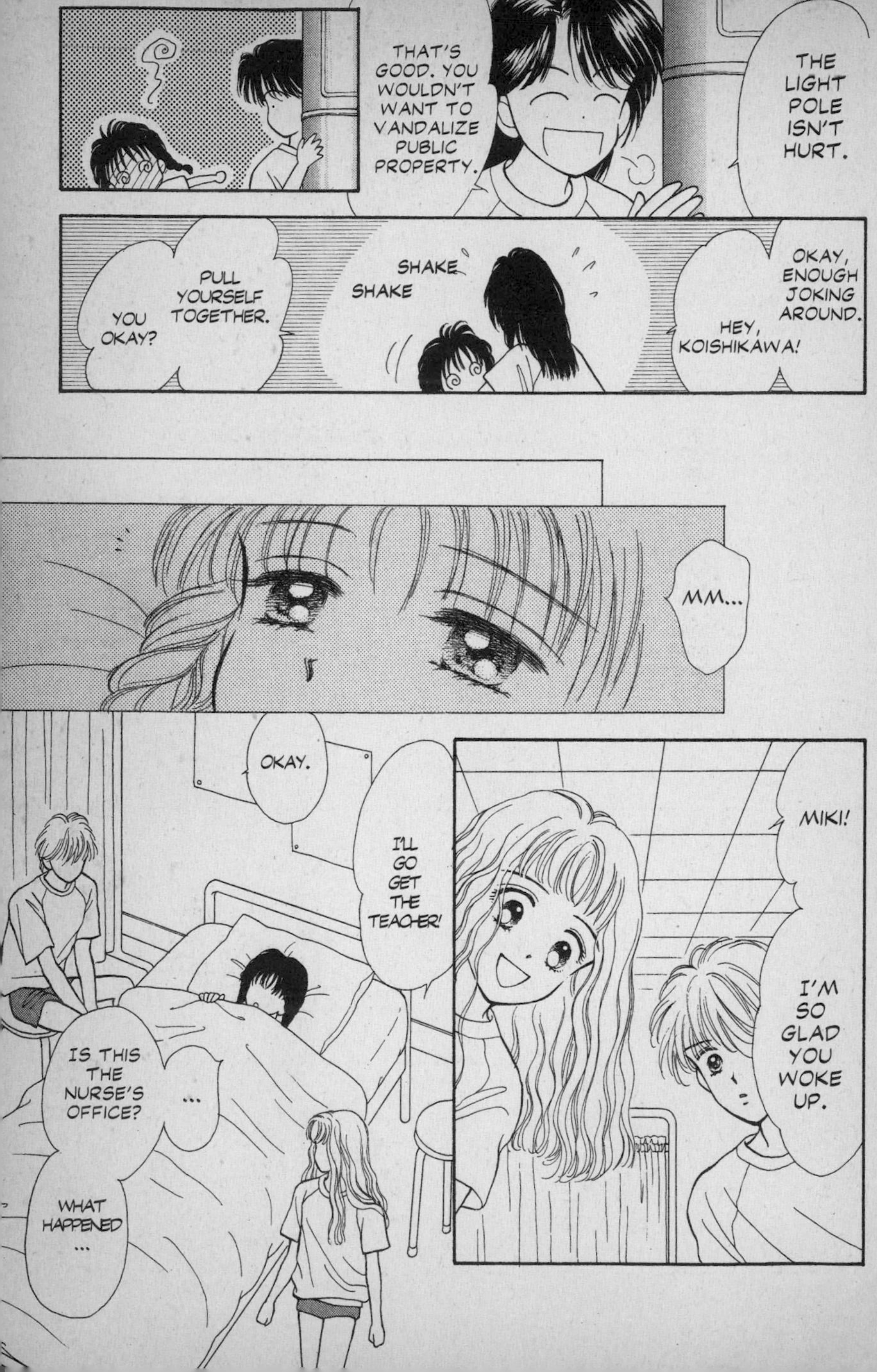
THE LIGHT POLE ISN'T HURT.
THAT'S GOOD. YOU WOULDN'T WANT TO VANDALIZE PUBLIC PROPERTY.
OKAY, ENOUGH JOKING AROUND.
HEY, KOISHIKAWA!
SHAKE
SHAKE
PULL YOURSELF TOGETHER.
YOU OKAY?
MM...
MIKI!
I'M SO GLAD YOU WOKE UP.
I'LL GO GET THE TEACHER!
OKAY.
...
IS THIS THE NURSE'S OFFICE?
WHAT HAPPENED ...

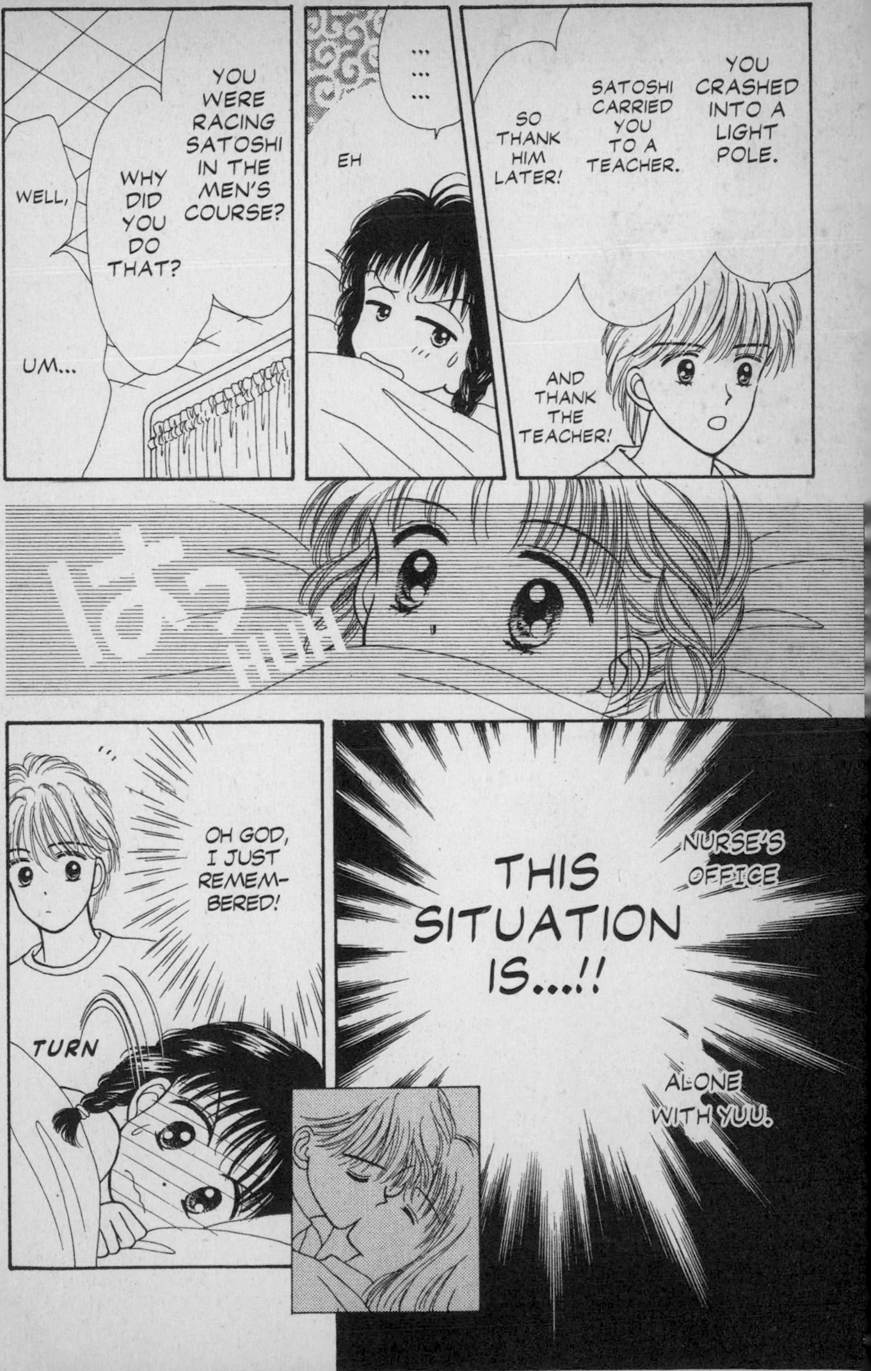
YOU CRASHED INTO A LIGHT POLE.
SATOSHI CARRIED YOU TO A TEACHER.
SO THANK HIM LATER!
AND THANK THE TEACHER!
......
......
......
EH
YOU WERE RACING SATOSHI IN THE MEN'S COURSE?
WHY DID YOU DO THAT?
WELL,
UM...
HUH
THIS SITUATION IS...!!
NURSE'S OFFICE
ALONE WITH YUU.
!!
OH GOD, I JUST REMEM-BERED!
TURN

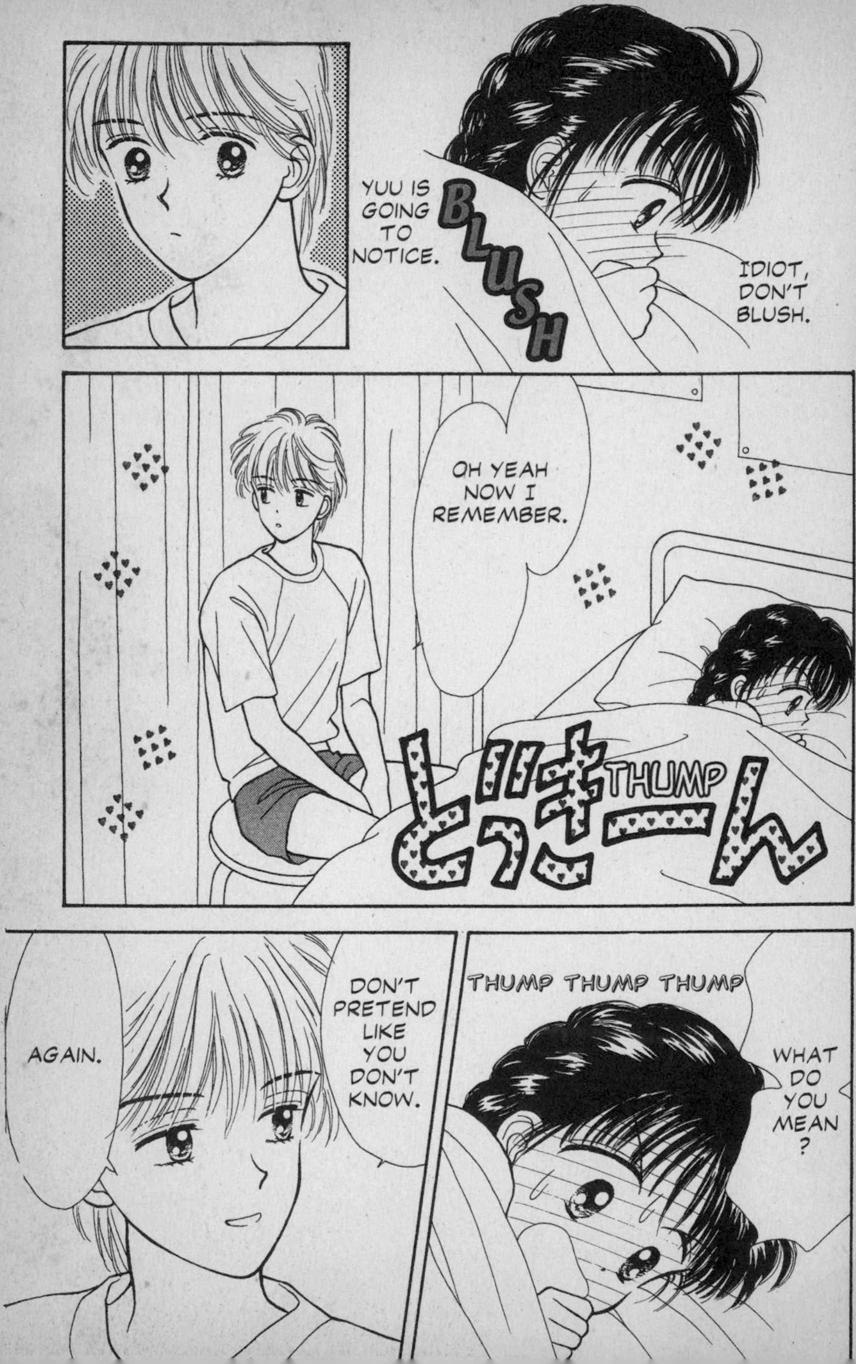
IDIOT, DON'T BLUSH.
BLUSH
YUU IS GOING TO NOTICE.
OH YEAH NOW I REMEMBER.
どっきーん
THUMP
THUMP THUMP THUMP
WHAT DO YOU MEAN?
DON'T PRETEND LIKE YOU DON'T KNOW.
AGAIN.

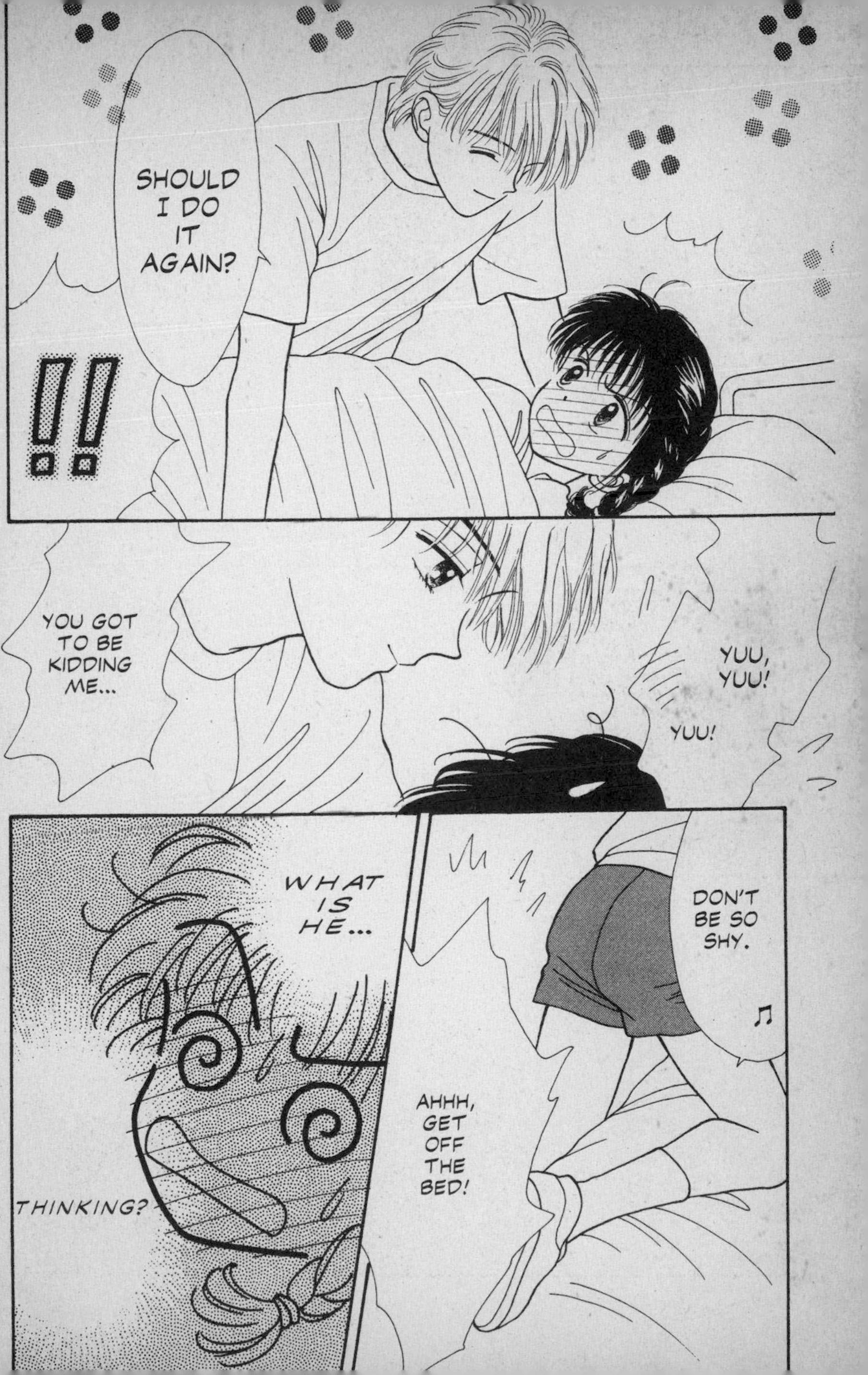
SHOULD I DO IT AGAIN?
!!
YUU, YUU!
YUU!
YOU GOT TO BE KIDDING ME...
DON'T BE SO SHY. ♫
AHHH, GET OFF THE BED!
WHAT IS HE... THINKING?

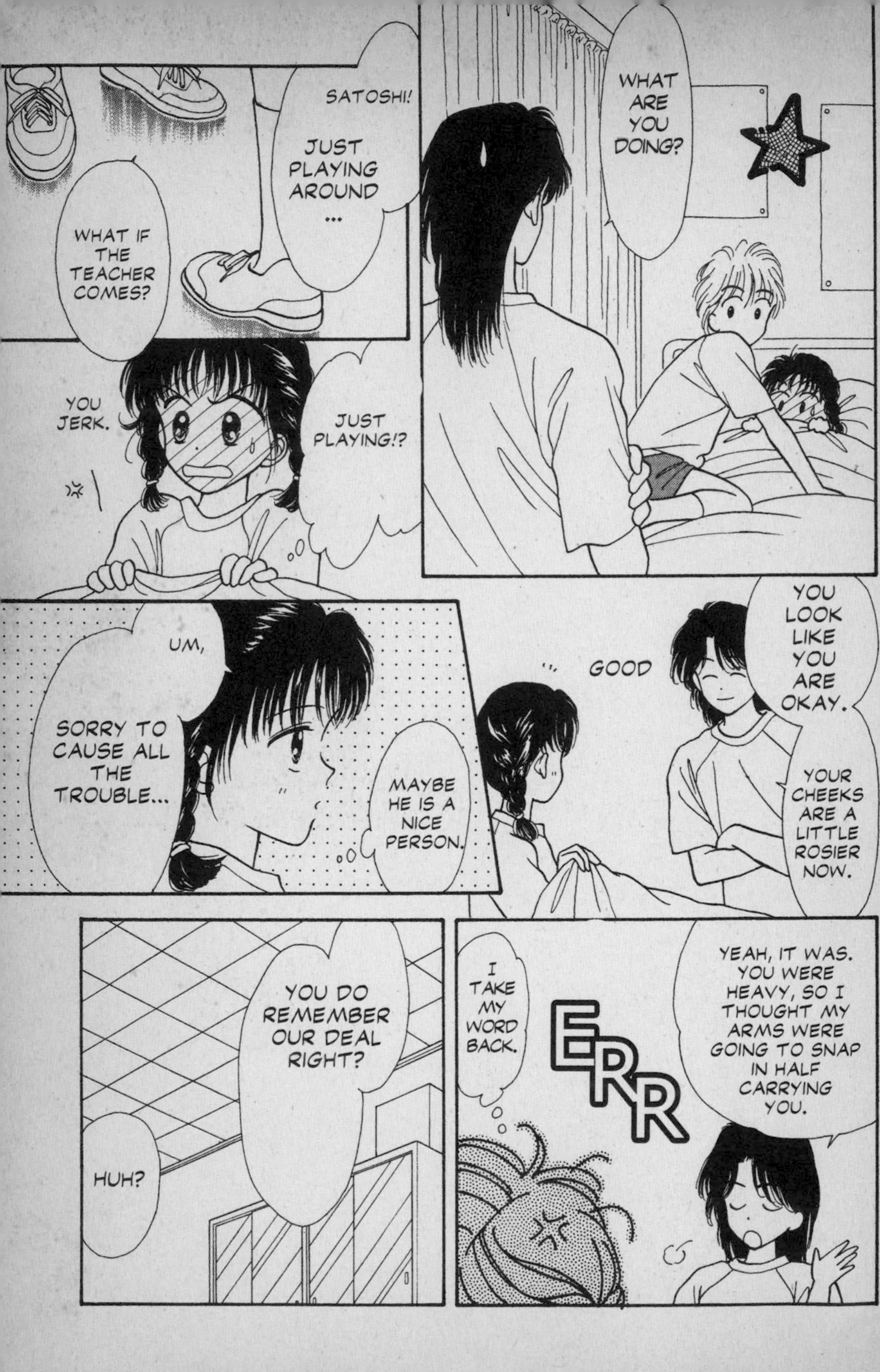
WHAT ARE YOU DOING?
SATOSHI!
JUST PLAYING AROUND ...
WHAT IF THE TEACHER COMES?
JUST PLAYING!?
YOU JERK.
YOU LOOK LIKE YOU ARE OKAY.
GOOD
YOUR CHEEKS ARE A LITTLE ROSIER NOW.
UM,
SORRY TO CAUSE ALL THE TROUBLE...
MAYBE HE IS A NICE PERSON.
YEAH, IT WAS. YOU WERE HEAVY, SO I THOUGHT MY ARMS WERE GOING TO SNAP IN HALF CARRYING YOU.
ERR
I TAKE MY WORD BACK.
YOU DO REMEMBER OUR DEAL RIGHT?
HUH?

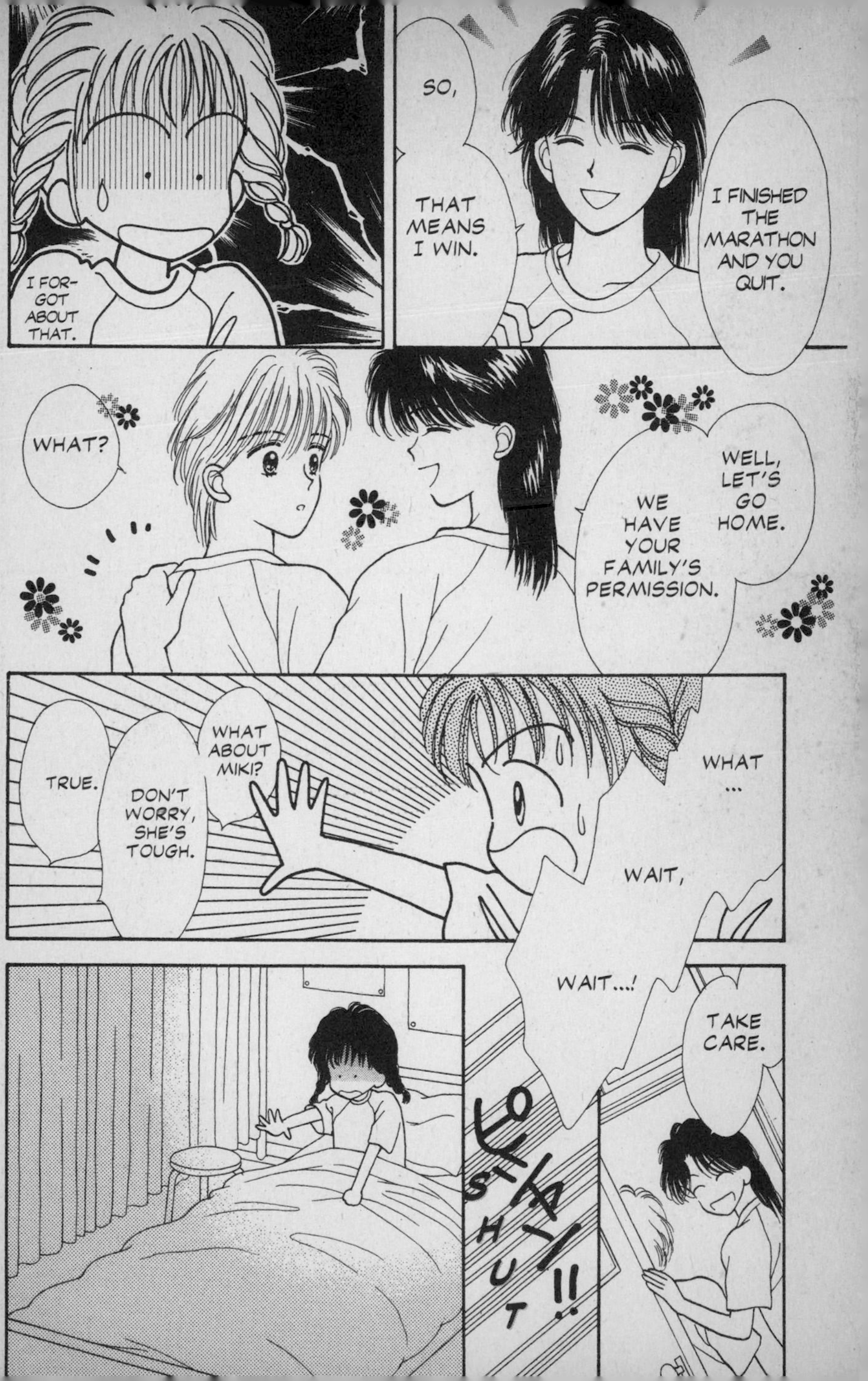
I FINISHED THE MARATHON AND YOU QUIT.
SO,
THAT MEANS I WIN.
I FOR-GOT ABOUT THAT.
WELL, LET'S GO HOME.
WE HAVE YOUR FAMILY'S PERMISSION.
WHAT?
WHAT...
WAIT,
WHAT ABOUT MIKI?
DON'T WORRY, SHE'S TOUGH.
TRUE.
WAIT...!
TAKE CARE.
SHUT!!

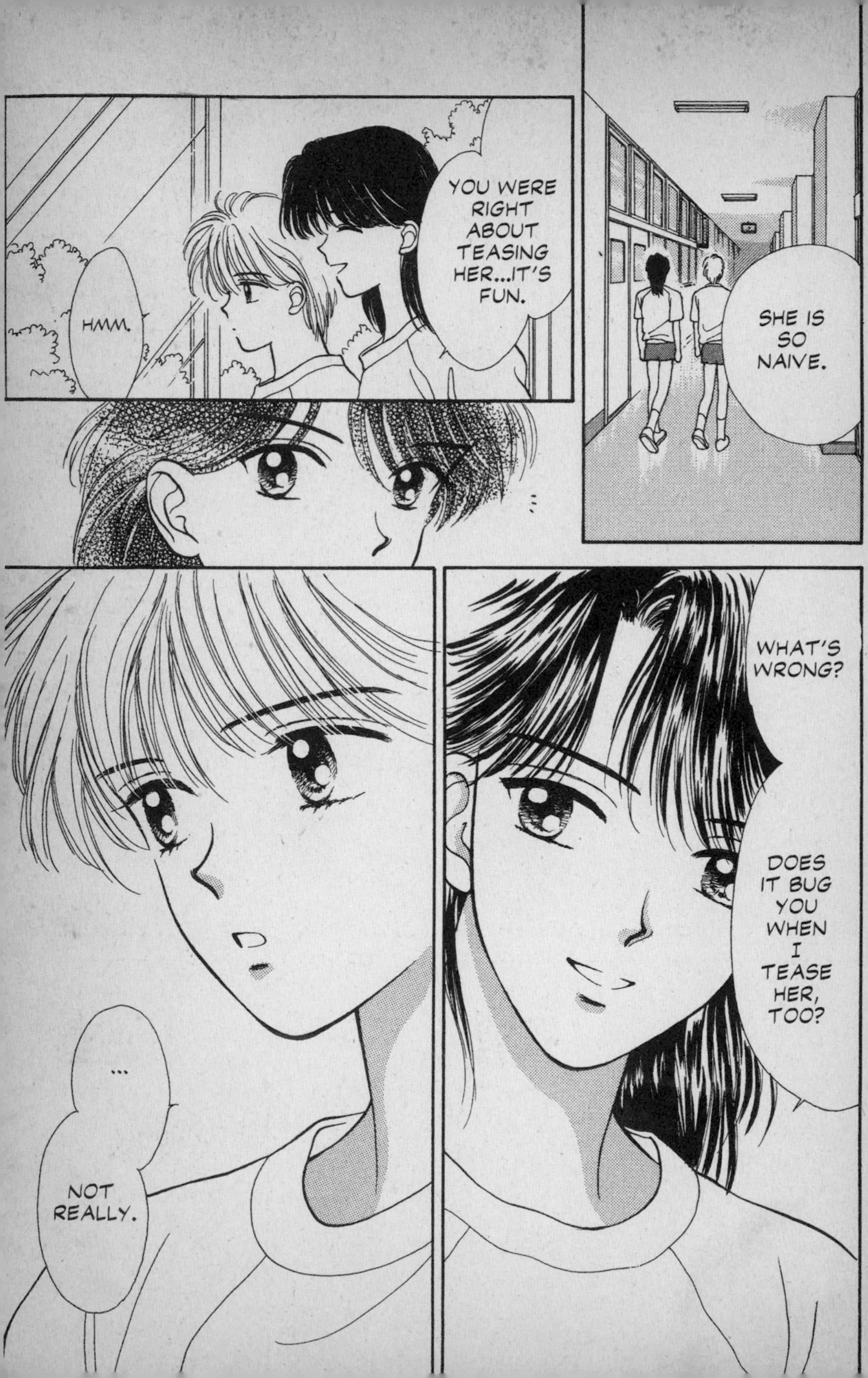
SHE IS SO NAIVE.
YOU WERE RIGHT ABOUT TEASING HER...IT'S FUN.
HMM.
WHAT'S WRONG?
DOES IT BUG YOU WHEN I TEASE HER, TOO?
...
NOT REALLY.

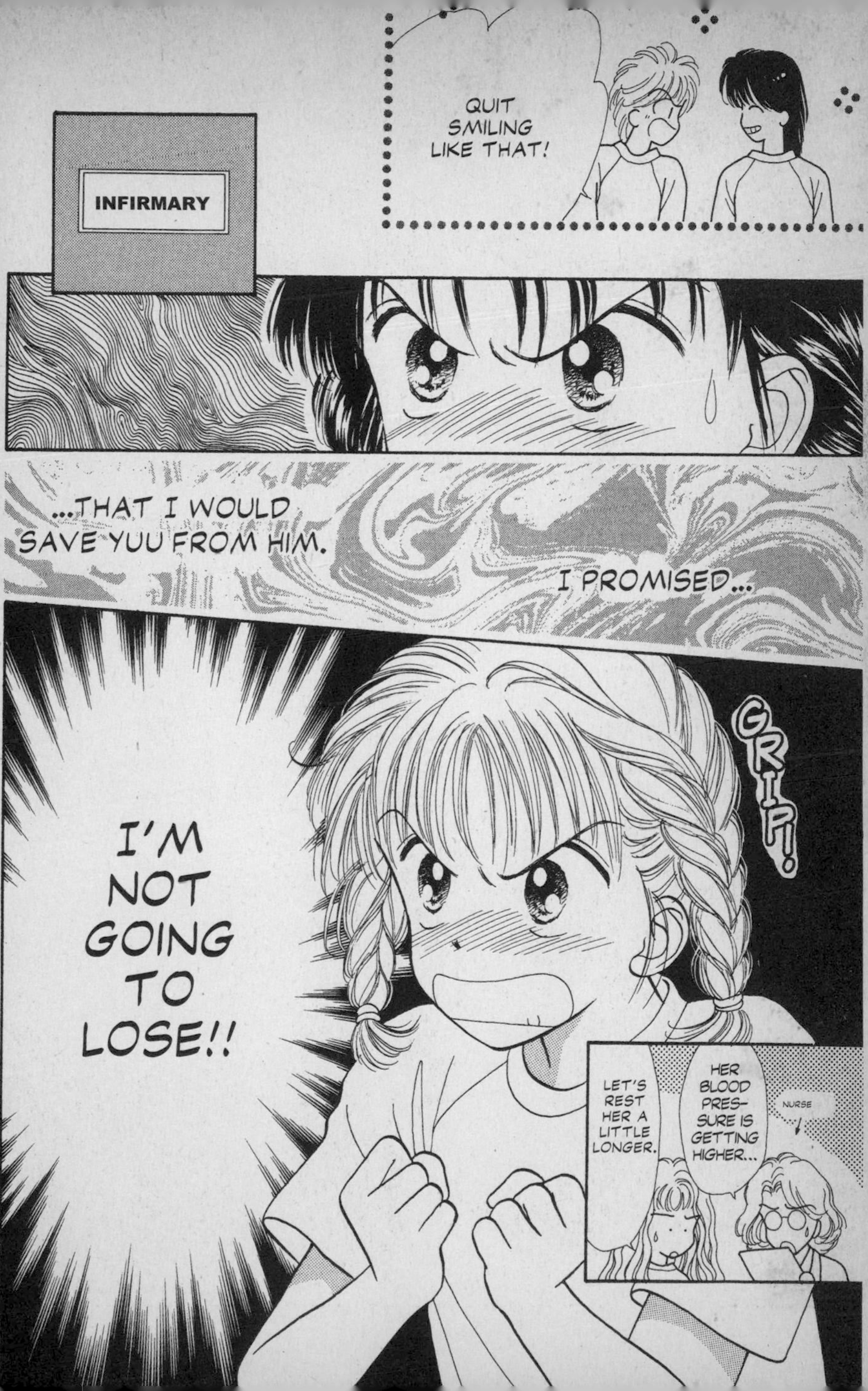
QUIT SMILING LIKE THAT!
INFIRMARY
I PROMISED...
...THAT I WOULD SAVE YUU FROM HIM.
GRIP!
I'M NOT GOING TO LOSE!!
NURSE
HER BLOOD PRES-SURE IS GETTING HIGHER...
LET'S REST HER A LITTLE LONGER.

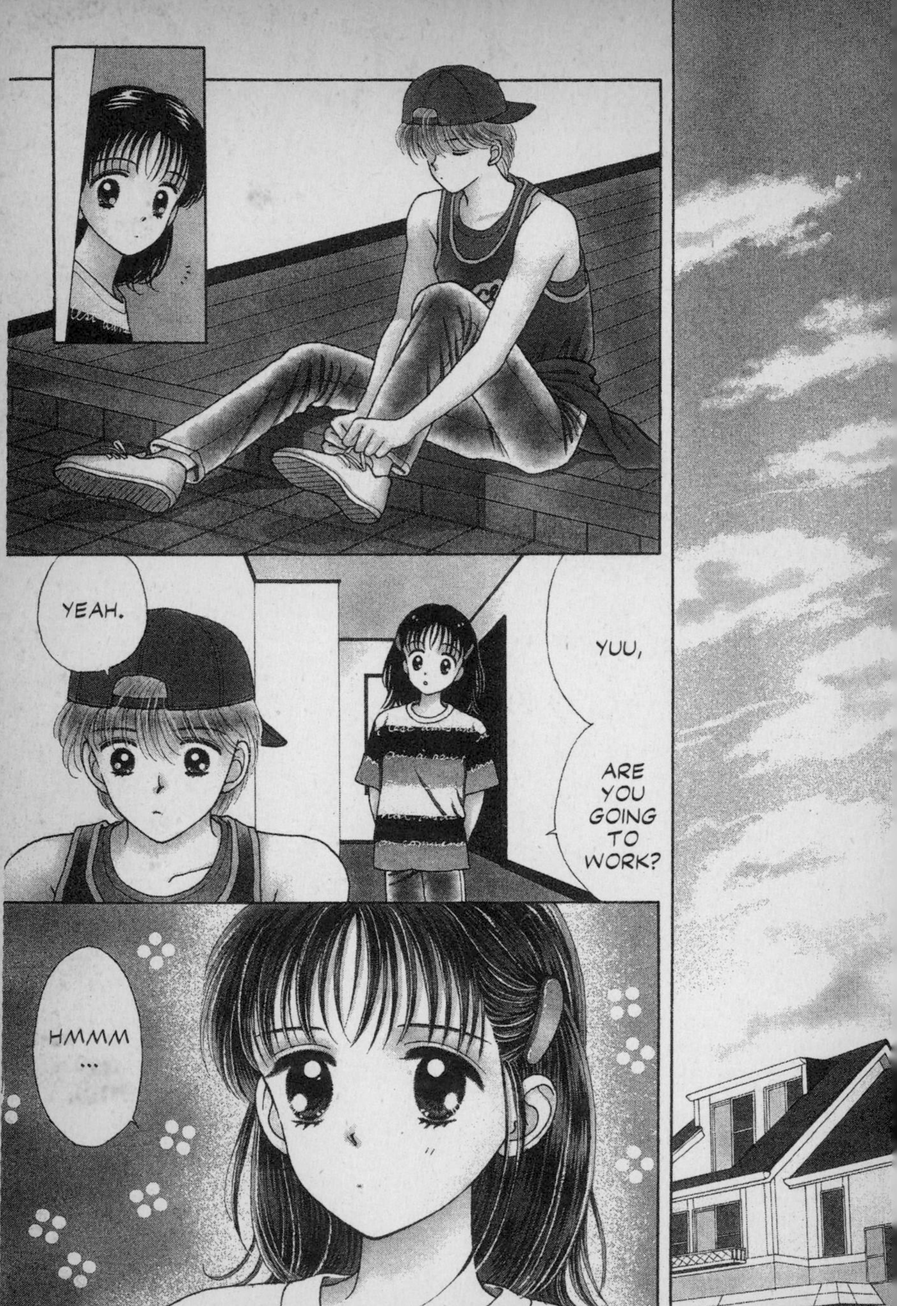
YUU,
ARE YOU GOING TO WORK?
YEAH.
HMMM ...

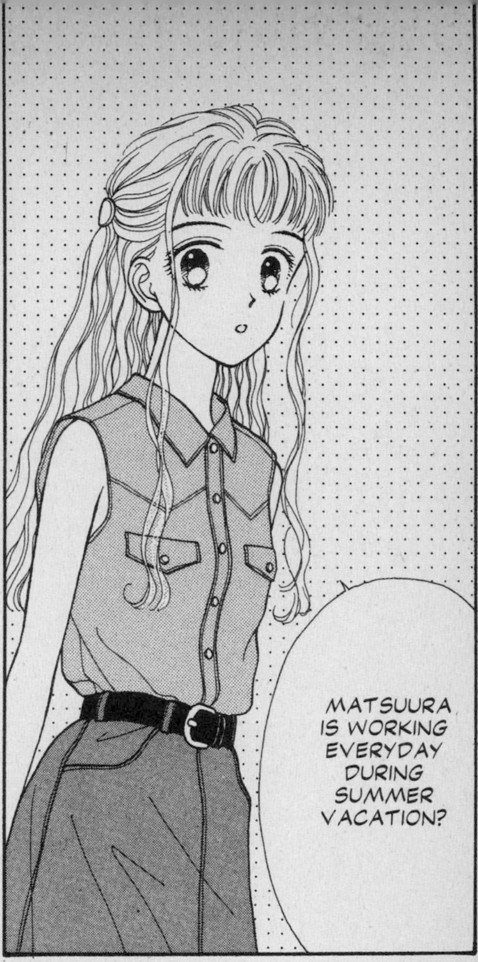
MATSUURA IS WORKING EVERYDAY DURING SUMMER VACATION?

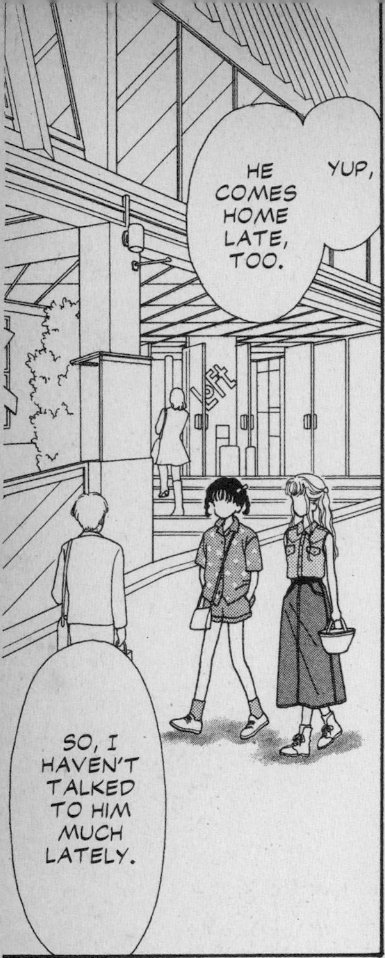
YUP, HE COMES HOME LATE, TOO.
SO, I HAVEN'T TALKED TO HIM MUCH LATELY.

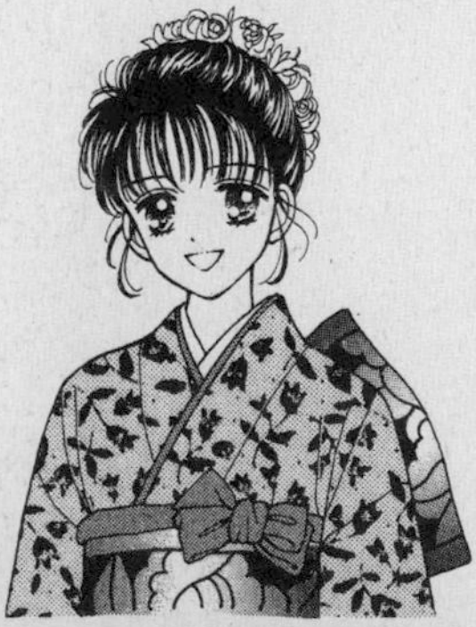

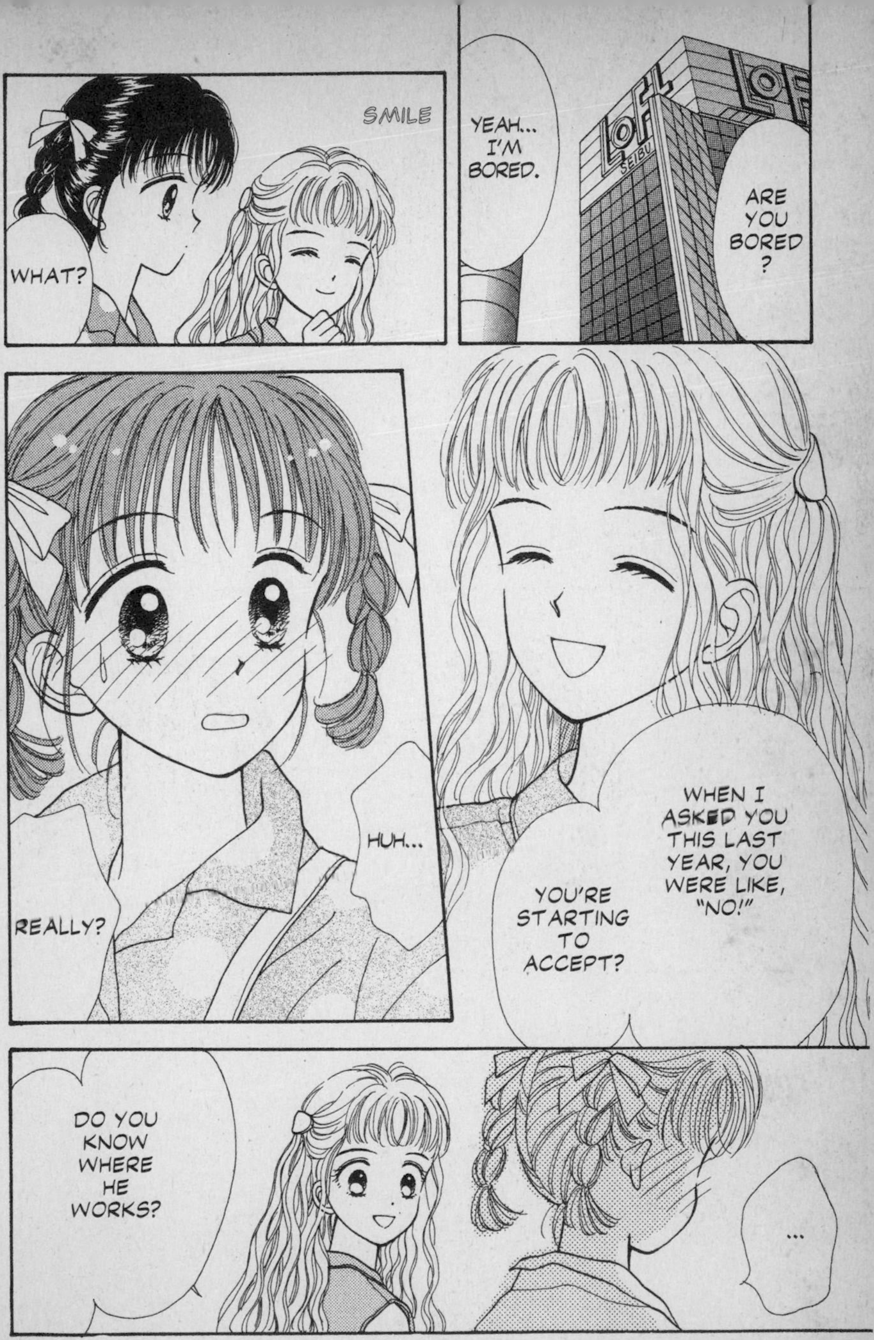
ARE YOU BORED?
YEAH... I'M BORED.
SEIBU
SMILE
WHAT?
WHEN I ASKED YOU THIS LAST YEAR, YOU WERE LIKE, "NO!"
YOU'RE STARTING TO ACCEPT?
HUH...
REALLY?
...
DO YOU KNOW WHERE HE WORKS?

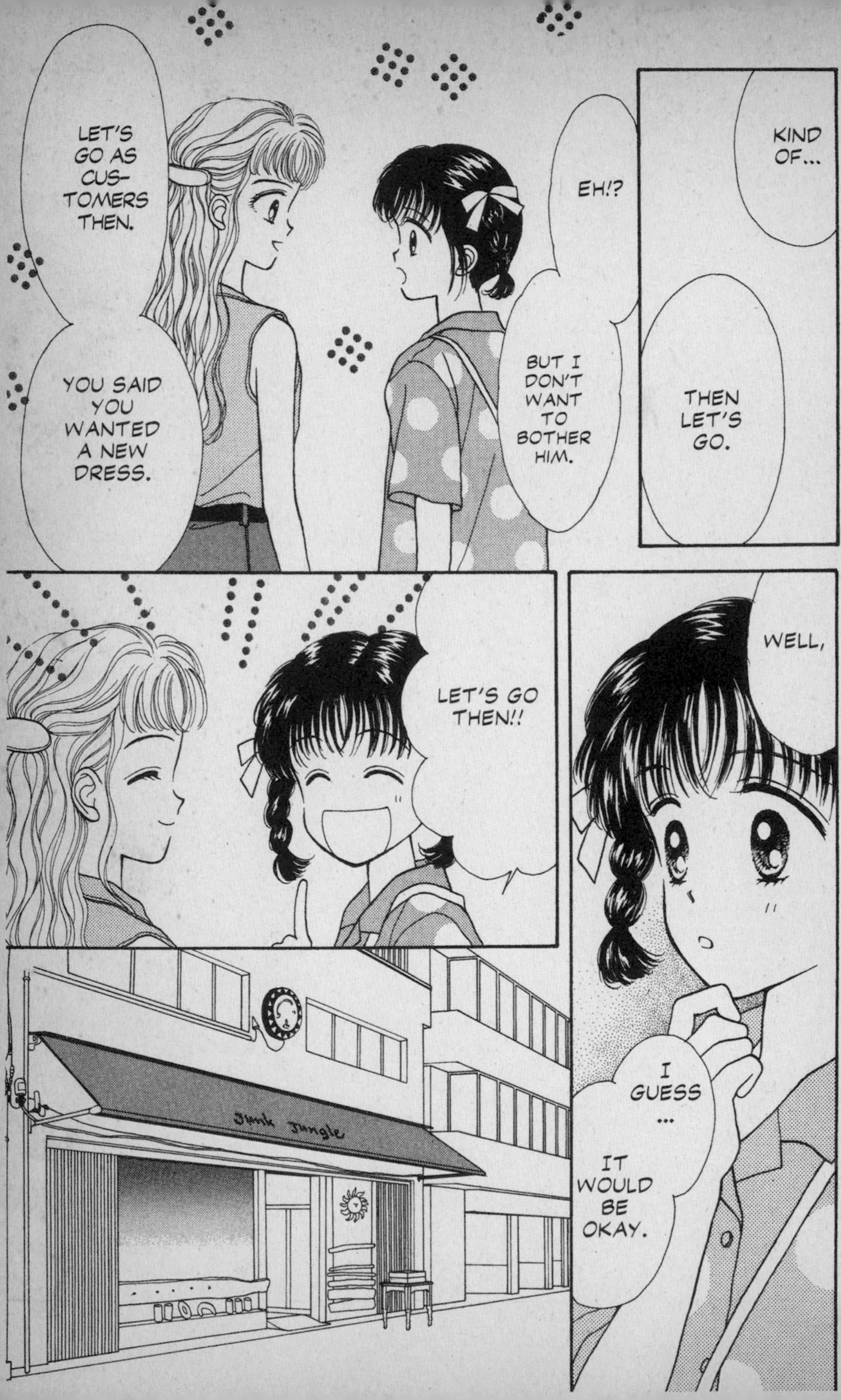
KIND OF...
THEN LET'S GO.
EH!?
BUT I DON'T WANT TO BOTHER HIM.
LET'S GO AS CUS-TOMERS THEN.
YOU SAID YOU WANTED A NEW DRESS.
WELL,
I GUESS ...
IT WOULD BE OKAY.
LET'S GO THEN!!
Junk Jungle

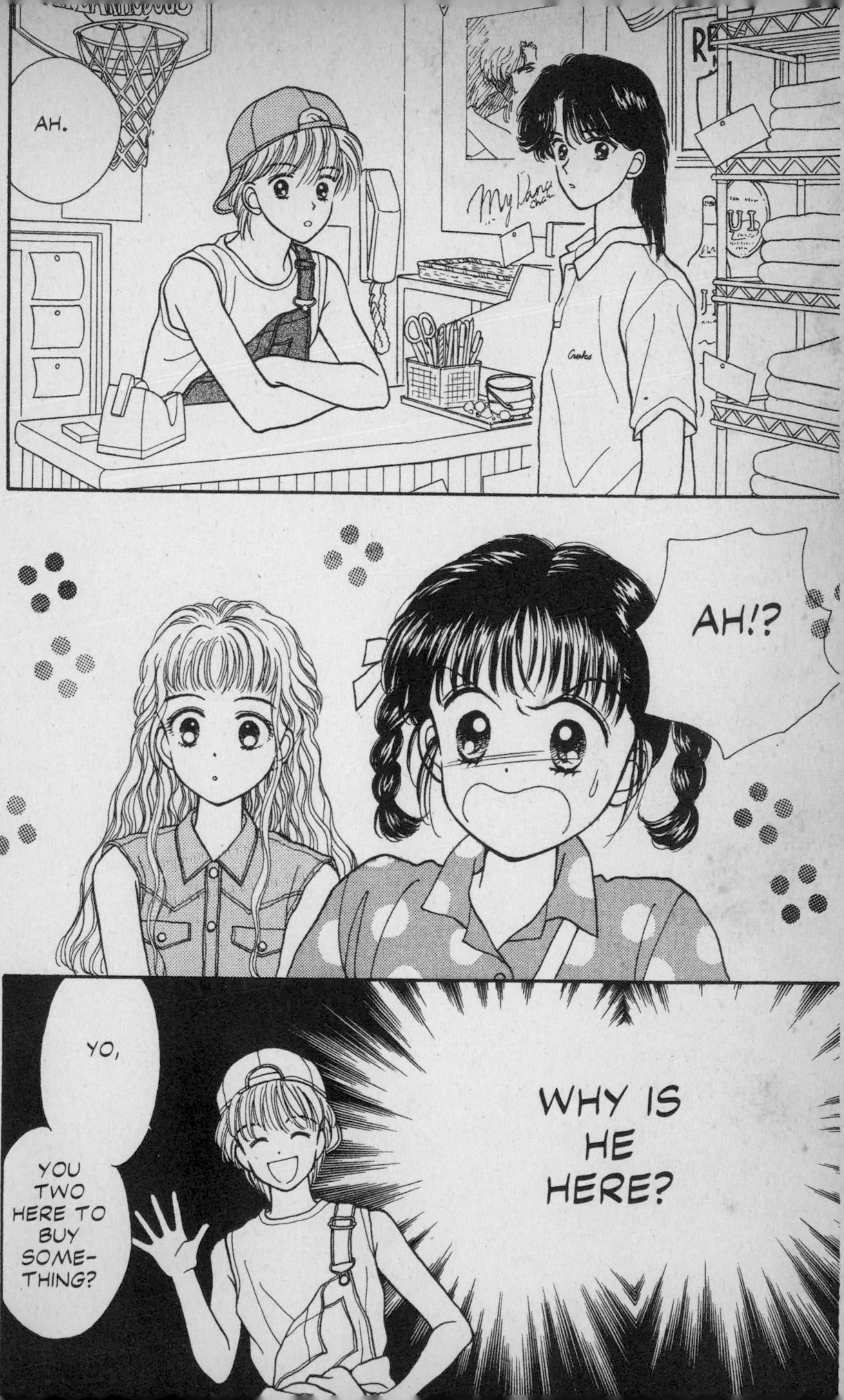
AH.
AH!?
WHY IS HE HERE?
YO,
YOU TWO HERE TO BUY SOME-THING?

FREE TALK ④

When Handsome Girlfriend became an animation video, we did not have much time so it became a serious video. But this time around, we have more time so there are lots of fun scenes and episodes. The animation director is really taking his time and creating the scripts so it should be a very good series.

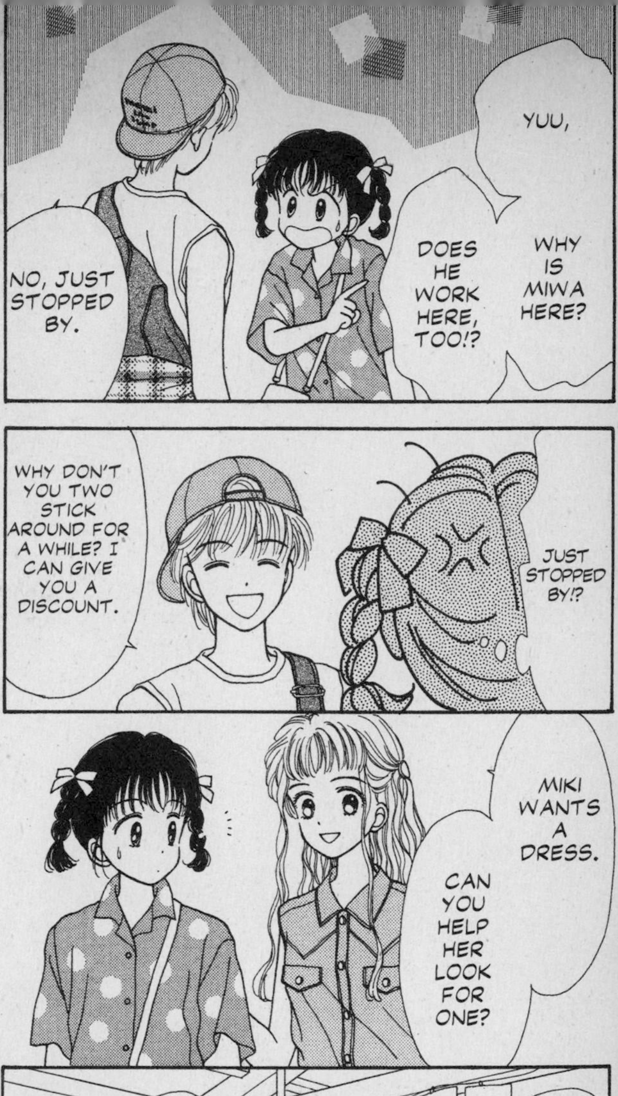
YUU,
WHY IS MIWA HERE?
DOES HE WORK HERE, TOO!?
NO, JUST STOPPED BY.
JUST STOPPED BY!?
WHY DON'T YOU TWO STICK AROUND FOR A WHILE? I CAN GIVE YOU A DISCOUNT.
MIKI WANTS A DRESS.
CAN YOU HELP HER LOOK FOR ONE?
WHAT KIND DO YOU WANT?
UM...
A COTTON ONE WITH A LARGE PRINT ...

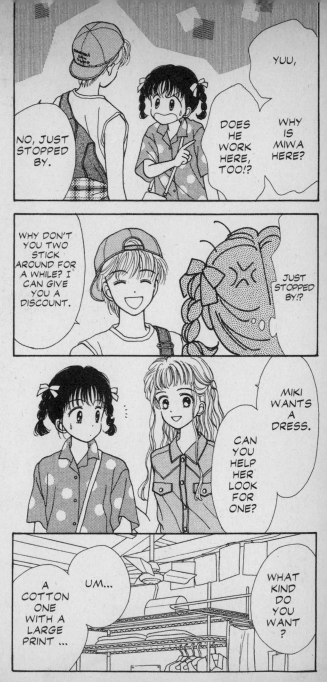

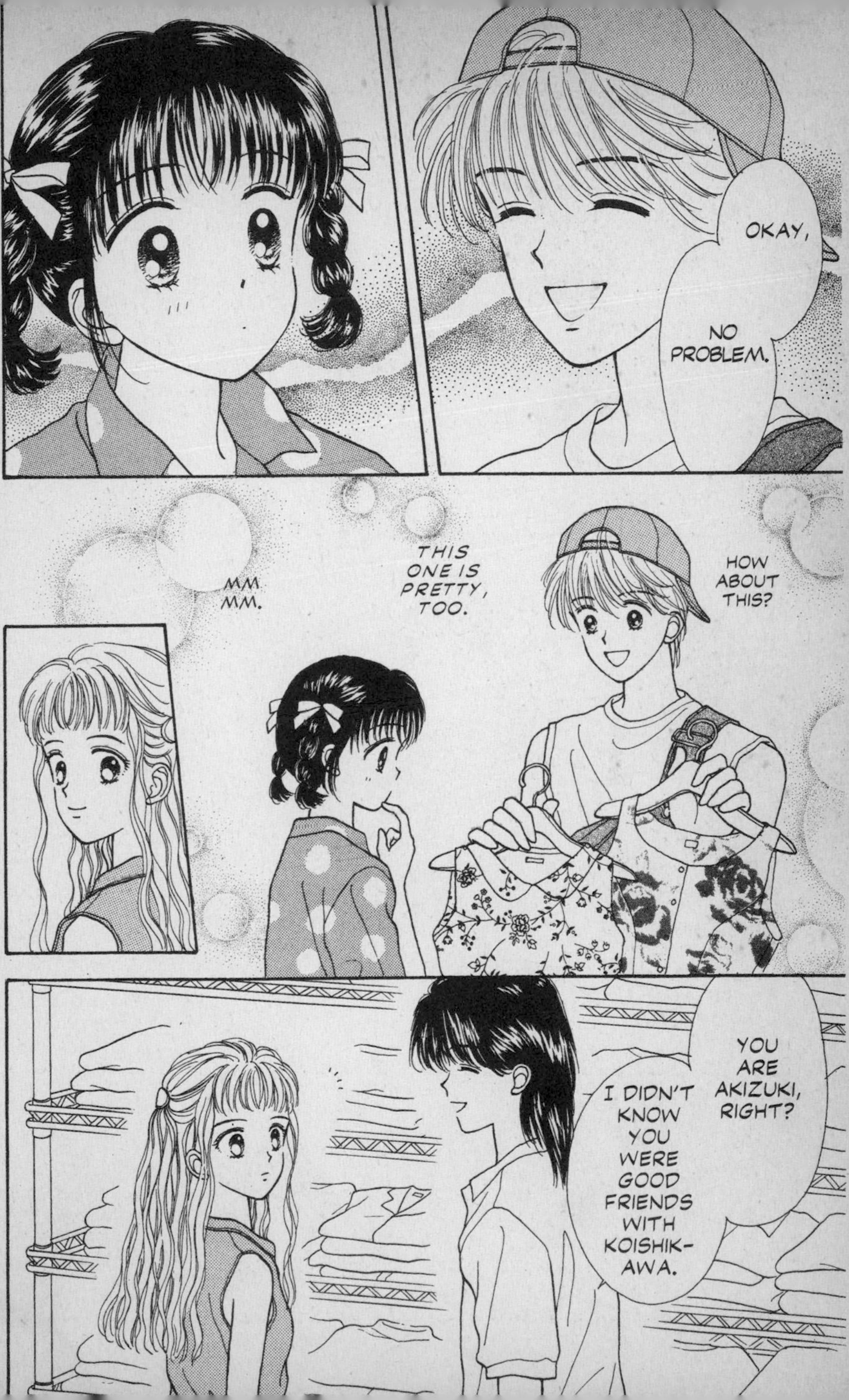
OKAY, NO PROBLEM.
HOW ABOUT THIS?
THIS ONE IS PRETTY, TOO.
MM MM.
YOU ARE AKIZUKI, RIGHT?
I DIDN'T KNOW YOU WERE GOOD FRIENDS WITH KOISHIK-AWA.

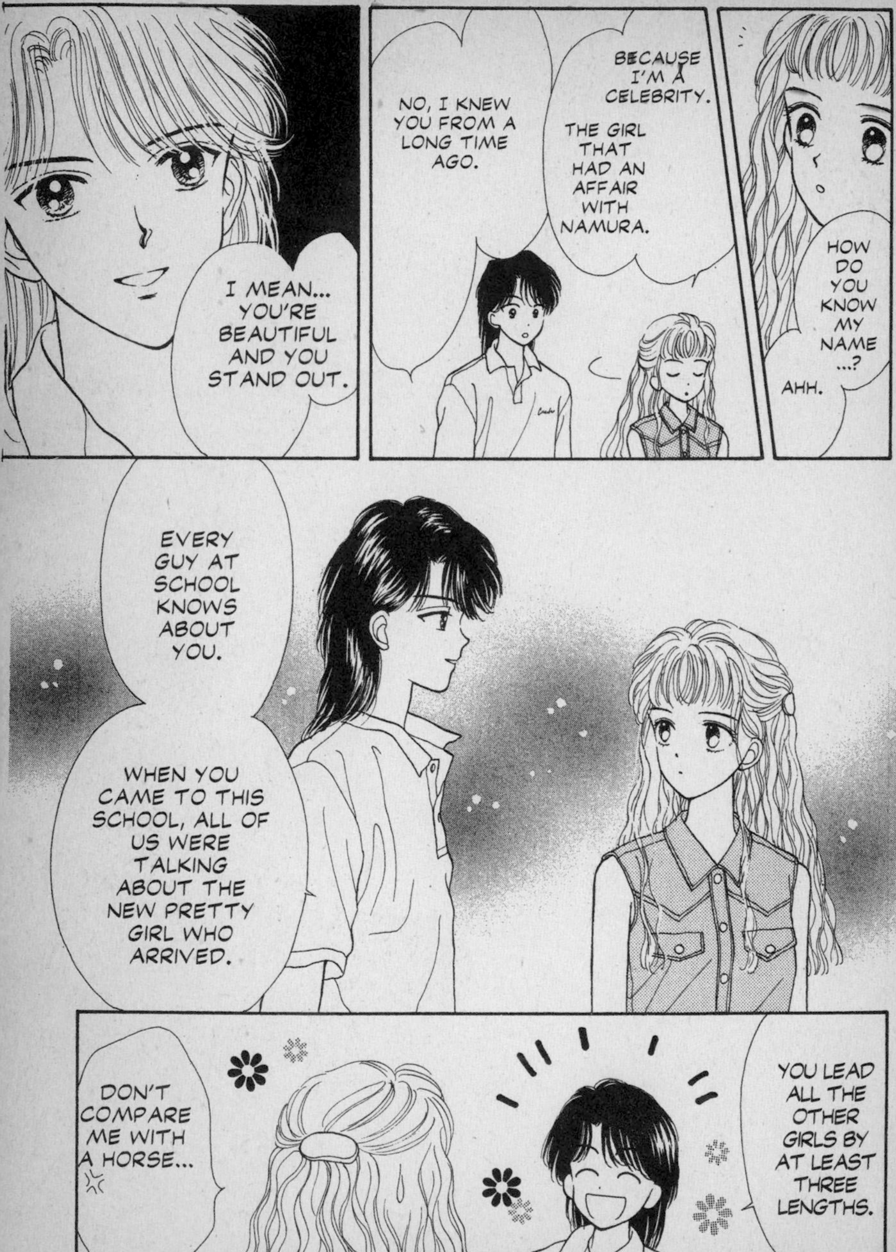
HOW DO YOU KNOW MY NAME ...?
AHH.
BECAUSE I'M A CELEBRITY.
THE GIRL THAT HAD AN AFFAIR WITH NAMURA.
NO, I KNEW YOU FROM A LONG TIME AGO.
I MEAN... YOU'RE BEAUTIFUL AND YOU STAND OUT.
EVERY GUY AT SCHOOL KNOWS ABOUT YOU.
WHEN YOU CAME TO THIS SCHOOL, ALL OF US WERE TALKING ABOUT THE NEW PRETTY GIRL WHO ARRIVED.
YOU LEAD ALL THE OTHER GIRLS BY AT LEAST THREE LENGTHS.
DON'T COMPARE ME WITH A HORSE...

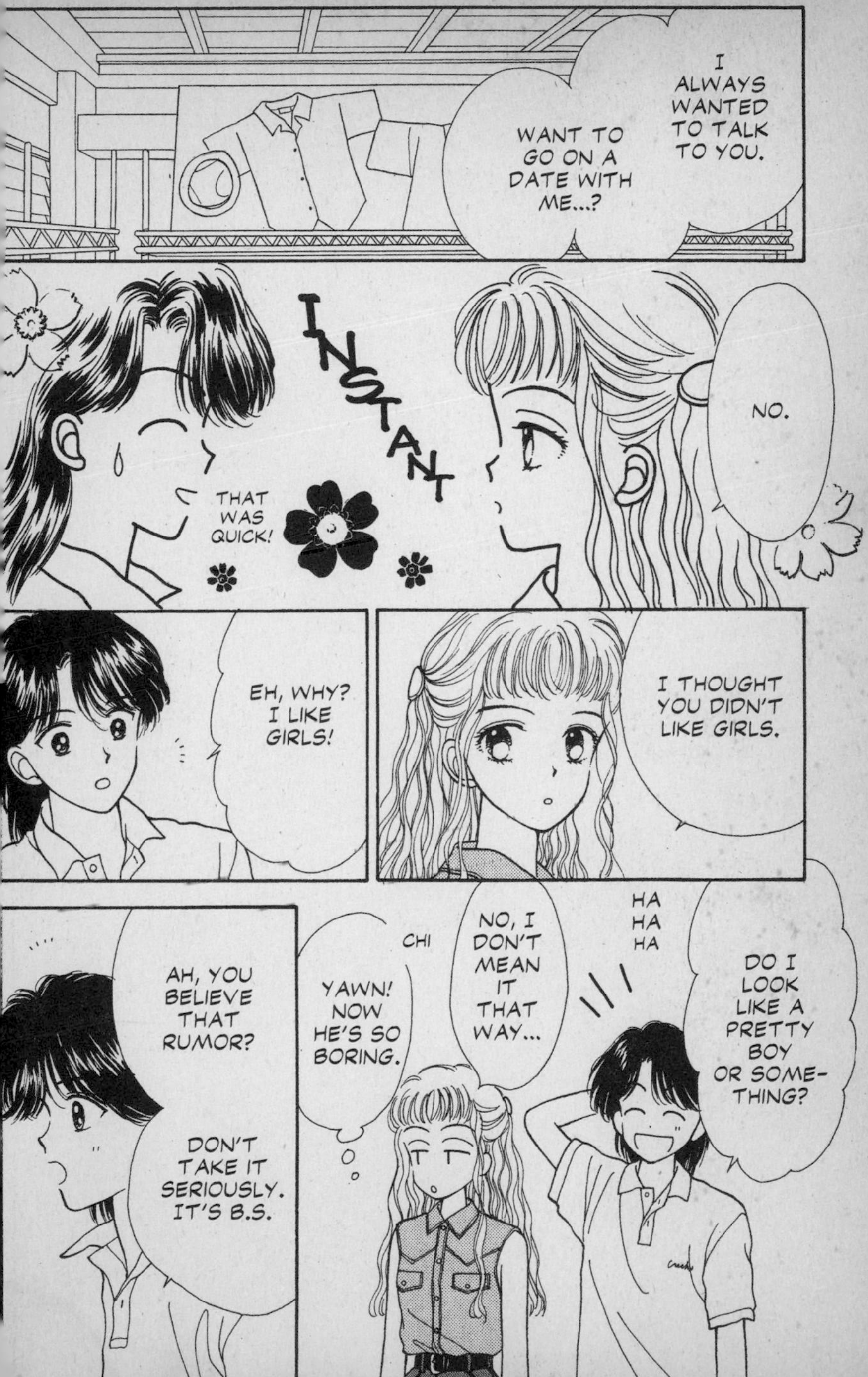
I ALWAYS WANTED TO TALK TO YOU.
WANT TO GO ON A DATE WITH ME...?
NO.
INSTANT
THAT WAS QUICK!
I THOUGHT YOU DIDN'T LIKE GIRLS.
EH, WHY? I LIKE GIRLS!
DO I LOOK LIKE A PRETTY BOY OR SOMETHING?
HA HA HA
NO, I DON'T MEAN IT THAT WAY...
CHI
YAWN! NOW HE'S SO BORING.
AH, YOU BELIEVE THAT RUMOR?
DON'T TAKE IT SERIOUSLY. IT'S B.S.

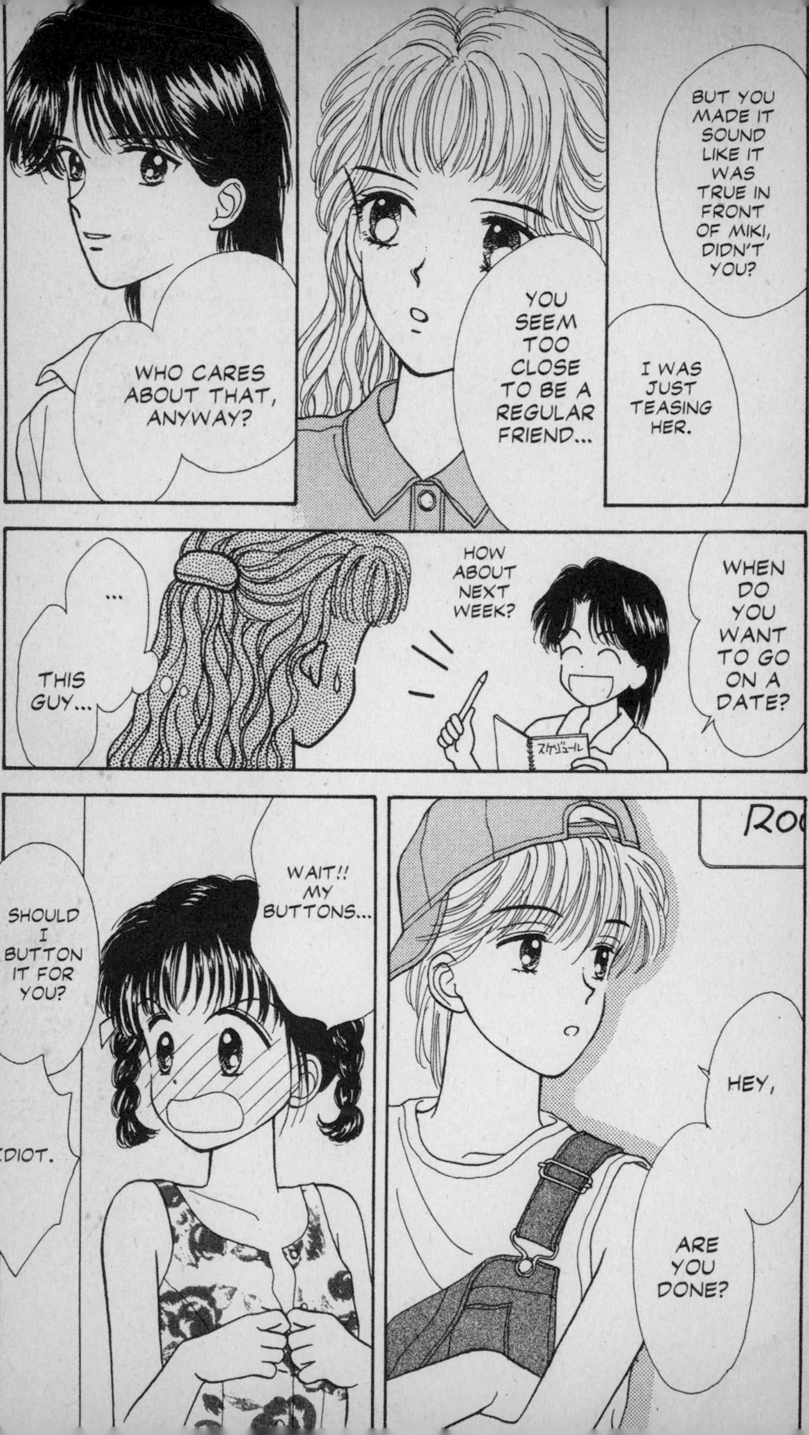
BUT YOU MADE IT SOUND LIKE IT WAS TRUE IN FRONT OF MIKI, DIDN'T YOU?
I WAS JUST TEASING HER.
YOU SEEM TOO CLOSE TO BE A REGULAR FRIEND...
WHO CARES ABOUT THAT, ANYWAY?
WHEN DO YOU WANT TO GO ON A DATE?
HOW ABOUT NEXT WEEK?
スケジュール
...
THIS GUY...
HEY,
ARE YOU DONE?
WAIT!! MY BUTTONS...
SHOULD I BUTTON IT FOR YOU?
IDIOT.

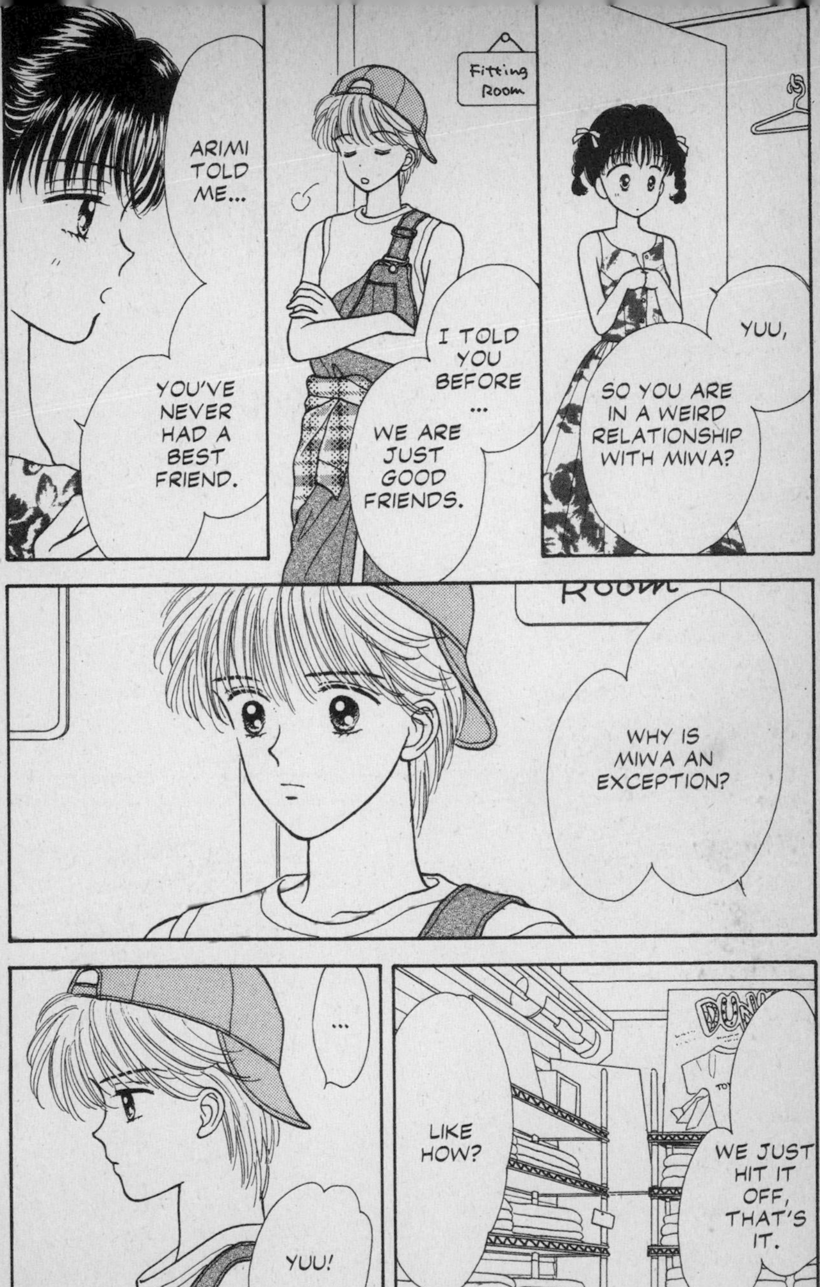
Fitting Room
YUU,
SO YOU ARE IN A WEIRD RELATIONSHIP WITH MIWA?
I TOLD YOU BEFORE ...
WE ARE JUST GOOD FRIENDS.
ARIMI TOLD ME...
YOU'VE NEVER HAD A BEST FRIEND.
WHY IS MIWA AN EXCEPTION?
WE JUST HIT IT OFF, THAT'S IT.
LIKE HOW?
...
YUU!

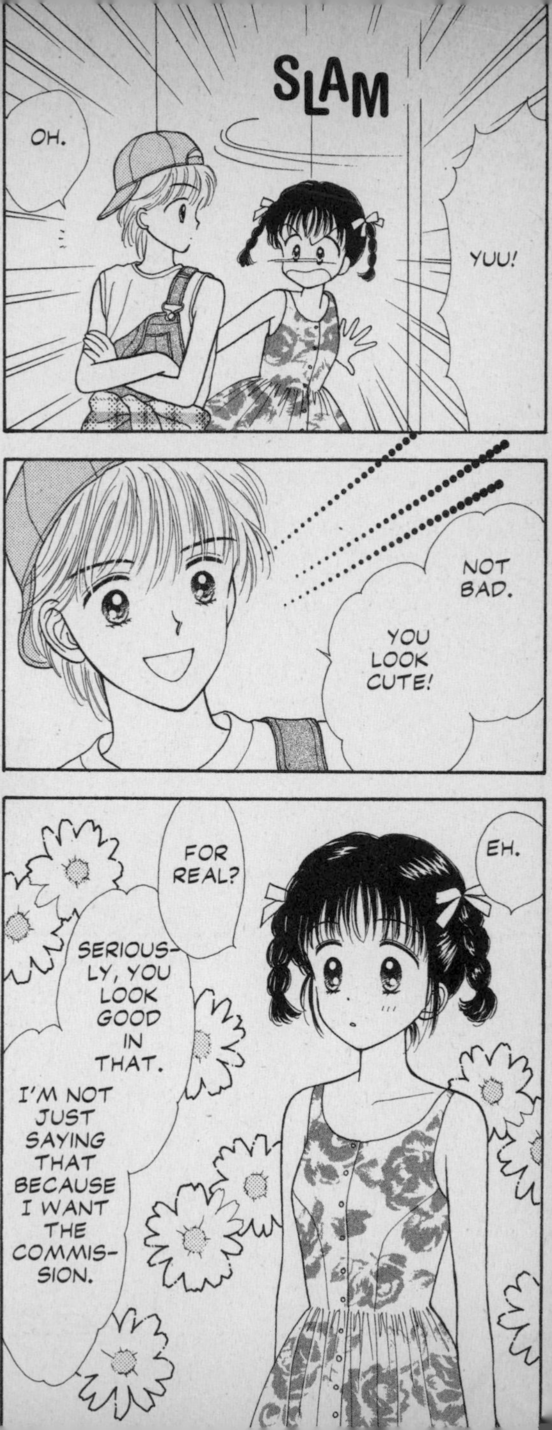
SLAM
YUU!
OH.
NOT BAD.
YOU LOOK CUTE!
EH.
FOR REAL?
SERIOUSLY, YOU LOOK GOOD IN THAT.
I'M NOT JUST SAYING THAT BECAUSE I WANT THE COMMISSION.

FREE TALK ⑤

It's funny—when I'm reading the scripts I can imagine how the scenes will come out. Like when the script said Rokutanada leans on Meiko because he is shocked by Arimi and Yuu's actions, I could picture that perfectly. Also there are scenes were Yuu and Miki accidentally meet in the shower. There are lots of corporations producing Marmalade Boy, like Toei, Katsu, ABC, and Bandai. I'm wondering if all these people actually like Marmalade Boy!

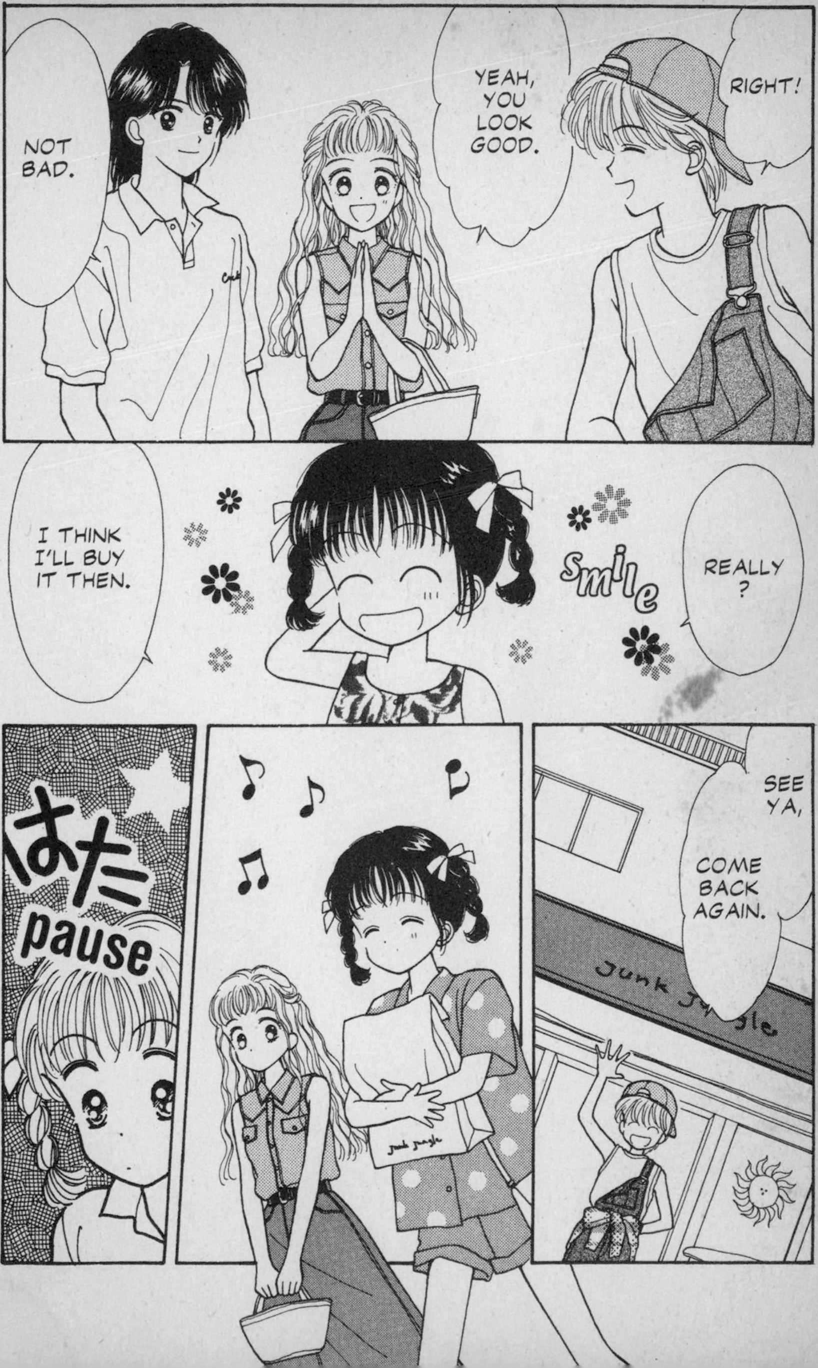
RIGHT!
YEAH, YOU LOOK GOOD.
NOT BAD.
REALLY ?
smile
I THINK I'LL BUY IT THEN.
SEE YA,
COME BACK AGAIN.
はた
pause

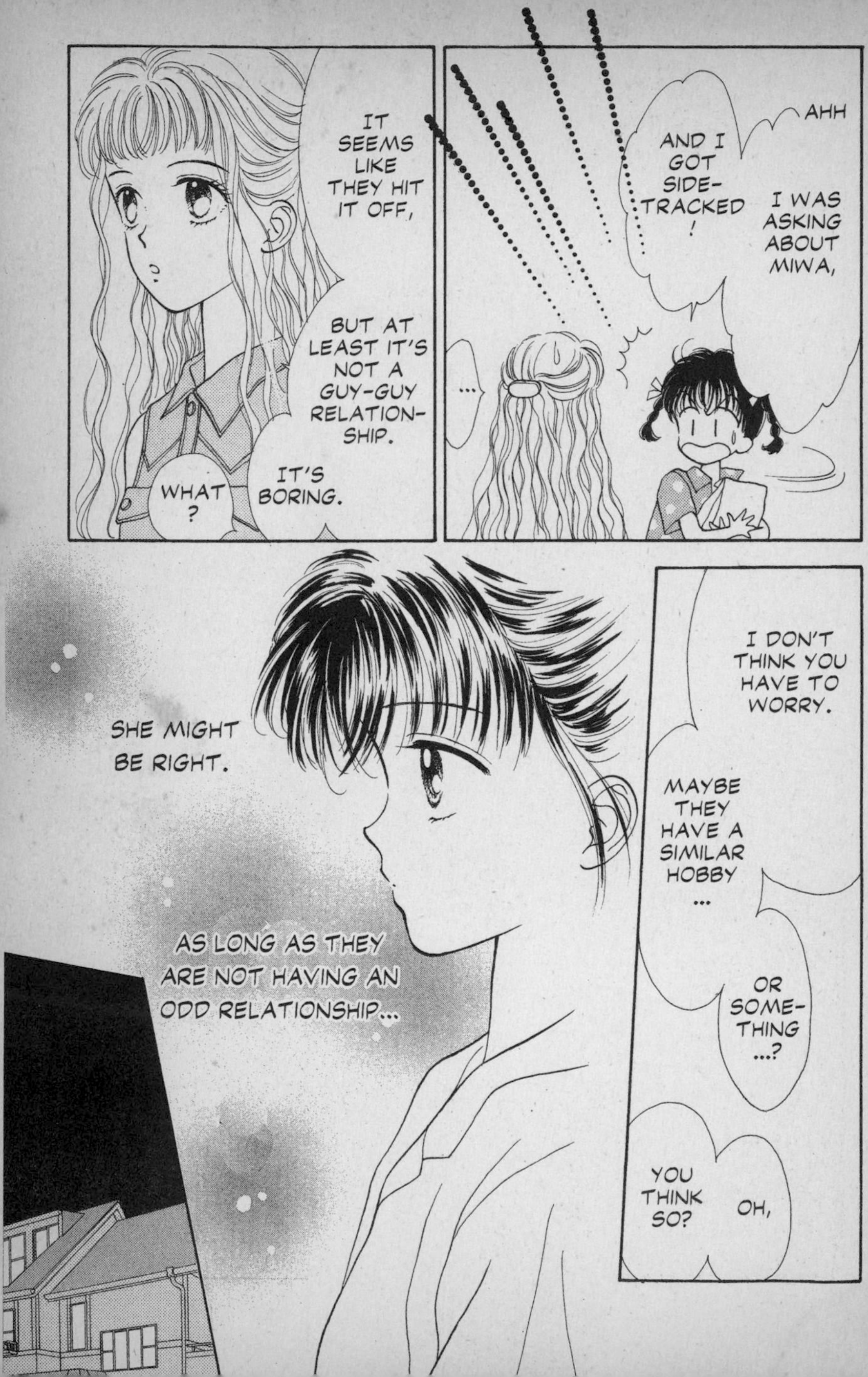
AHH
I WAS ASKING ABOUT MIWA,
AND I GOT SIDE-TRACKED!
...
IT SEEMS LIKE THEY HIT IT OFF,
BUT AT LEAST IT'S NOT A GUY-GUY RELATIONSHIP.
IT'S BORING.
WHAT?
I DON'T THINK YOU HAVE TO WORRY.
MAYBE THEY HAVE A SIMILAR HOBBY...
OR SOMETHING...?
OH,
YOU THINK SO?
SHE MIGHT BE RIGHT.
AS LONG AS THEY ARE NOT HAVING AN ODD RELATIONSHIP...

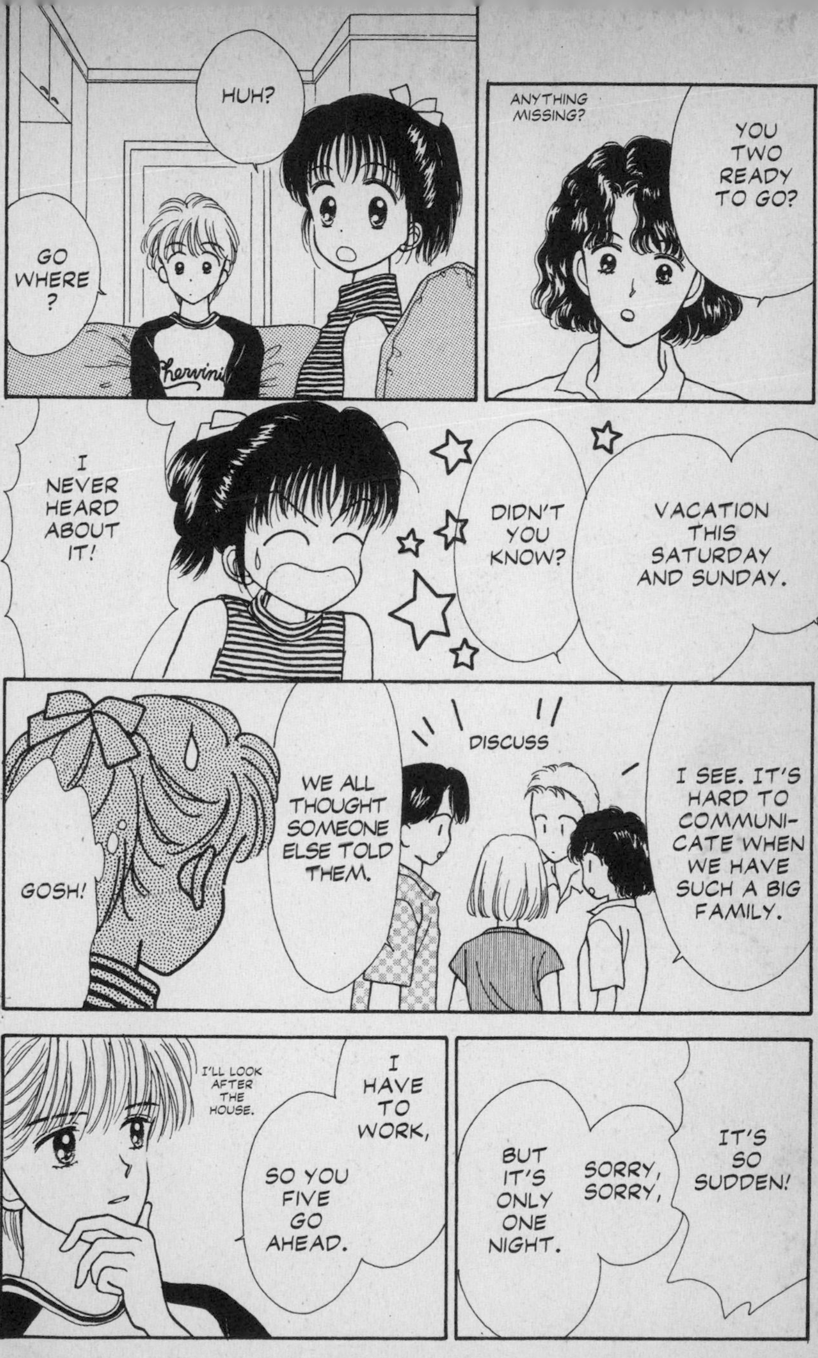
YOU TWO READY TO GO?
ANYTHING MISSING?
HUH?
GO WHERE?
VACATION THIS SATURDAY AND SUNDAY.
DIDN'T YOU KNOW?
I NEVER HEARD ABOUT IT!
I SEE. IT'S HARD TO COMMUNI-CATE WHEN WE HAVE SUCH A BIG FAMILY.
DISCUSS
WE ALL THOUGHT SOMEONE ELSE TOLD THEM.
GOSH!
IT'S SO SUDDEN!
SORRY, SORRY,
BUT IT'S ONLY ONE NIGHT.
I HAVE TO WORK,
SO YOU FIVE GO AHEAD.
I'LL LOOK AFTER THE HOUSE.

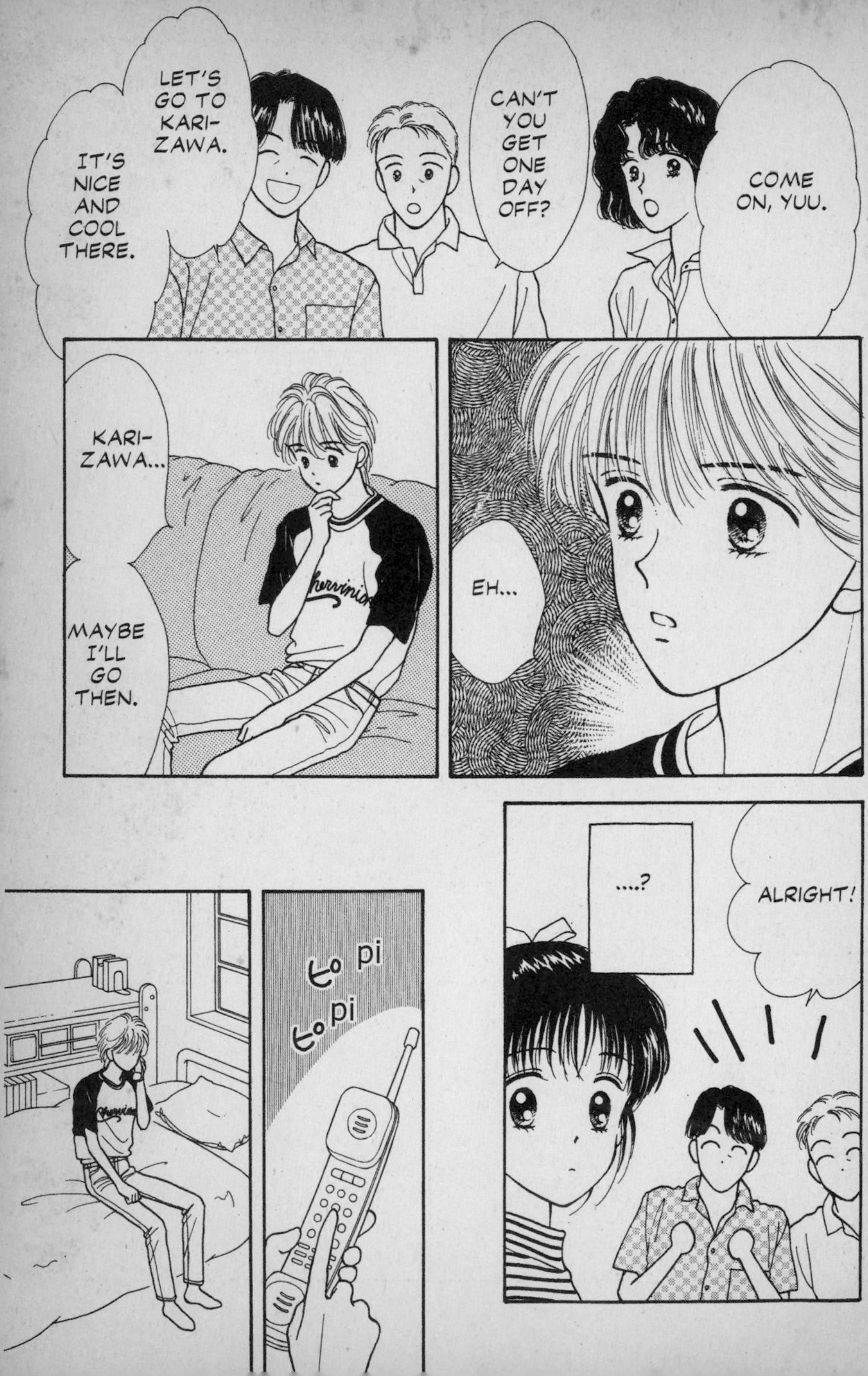
COME ON, YUU.
CAN'T YOU GET ONE DAY OFF?
LET'S GO TO KARI-ZAWA.
IT'S NICE AND COOL THERE.
EH...
KARI-ZAWA...
MAYBE I'LL GO THEN.
ALRIGHT!
....?
ピ pi
ピ pi

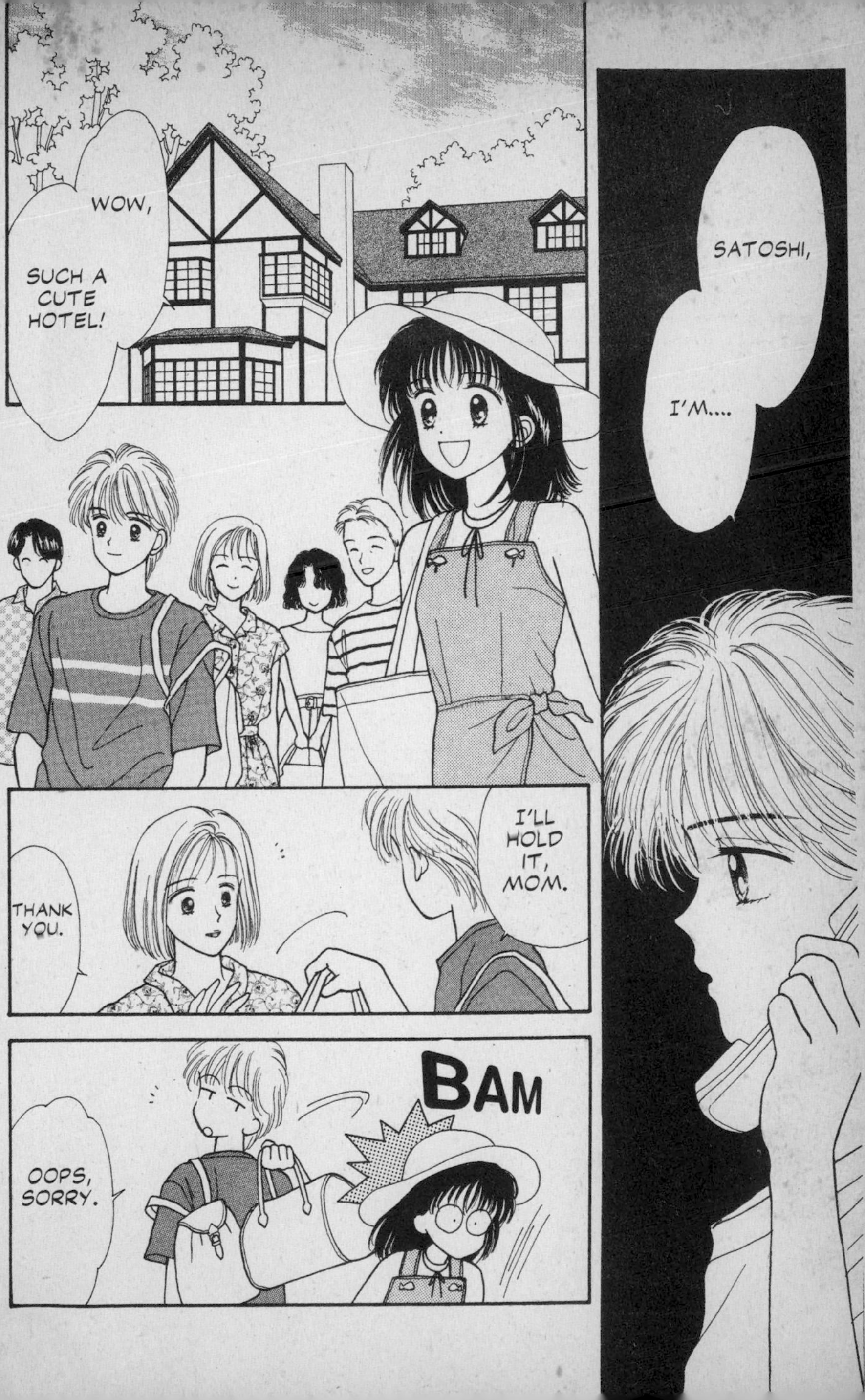
SATOSHI,
I'M....
WOW,
SUCH A CUTE HOTEL!
I'LL HOLD IT, MOM.
THANK YOU.
BAM
OOPS, SORRY.

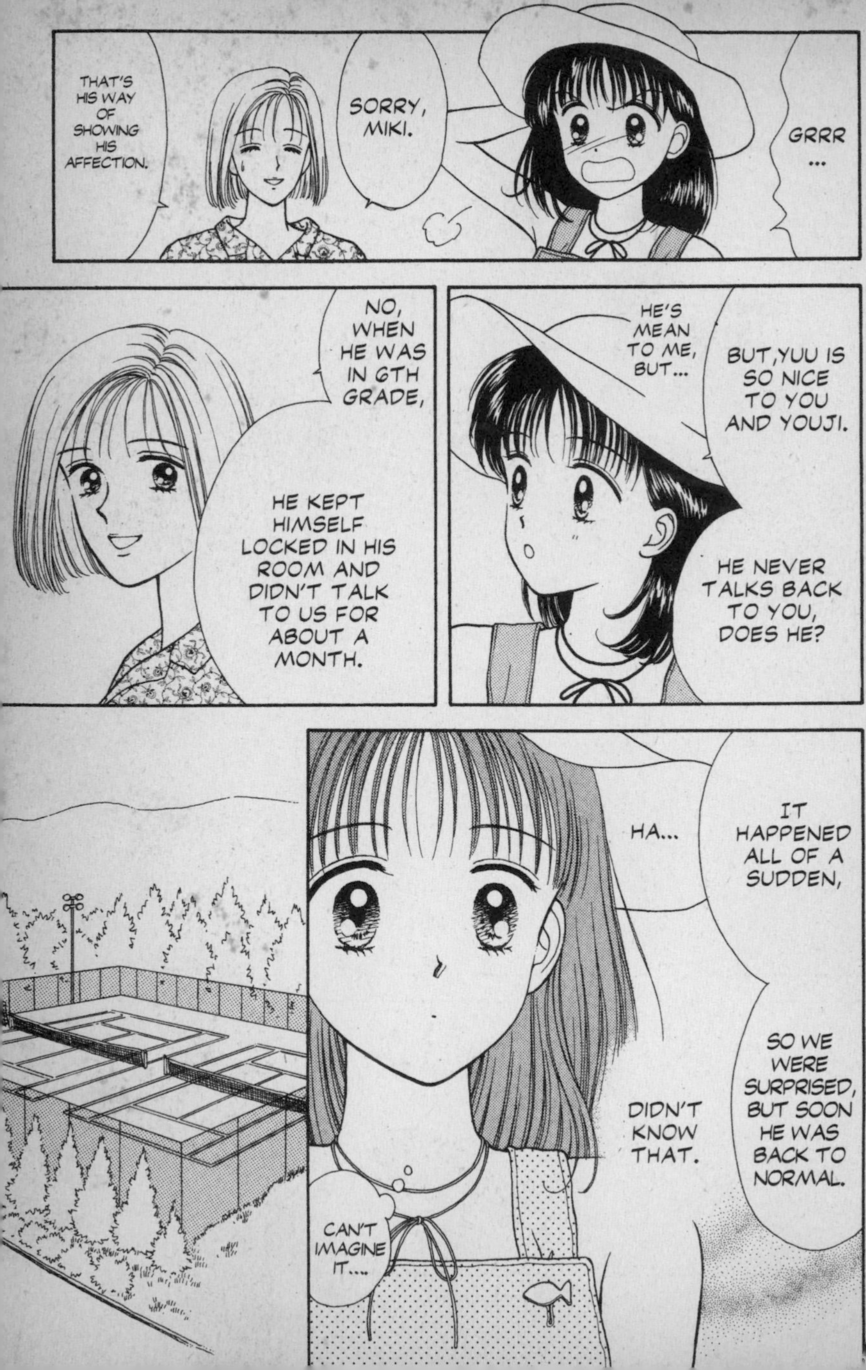
GRRR ...
SORRY, MIKI.
THAT'S HIS WAY OF SHOWING HIS AFFECTION.
BUT,YUU IS SO NICE TO YOU AND YOUJI.
HE NEVER TALKS BACK TO YOU, DOES HE?
HE'S MEAN TO ME, BUT...
NO, WHEN HE WAS IN 6TH GRADE,
HE KEPT HIMSELF LOCKED IN HIS ROOM AND DIDN'T TALK TO US FOR ABOUT A MONTH.
IT HAPPENED ALL OF A SUDDEN,
SO WE WERE SURPRISED, BUT SOON HE WAS BACK TO NORMAL.
HA...
DIDN'T KNOW THAT.
CAN'T IMAGINE IT....

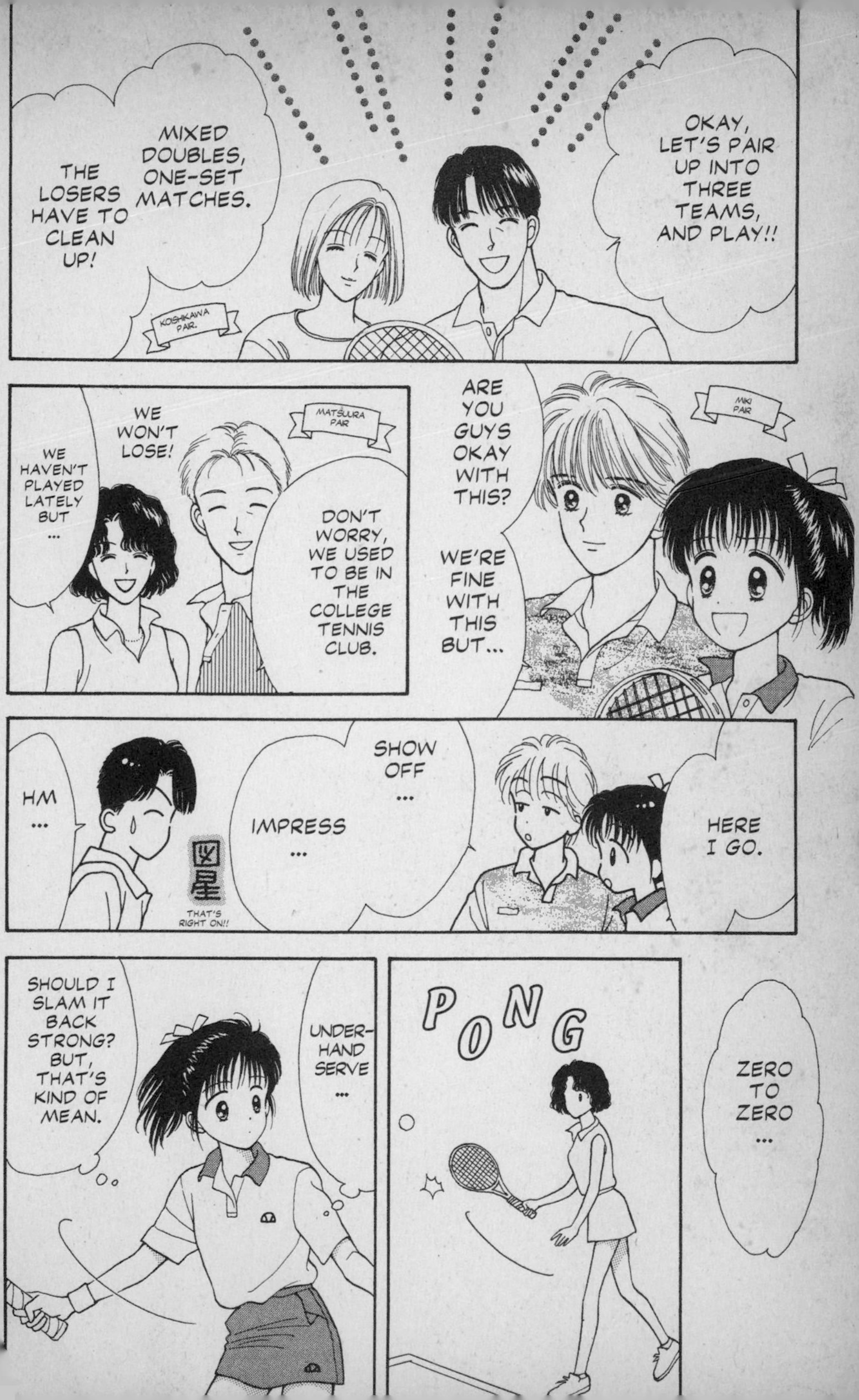
OKAY, LET'S PAIR UP INTO THREE TEAMS, AND PLAY!!
MIXED DOUBLES, ONE-SET MATCHES.
THE LOSERS HAVE TO CLEAN UP!
KOSHIKAWA PAIR.
MIKI PAIR
ARE YOU GUYS OKAY WITH THIS?
WE'RE FINE WITH THIS BUT...
MATSUURA PAIR
DON'T WORRY, WE USED TO BE IN THE COLLEGE TENNIS CLUB.
WE WON'T LOSE!
WE HAVEN'T PLAYED LATELY BUT ...
HERE I GO.
SHOW OFF ...
IMPRESS ...
図星
THAT'S RIGHT ON!!
HM ...
PONG
ZERO TO ZERO ...
UNDER-HAND SERVE ...
SHOULD I SLAM IT BACK STRONG? BUT, THAT'S KIND OF MEAN.

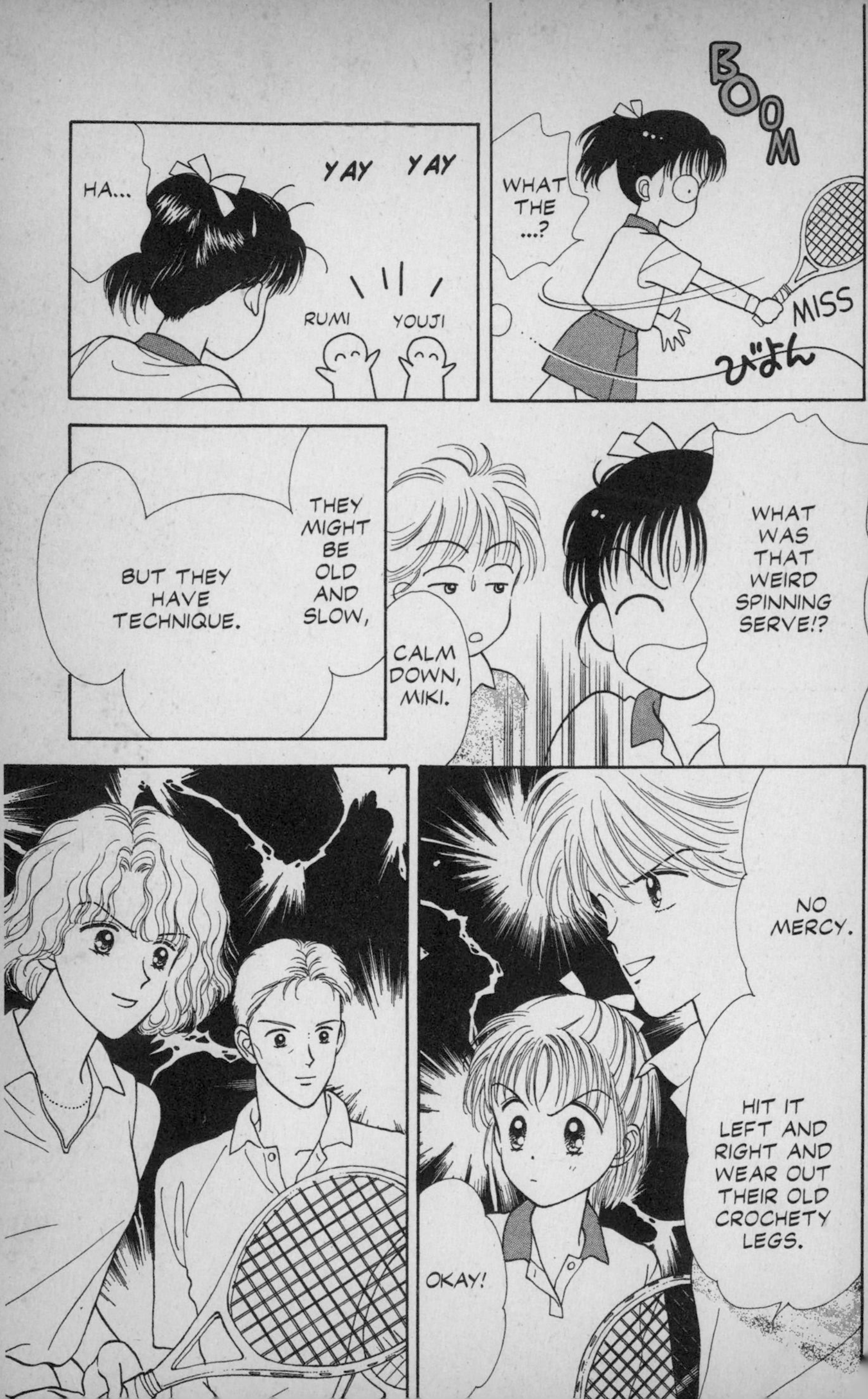
BOOM
WHAT THE ...?
MISS
びよん
HA...
YAY YAY
RUMI
YOUJI
WHAT WAS THAT WEIRD SPINNING SERVE!?
CALM DOWN, MIKI.
THEY MIGHT BE OLD AND SLOW,
BUT THEY HAVE TECHNIQUE.
NO MERCY.
HIT IT LEFT AND RIGHT AND WEAR OUT THEIR OLD CROCHETY LEGS.
OKAY!

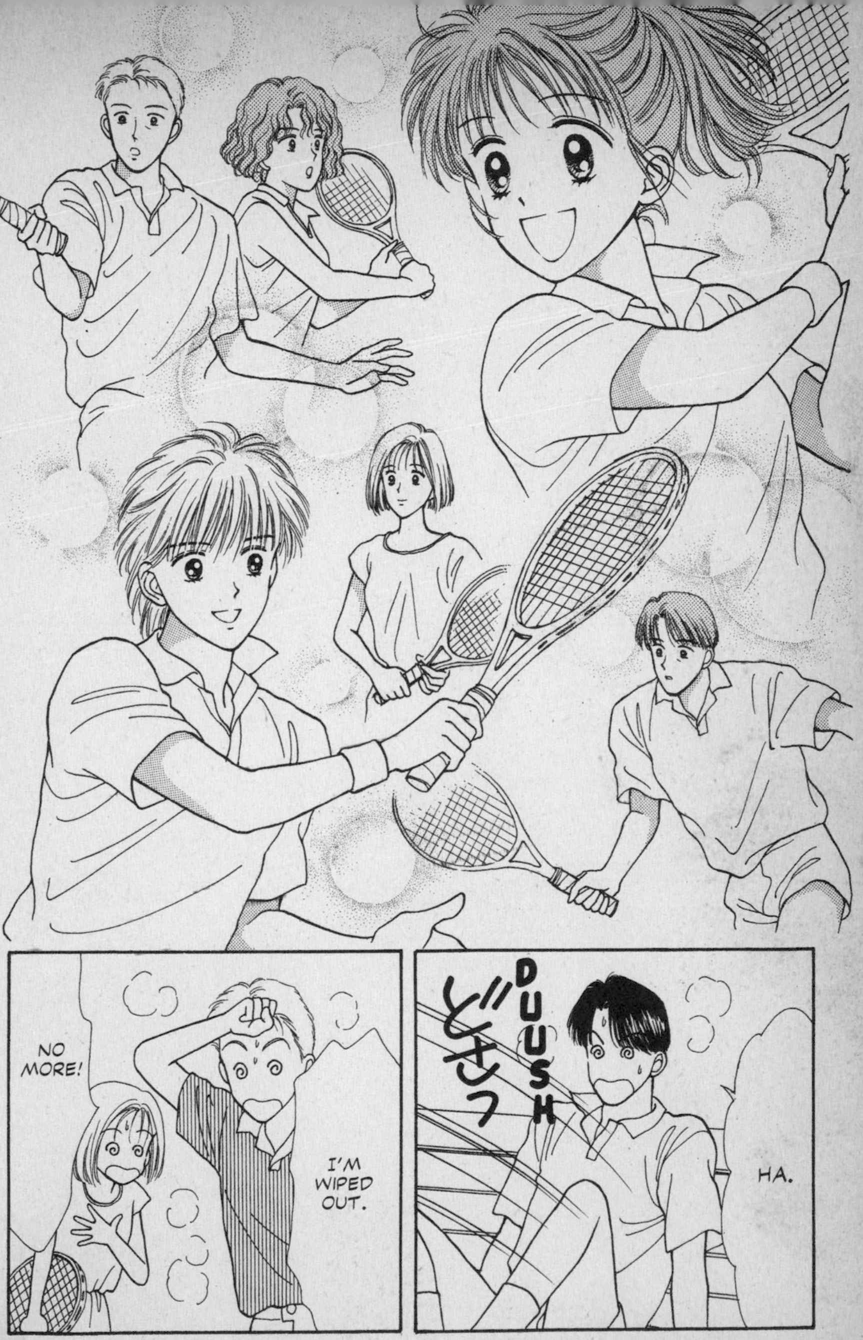
DUUSH
どきっ
HA.
NO MORE!
I'M WIPED OUT.

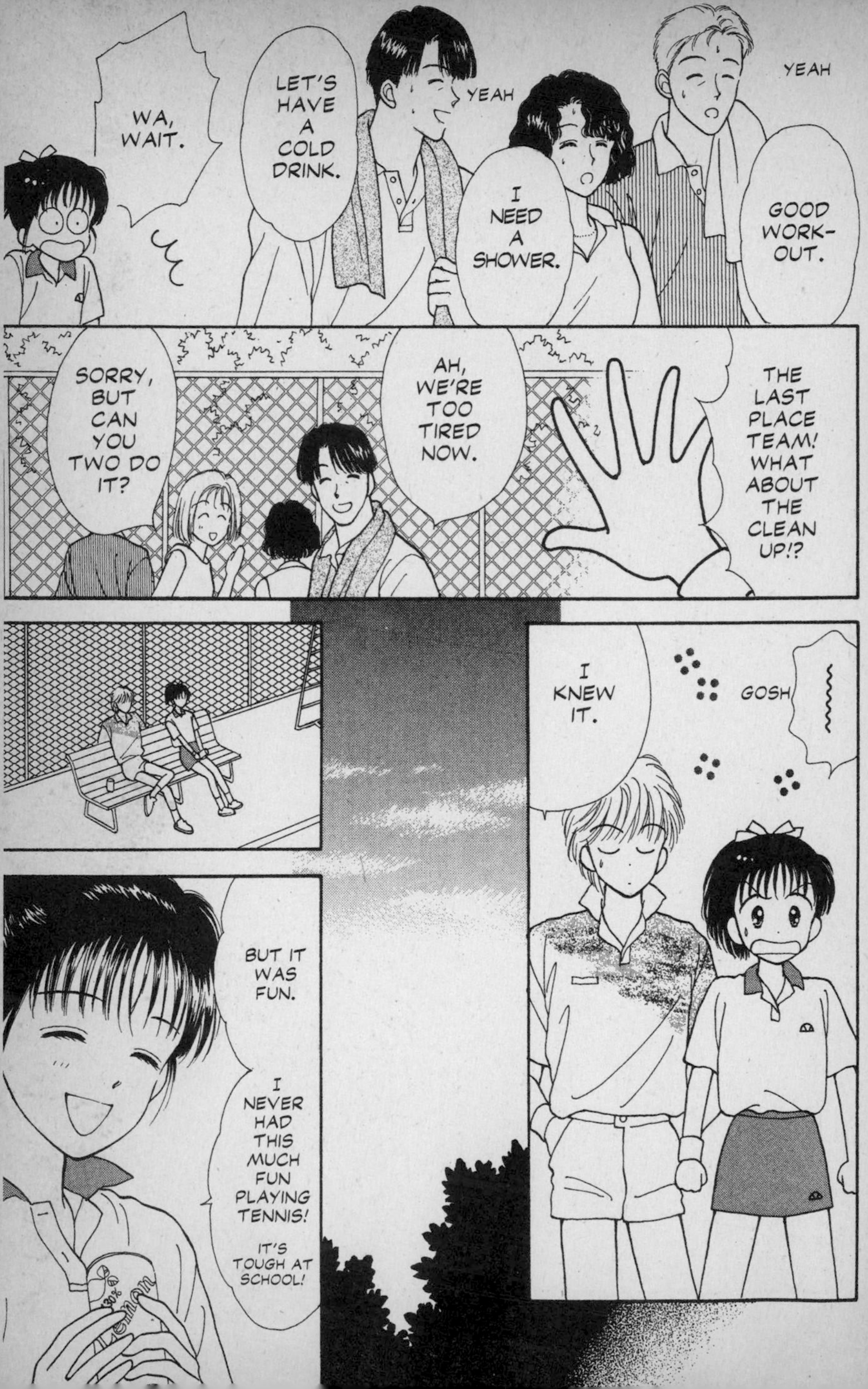
YEAH
GOOD WORK-OUT.
I NEED A SHOWER.
YEAH
LET'S HAVE A COLD DRINK.
WA, WAIT.
THE LAST PLACE TEAM! WHAT ABOUT THE CLEAN UP!?
AH, WE'RE TOO TIRED NOW.
SORRY, BUT CAN YOU TWO DO IT?
GOSH
I KNEW IT.
BUT IT WAS FUN.
I NEVER HAD THIS MUCH FUN PLAYING TENNIS!
IT'S TOUGH AT SCHOOL!

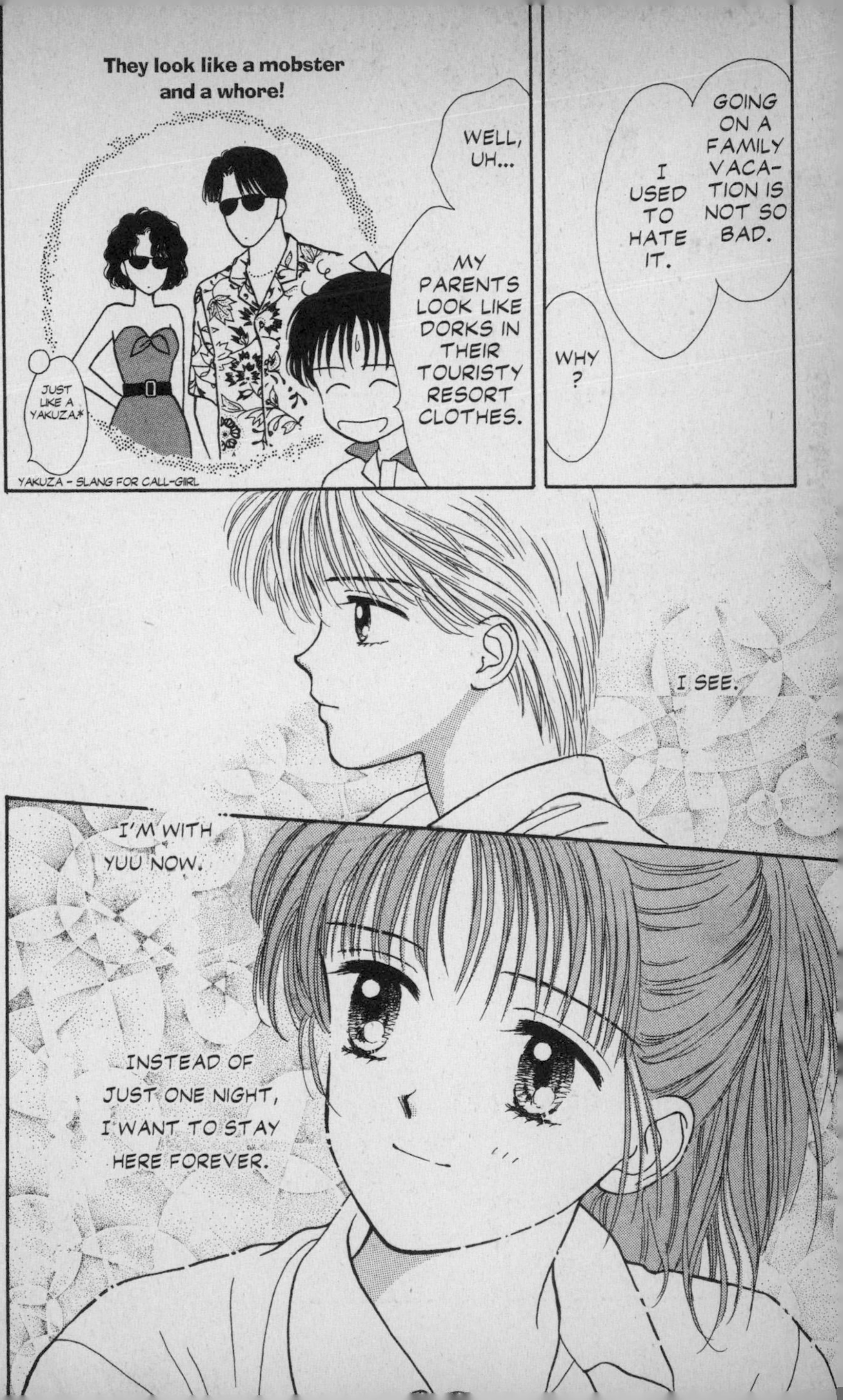
GOING ON A FAMILY VACATION IS NOT SO BAD.
I USED TO HATE IT.
WHY?
WELL, UH...
MY PARENTS LOOK LIKE DORKS IN THEIR TOURISTY RESORT CLOTHES.
They look like a mobster and a whore!
JUST LIKE A YAKUZA.*
YAKUZA - SLANG FOR CALL-GIIRL
I SEE.
I'M WITH YUU NOW.
INSTEAD OF JUST ONE NIGHT, I WANT TO STAY HERE FOREVER.

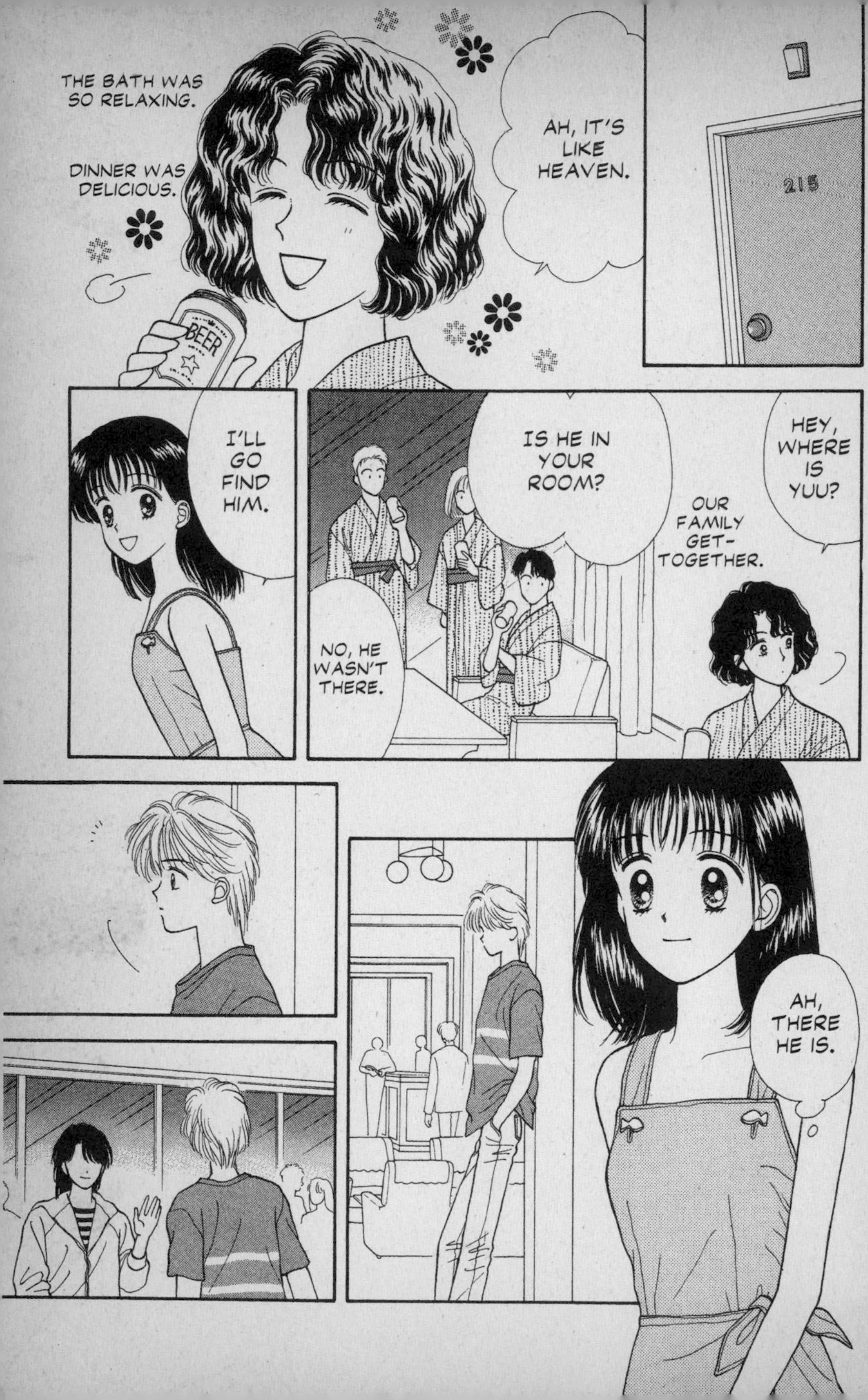
AH, IT'S LIKE HEAVEN.
THE BATH WAS SO RELAXING.
DINNER WAS DELICIOUS.
BEER
HEY, WHERE IS YUU?
OUR FAMILY GET-TOGETHER.
IS HE IN YOUR ROOM?
NO, HE WASN'T THERE.
I'LL GO FIND HIM.
AH, THERE HE IS.

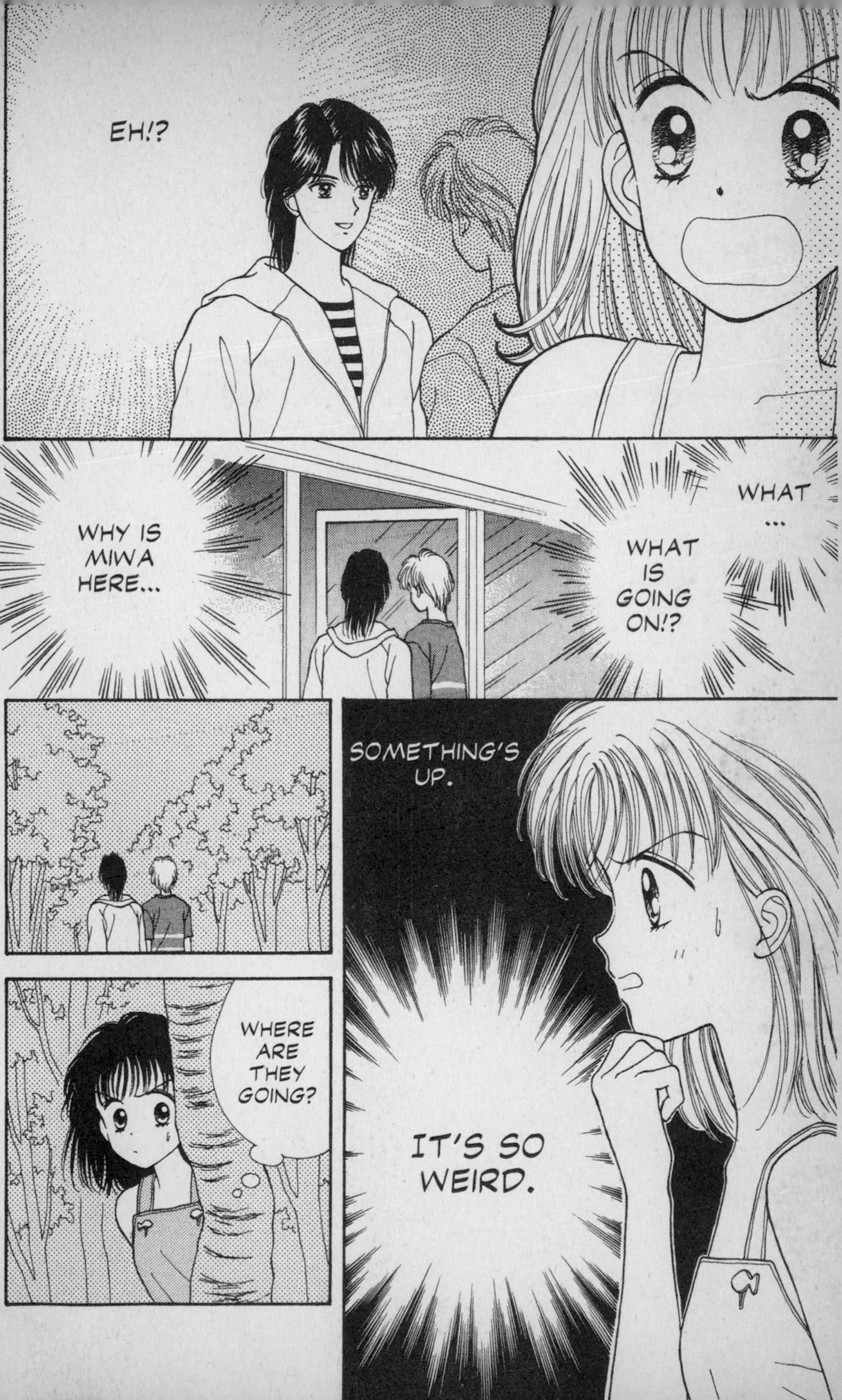
EH!?
WHAT ...
WHAT IS GOING ON!?
WHY IS MIWA HERE...
SOMETHING'S UP.
IT'S SO WEIRD.
WHERE ARE THEY GOING?

FREE TALK ⑥

When you make animation, you need a sponsor no matter what. For Marmalade Boy, we got Bandai as a sponsor. Since Bandai became the sponsor, they have all the rights for products related to Marmalade Boy in Japan. If the products don't sell, that's a big problem.

** Look for the Marmalade Boy anime coming in 2003 from TOKYOPOP.

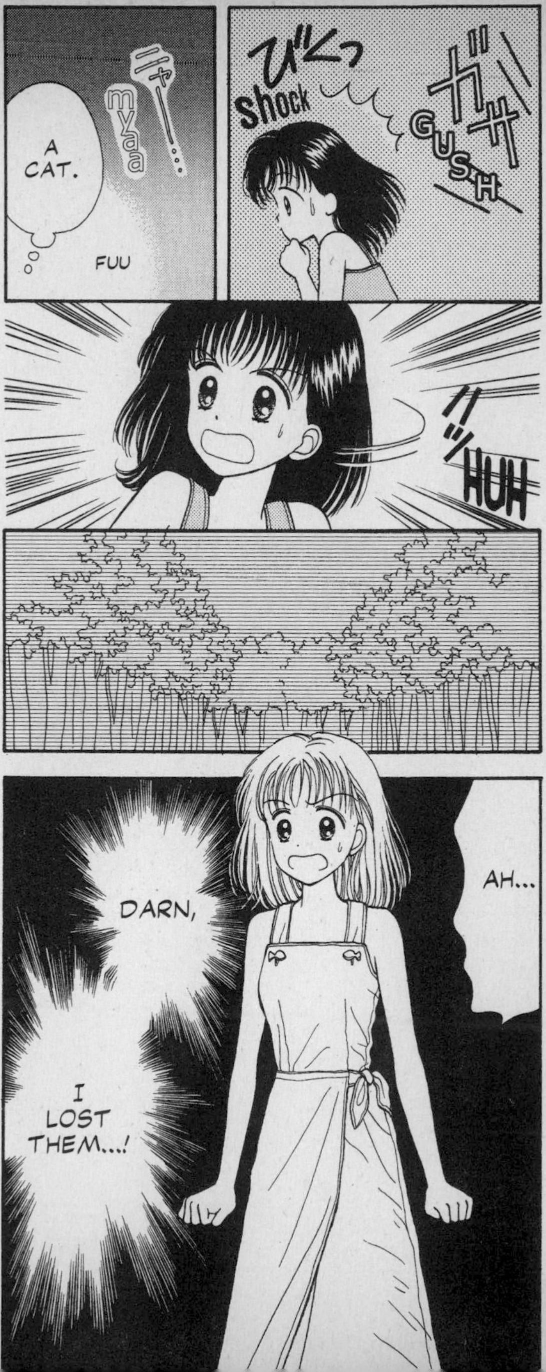
びくっ
Shock
ガサ
GUSH
ニャー…
myaa
A CAT.
FUU
ハッ
HUH
AH...
DARN,
I LOST THEM...!

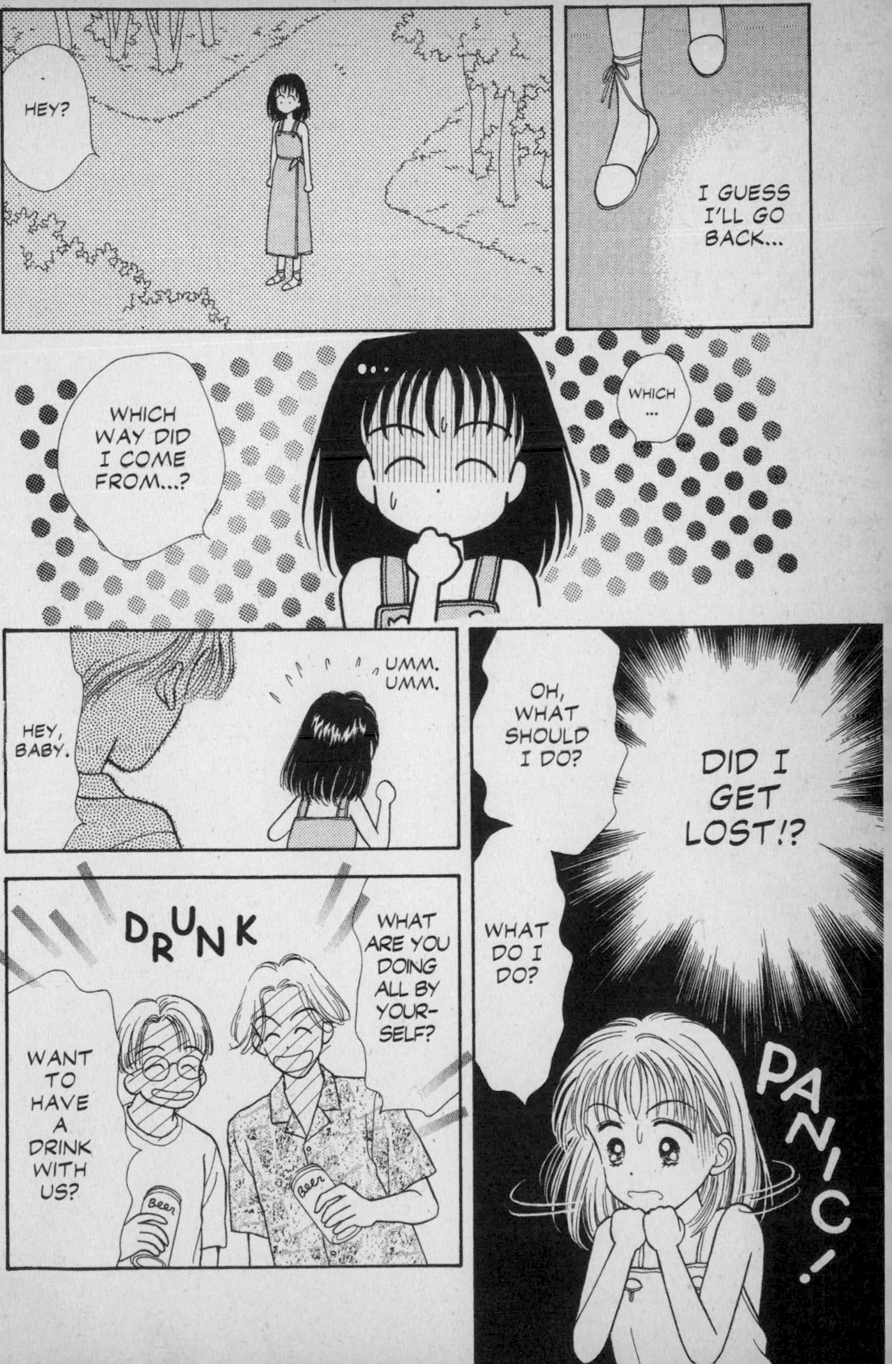
I GUESS I'LL GO BACK...
HEY?
WHICH ...
WHICH WAY DID I COME FROM...?
DID I GET LOST!?
OH, WHAT SHOULD I DO?
WHAT DO I DO?
PANIC!
UMM. UMM.
HEY, BABY.
WHAT ARE YOU DOING ALL BY YOUR-SELF?
DRUNK
WANT TO HAVE A DRINK WITH US?

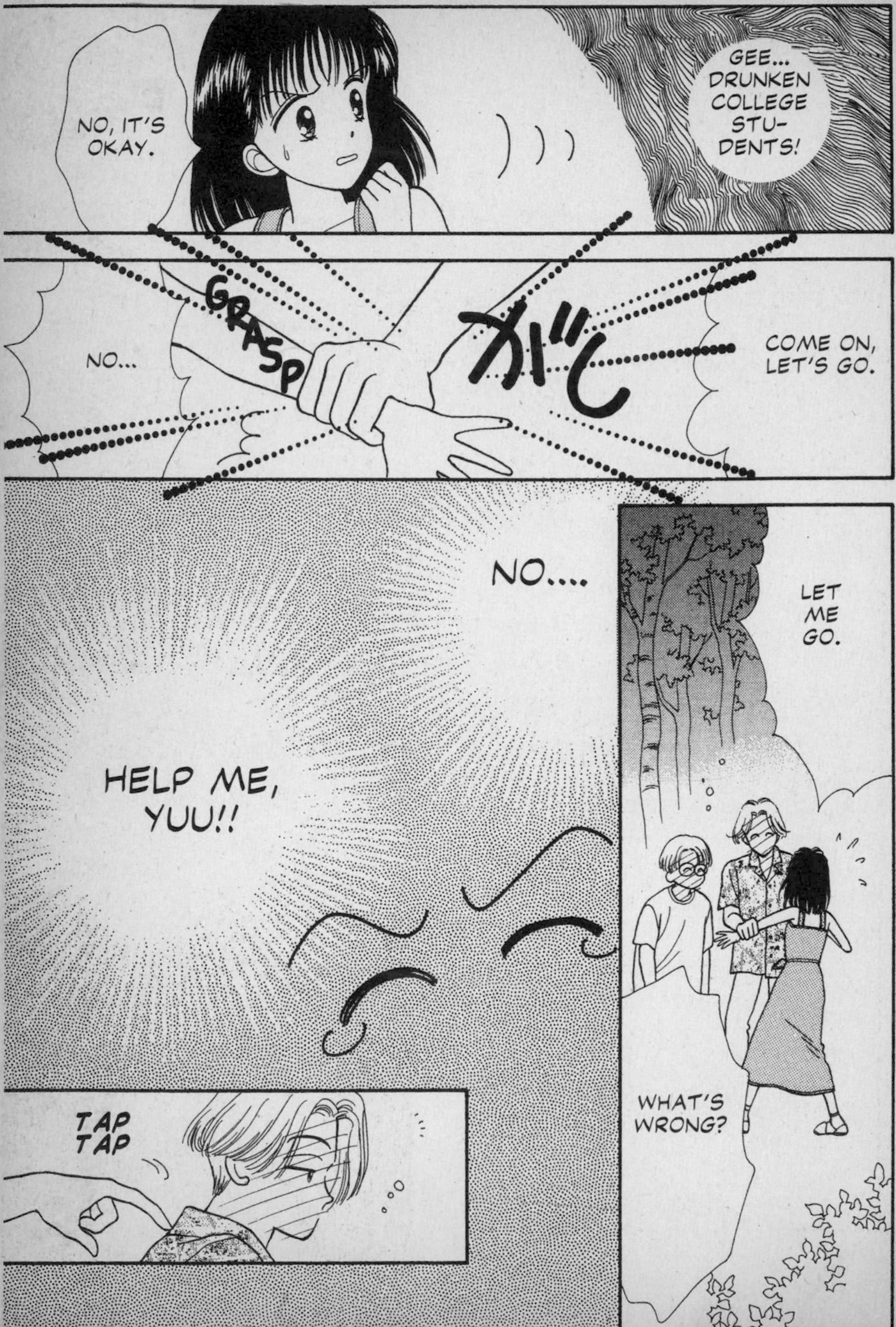
GEE... DRUNKEN COLLEGE STU- DENTS!
NO, IT'S OKAY.
COME ON, LET'S GO.
がし
GRASP
NO...
LET ME GO.
WHAT'S WRONG?
NO....
HELP ME, YUU!!
TAP TAP

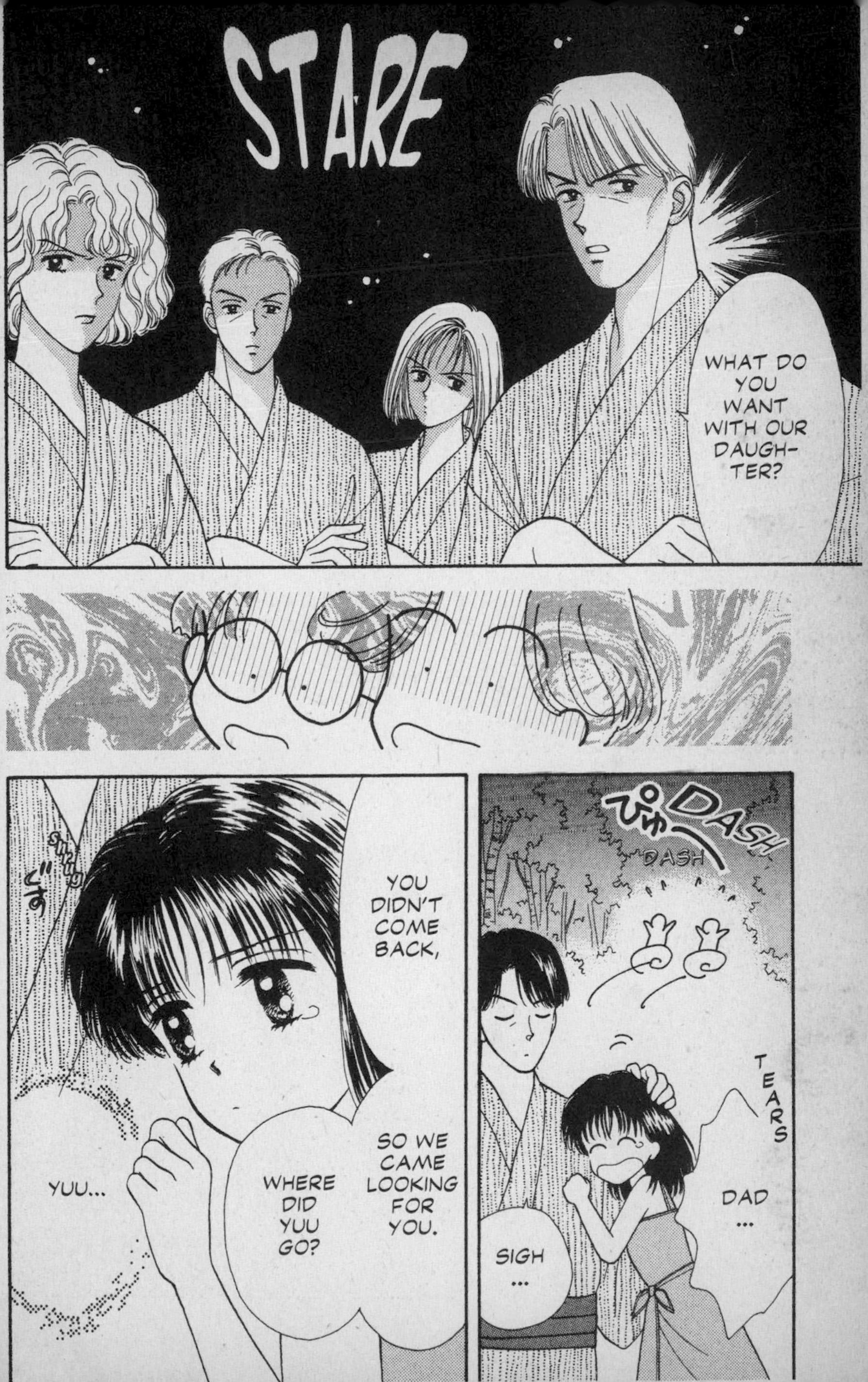
STARE
WHAT DO YOU WANT WITH OUR DAUGHTER?
ぴゅー
DASH
DASH
TEARS
DAD ...
SIGH ...
YOU DIDN'T COME BACK,
SO WE CAME LOOKING FOR YOU.
WHERE DID YUU GO?
shrug
ぐす
YUU...

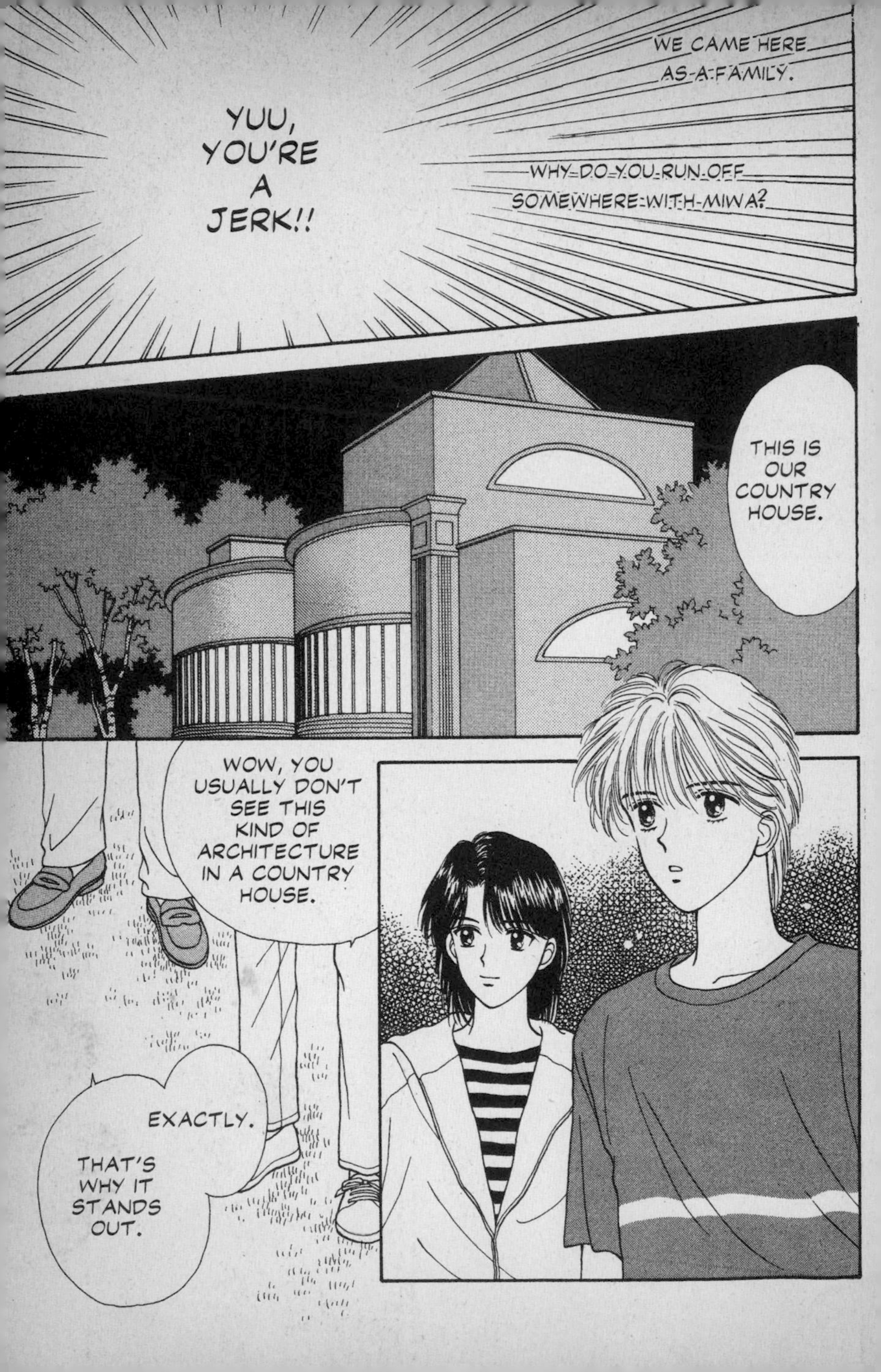
WE CAME HERE AS A FAMILY.
WHY DO YOU RUN OFF SOMEWHERE WITH MIWA?
YUU, YOU'RE A JERK!!
THIS IS OUR COUNTRY HOUSE.
WOW, YOU USUALLY DON'T SEE THIS KIND OF ARCHITECTURE IN A COUNTRY HOUSE.
EXACTLY.
THAT'S WHY IT STANDS OUT.

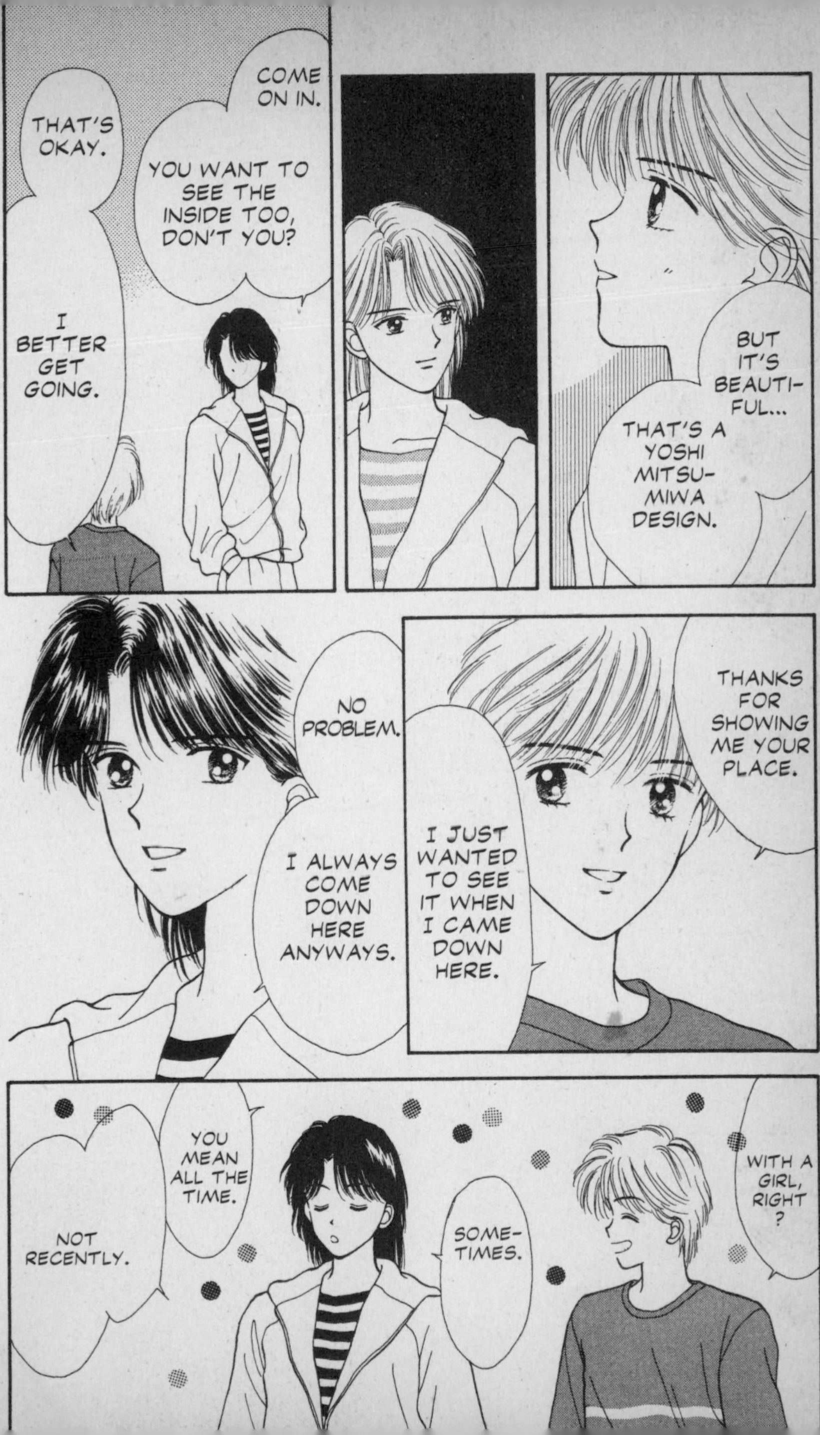
BUT IT'S BEAUTIFUL...
THAT'S A YOSHI MITSUMIWA DESIGN.
COME ON IN.
YOU WANT TO SEE THE INSIDE TOO, DON'T YOU?
THAT'S OKAY.
I BETTER GET GOING.
THANKS FOR SHOWING ME YOUR PLACE.
I JUST WANTED TO SEE IT WHEN I CAME DOWN HERE.
NO PROBLEM.
I ALWAYS COME DOWN HERE ANYWAYS.
WITH A GIRL, RIGHT?
SOMETIMES.
YOU MEAN ALL THE TIME.
NOT RECENTLY.

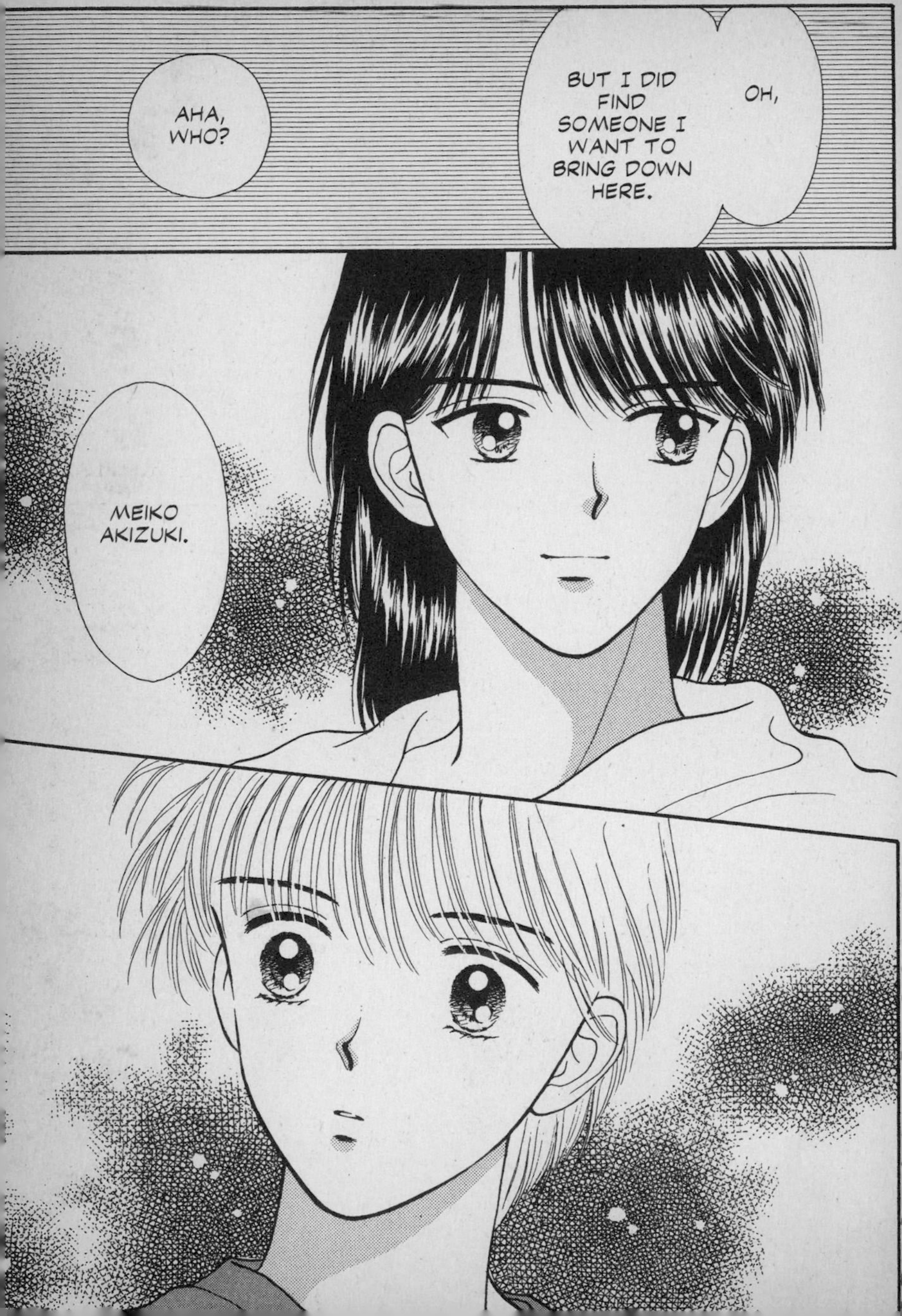
OH,
BUT I DID FIND SOMEONE I WANT TO BRING DOWN HERE.
AHA, WHO?
MEIKO AKIZUKI.

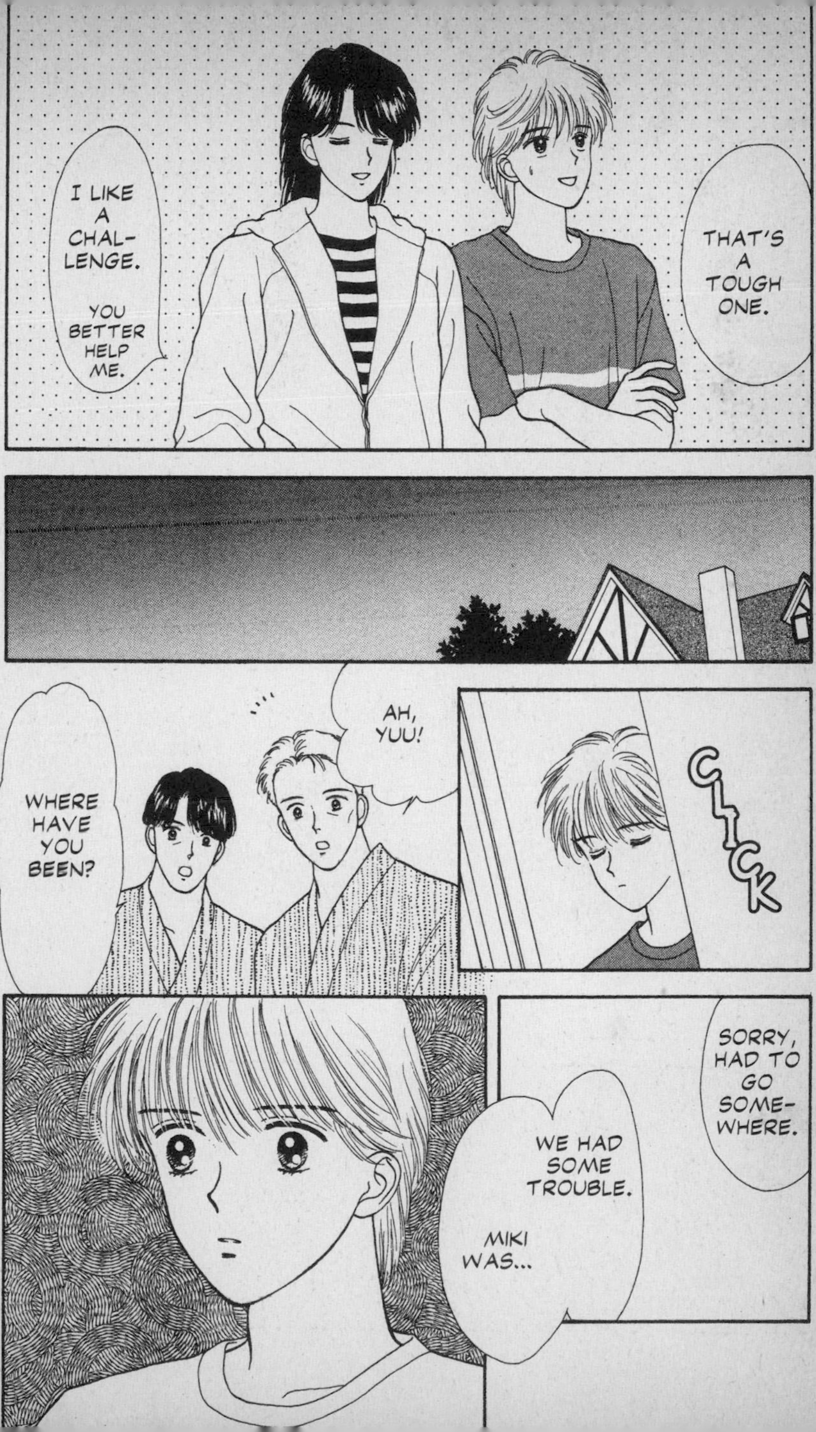
THAT'S A TOUGH ONE.
I LIKE A CHAL-LENGE.
YOU BETTER HELP ME.
CLICK
AH, YUU!
WHERE HAVE YOU BEEN?
SORRY, HAD TO GO SOME-WHERE.
WE HAD SOME TROUBLE.
MIKI WAS...

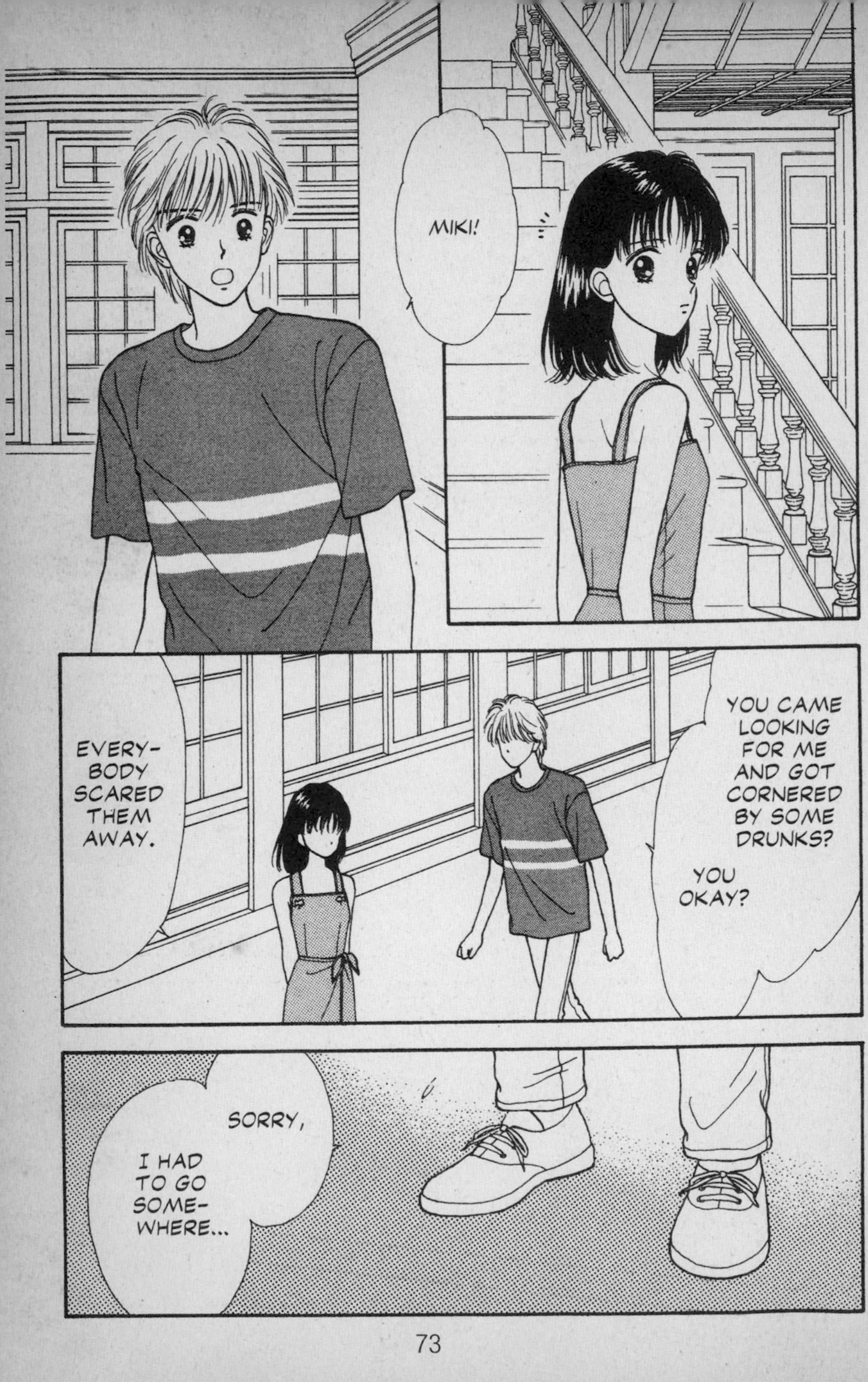
MIKI!
YOU CAME LOOKING FOR ME AND GOT CORNERED BY SOME DRUNKS?
YOU OKAY?
EVERY-BODY SCARED THEM AWAY.
SORRY,
I HAD TO GO SOME-WHERE...

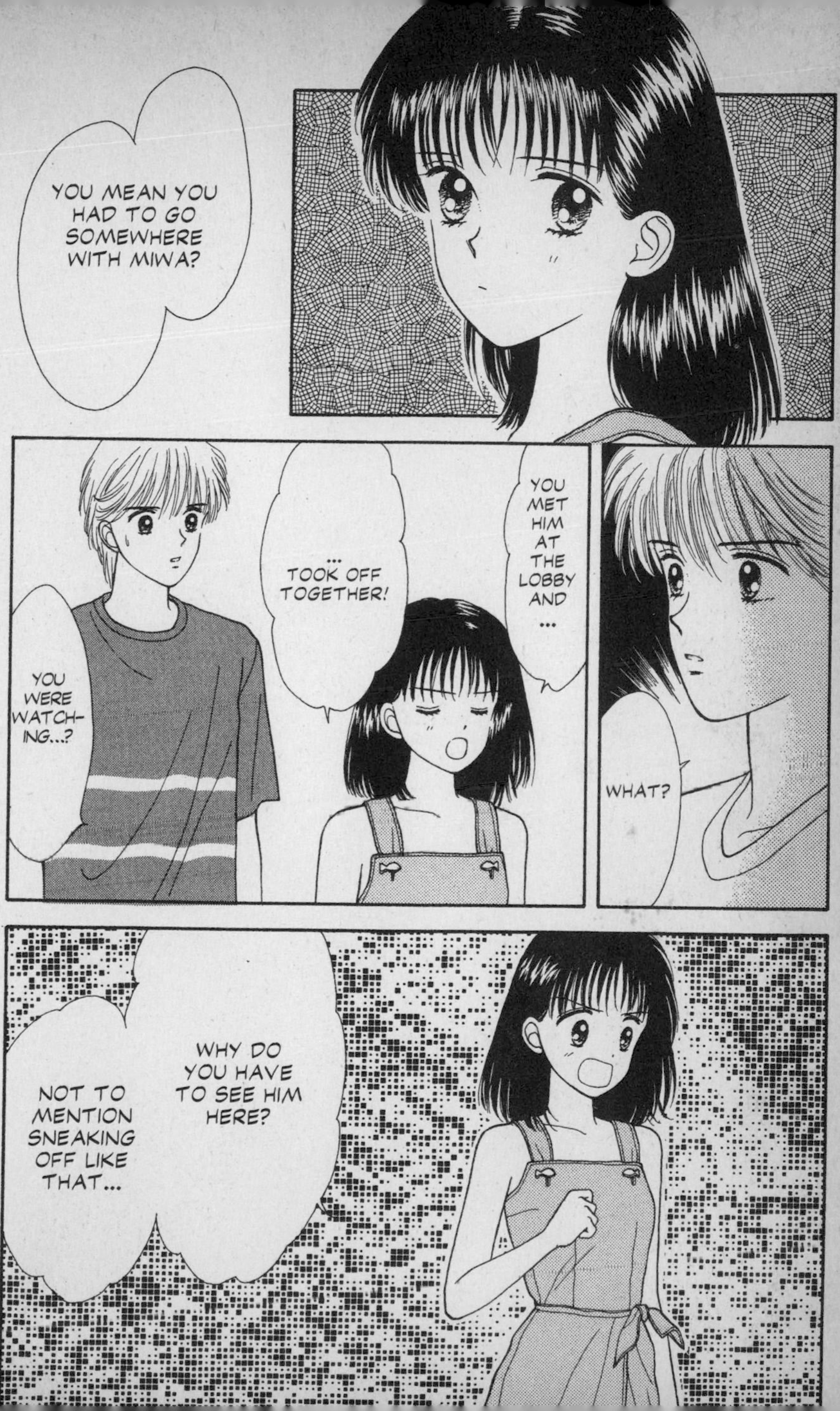
YOU MEAN YOU HAD TO GO SOMEWHERE WITH MIWA?
WHAT?
YOU MET HIM AT THE LOBBY AND ...
... TOOK OFF TOGETHER!
YOU WERE WATCHING...?
WHY DO YOU HAVE TO SEE HIM HERE?
NOT TO MENTION SNEAKING OFF LIKE THAT...

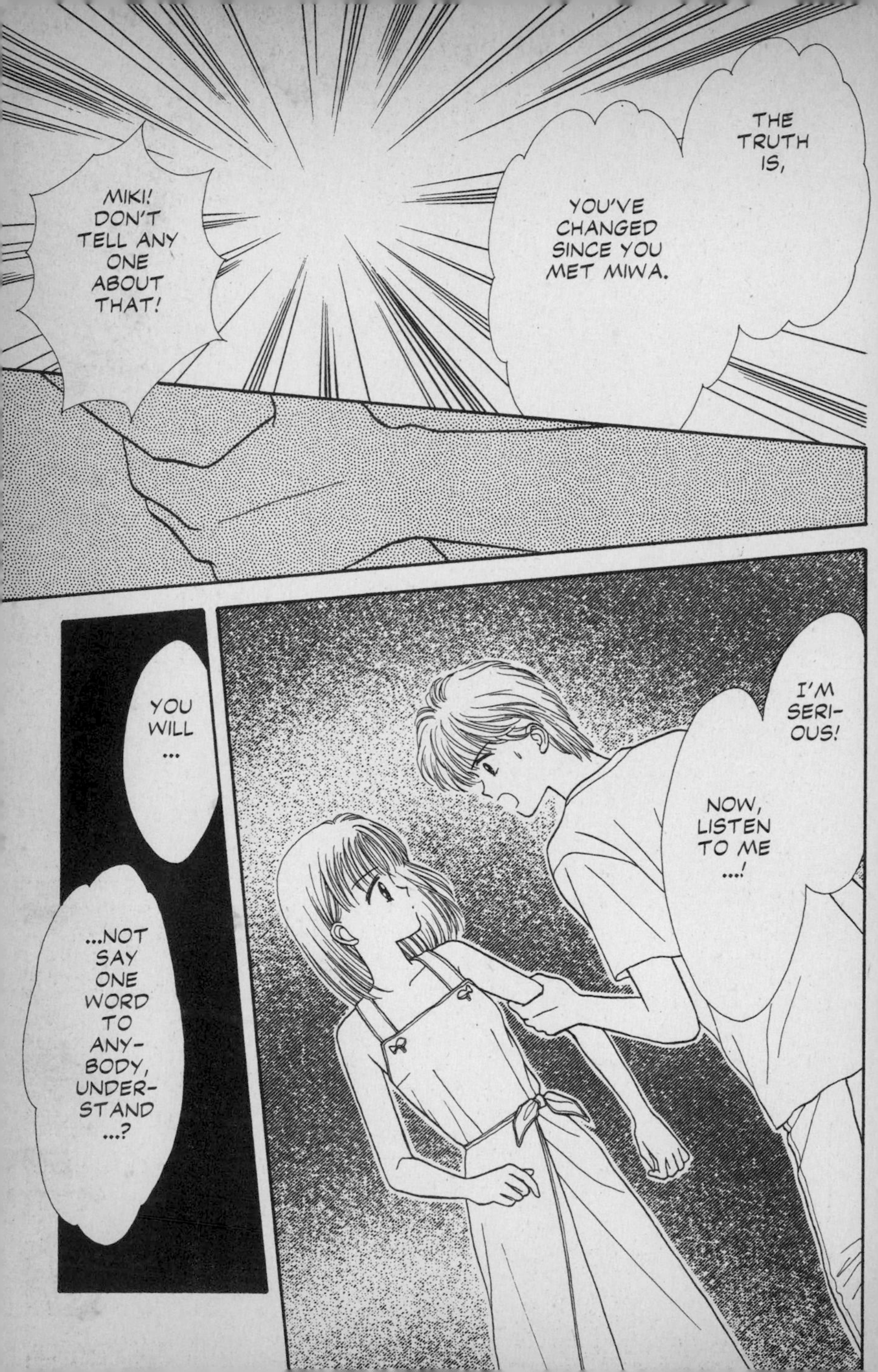
THE TRUTH IS,
YOU'VE CHANGED SINCE YOU MET MIWA.
MIKI! DON'T TELL ANY ONE ABOUT THAT!
I'M SERI-OUS!
NOW, LISTEN TO ME ...!
YOU WILL ...
...NOT SAY ONE WORD TO ANY-BODY, UNDER-STAND ...?

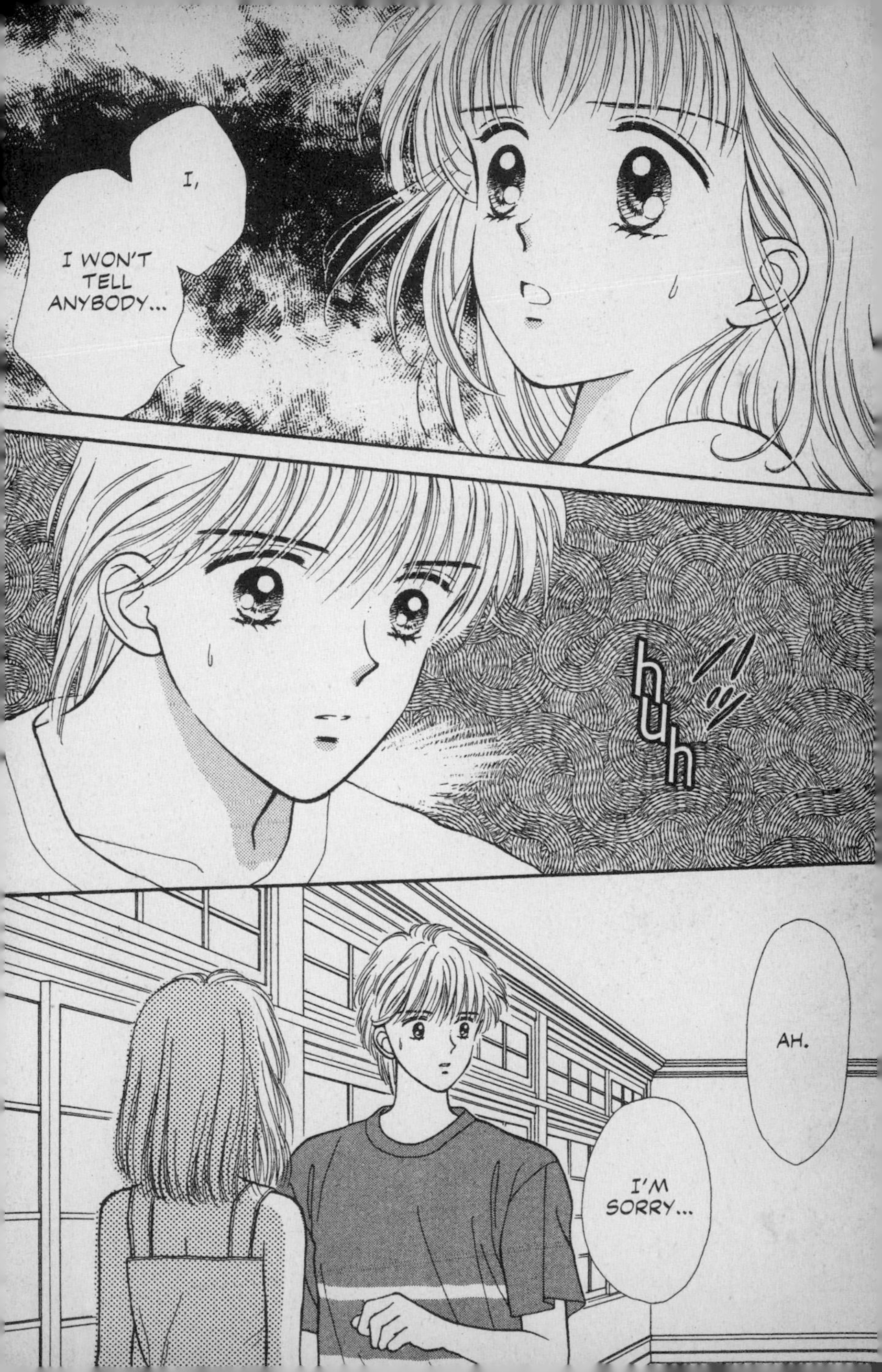
I,
I WON'T TELL ANYBODY...
huh
AH.
I'M SORRY...

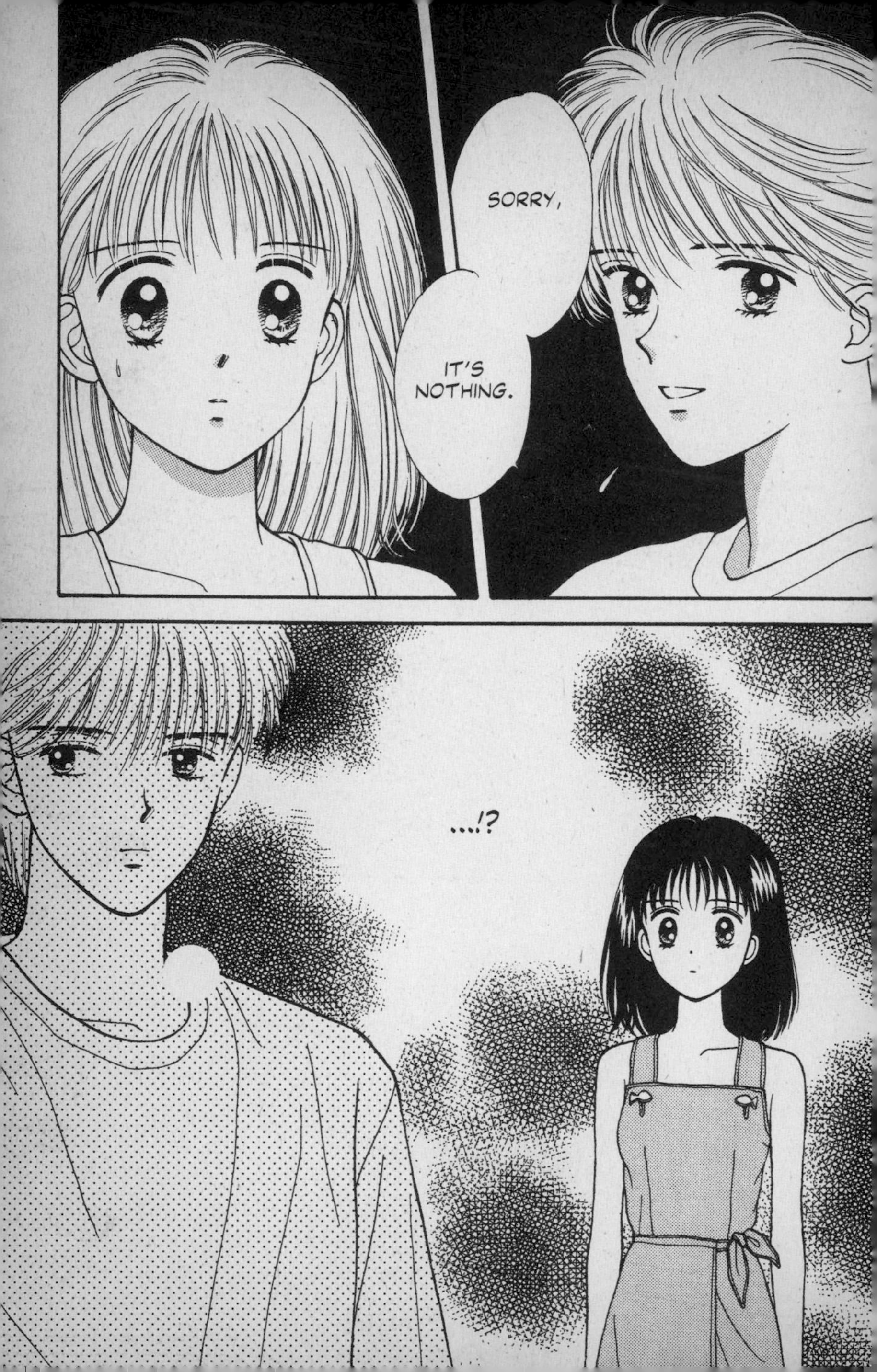
SORRY,
IT'S NOTHING.
...!?

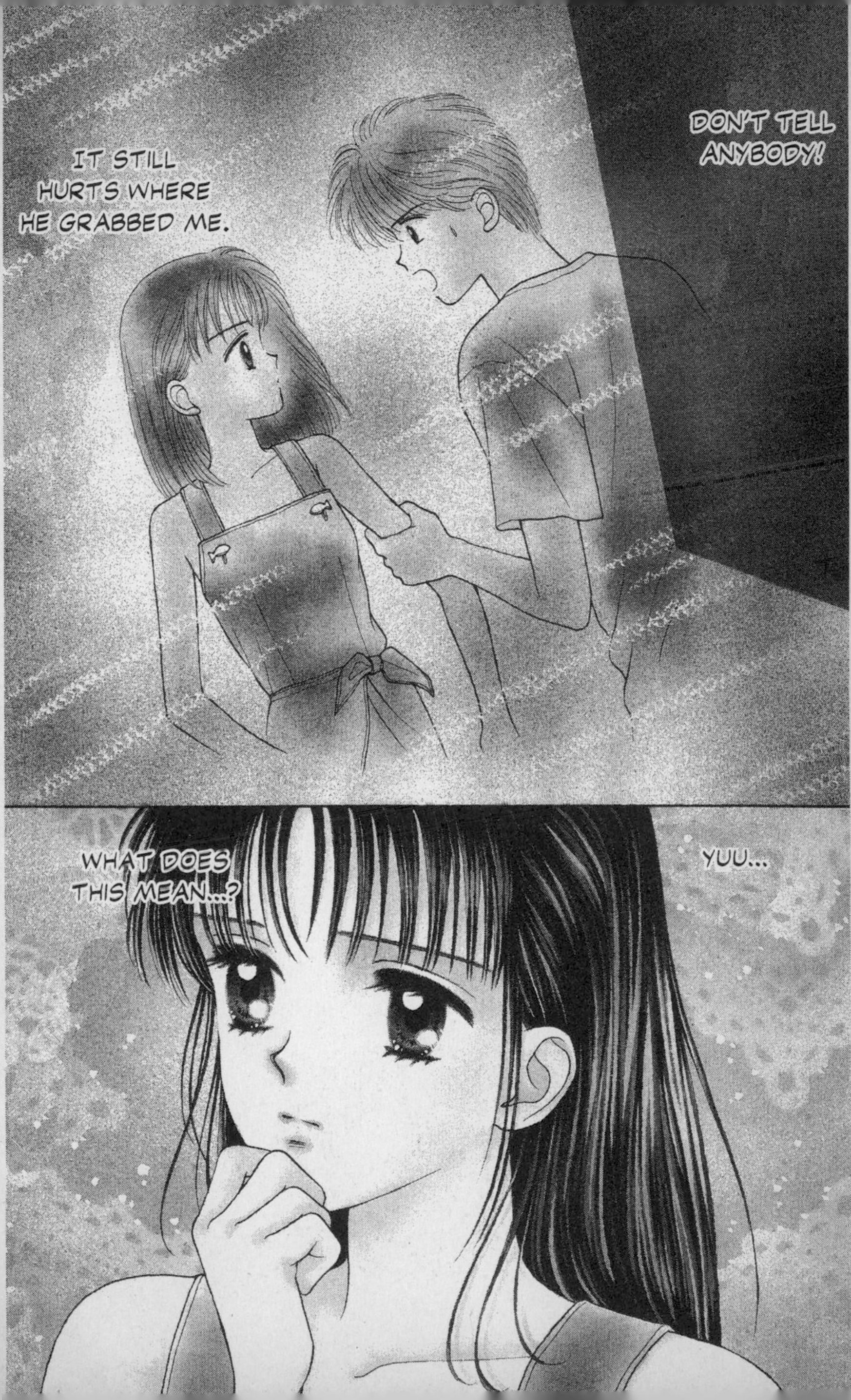
DON'T TELL ANYBODY!
IT STILL HURTS WHERE HE GRABBED ME.
YUU...
WHAT DOES THIS MEAN...?

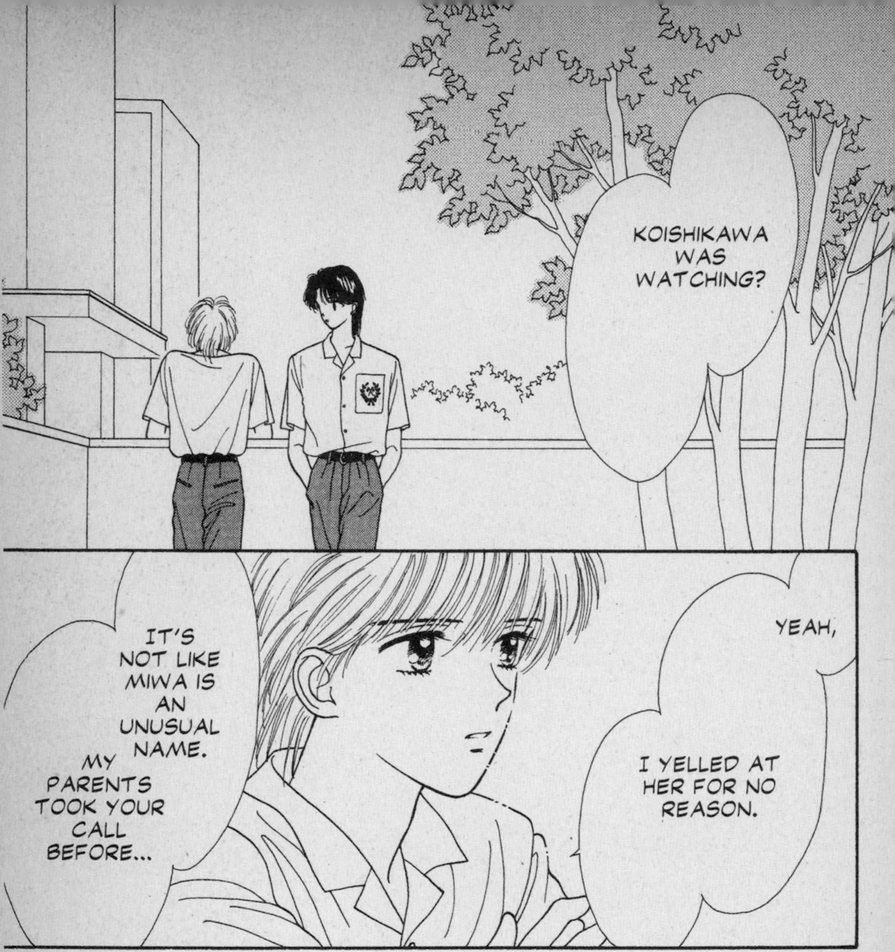
KOISHIKAWA WAS WATCHING?
YEAH,
I YELLED AT HER FOR NO REASON.
IT'S NOT LIKE MIWA IS AN UNUSUAL NAME.
MY PARENTS TOOK YOUR CALL BEFORE...

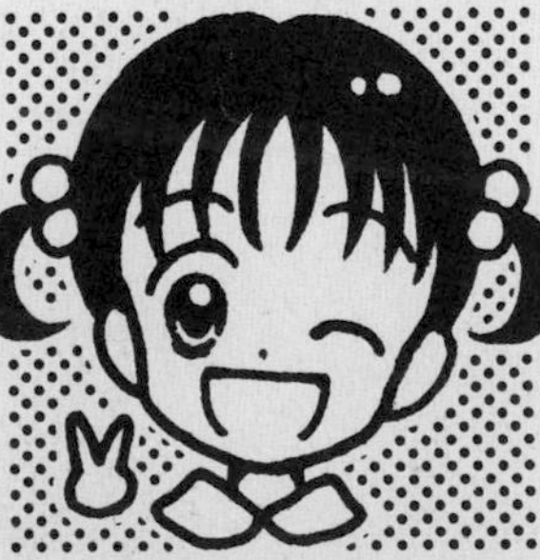

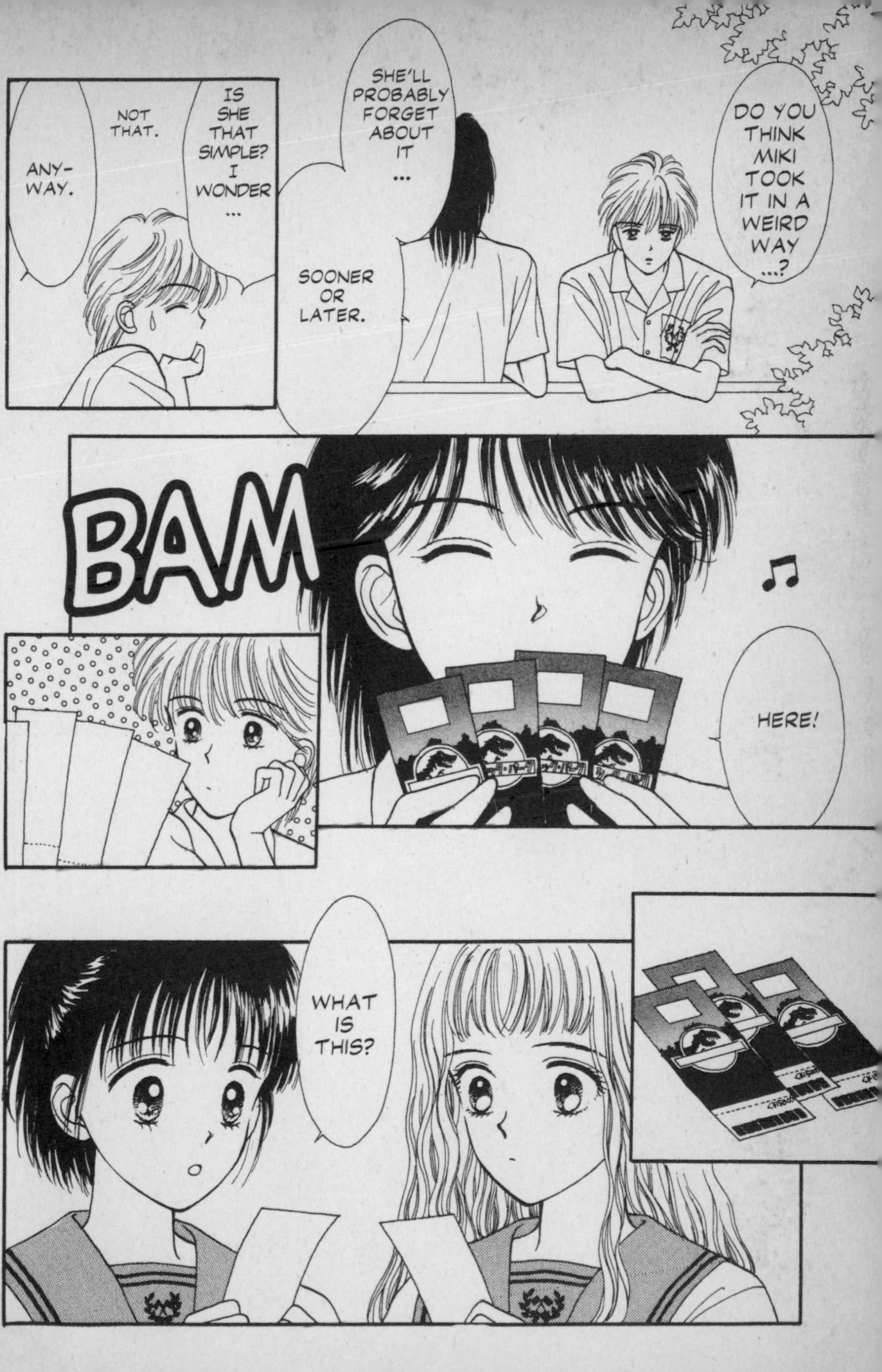
DO YOU THINK MIKI TOOK IT IN A WEIRD WAY ...?
SHE'LL PROBABLY FORGET ABOUT IT ...
SOONER OR LATER.
IS SHE THAT SIMPLE? I WONDER ...
NOT THAT.
ANY-WAY.
BAM
♪
HERE!
WHAT IS THIS?

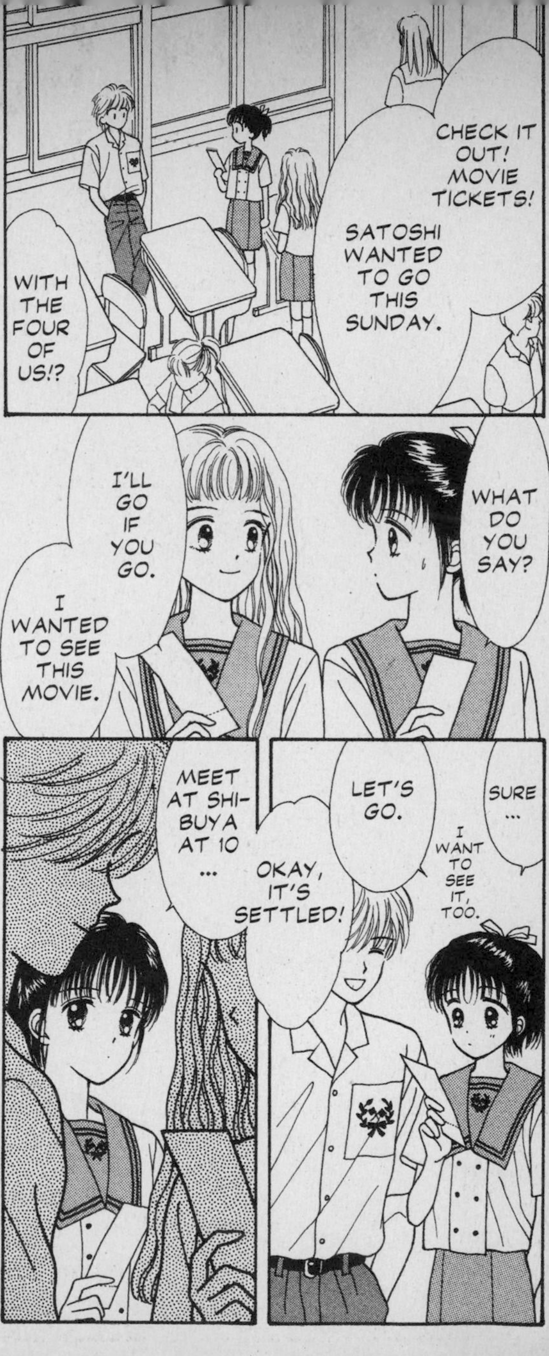
CHECK IT OUT! MOVIE TICKETS!
SATOSHI WANTED TO GO THIS SUNDAY.
WITH THE FOUR OF US!?
WHAT DO YOU SAY?
I'LL GO IF YOU GO.
I WANTED TO SEE THIS MOVIE.
SURE ...
I WANT TO SEE IT, TOO.
LET'S GO.
OKAY, IT'S SETTLED!
MEET AT SHI-BUYA AT 10 ...

FREE TALK ⑦

If the merchandise for Marmalade Boy doesn't sell well, Bandai will lose money. I hope it sells!
If it was a magical phantasm-type animation, Bandai can sell some toys and clothes, but Marmalade Boy...

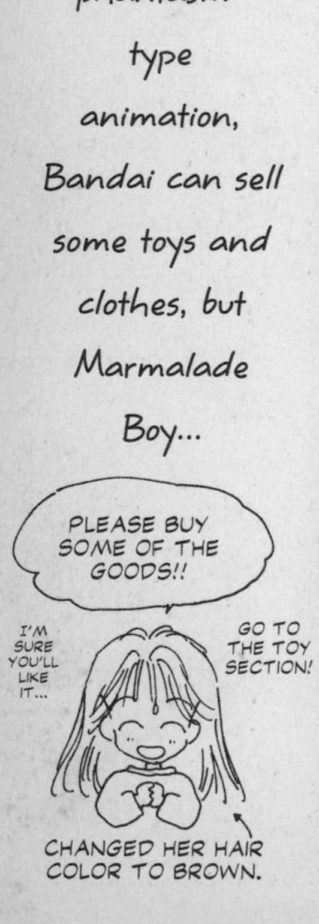
PLEASE BUY SOME OF THE GOODS!!
I'M SURE YOU'LL LIKE IT...
GO TO THE TOY SECTION!
CHANGED HER HAIR COLOR TO BROWN.

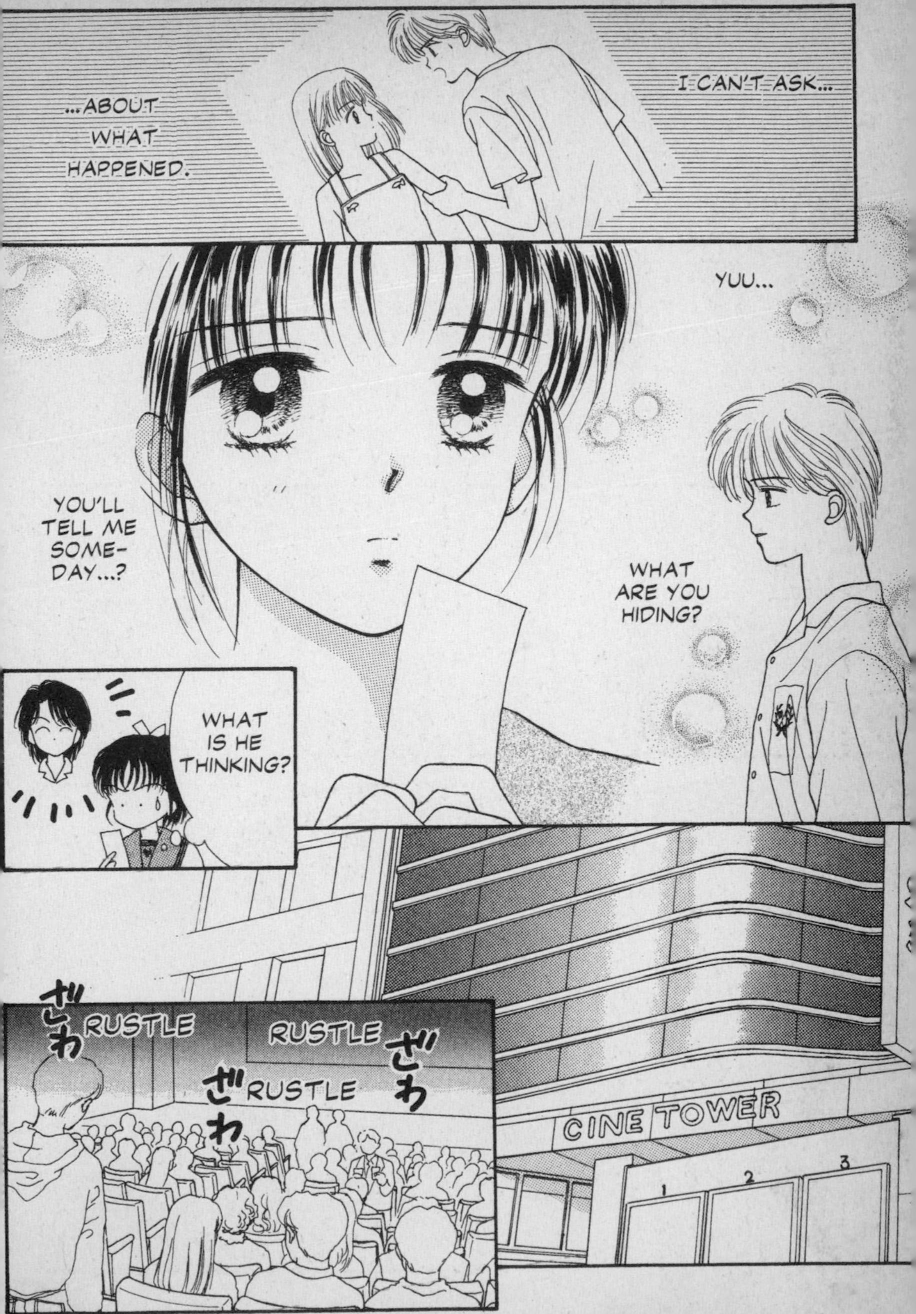
I CAN'T ASK...
...ABOUT WHAT HAPPENED.
YUU...
WHAT ARE YOU HIDING?
YOU'LL TELL ME SOME-DAY...?
WHAT IS HE THINKING?
CINE TOWER
1
2
3
RUSTLE ざわ
ざわ RUSTLE
ざわ RUSTLE

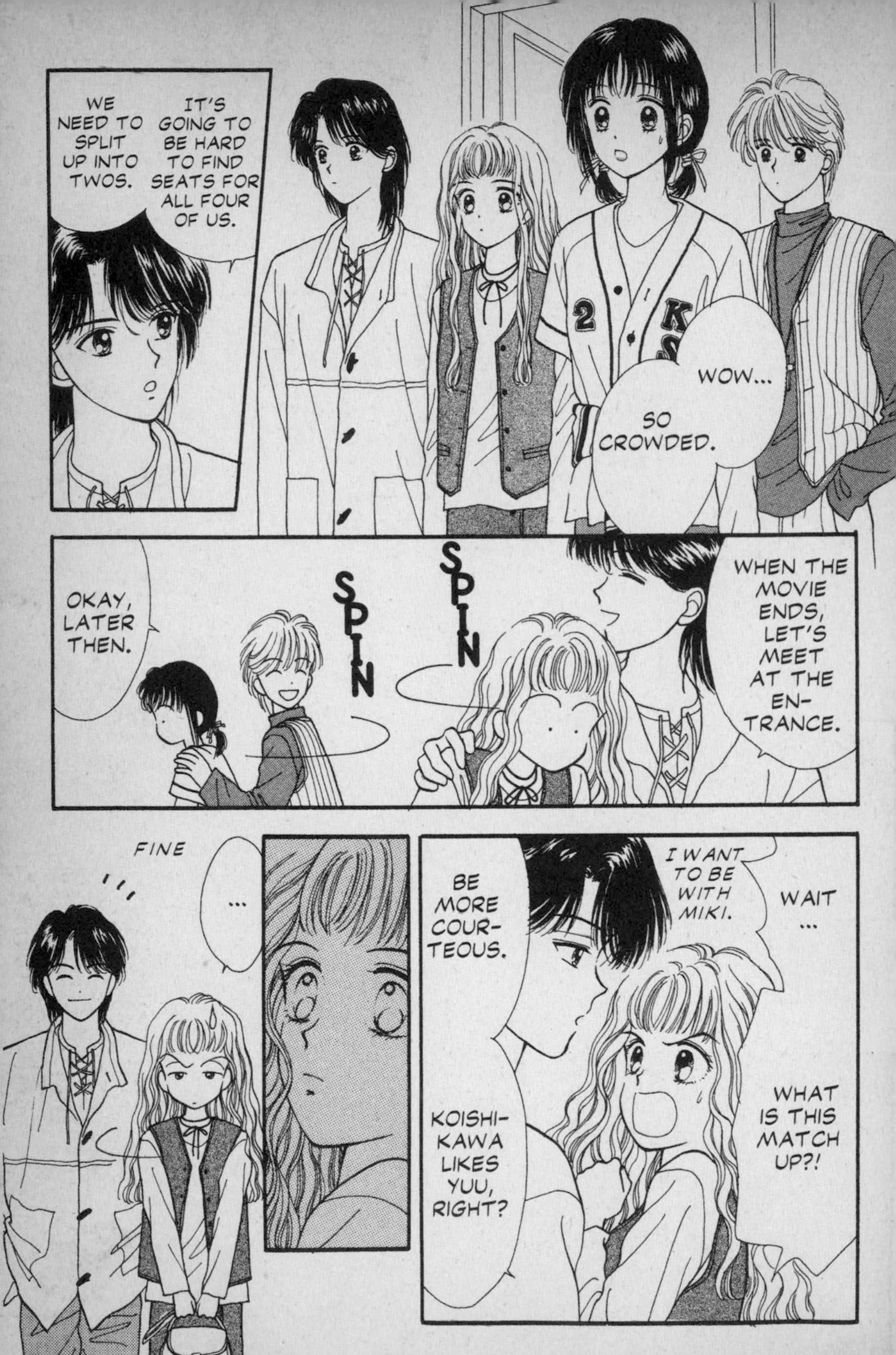
WOW...
SO CROWDED.
IT'S GOING TO BE HARD TO FIND SEATS FOR ALL FOUR OF US.
WE NEED TO SPLIT UP INTO TWOS.
WHEN THE MOVIE ENDS, LET'S MEET AT THE EN-TRANCE.
SPIN
SPIN
OKAY, LATER THEN.
WAIT ...
I WANT TO BE WITH MIKI.
WHAT IS THIS MATCH UP?!
BE MORE COUR-TEOUS.
KOISHI-KAWA LIKES YUU, RIGHT?
...
FINE

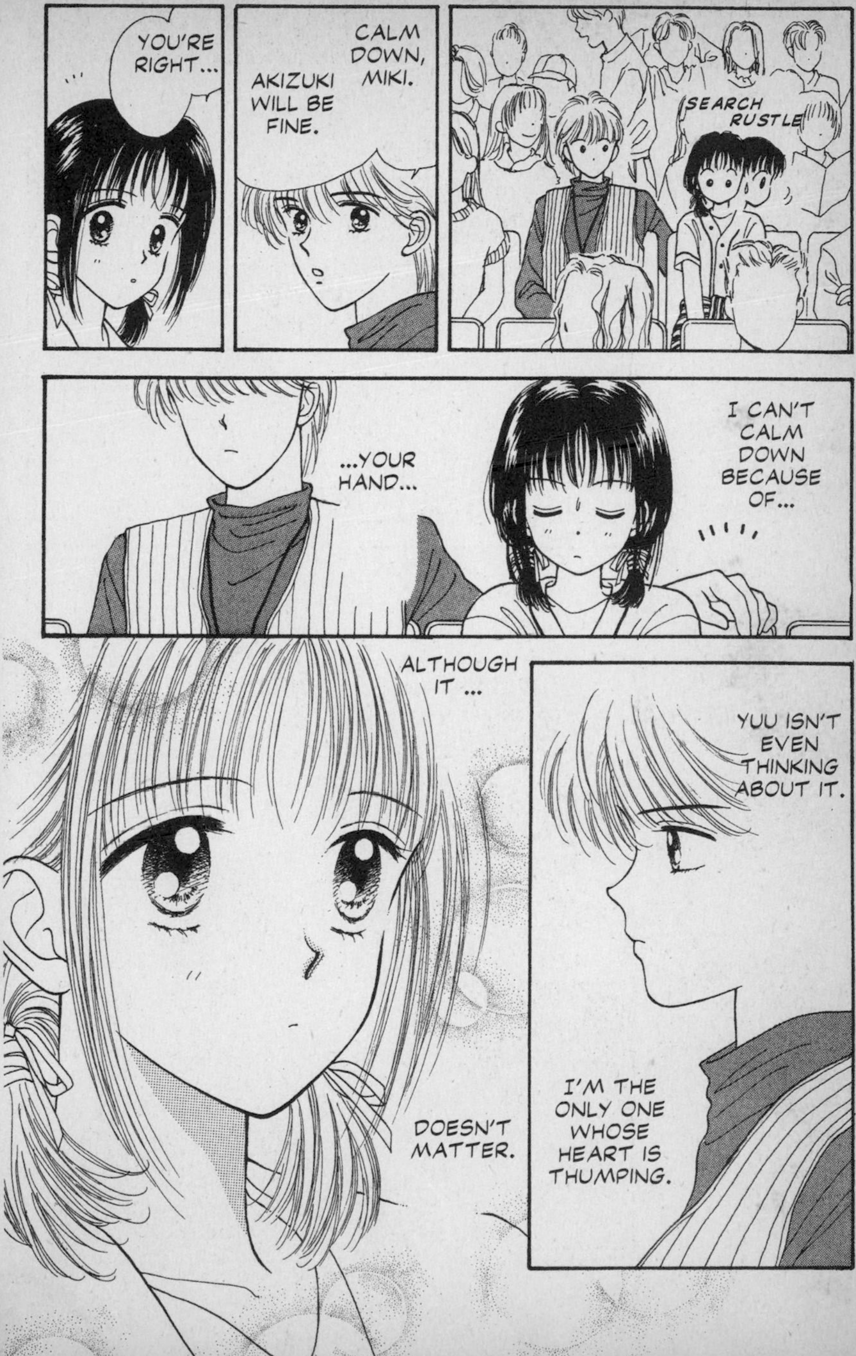
SEARCH
RUSTLE
CALM DOWN, MIKI.
AKIZUKI WILL BE FINE.
YOU'RE RIGHT...
I CAN'T CALM DOWN BECAUSE OF...
...YOUR HAND...
YUU ISN'T EVEN THINKING ABOUT IT.
I'M THE ONLY ONE WHOSE HEART IS THUMPING.
ALTHOUGH IT ...
DOESN'T MATTER.

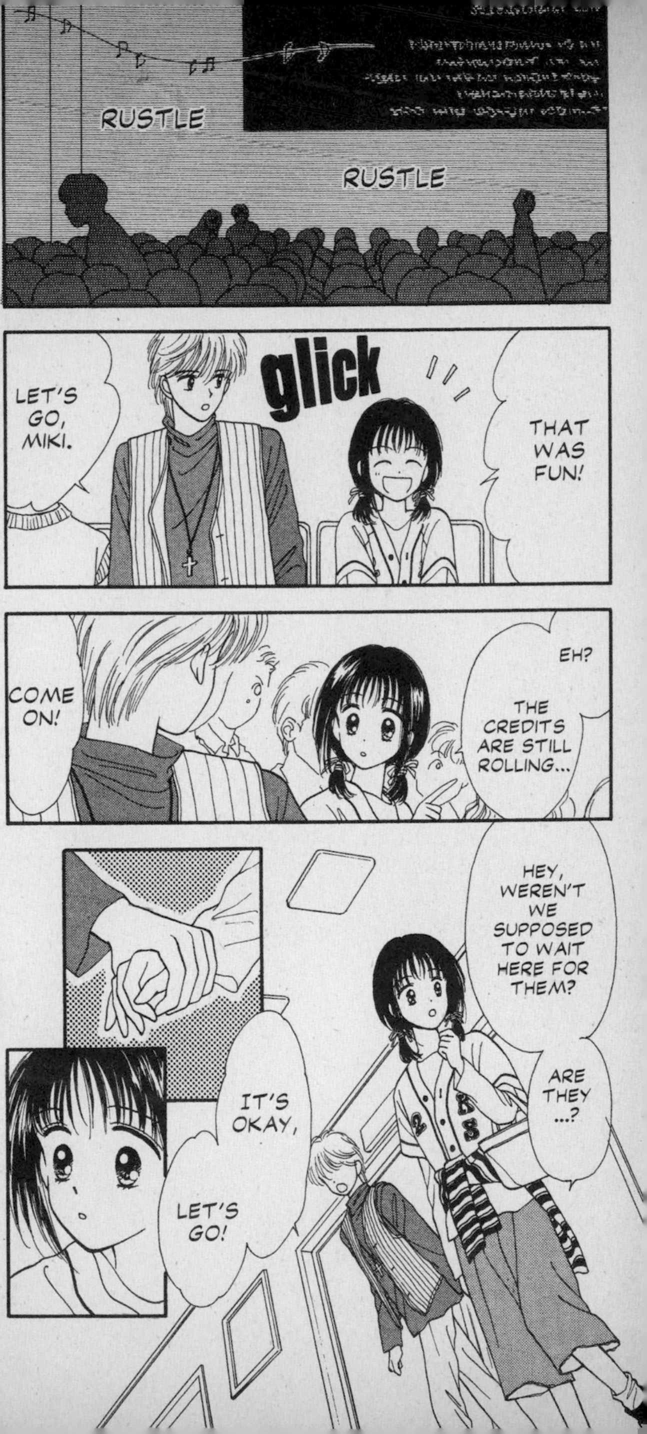
RUSTLE
RUSTLE
THAT WAS FUN!
glick
LET'S GO, MIKI.
EH?
THE CREDITS ARE STILL ROLLING...
COME ON!
HEY, WEREN'T WE SUPPOSED TO WAIT HERE FOR THEM?
ARE THEY ...?
IT'S OKAY,
LET'S GO!

FREE TALK ⑧

Goods that are going to be sold:

Notebook

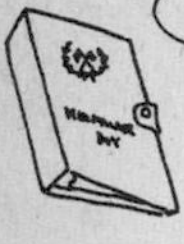

It has Miki's school's symbol on it. In the animation, Miki uses it.

Voice memo device

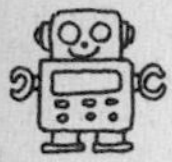

A robot- shaped tape recorder. There are blue, red, and yellow colors.

bag

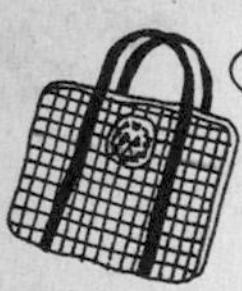

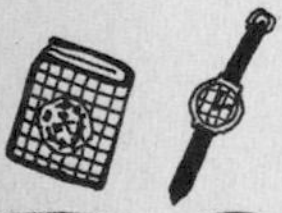

wallet

watch

The watch comes with a golden mini accessory.

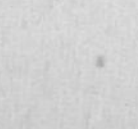

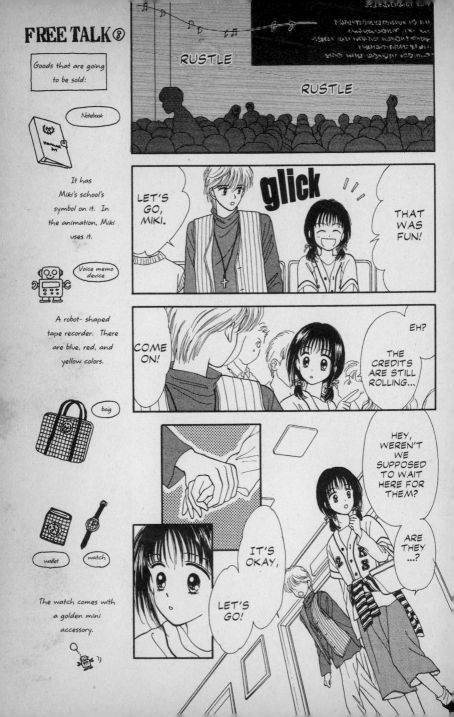

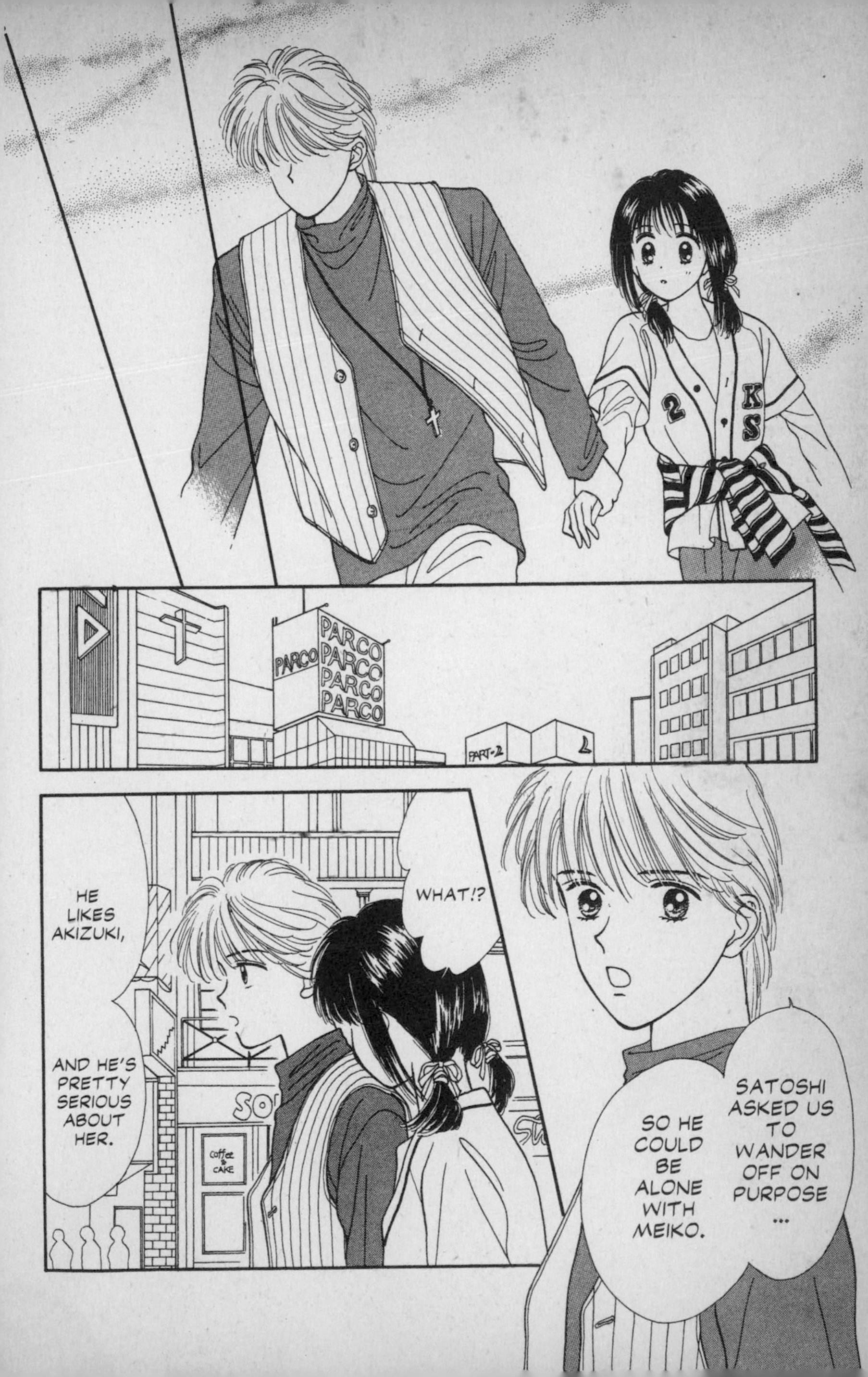
PARCO
PARCO PARCO PARCO PARCO
PART-2
SATOSHI ASKED US TO WANDER OFF ON PURPOSE ...
SO HE COULD BE ALONE WITH MEIKO.
WHAT!?
HE LIKES AKIZUKI,
AND HE'S PRETTY SERIOUS ABOUT HER.
Coffee & CAKE

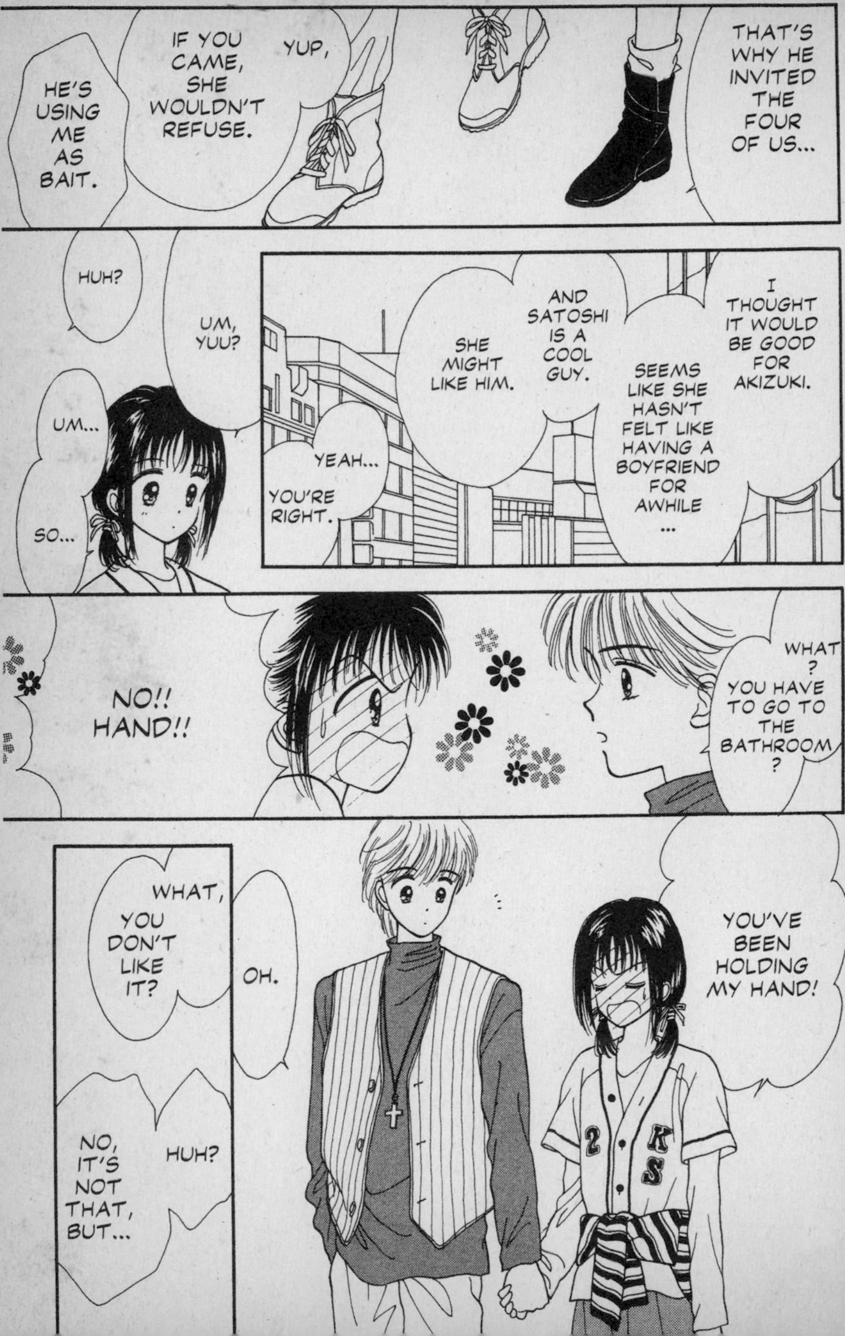
THAT'S WHY HE INVITED THE FOUR OF US...
YUP,
IF YOU CAME, SHE WOULDN'T REFUSE.
HE'S USING ME AS BAIT.
I THOUGHT IT WOULD BE GOOD FOR AKIZUKI.
SEEMS LIKE SHE HASN'T FELT LIKE HAVING A BOYFRIEND FOR AWHILE ...
AND SATOSHI IS A COOL GUY.
SHE MIGHT LIKE HIM.
YEAH... YOU'RE RIGHT.
UM, YUU?
HUH?
UM... SO...
WHAT? YOU HAVE TO GO TO THE BATHROOM?
NO!! HAND!!
YOU'VE BEEN HOLDING MY HAND!
OH.
WHAT, YOU DON'T LIKE IT?
HUH?
NO, IT'S NOT THAT, BUT...

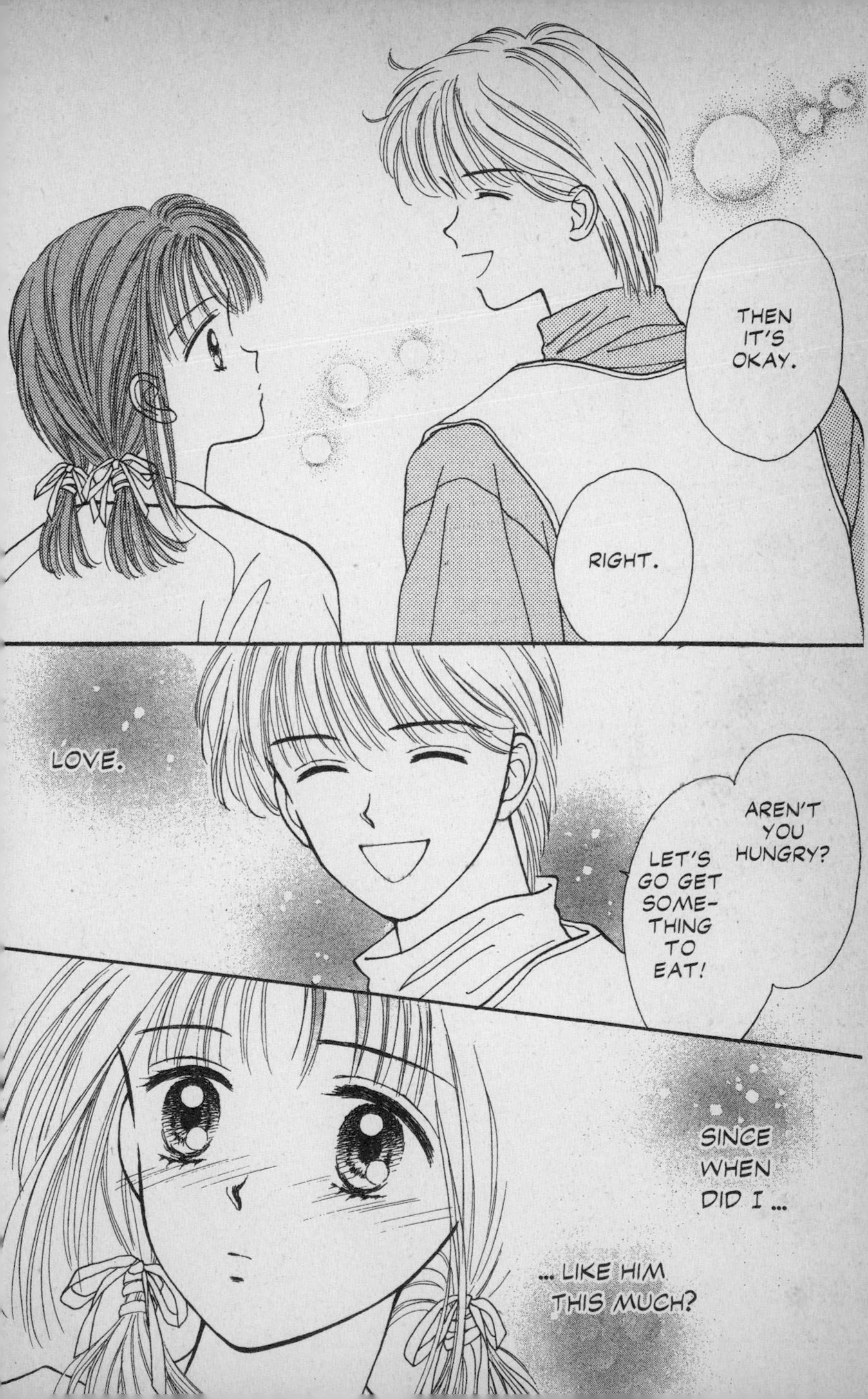

THEN IT'S OKAY.
RIGHT.
AREN'T YOU HUNGRY?
LET'S GO GET SOME-THING TO EAT!
LOVE.
SINCE WHEN DID I ...
... LIKE HIM THIS MUCH?

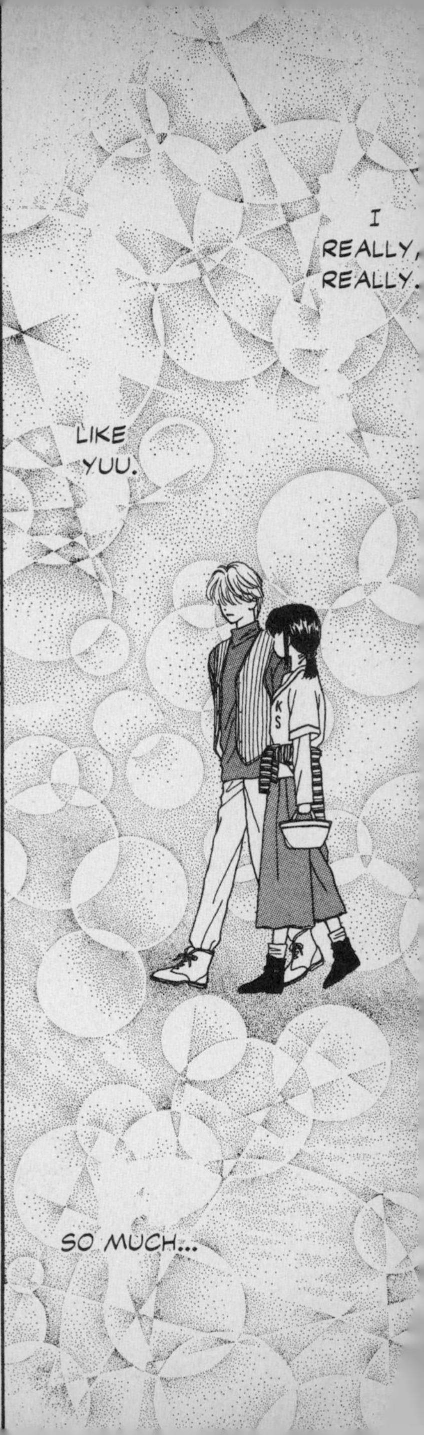
I REALLY, REALLY
LIKE YUU.
SO MUCH...

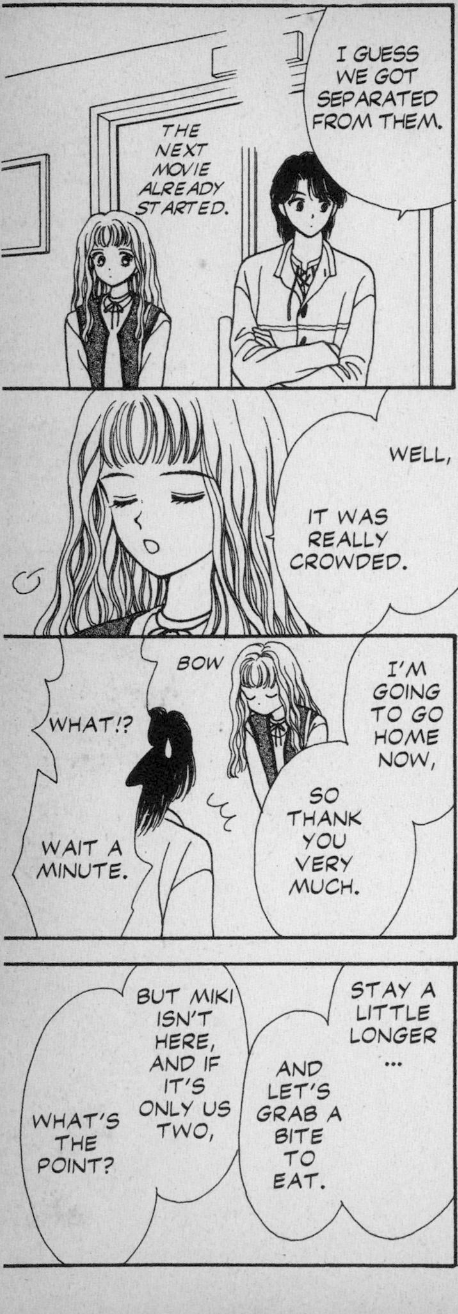
I GUESS WE GOT SEPARATED FROM THEM.
THE NEXT MOVIE ALREADY STARTED.
WELL,
IT WAS REALLY CROWDED.
I'M GOING TO GO HOME NOW,
SO THANK YOU VERY MUCH.
BOW
WHAT!?
WAIT A MINUTE.
STAY A LITTLE LONGER ...
AND LET'S GRAB A BITE TO EAT.
BUT MIKI ISN'T HERE, AND IF IT'S ONLY US TWO,
WHAT'S THE POINT?

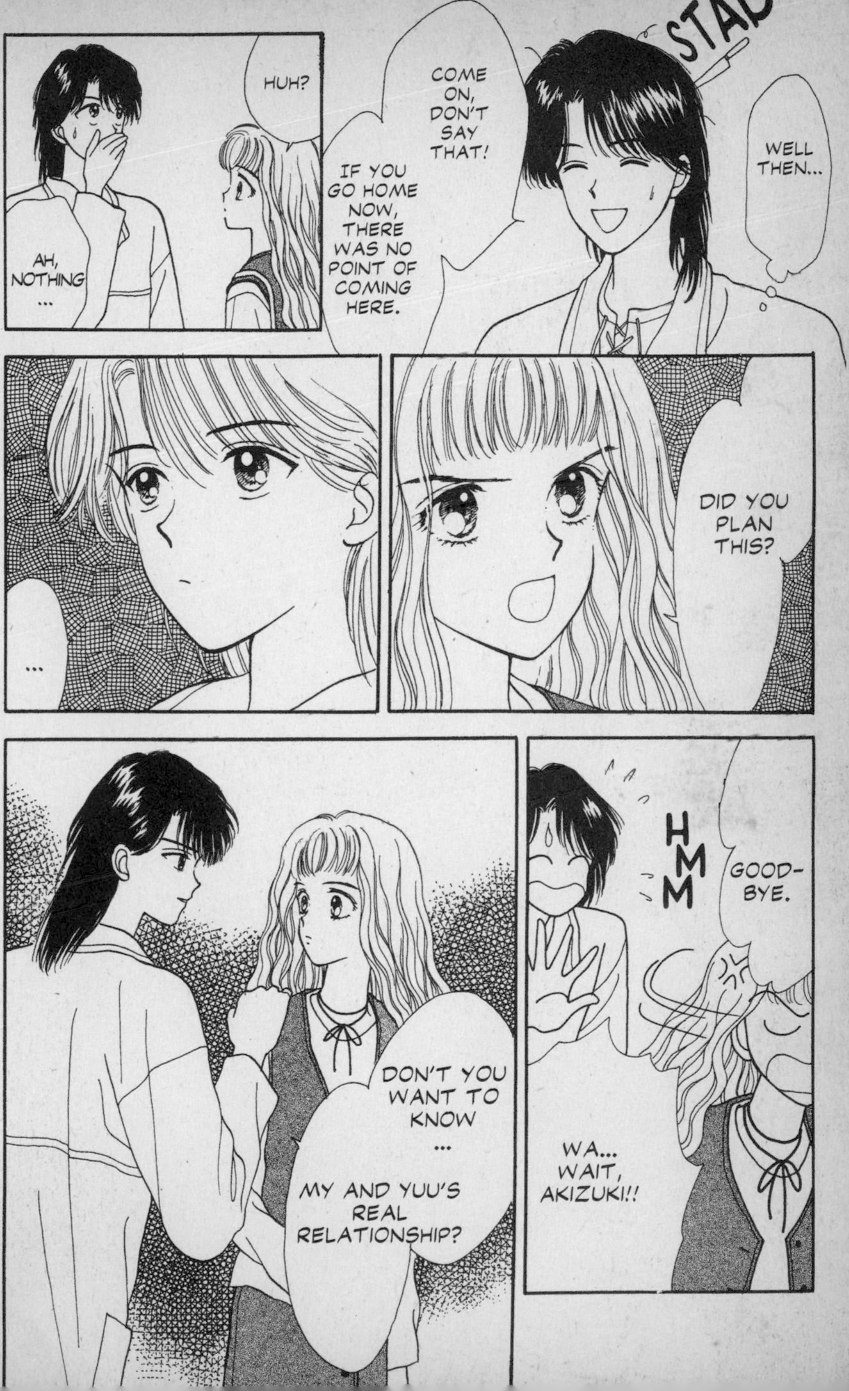
STAB
WELL THEN...
COME ON, DON'T SAY THAT!
IF YOU GO HOME NOW, THERE WAS NO POINT OF COMING HERE.
HUH?
AH, NOTHING ...
DID YOU PLAN THIS?
...
HMM
GOOD-BYE.
WA... WAIT, AKIZUKI!!
DON'T YOU WANT TO KNOW ...
MY AND YUU'S REAL RELATIONSHIP?

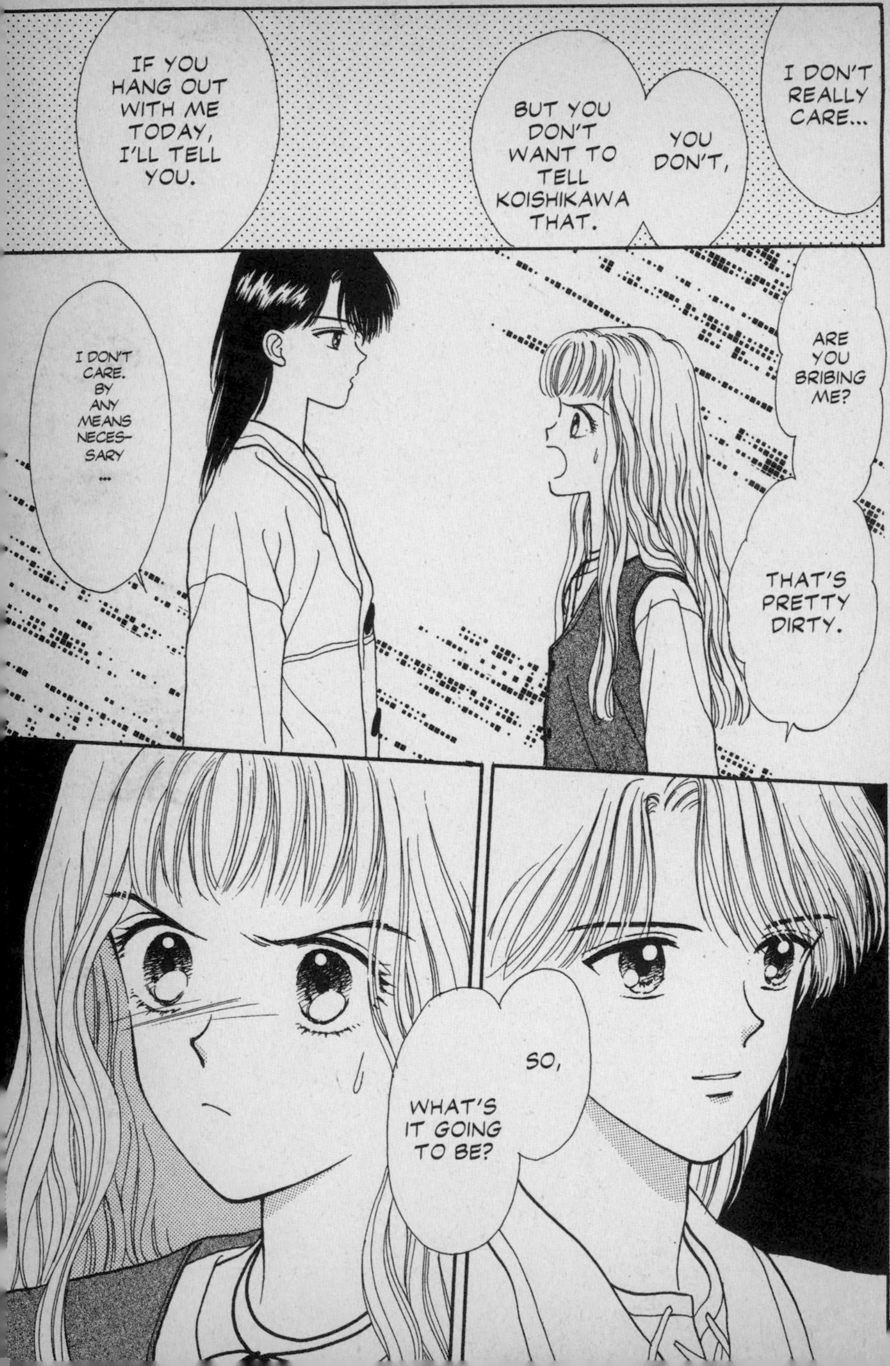
I DON'T REALLY CARE...
YOU DON'T,
BUT YOU DON'T WANT TO TELL KOISHIKAWA THAT.
IF YOU HANG OUT WITH ME TODAY, I'LL TELL YOU.
ARE YOU BRIBING ME?
THAT'S PRETTY DIRTY.
I DON'T CARE. BY ANY MEANS NECES-SARY ...
SO,
WHAT'S IT GOING TO BE?

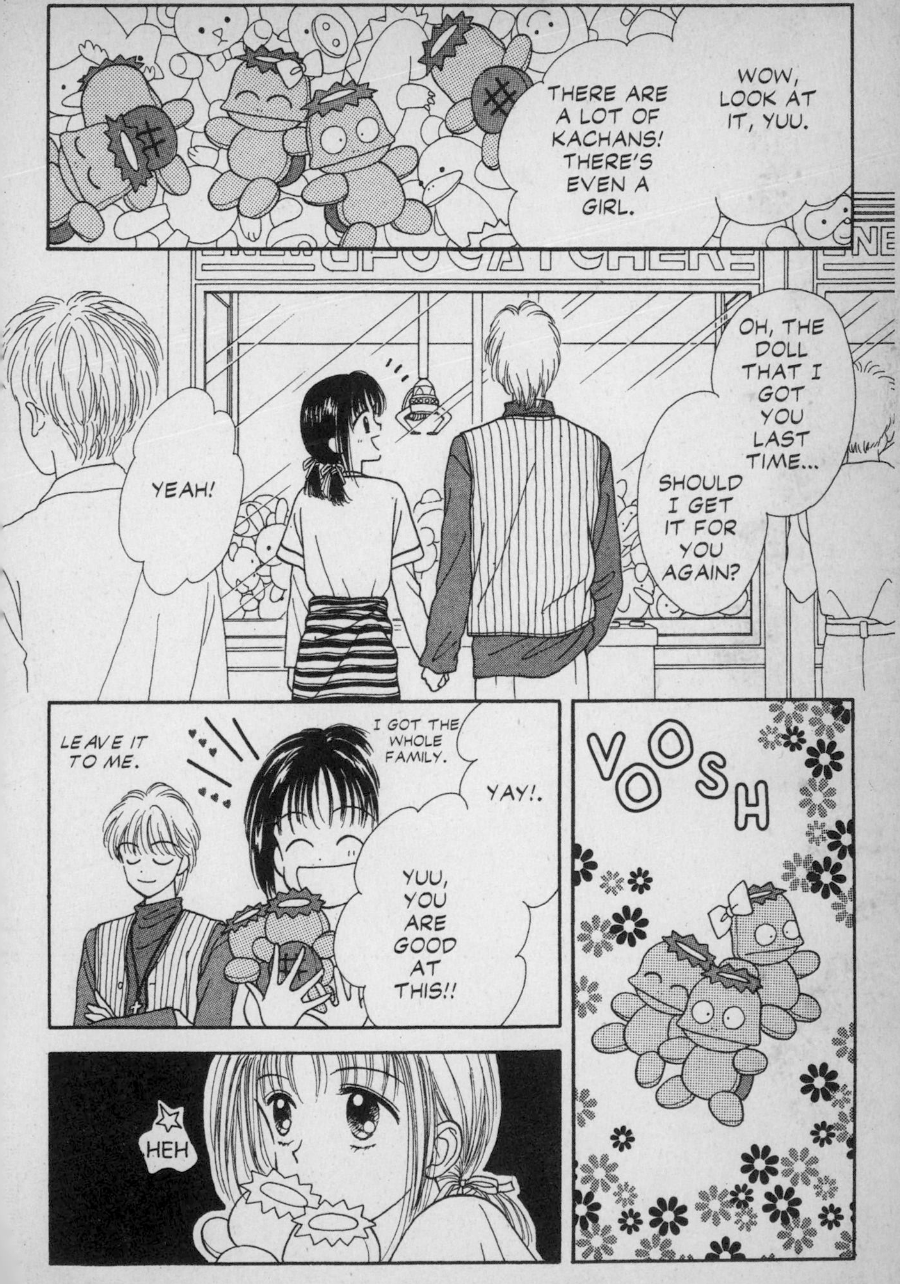
WOW, LOOK AT IT, YUU.
THERE ARE A LOT OF KACHANS! THERE'S EVEN A GIRL.
OH, THE DOLL THAT I GOT YOU LAST TIME...
SHOULD I GET IT FOR YOU AGAIN?
YEAH!
VOOSH
I GOT THE WHOLE FAMILY.
YAY!.
LEAVE IT TO ME.
YUU, YOU ARE GOOD AT THIS!!
HEH

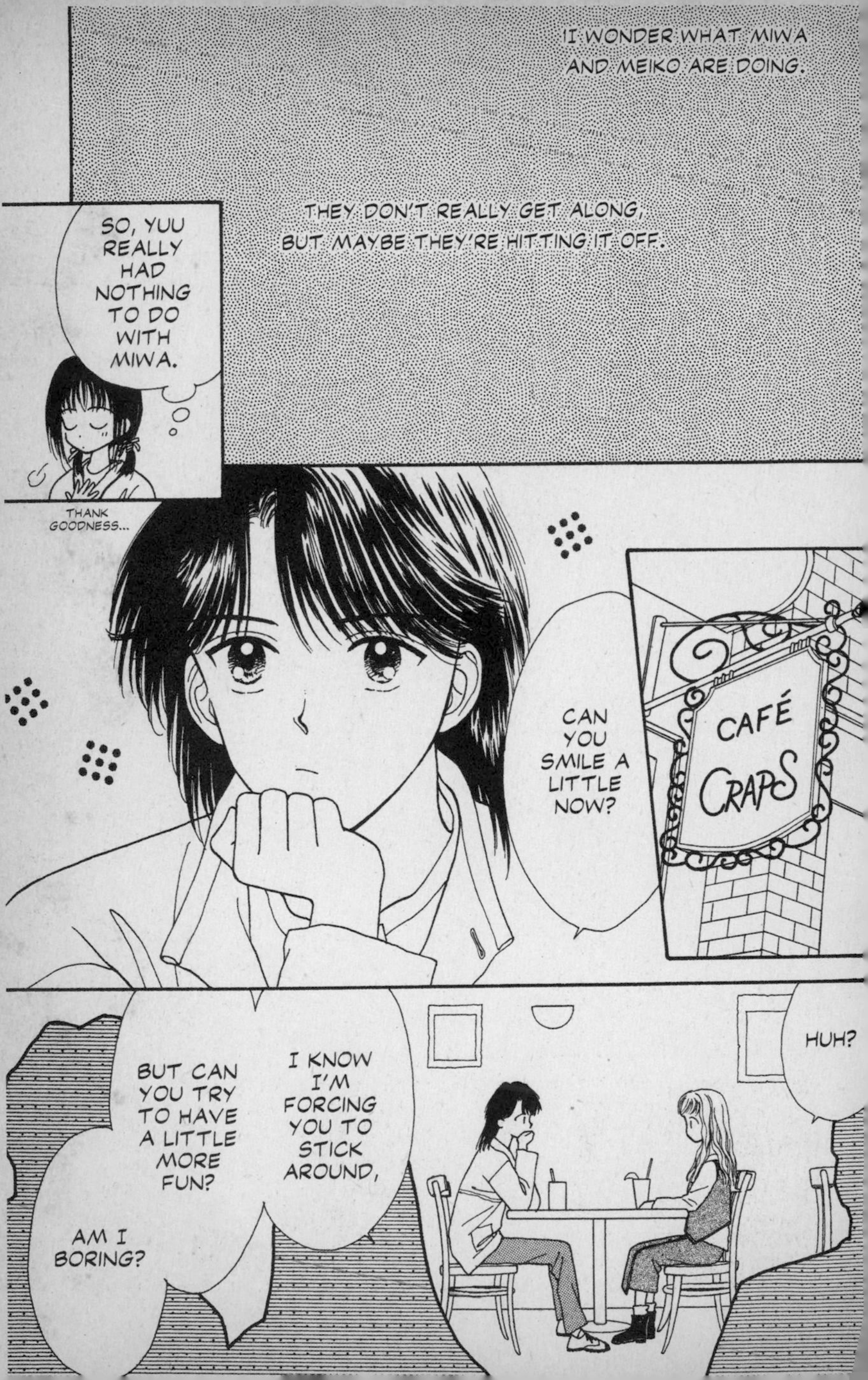
I WONDER WHAT MIWA AND MEIKO ARE DOING.
THEY DON'T REALLY GET ALONG, BUT MAYBE THEY'RE HITTING IT OFF.
SO, YUU REALLY HAD NOTHING TO DO WITH MIWA.
THANK GOODNESS...
CAFÉ CRAPS
CAN YOU SMILE A LITTLE NOW?
HUH?
I KNOW I'M FORCING YOU TO STICK AROUND,
BUT CAN YOU TRY TO HAVE A LITTLE MORE FUN?
AM I BORING?

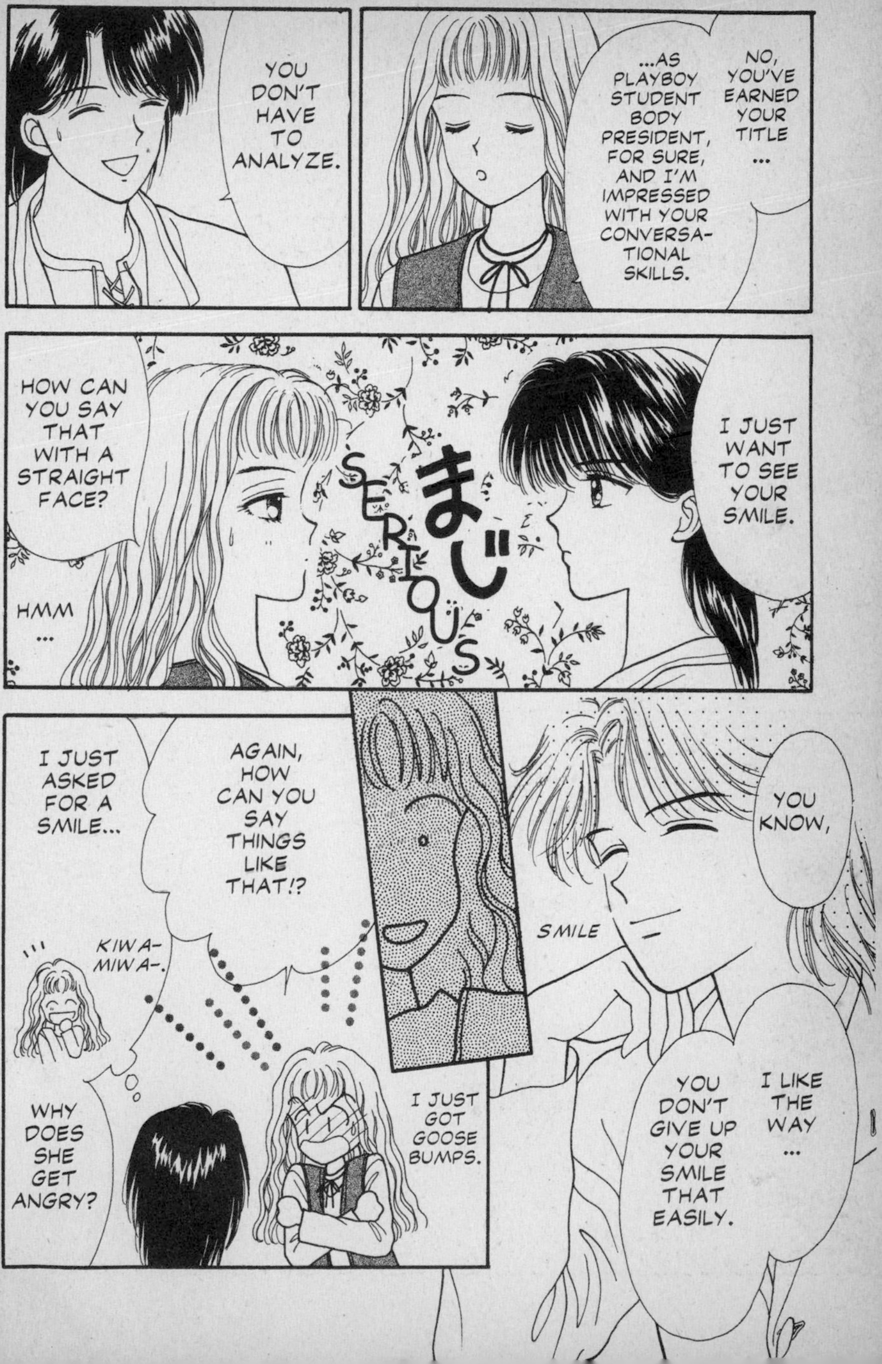
NO, YOU'VE EARNED YOUR TITLE ...
...AS PLAYBOY STUDENT BODY PRESIDENT, FOR SURE, AND I'M IMPRESSED WITH YOUR CONVERSATIONAL SKILLS.
YOU DON'T HAVE TO ANALYZE.
I JUST WANT TO SEE YOUR SMILE.
まじ
SERIOUS
HOW CAN YOU SAY THAT WITH A STRAIGHT FACE?
HMM ...
YOU KNOW,
I LIKE THE WAY ...
YOU DON'T GIVE UP YOUR SMILE THAT EASILY.
SMILE
AGAIN, HOW CAN YOU SAY THINGS LIKE THAT!?
I JUST ASKED FOR A SMILE...
KIWA-MIWA-.
...
I JUST GOT GOOSE BUMPS.
WHY DOES SHE GET ANGRY?

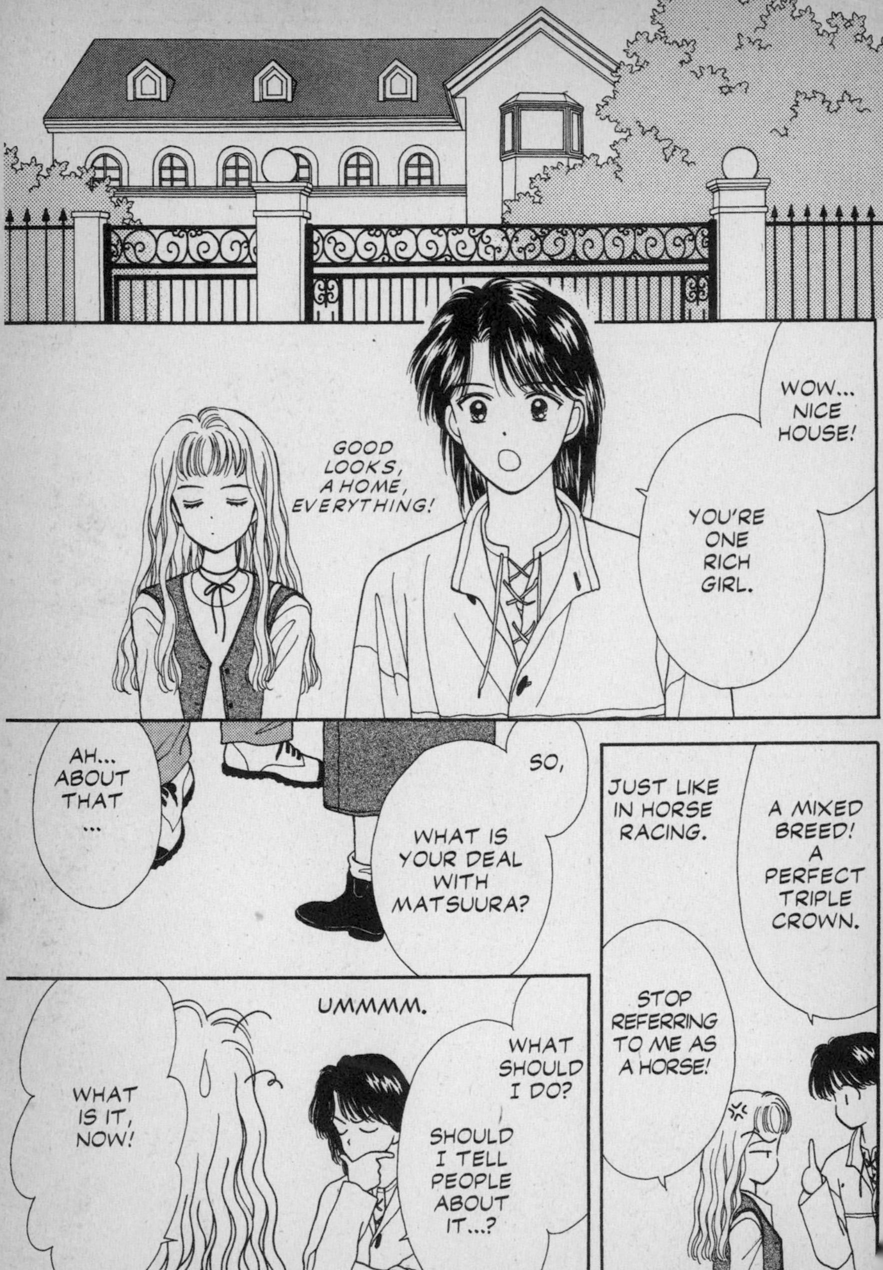
WOW... NICE HOUSE!
YOU'RE ONE RICH GIRL.
GOOD LOOKS, A HOME, EVERYTHING!
A MIXED BREED! A PERFECT TRIPLE CROWN.
JUST LIKE IN HORSE RACING.
STOP REFERRING TO ME AS A HORSE!
SO,
WHAT IS YOUR DEAL WITH MATSUURA?
AH... ABOUT THAT ...
UMMMM.
WHAT SHOULD I DO?
SHOULD I TELL PEOPLE ABOUT IT...?
WHAT IS IT, NOW!

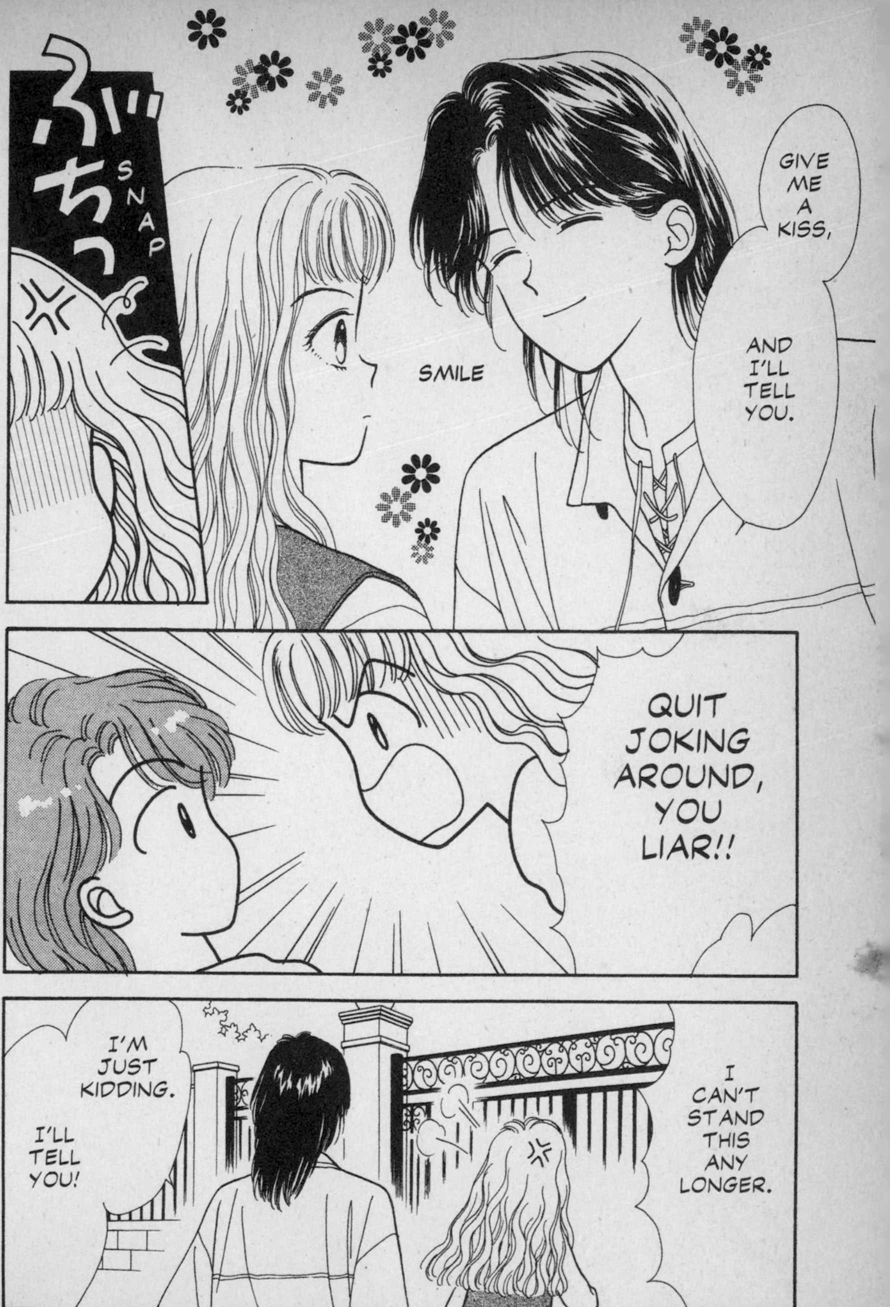
GIVE ME A KISS,
AND I'LL TELL YOU.
SMILE
SNAP
QUIT JOKING AROUND, YOU LIAR!!
I CAN'T STAND THIS ANY LONGER.
I'M JUST KIDDING.
I'LL TELL YOU!

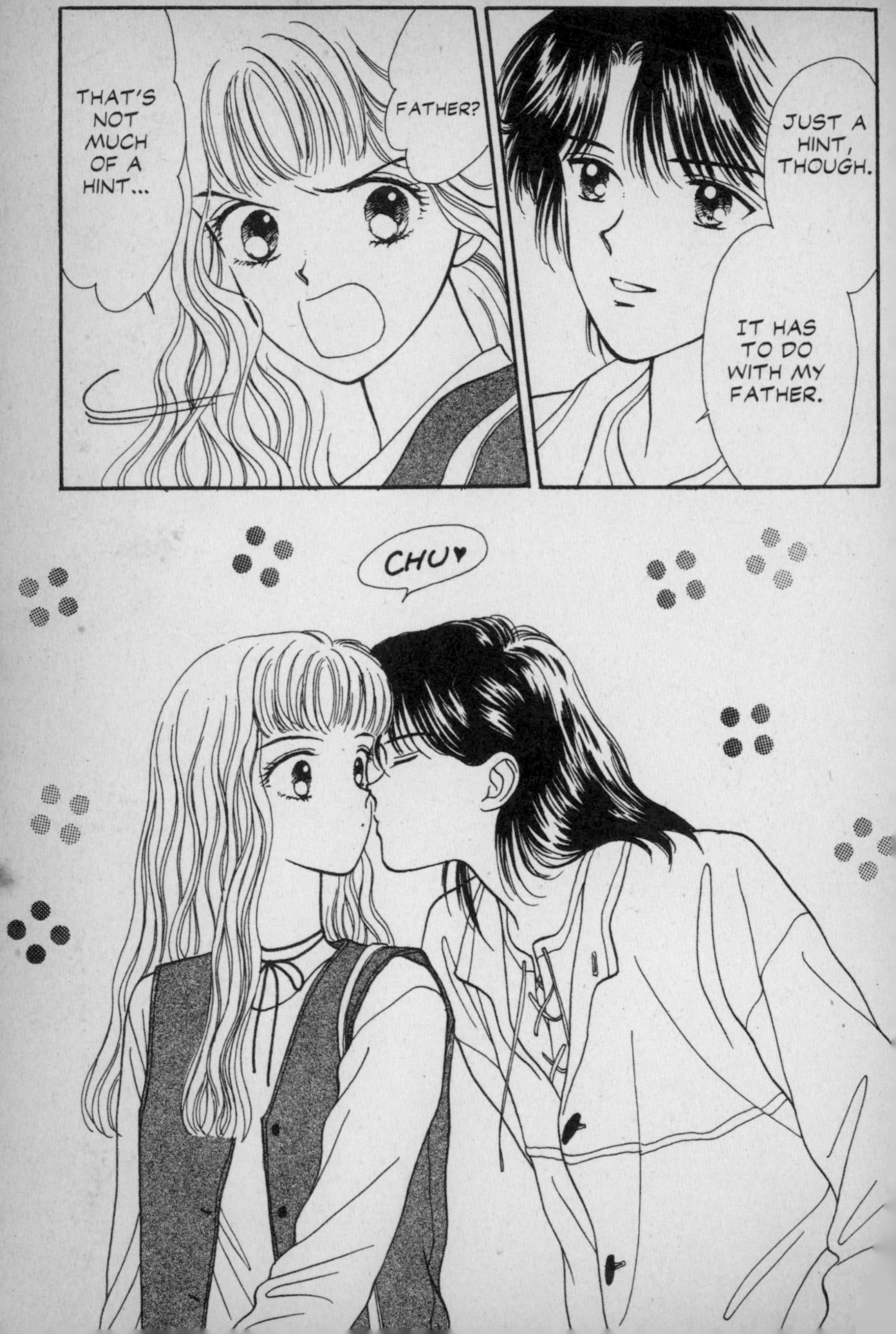
JUST A HINT, THOUGH.
IT HAS TO DO WITH MY FATHER.
FATHER?
THAT'S NOT MUCH OF A HINT...
CHU♥

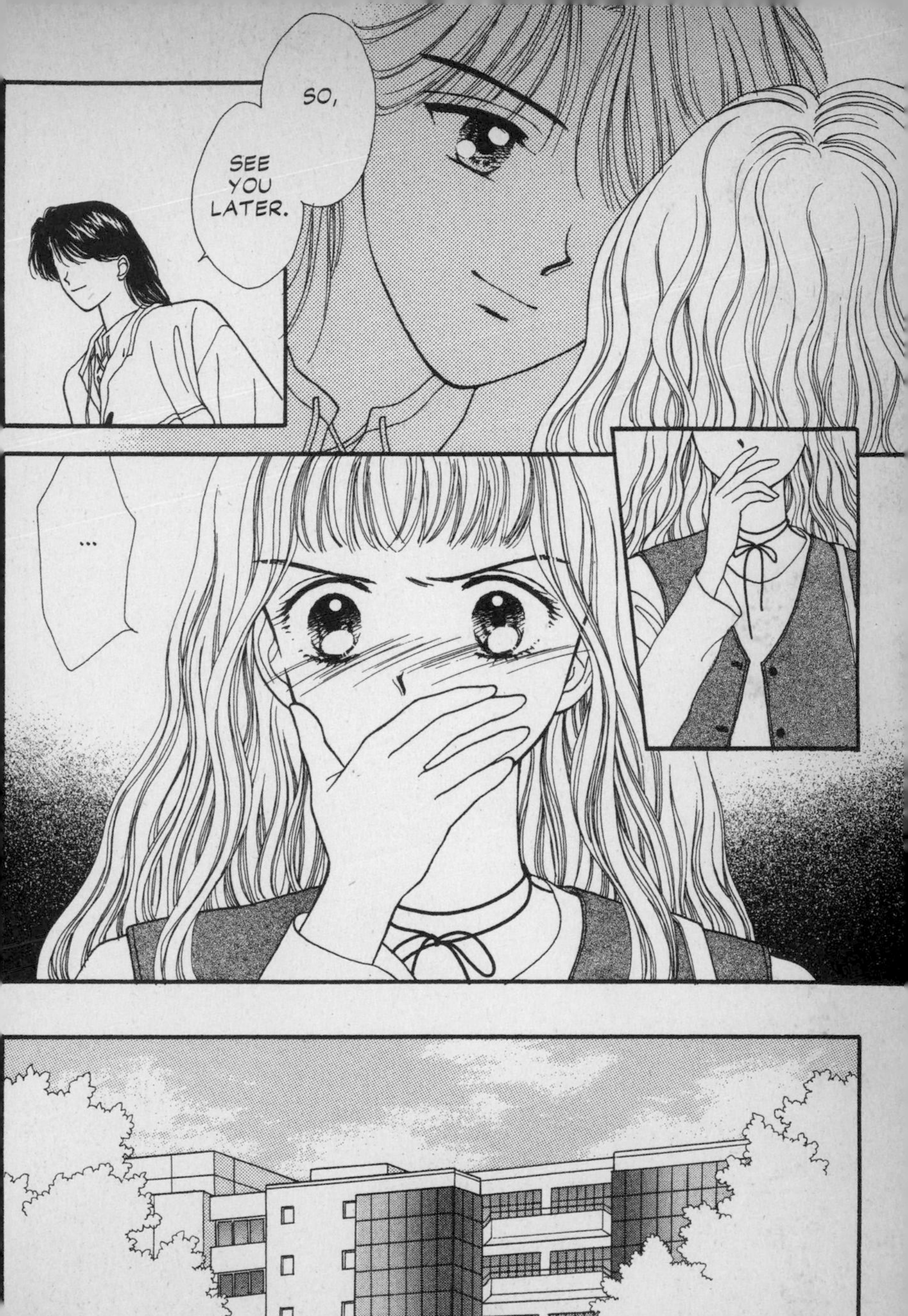
SO,
SEE YOU LATER.
...

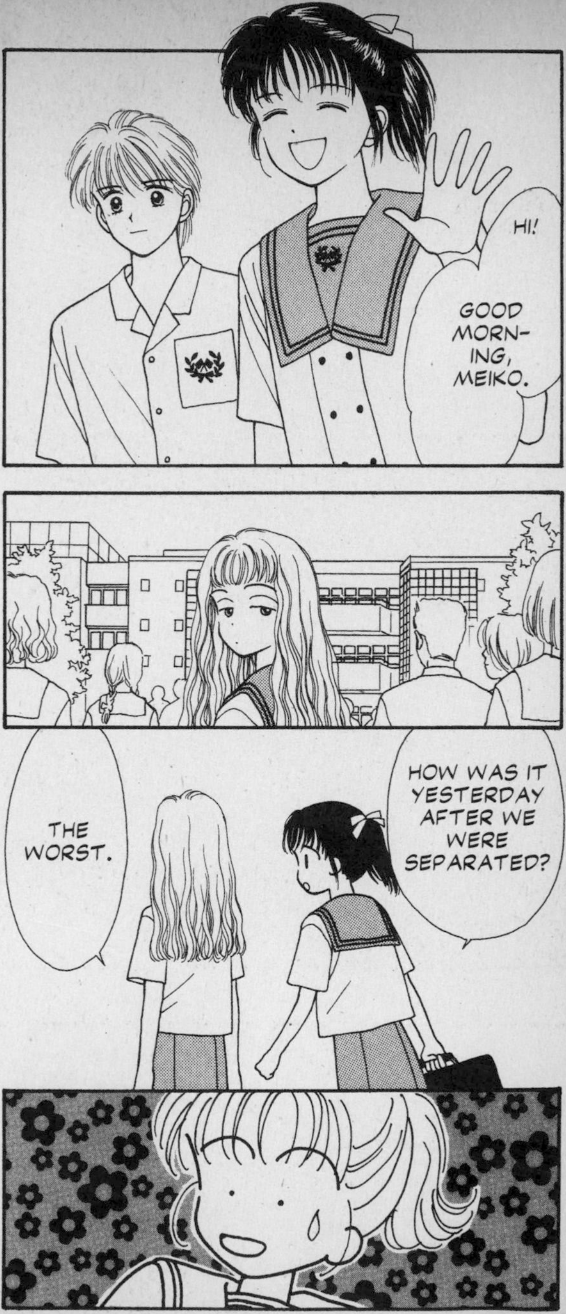
HI!
GOOD MORN-ING, MEIKO.
HOW WAS IT YESTERDAY AFTER WE WERE SEPARATED?
THE WORST.

FREE TALK ⑨

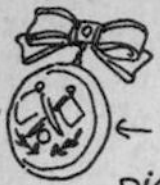

Medal

← You can put a picture inside. It is given to all the students in the animation series as a good-luck charm.

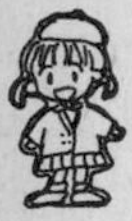

Badge

They used the design I produced.

These are some of the items that are going to be sold. What I am waiting for are the Miki and Yuu dolls. They're made so they would actually stand straight up. I hope they come out looking cute.

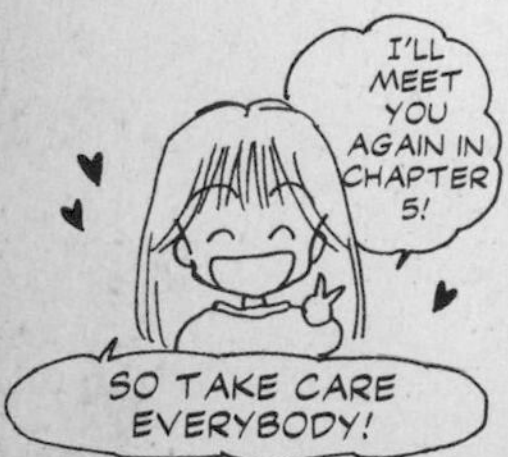
I'LL MEET YOU AGAIN IN CHAPTER 5!
SO TAKE CARE EVERYBODY!

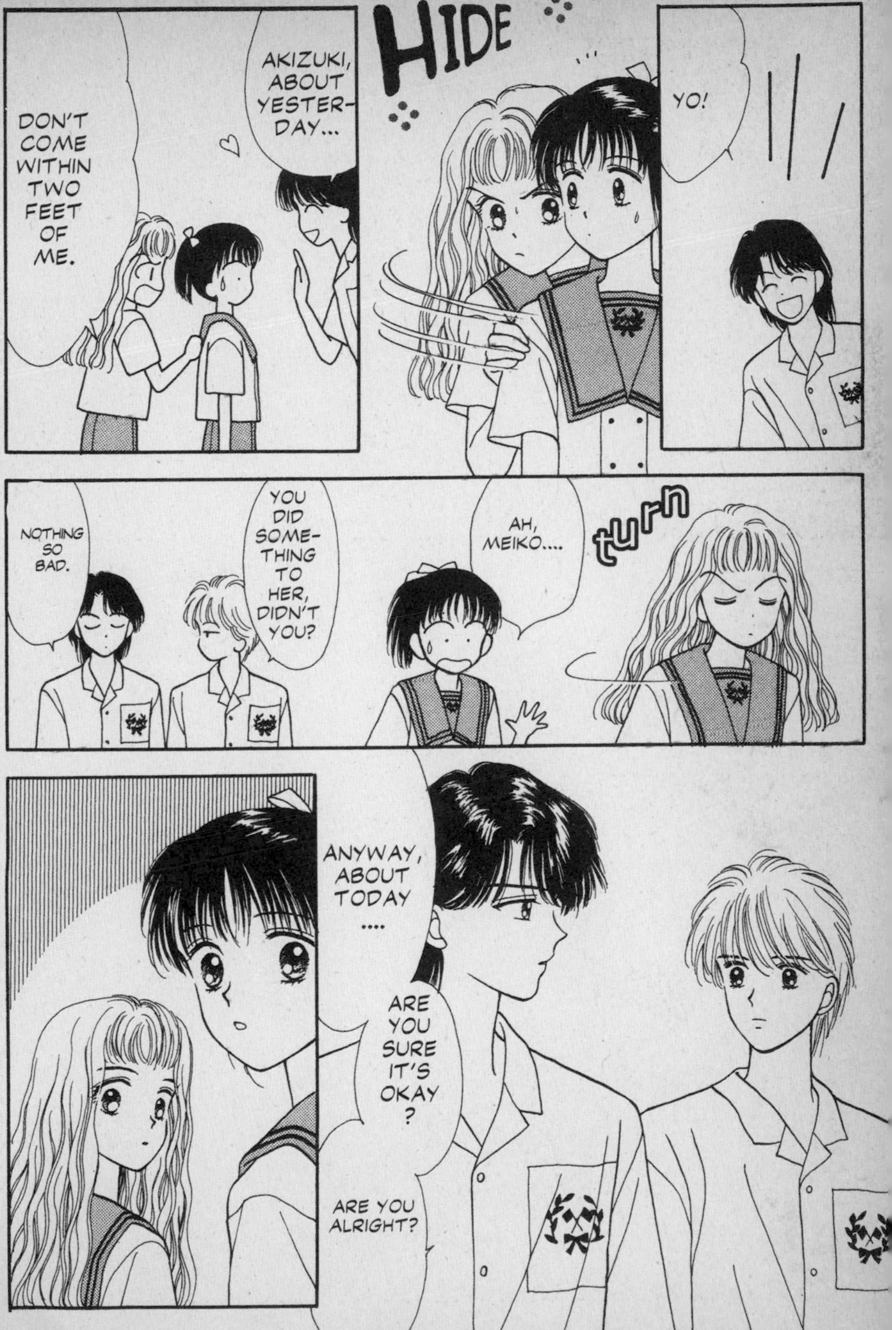
YO!
HIDE
AKIZUKI, ABOUT YESTER-DAY...
DON'T COME WITHIN TWO FEET OF ME.
turn
AH, MEIKO....
YOU DID SOME-THING TO HER, DIDN'T YOU?
NOTHING SO BAD.
ANYWAY, ABOUT TODAY ....
ARE YOU SURE IT'S OKAY ?
ARE YOU ALRIGHT?

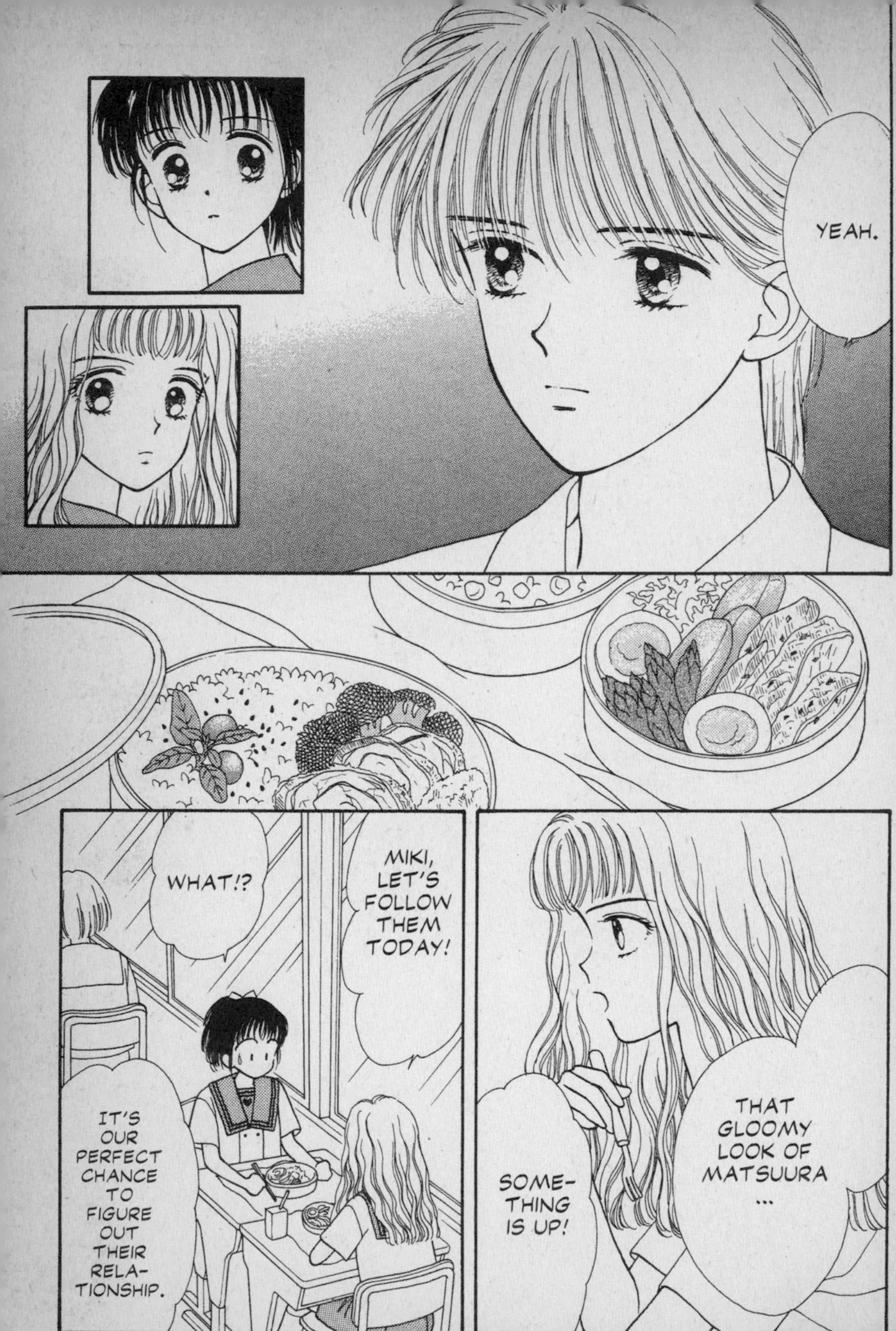
YEAH.
THAT GLOOMY LOOK OF MATSUURA ...
SOME-THING IS UP!
MIKI, LET'S FOLLOW THEM TODAY!
WHAT!?
IT'S OUR PERFECT CHANCE TO FIGURE OUT THEIR RELA-TIONSHIP.

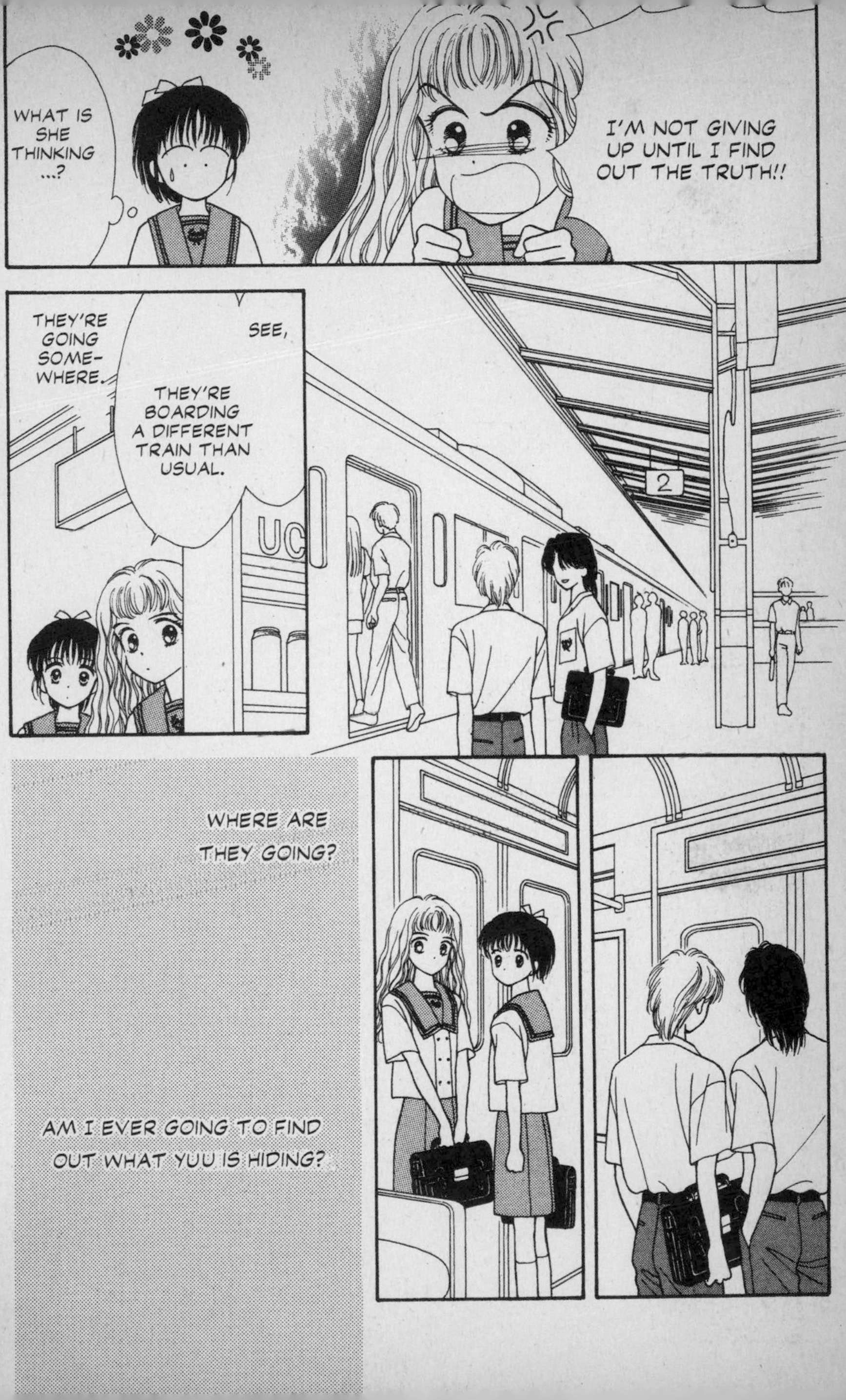
I'M NOT GIVING UP UNTIL I FIND OUT THE TRUTH!!
WHAT IS SHE THINKING ...?
SEE, THEY'RE BOARDING A DIFFERENT TRAIN THAN USUAL.
THEY'RE GOING SOME-WHERE.
2
WHERE ARE THEY GOING?
AM I EVER GOING TO FIND OUT WHAT YUU IS HIDING?

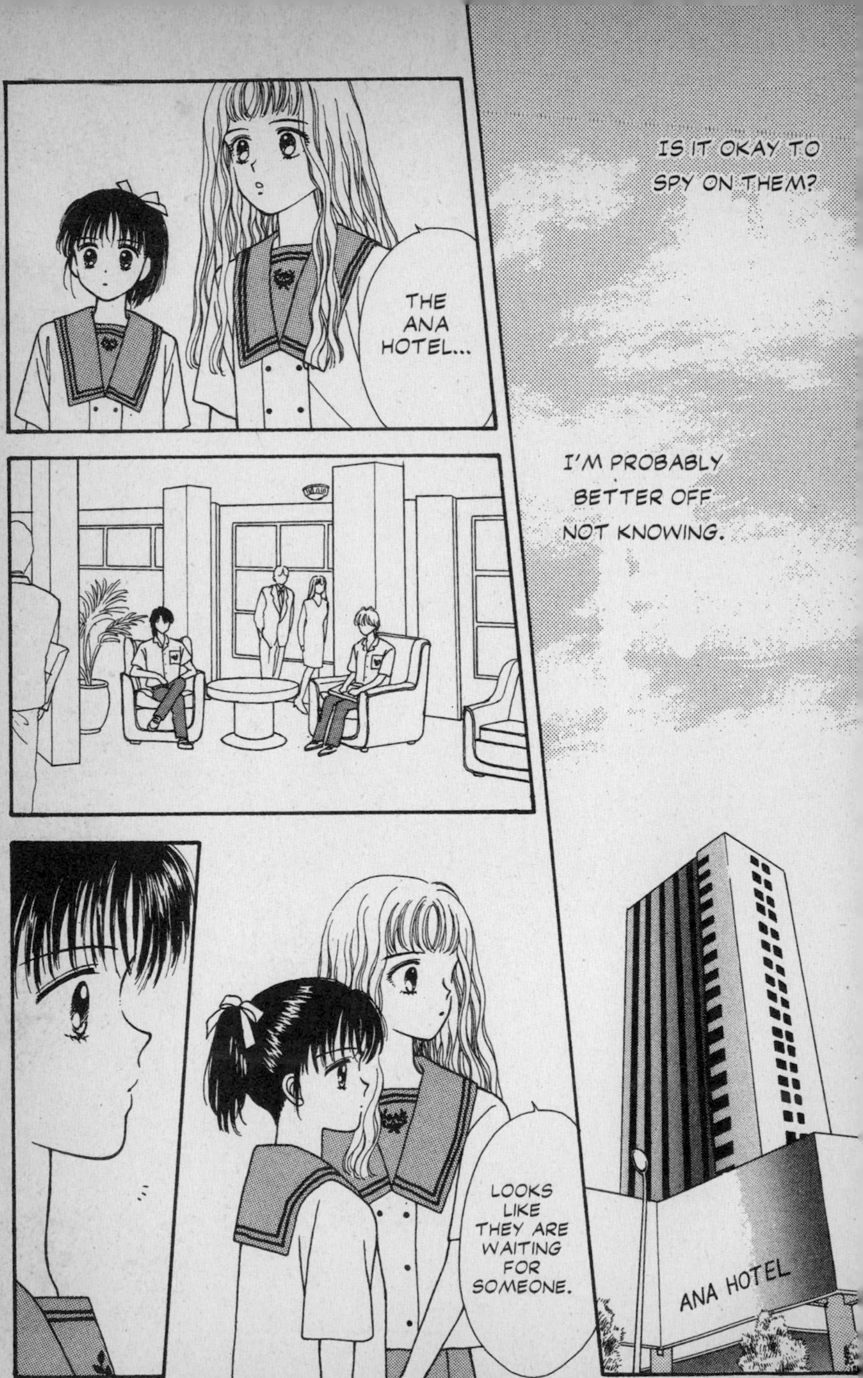
IS IT OKAY TO SPY ON THEM?
I'M PROBABLY BETTER OFF NOT KNOWING.
ANA HOTEL
THE ANA HOTEL...
LOOKS LIKE THEY ARE WAITING FOR SOMEONE.

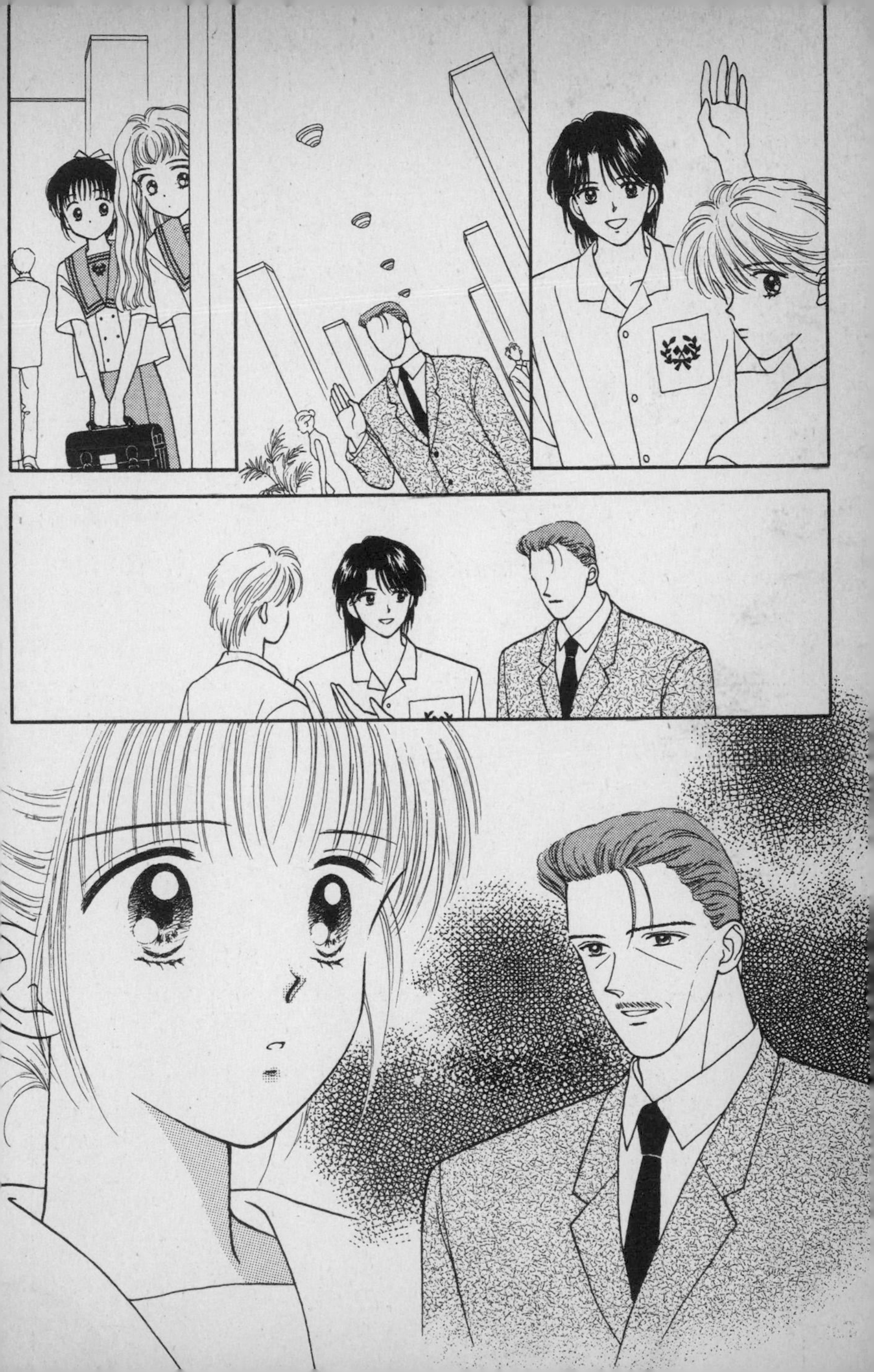

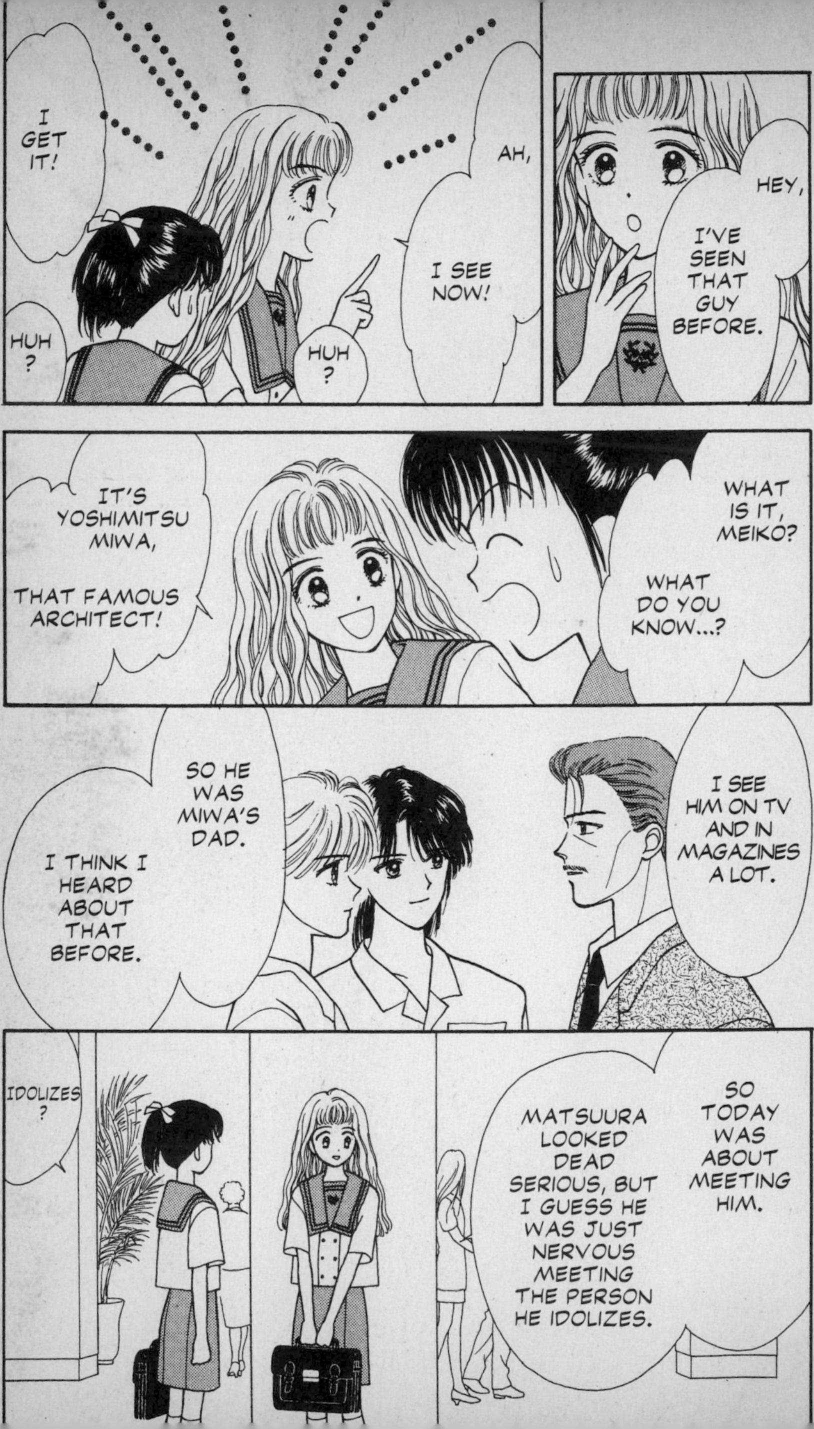
HEY, I'VE SEEN THAT GUY BEFORE.
AH, I SEE NOW!
I GET IT!
HUH?
HUH?
WHAT IS IT, MEIKO?
WHAT DO YOU KNOW...?
IT'S YOSHIMITSU MIWA, THAT FAMOUS ARCHITECT!
I SEE HIM ON TV AND IN MAGAZINES A LOT.
SO HE WAS MIWA'S DAD.
I THINK I HEARD ABOUT THAT BEFORE.
SO TODAY WAS ABOUT MEETING HIM.
MATSUURA LOOKED DEAD SERIOUS, BUT I GUESS HE WAS JUST NERVOUS MEETING THE PERSON HE IDOLIZES.
IDOLIZES?

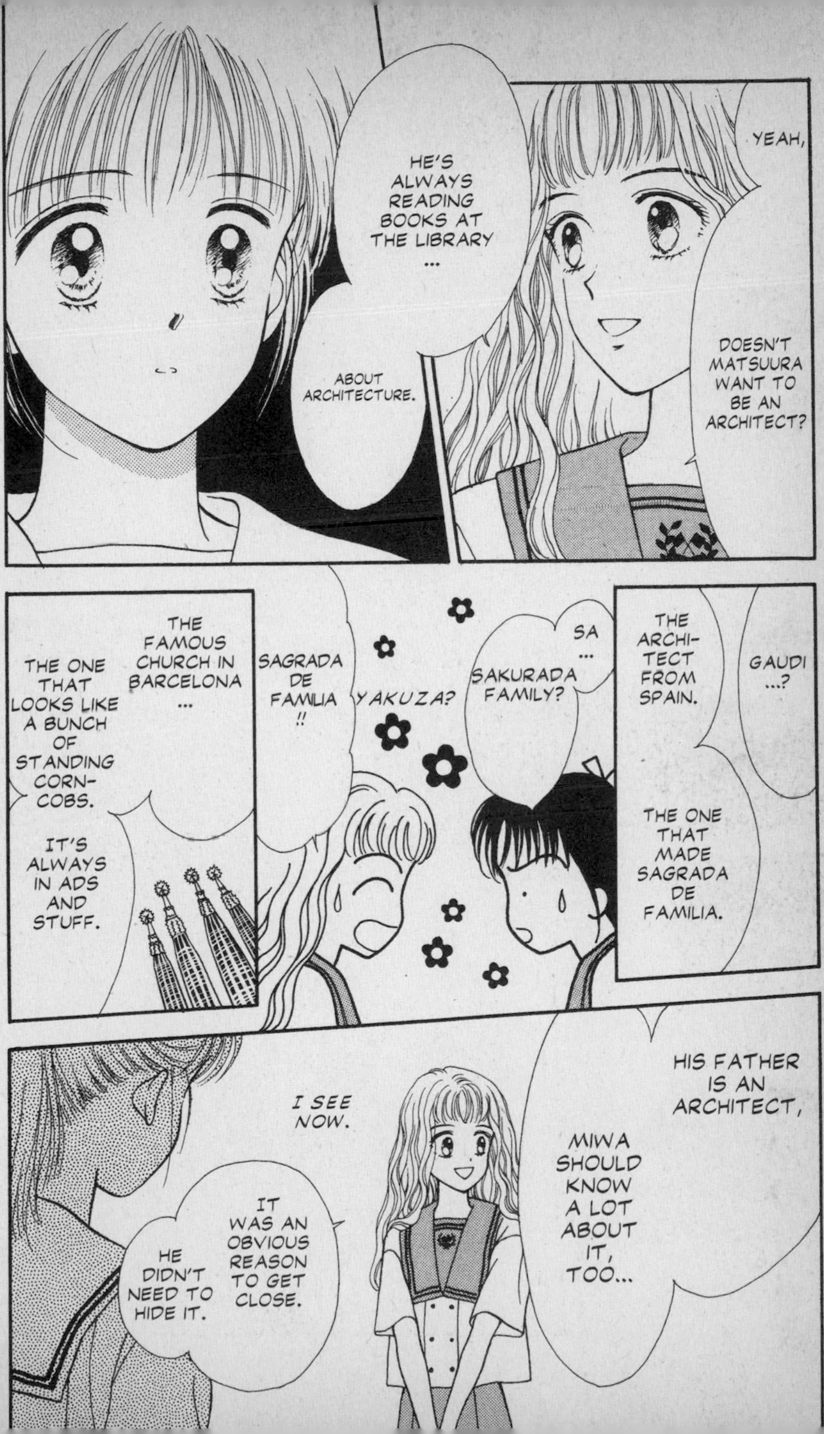
YEAH,
DOESN'T MATSUURA WANT TO BE AN ARCHITECT?
HE'S ALWAYS READING BOOKS AT THE LIBRARY ...
ABOUT ARCHITECTURE.
GAUDI ...?
THE ARCHI- TECT FROM SPAIN.
THE ONE THAT MADE SAGRADA DE FAMILIA.
SA ...
SAKURADA FAMILY?
YAKUZA?
SAGRADA DE FAMILIA !!
THE FAMOUS CHURCH IN BARCELONA ...
THE ONE THAT LOOKS LIKE A BUNCH OF STANDING CORN- COBS.
IT'S ALWAYS IN ADS AND STUFF.
HIS FATHER IS AN ARCHITECT,
MIWA SHOULD KNOW A LOT ABOUT IT, TOO...
I SEE NOW.
IT WAS AN OBVIOUS REASON TO GET CLOSE.
HE DIDN'T NEED TO HIDE IT.

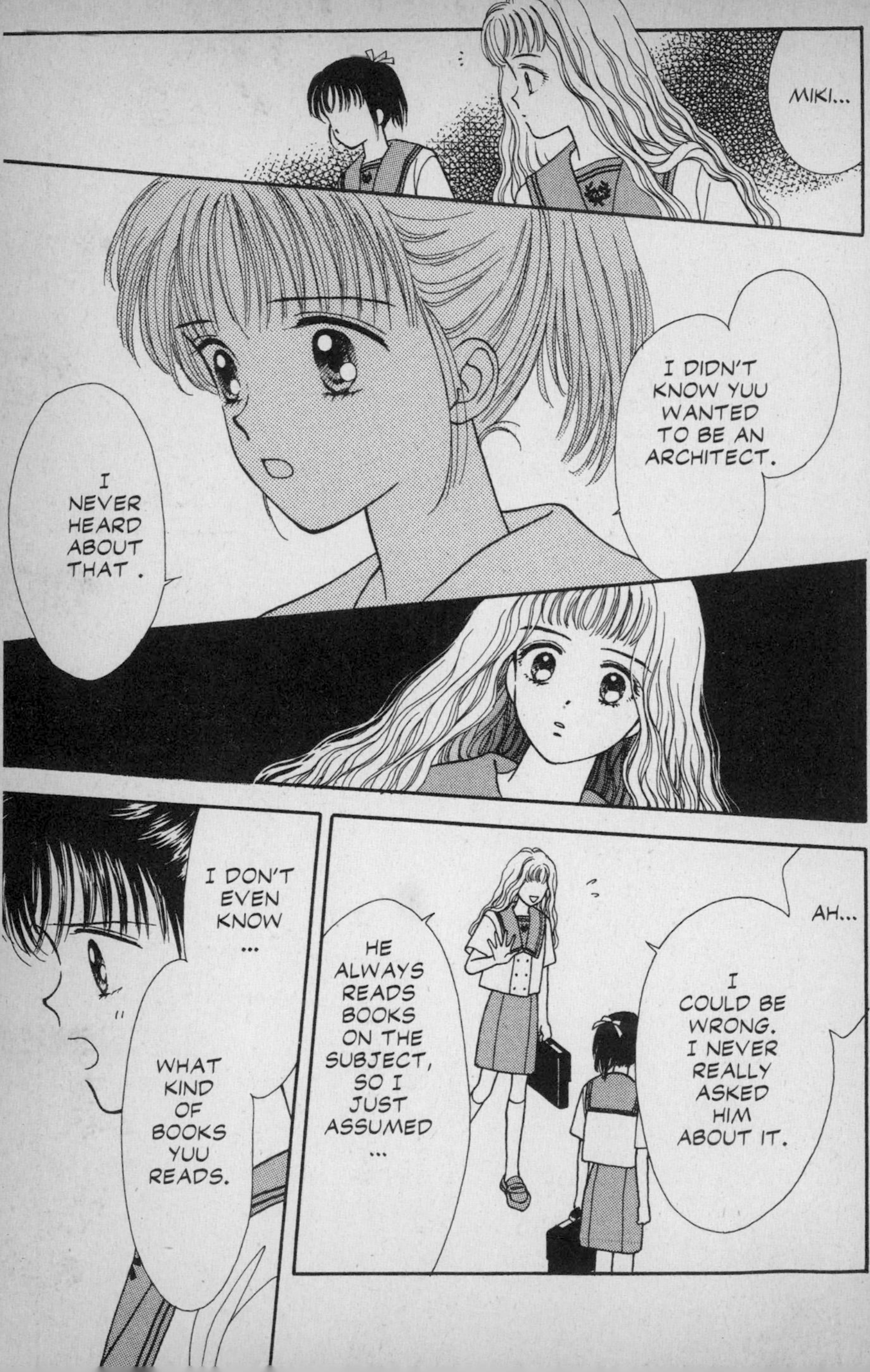
MIKI...
I DIDN'T KNOW YUU WANTED TO BE AN ARCHITECT.
I NEVER HEARD ABOUT THAT.
AH...
I COULD BE WRONG. I NEVER REALLY ASKED HIM ABOUT IT.
HE ALWAYS READS BOOKS ON THE SUBJECT, SO I JUST ASSUMED ...
I DON'T EVEN KNOW ...
WHAT KIND OF BOOKS YUU READS.

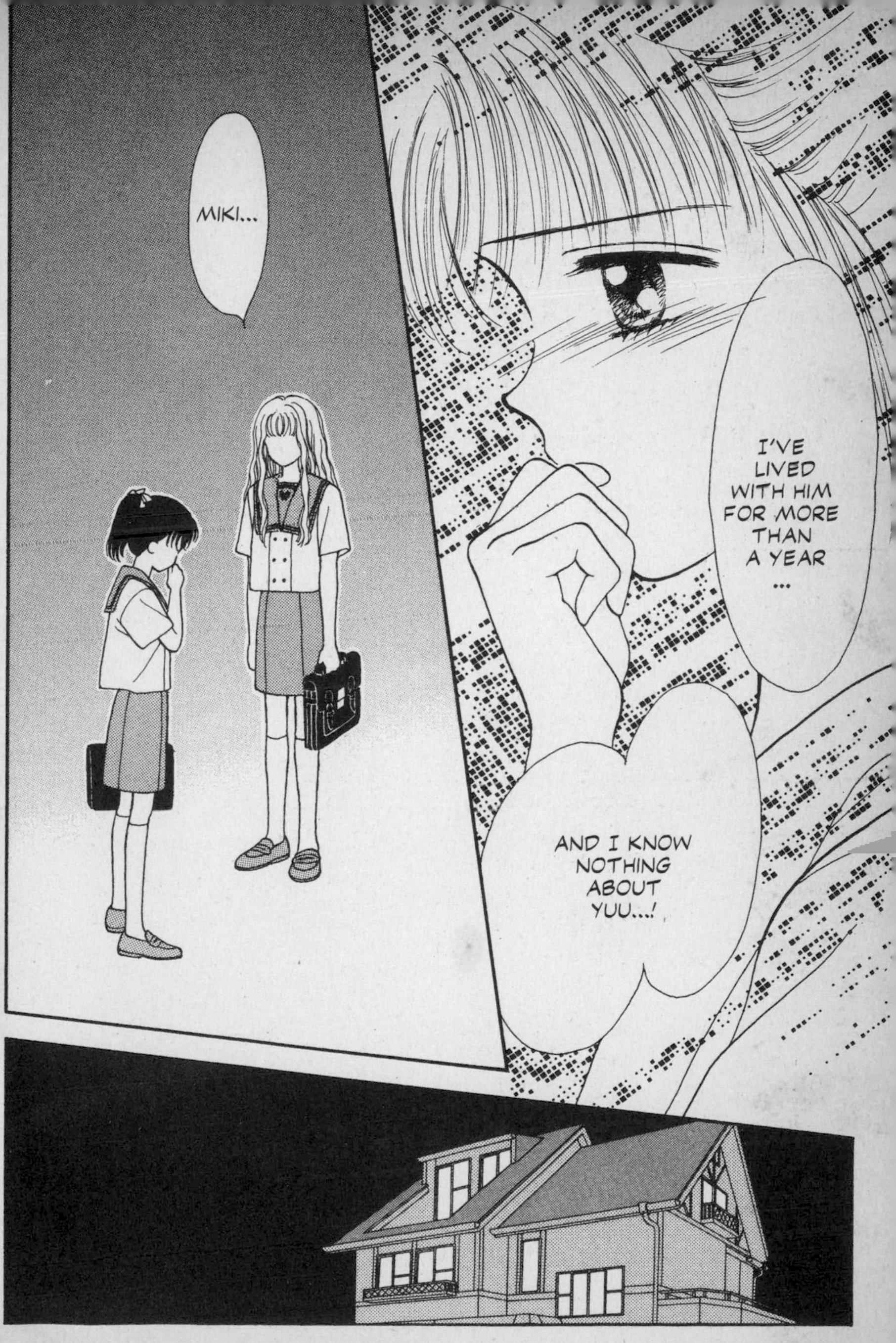
I'VE LIVED WITH HIM FOR MORE THAN A YEAR ...
AND I KNOW NOTHING ABOUT YUU...!
MIKI...

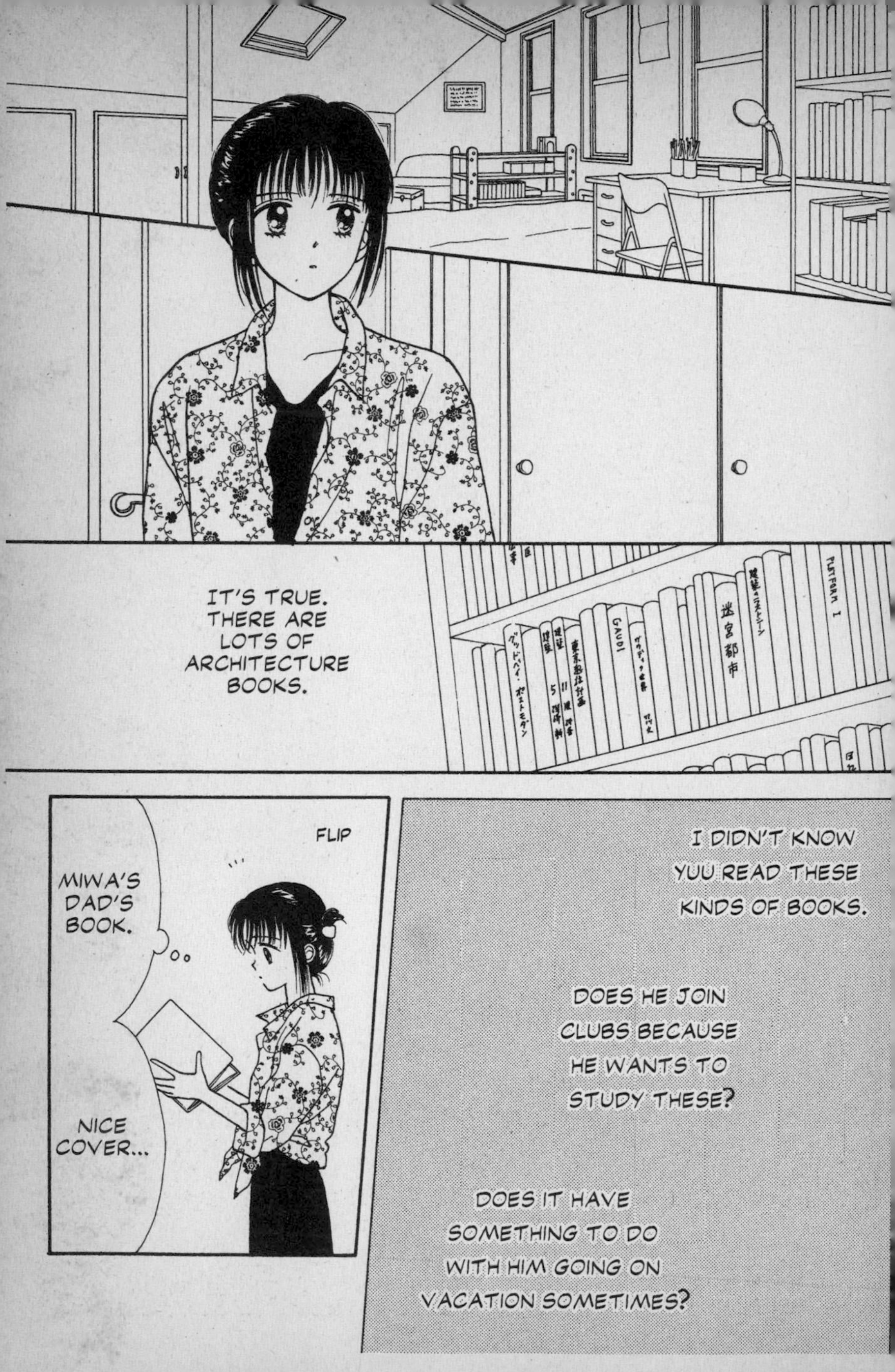
IT'S TRUE. THERE ARE LOTS OF ARCHITECTURE BOOKS.
GAUDI
迷宮都市
PLATFORM I
I DIDN'T KNOW YUU READ THESE KINDS OF BOOKS.
DOES HE JOIN CLUBS BECAUSE HE WANTS TO STUDY THESE?
DOES IT HAVE SOMETHING TO DO WITH HIM GOING ON VACATION SOMETIMES?
FLIP
MIWA'S DAD'S BOOK.
NICE COVER...

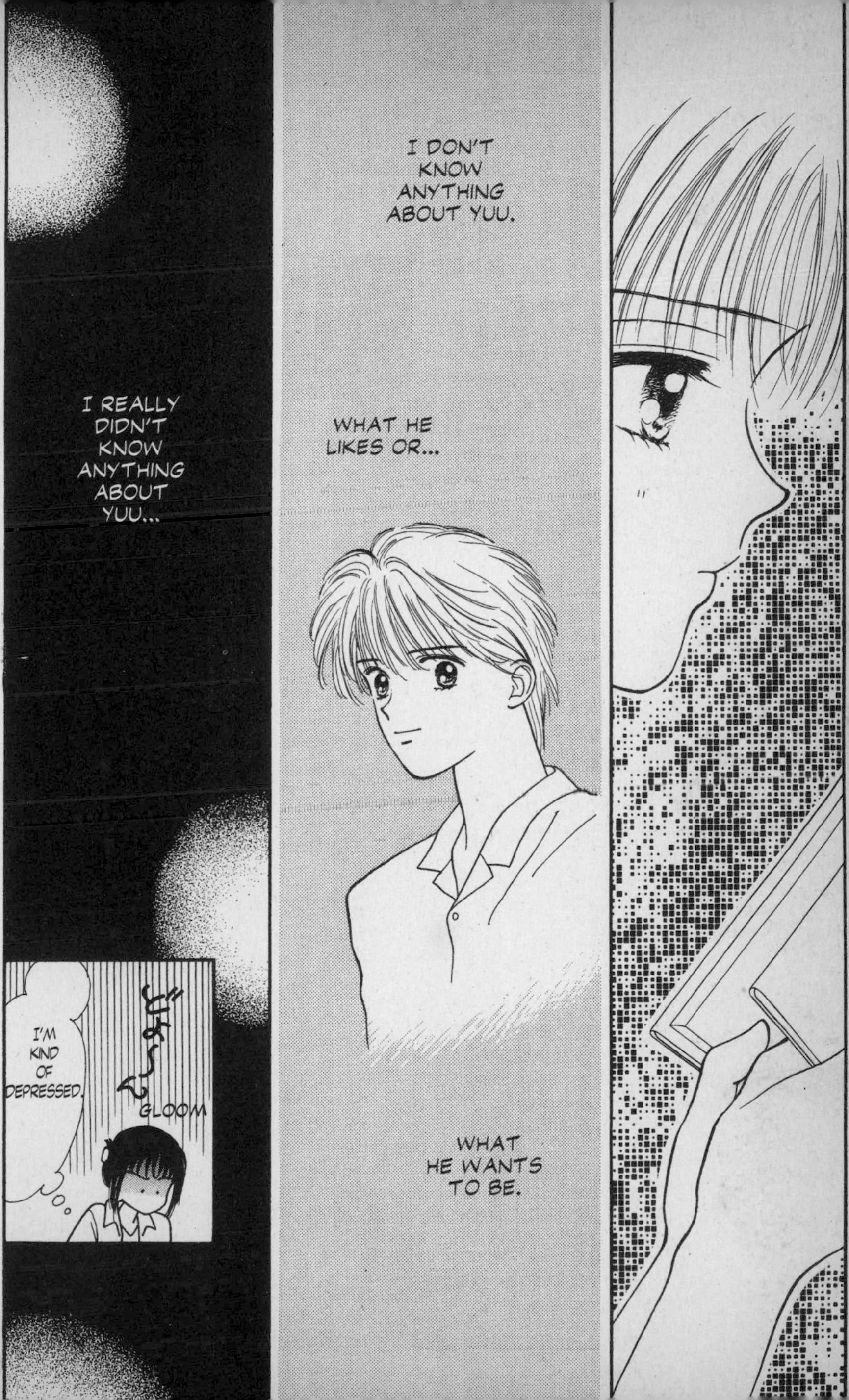
I DON'T KNOW ANYTHING ABOUT YUU.
WHAT HE LIKES OR...
WHAT HE WANTS TO BE.
I REALLY DIDN'T KNOW ANYTHING ABOUT YUU...
I'M KIND OF DEPRESSED.
GLOOM

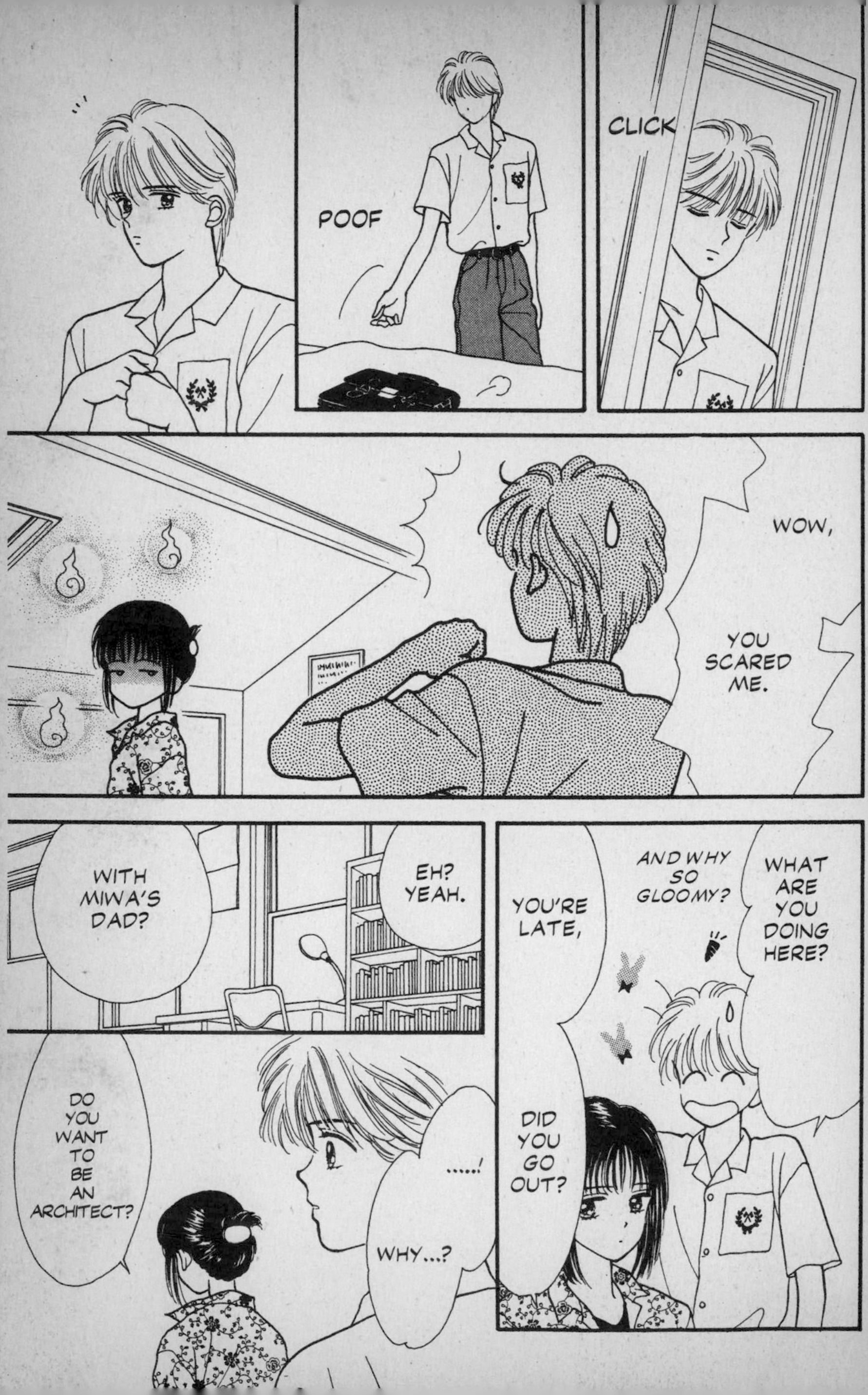
CLICK
POOF
WOW,
YOU SCARED ME.
WHAT ARE YOU DOING HERE?
AND WHY SO GLOOMY?
YOU'RE LATE,
DID YOU GO OUT?
EH? YEAH.
WITH MIWA'S DAD?
......!
WHY...?
DO YOU WANT TO BE AN ARCHITECT?

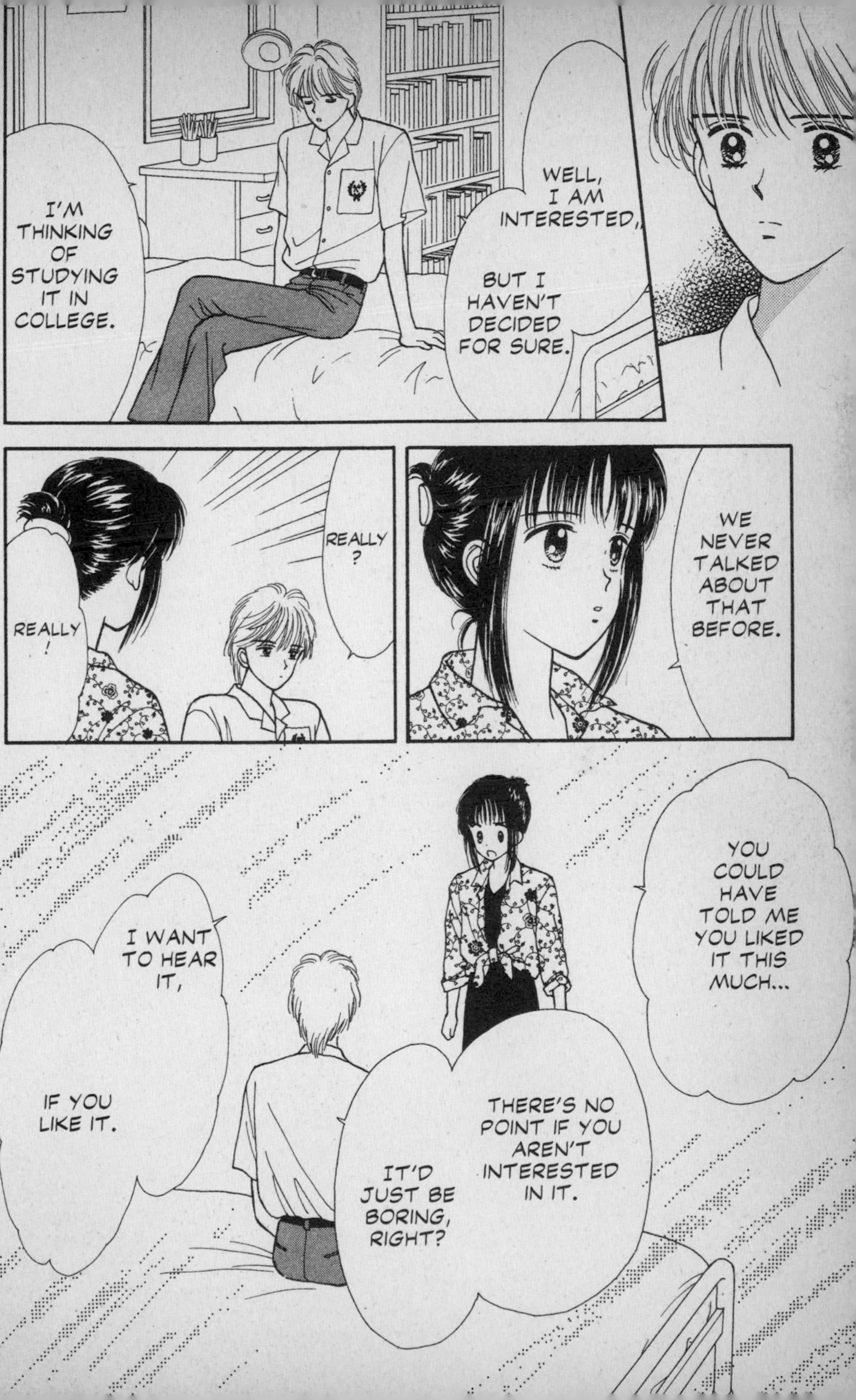
WELL, I AM INTERESTED,
BUT I HAVEN'T DECIDED FOR SURE.
I'M THINKING OF STUDYING IT IN COLLEGE.
WE NEVER TALKED ABOUT THAT BEFORE.
REALLY?
REALLY!
YOU COULD HAVE TOLD ME YOU LIKED IT THIS MUCH...
I WANT TO HEAR IT,
IF YOU LIKE IT.
THERE'S NO POINT IF YOU AREN'T INTERESTED IN IT.
IT'D JUST BE BORING, RIGHT?

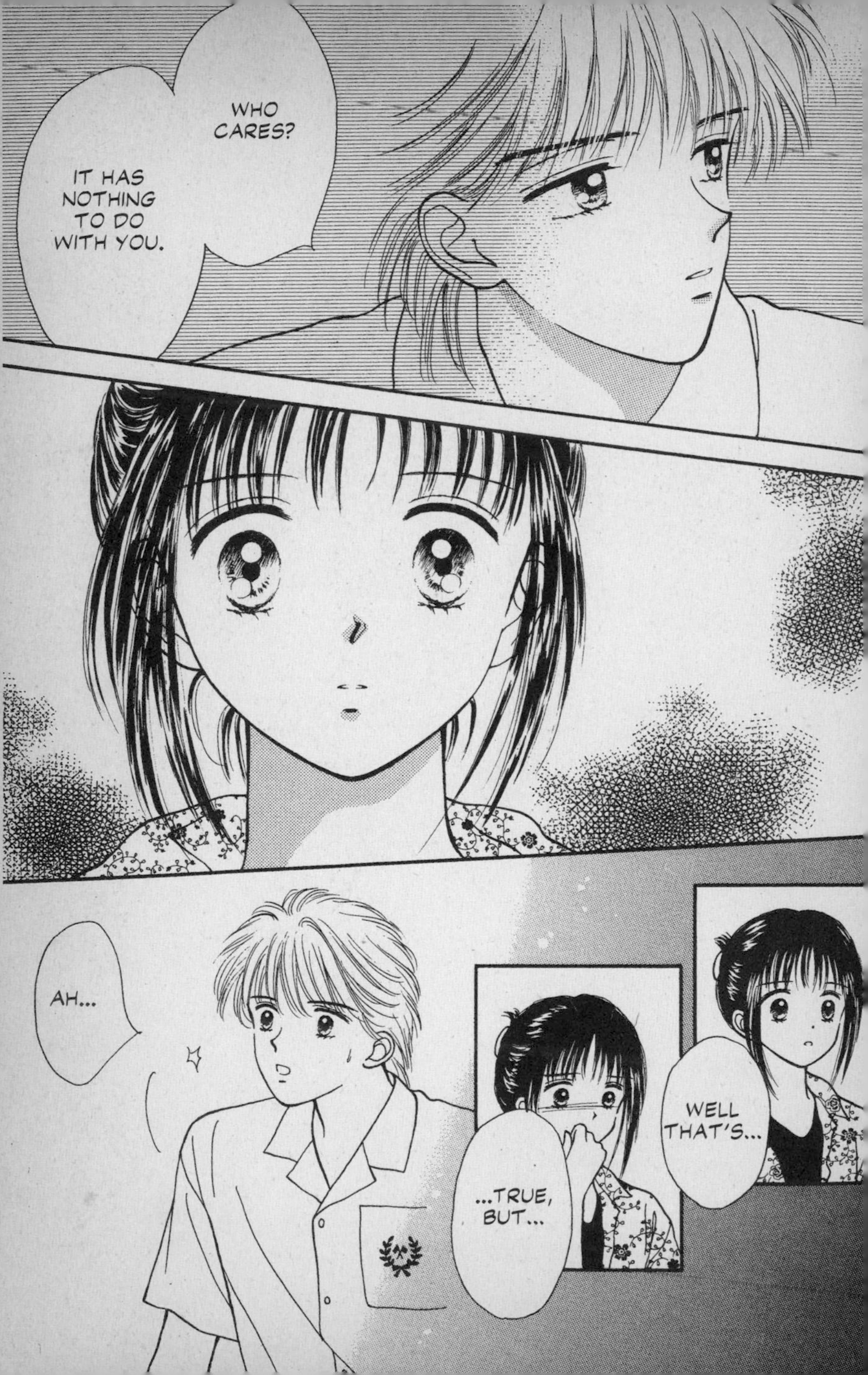
WHO CARES?
IT HAS NOTHING TO DO WITH YOU.
WELL THAT'S...
...TRUE, BUT...
AH...

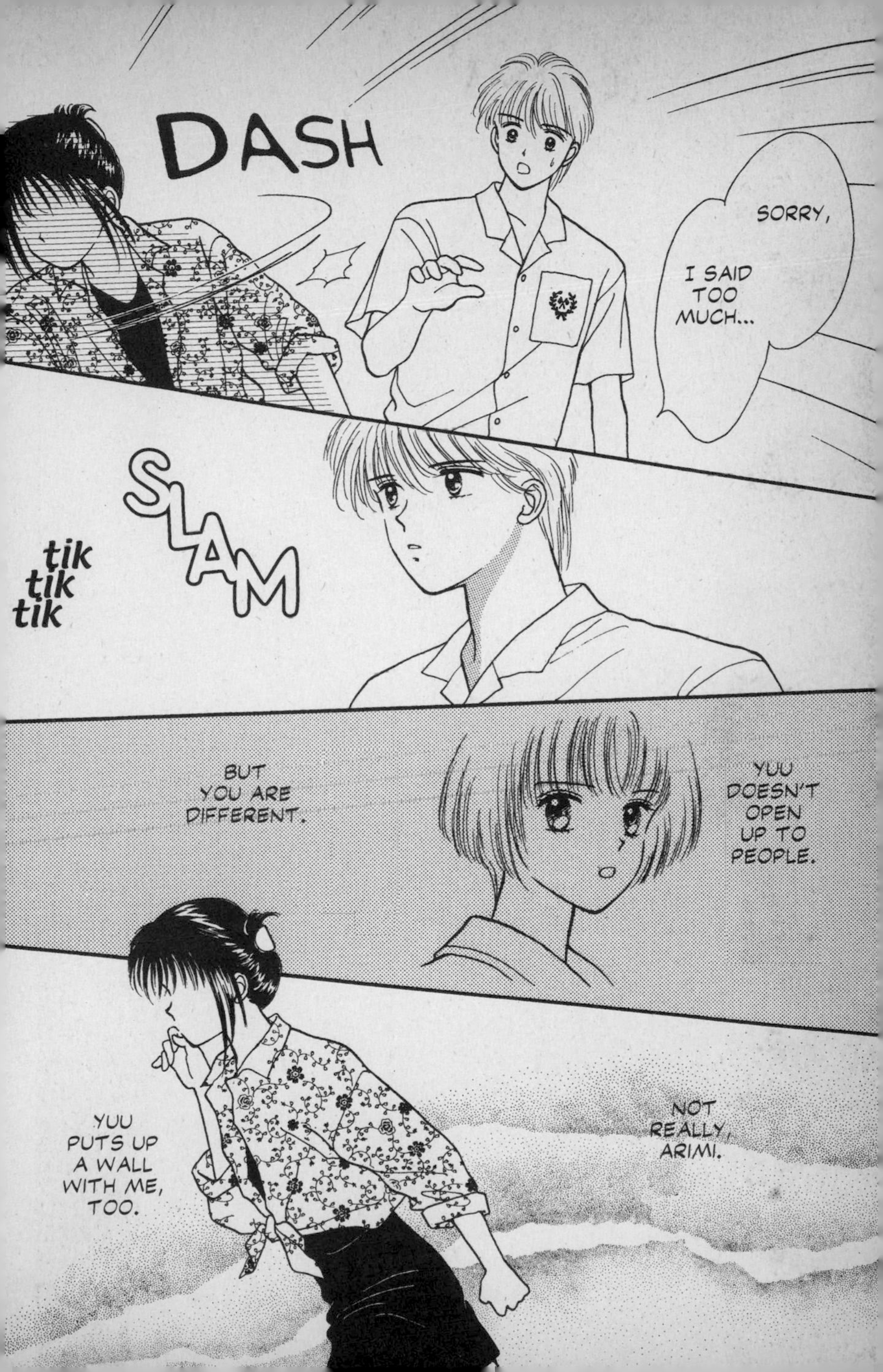
SORRY,
I SAID TOO MUCH...
DASH
SLAM
tik tik tik
YUU DOESN'T OPEN UP TO PEOPLE.
BUT YOU ARE DIFFERENT.
NOT REALLY, ARIMI.
YUU PUTS UP A WALL WITH ME, TOO.

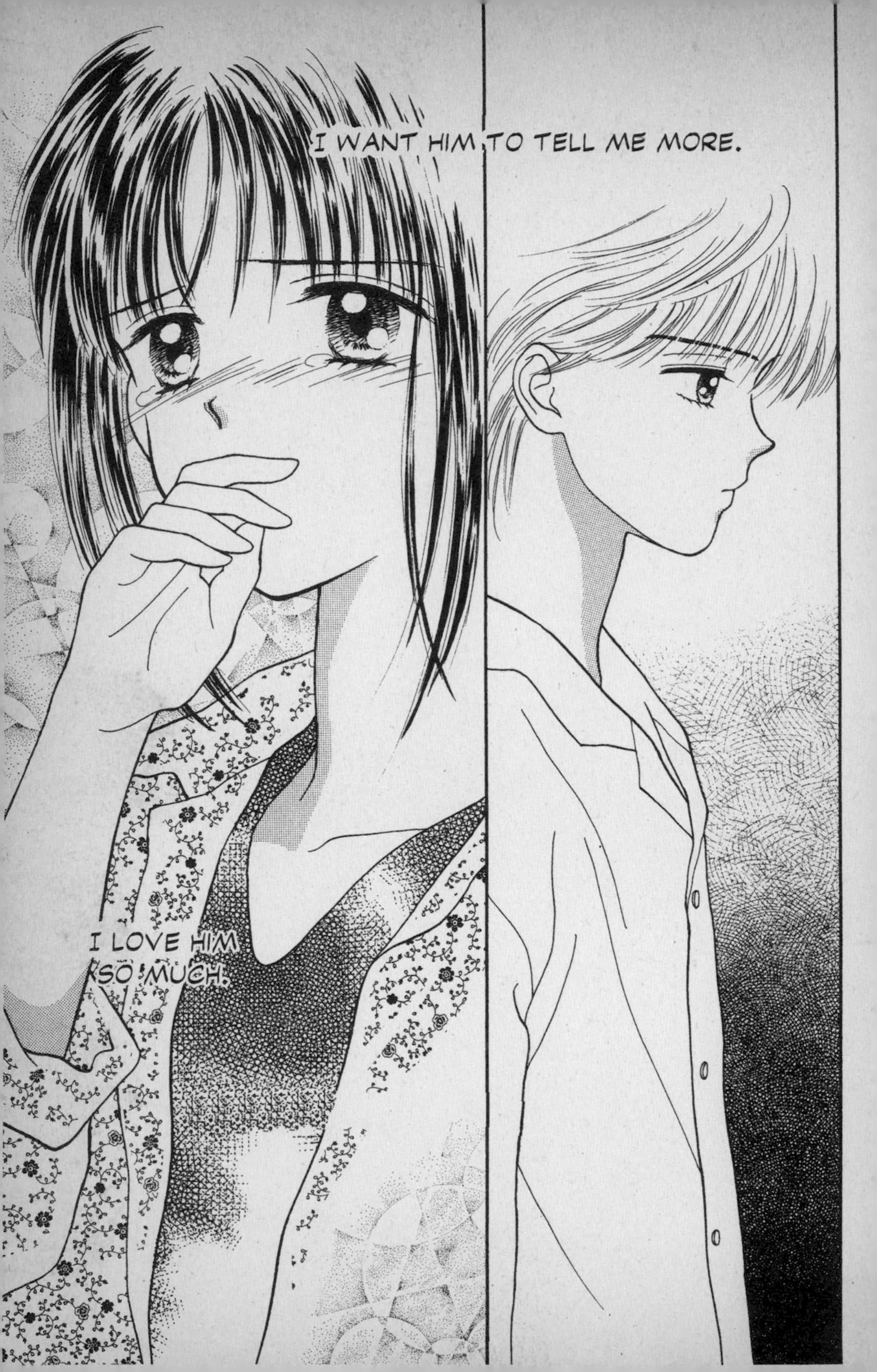
I WANT HIM TO TELL ME MORE.
I LOVE HIM SO MUCH.

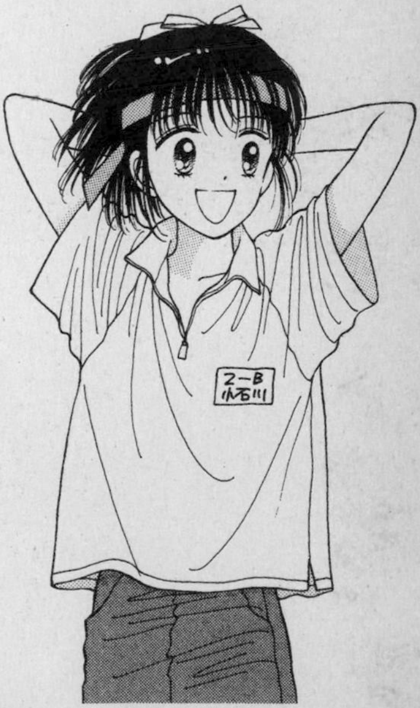
2—B
小石川

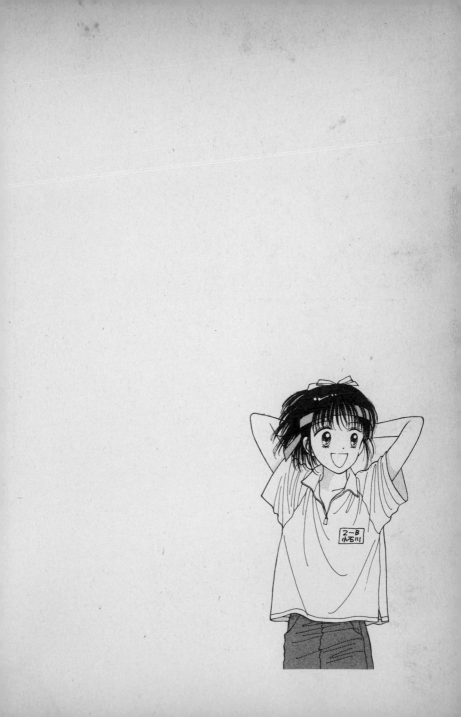

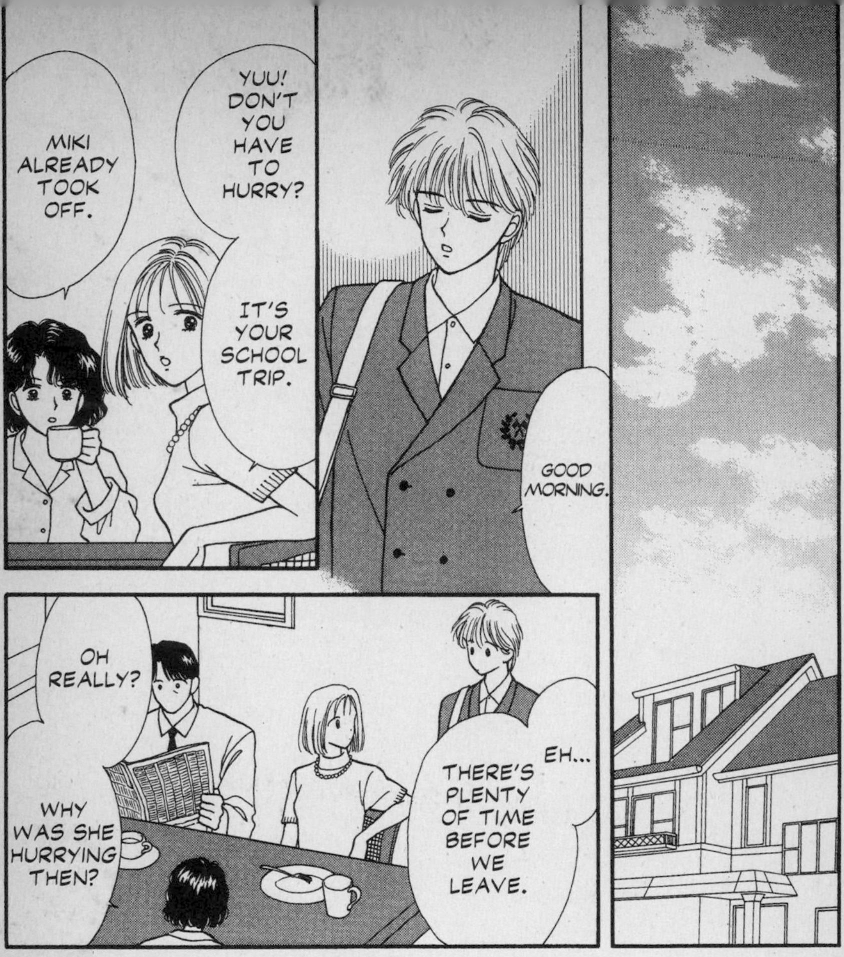
GOOD MORNING.
YUU! DON'T YOU HAVE TO HURRY?
IT'S YOUR SCHOOL TRIP.
MIKI ALREADY TOOK OFF.
EH... THERE'S PLENTY OF TIME BEFORE WE LEAVE.
OH REALLY?
WHY WAS SHE HURRYING THEN?

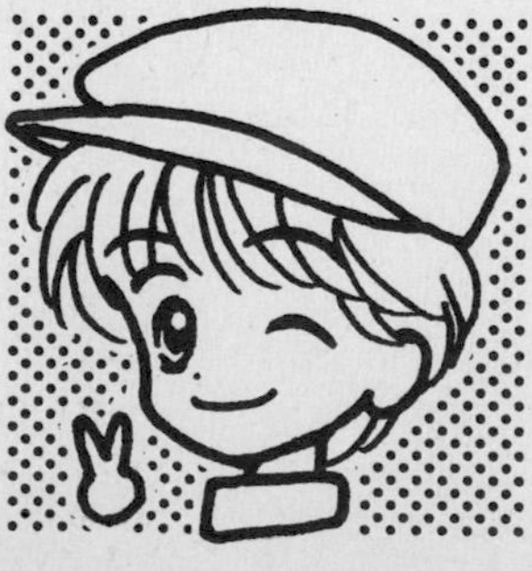

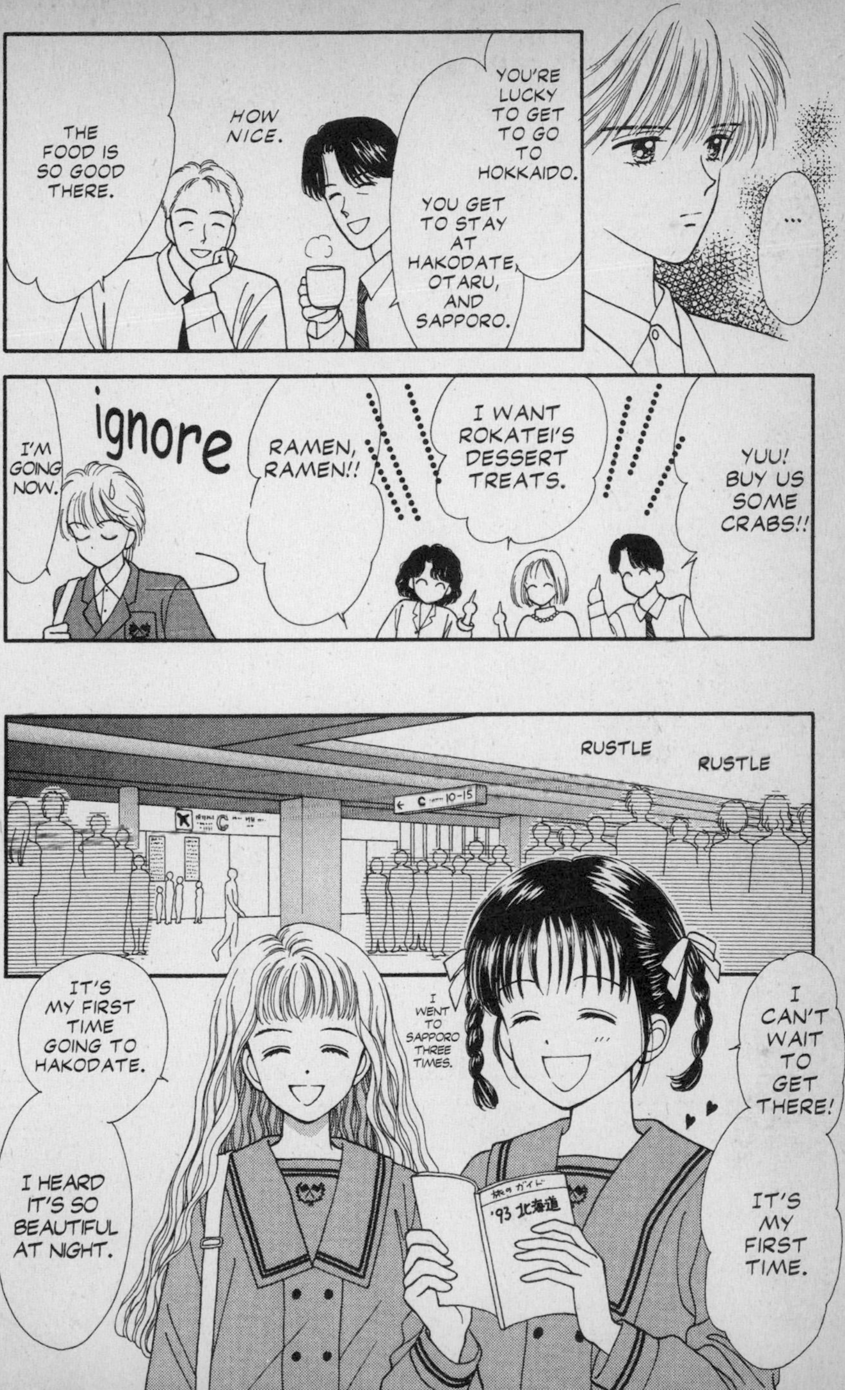
...
YOU'RE LUCKY TO GET TO GO TO HOKKAIDO.
YOU GET TO STAY AT HAKODATE, OTARU, AND SAPPORO.
HOW NICE.
THE FOOD IS SO GOOD THERE.
YUU! BUY US SOME CRABS!!
I WANT ROKATEI'S DESSERT TREATS.
RAMEN, RAMEN!!
ignore
I'M GOING NOW.
RUSTLE
RUSTLE
C 10-15
I CAN'T WAIT TO GET THERE!
IT'S MY FIRST TIME.
旅のガイド
'93 北海道
I WENT TO SAPPORO THREE TIMES.
IT'S MY FIRST TIME GOING TO HAKODATE.
I HEARD IT'S SO BEAUTIFUL AT NIGHT.

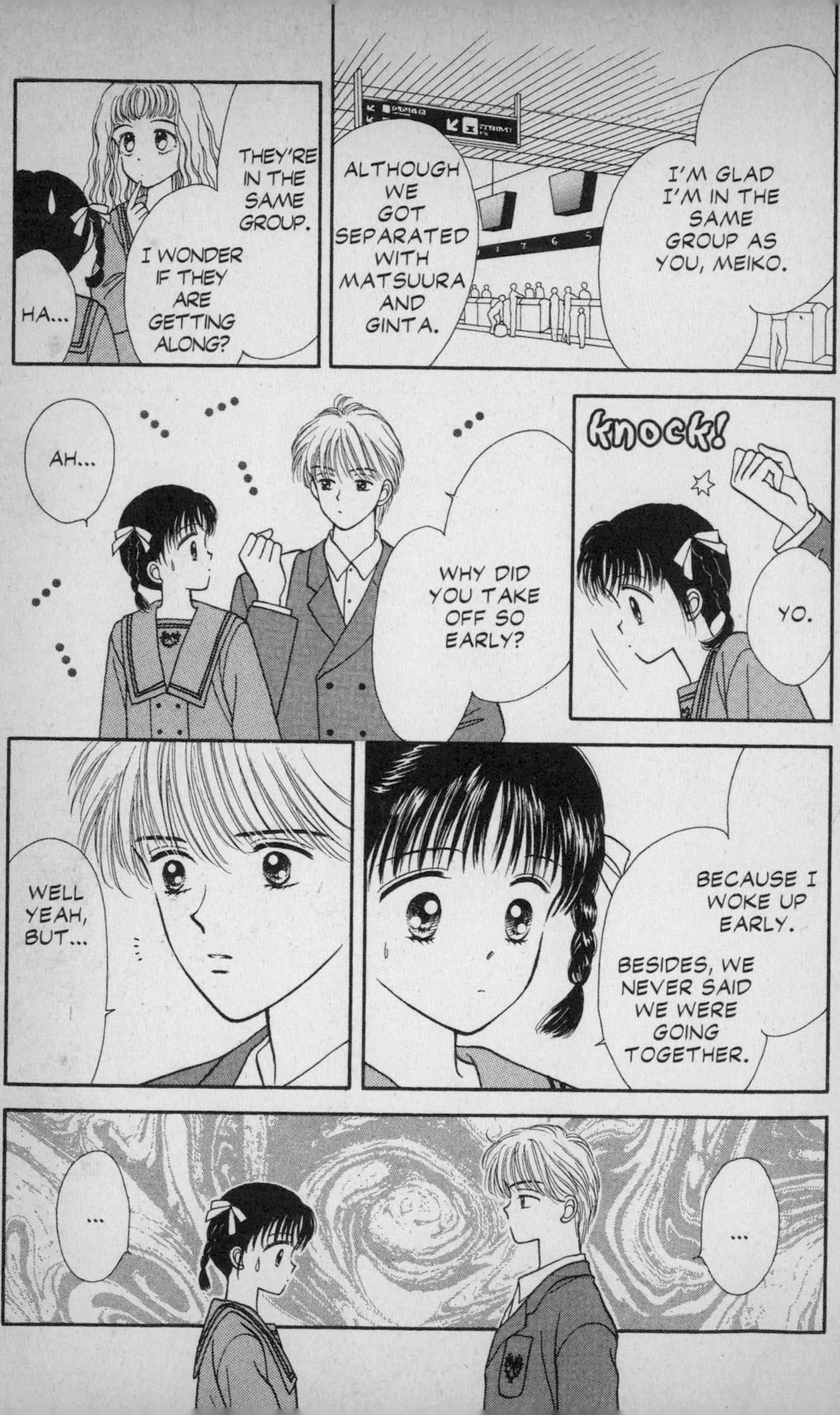
I'M GLAD I'M IN THE SAME GROUP AS YOU, MEIKO.
ALTHOUGH WE GOT SEPARATED WITH MATSUURA AND GINTA.
THEY'RE IN THE SAME GROUP.
I WONDER IF THEY ARE GETTING ALONG?
HA...
KNOCK!
YO.
WHY DID YOU TAKE OFF SO EARLY?
AH...
BECAUSE I WOKE UP EARLY.
BESIDES, WE NEVER SAID WE WERE GOING TOGETHER.
WELL YEAH, BUT...
...
...

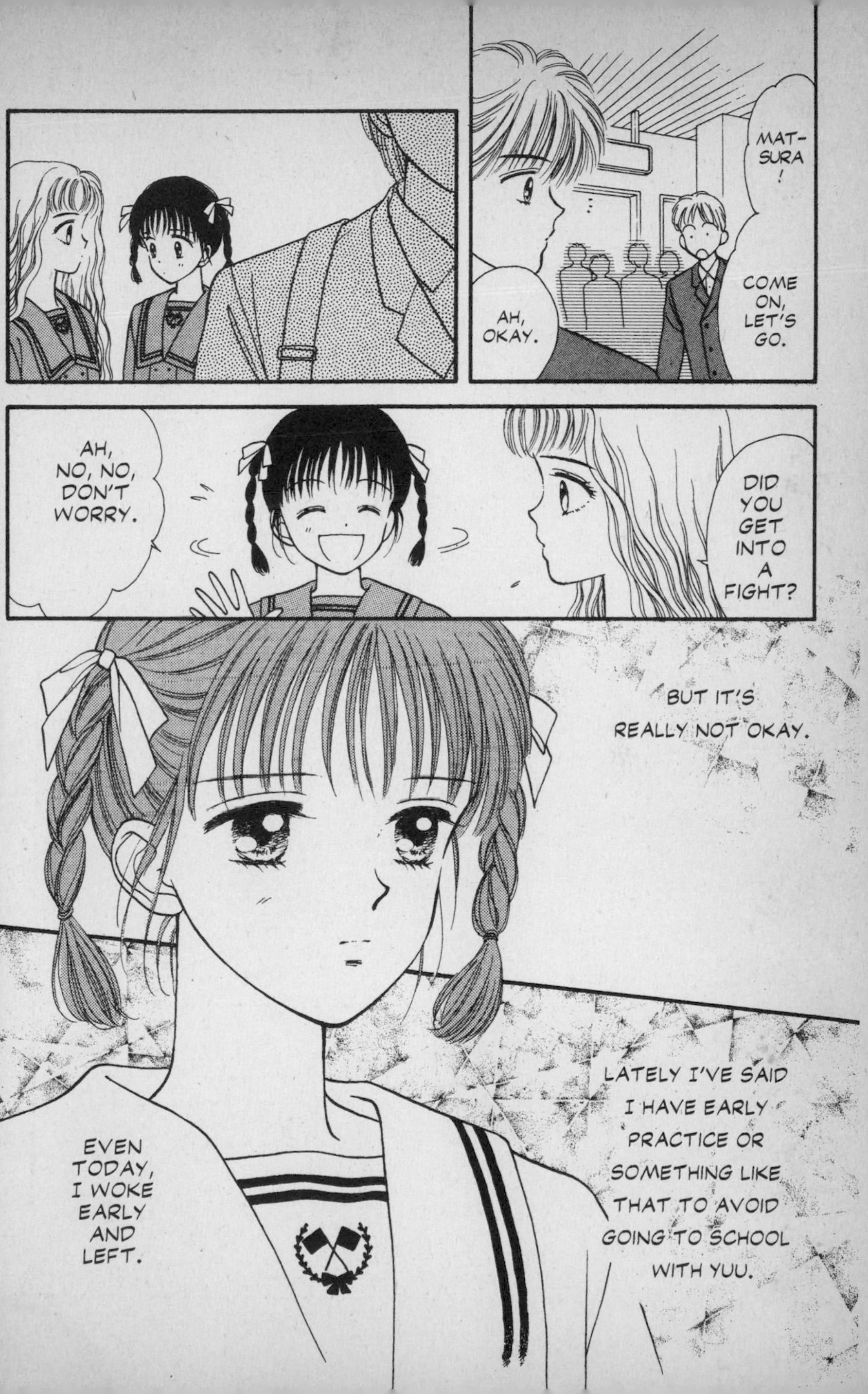
MAT-SURA!
COME ON, LET'S GO.
AH, OKAY.
DID YOU GET INTO A FIGHT?
AH, NO, NO, DON'T WORRY.
BUT IT'S REALLY NOT OKAY.
LATELY I'VE SAID I HAVE EARLY PRACTICE OR SOMETHING LIKE THAT TO AVOID GOING TO SCHOOL WITH YUU.
EVEN TODAY, I WOKE EARLY AND LEFT.

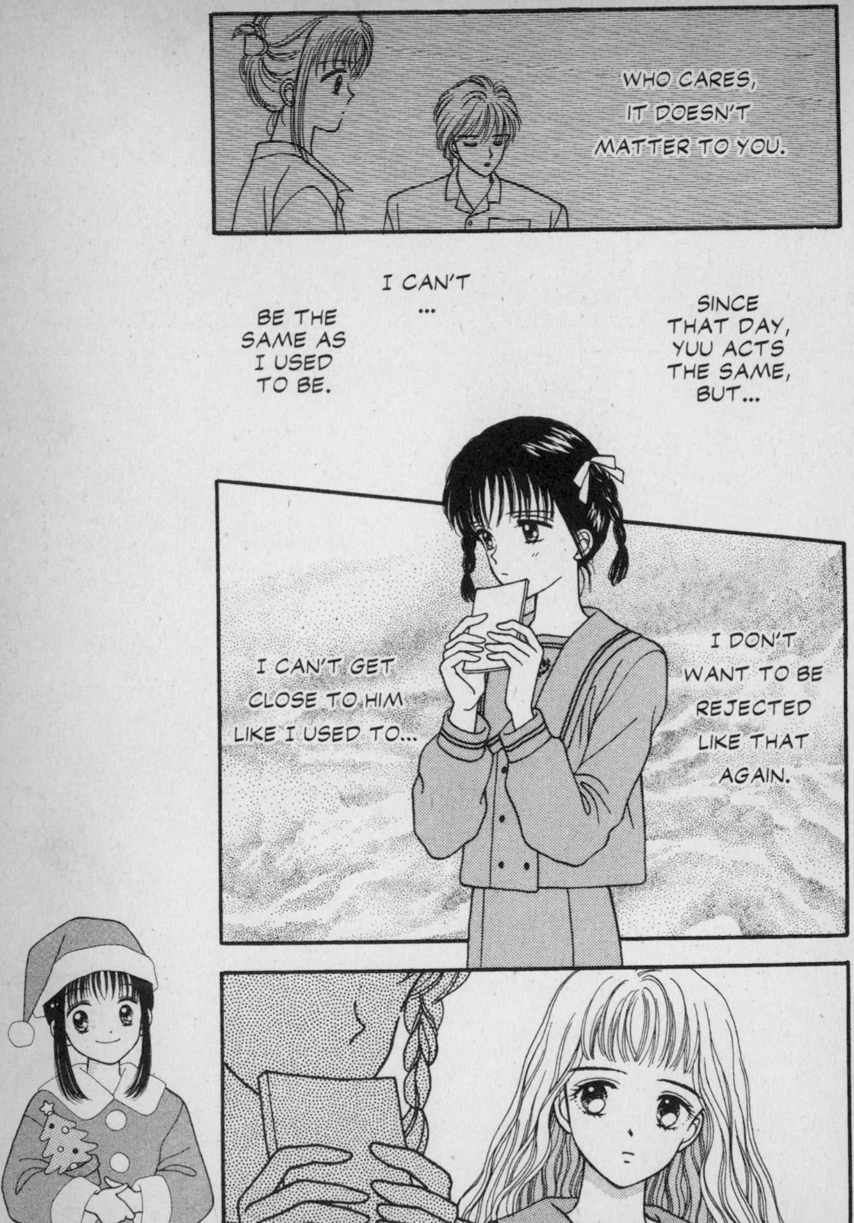
WHO CARES, IT DOESN'T MATTER TO YOU.
SINCE THAT DAY, YUU ACTS THE SAME, BUT...
I CAN'T ...
BE THE SAME AS I USED TO BE.
I DON'T WANT TO BE REJECTED LIKE THAT AGAIN.
I CAN'T GET CLOSE TO HIM LIKE I USED TO...

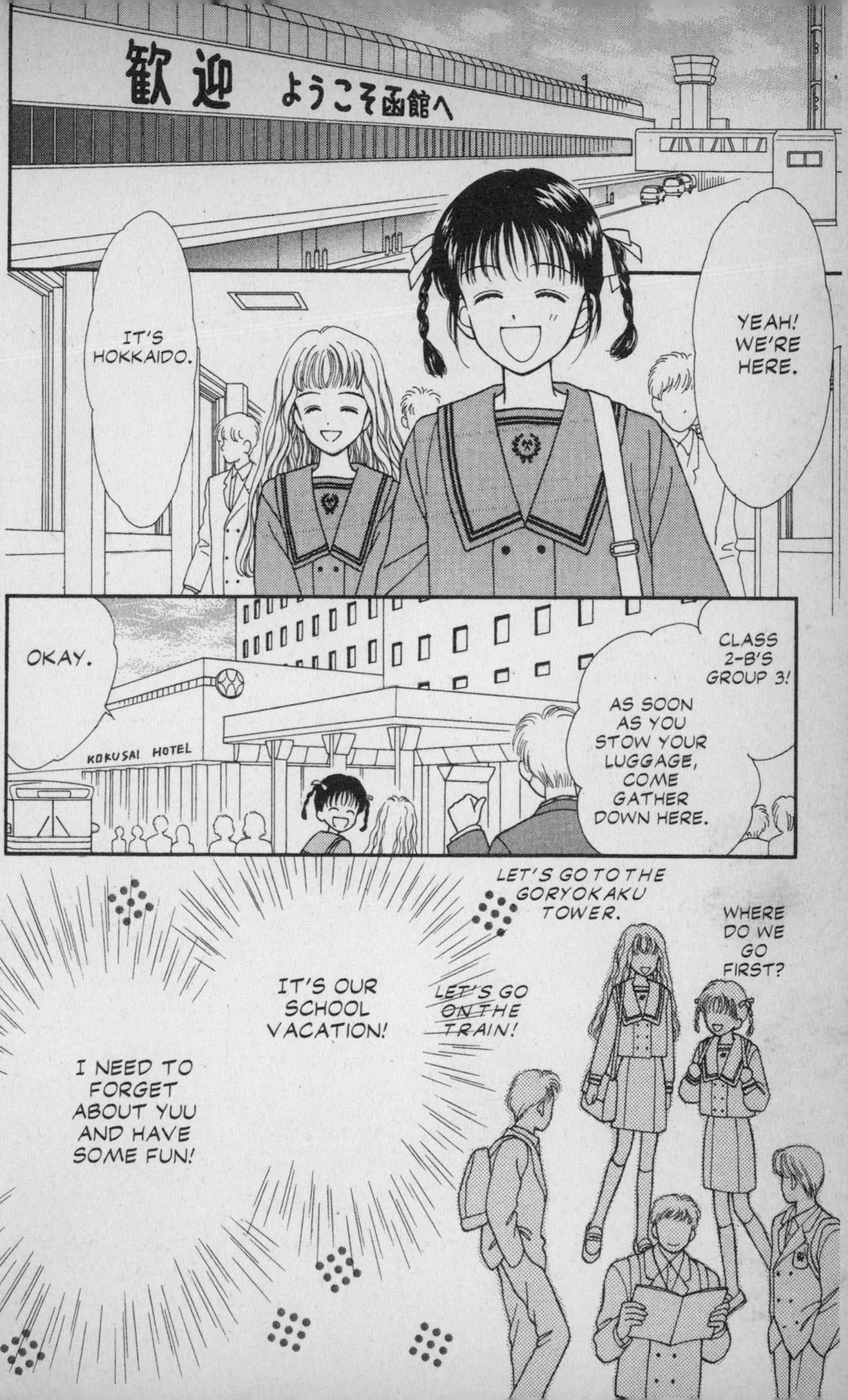
歓迎 ようこそ函館へ
YEAH! WE'RE HERE.
IT'S HOKKAIDO.
CLASS 2-B'S GROUP 3!
AS SOON AS YOU STOW YOUR LUGGAGE, COME GATHER DOWN HERE.
KOKUSAI HOTEL
OKAY.
WHERE DO WE GO FIRST?
LET'S GO TO THE GORYOKAKU TOWER.
LET'S GO ON THE TRAIN!
IT'S OUR SCHOOL VACATION!
I NEED TO FORGET ABOUT YUU AND HAVE SOME FUN!

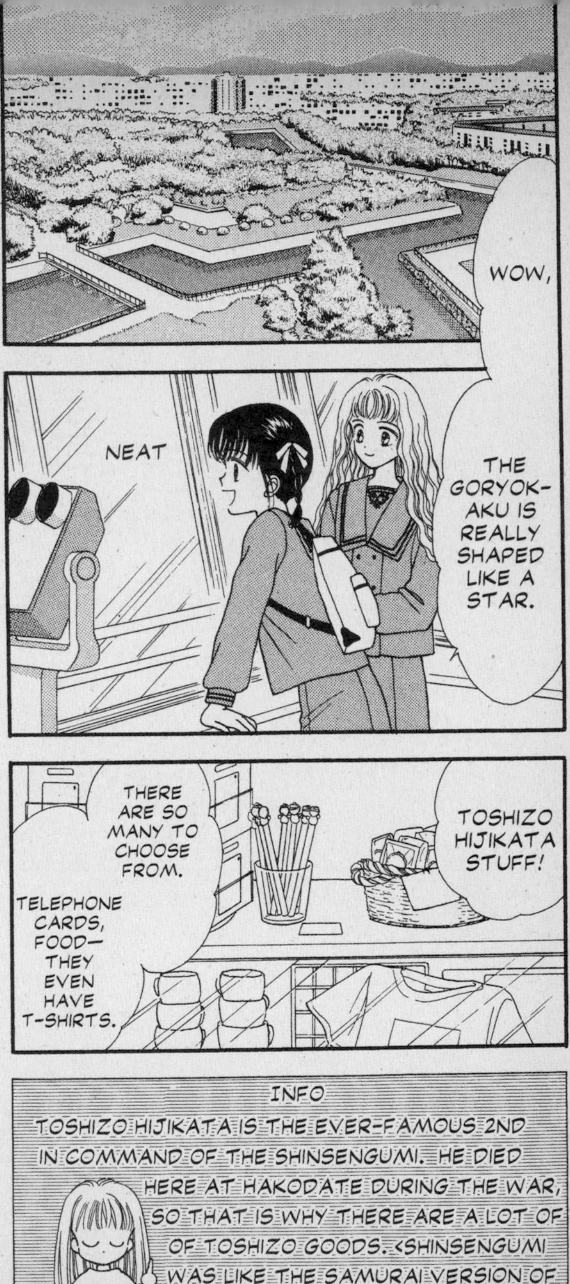
WOW,
THE GORYOK-AKU IS REALLY SHAPED LIKE A STAR.
NEAT
TOSHIZO HIJIKATA STUFF!
THERE ARE SO MANY TO CHOOSE FROM.
TELEPHONE CARDS, FOOD— THEY EVEN HAVE T-SHIRTS.
INFO
TOSHIZO HIJIKATA IS THE EVER-FAMOUS 2ND IN COMMAND OF THE SHINSENGUMI. HE DIED HERE AT HAKODATE DURING THE WAR, SO THAT IS WHY THERE ARE A LOT OF OF TOSHIZO GOODS. <SHINSENGUMI WAS LIKE THE SAMURAI VERSION OF KGB BACK IN THE OLD DAYS.>
吉住

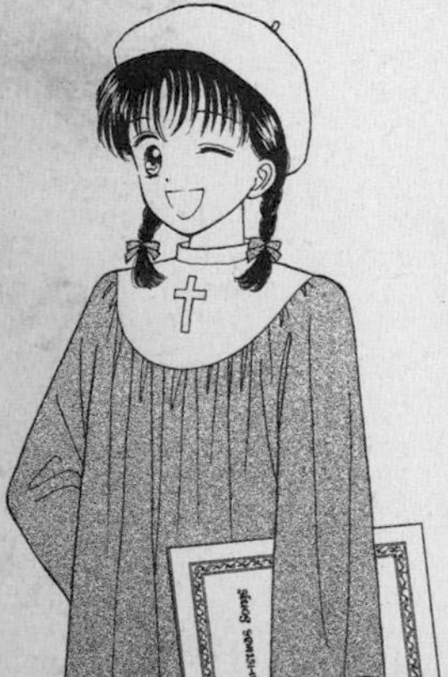

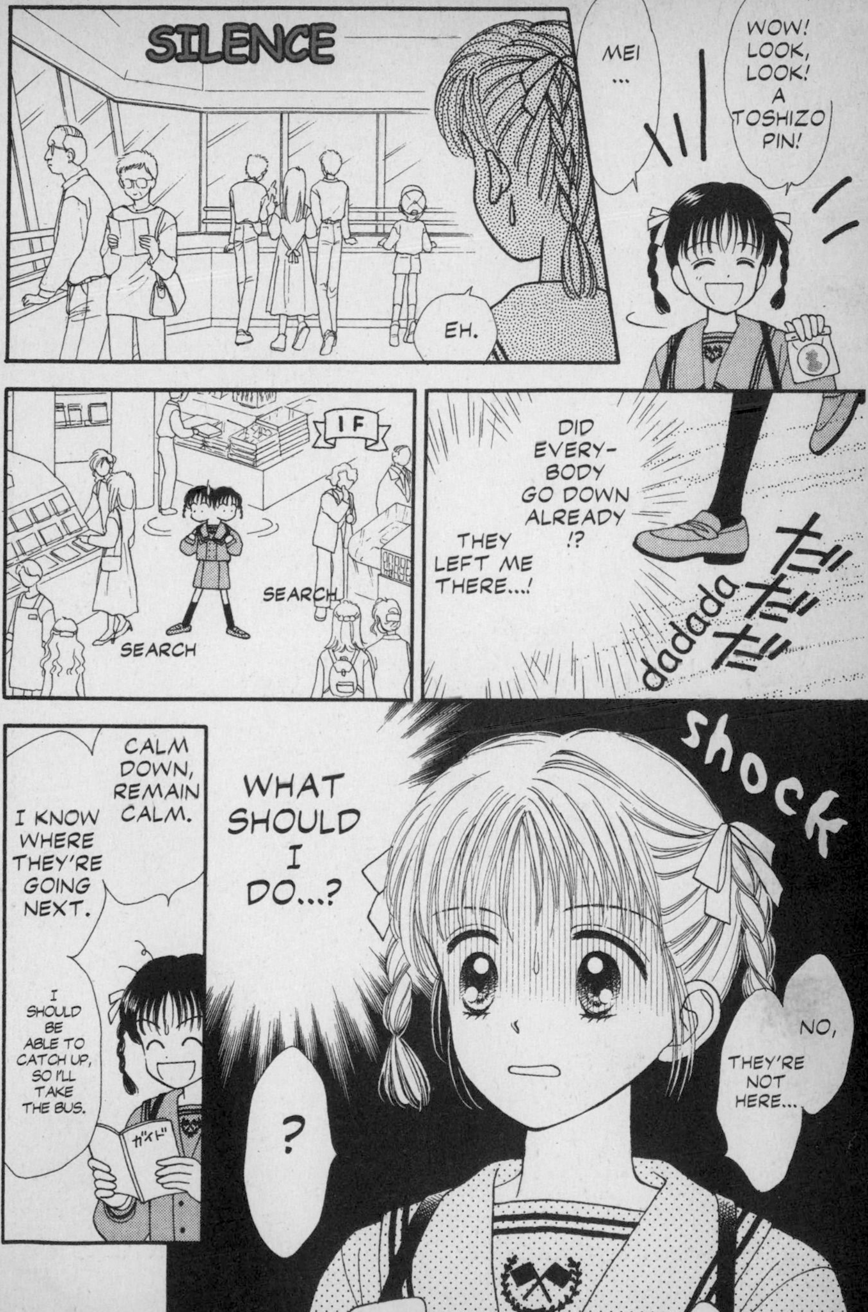
WOW! LOOK, LOOK! A TOSHIZO PIN!
MEI ...
EH.
SILENCE
DID EVERY-BODY GO DOWN ALREADY !?
THEY LEFT ME THERE...!
だだだ
dadada
IF
SEARCH
SEARCH
shock
NO, THEY'RE NOT HERE...
?
WHAT SHOULD I DO...?
CALM DOWN, REMAIN CALM.
I KNOW WHERE THEY'RE GOING NEXT.
I SHOULD BE ABLE TO CATCH UP, SO I'LL TAKE THE BUS.
ガイド

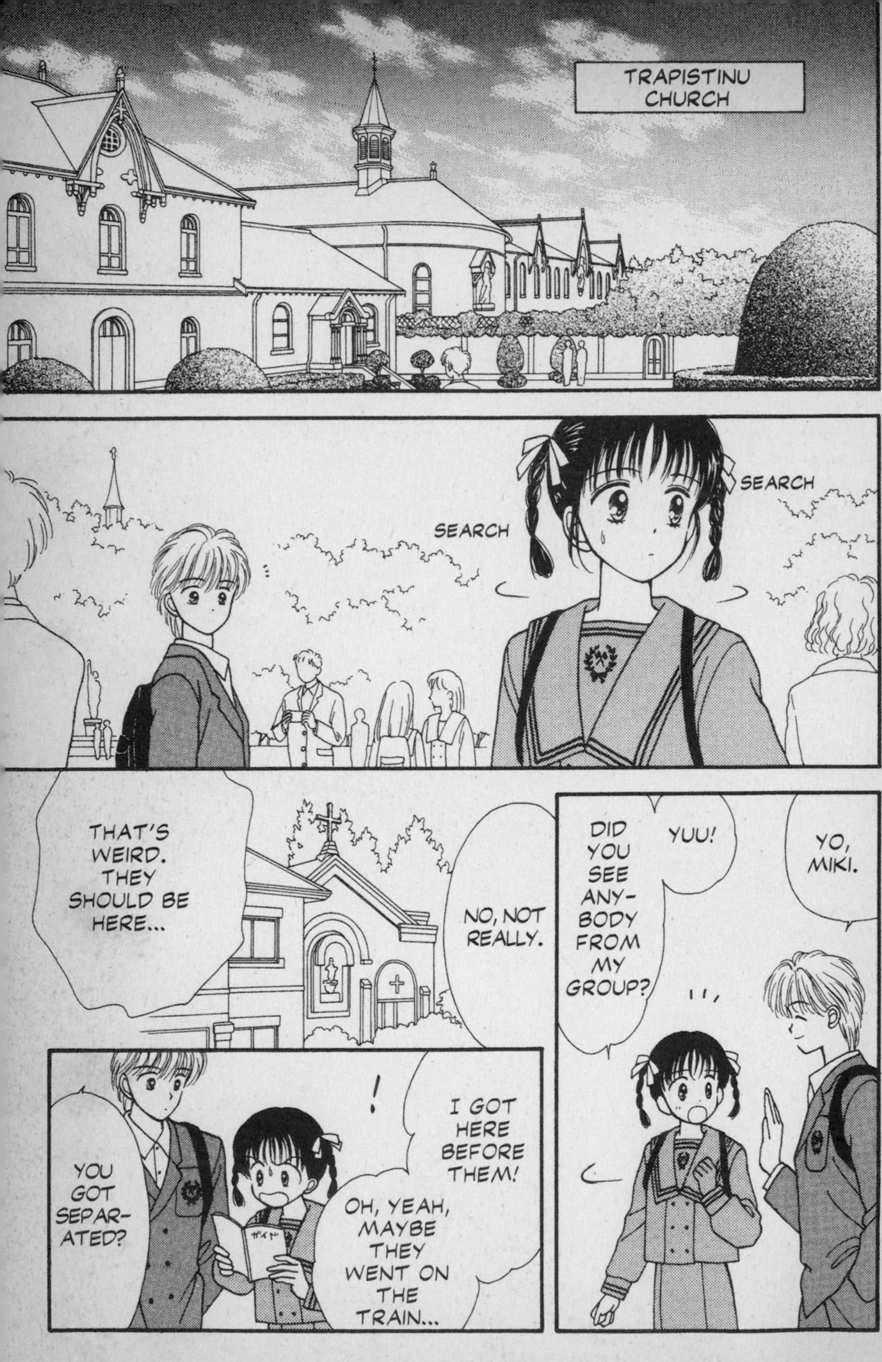
TRAPISTINU CHURCH
SEARCH
SEARCH
YO, MIKI.
YUU!
DID YOU SEE ANYBODY FROM MY GROUP?
NO, NOT REALLY.
THAT'S WEIRD. THEY SHOULD BE HERE...
!
I GOT HERE BEFORE THEM!
OH, YEAH, MAYBE THEY WENT ON THE TRAIN...
YOU GOT SEPARATED?

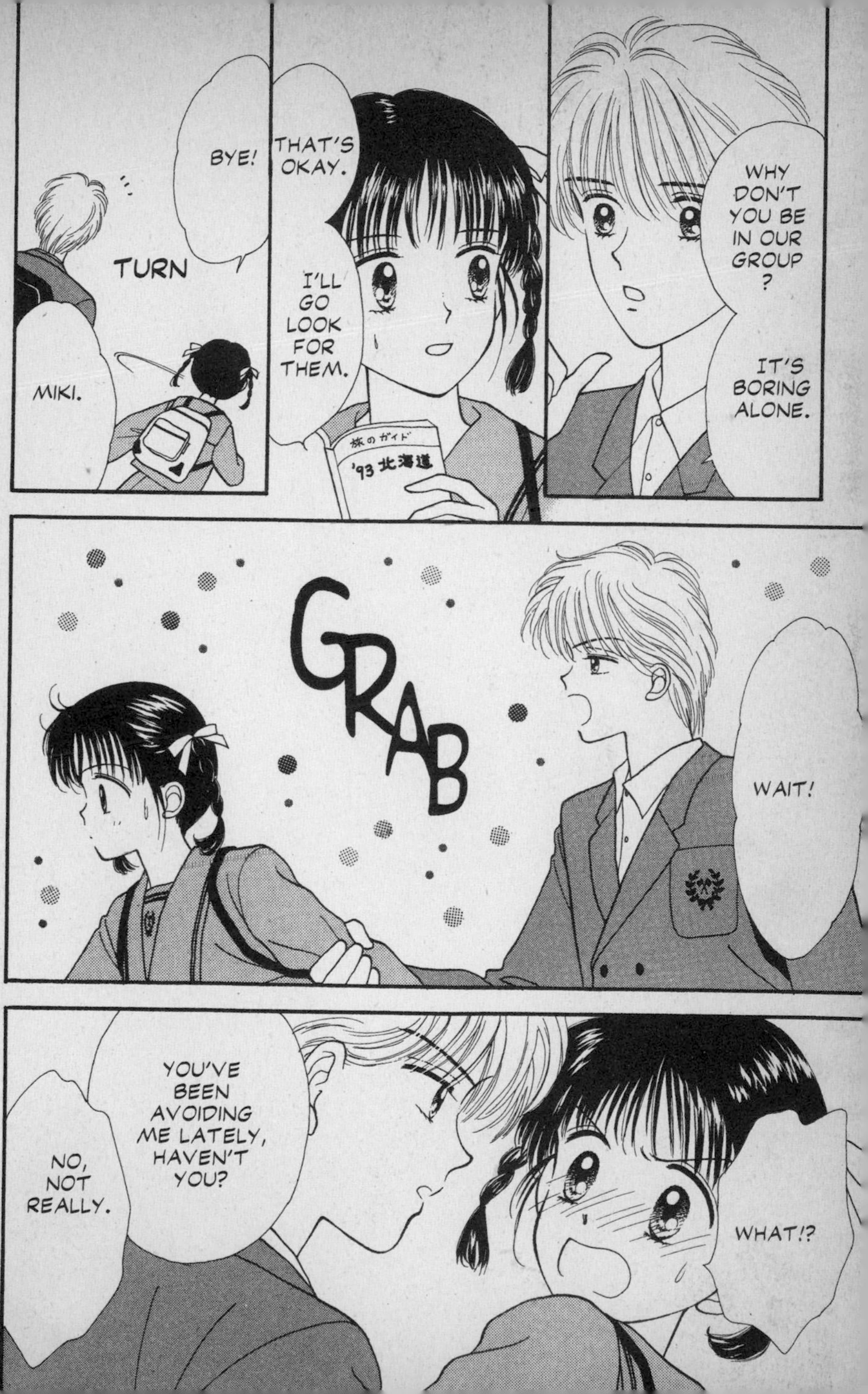
WHY DON'T YOU BE IN OUR GROUP?
IT'S BORING ALONE.
THAT'S OKAY.
I'LL GO LOOK FOR THEM.
旅のガイド
'93 北海道
BYE!
TURN
MIKI.
WAIT!
GRAB
WHAT!?
YOU'VE BEEN AVOIDING ME LATELY, HAVEN'T YOU?
NO, NOT REALLY.

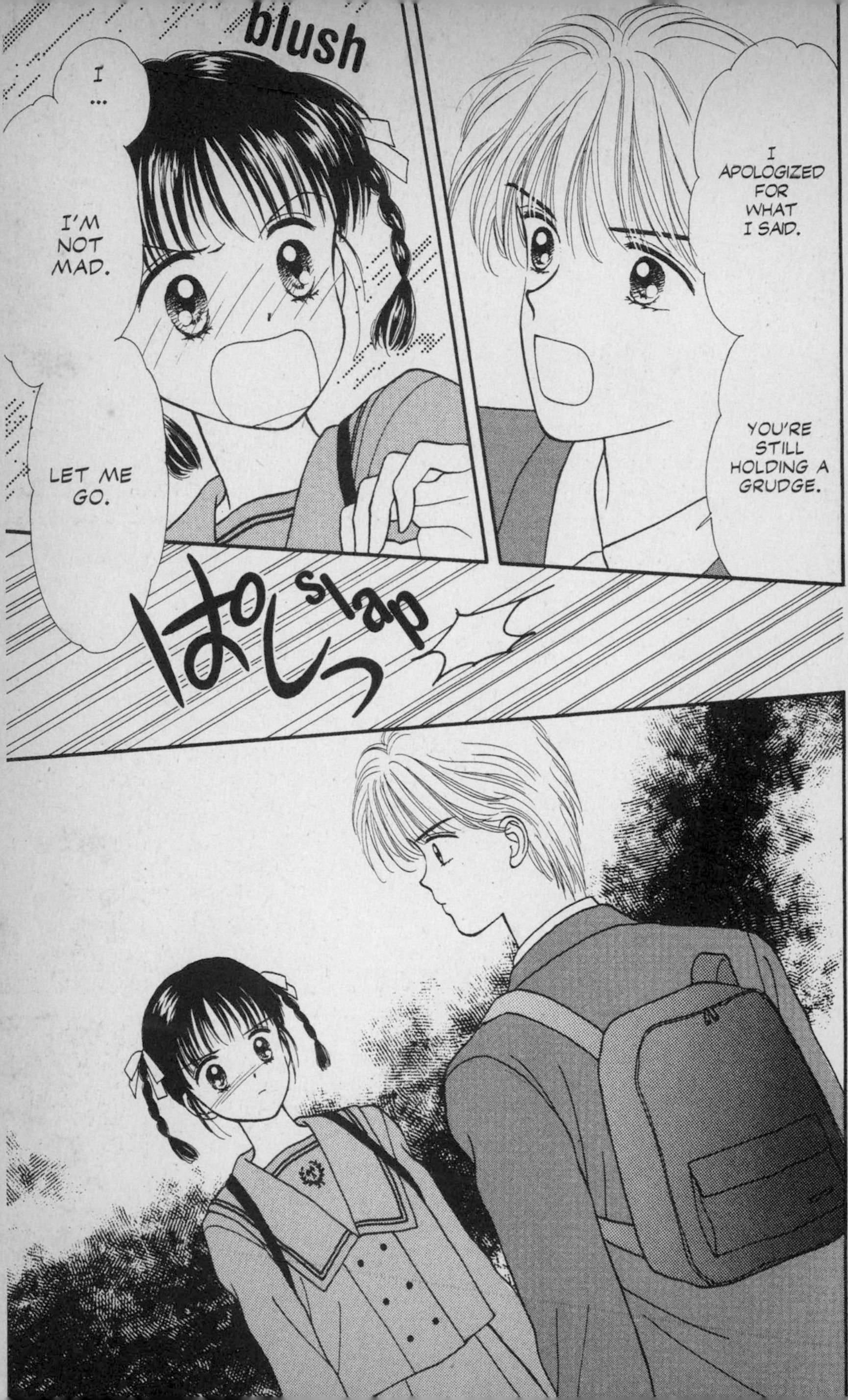
I APOLOGIZED FOR WHAT I SAID.
YOU'RE STILL HOLDING A GRUDGE.
blush
I ...
I'M NOT MAD.
LET ME GO.
ぱしっ
slap

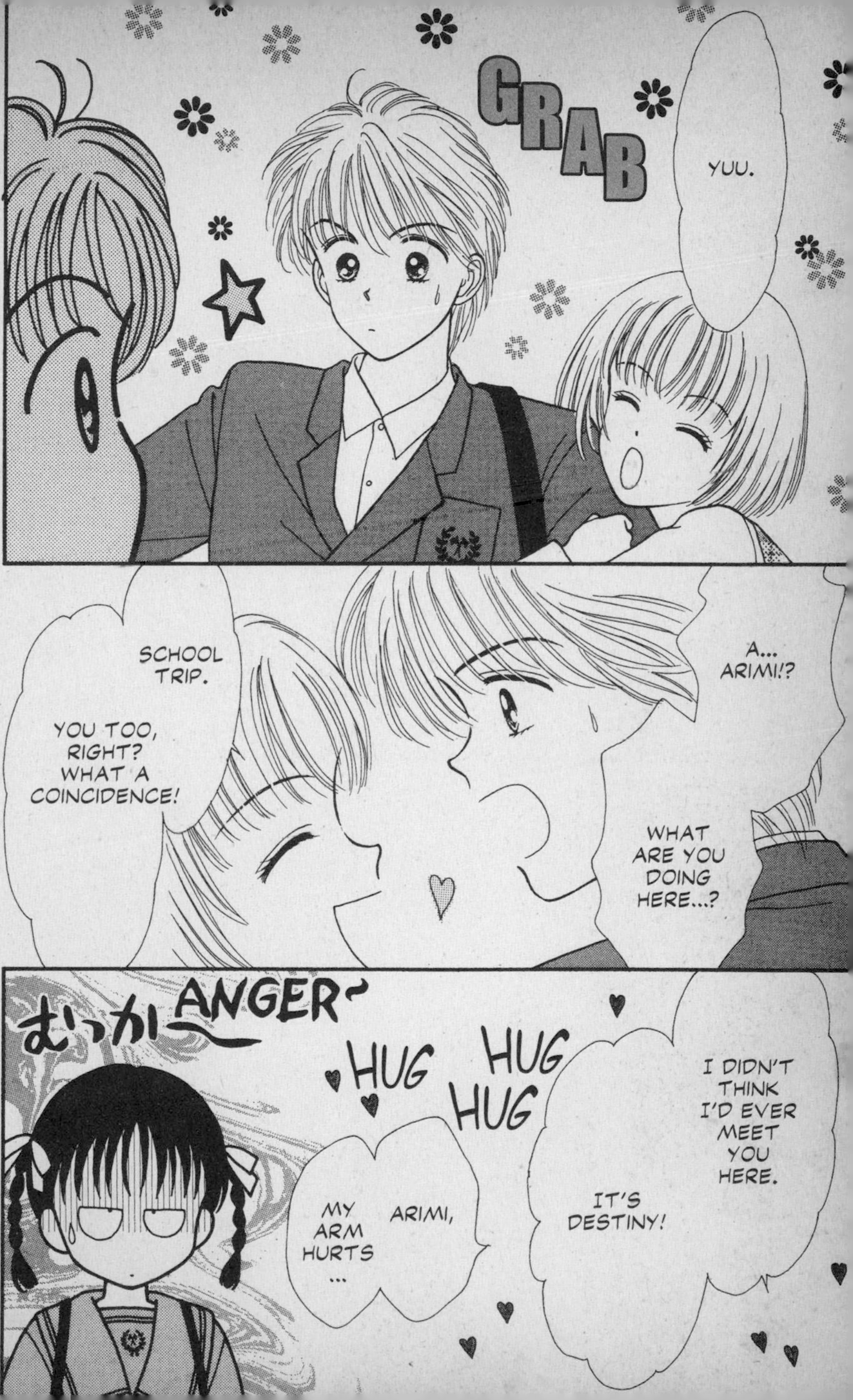
GRAB
YUU.
A... ARIMI!?
WHAT ARE YOU DOING HERE...?
SCHOOL TRIP.
YOU TOO, RIGHT? WHAT A COINCIDENCE!
I DIDN'T THINK I'D EVER MEET YOU HERE.
IT'S DESTINY!
HUG HUG HUG
ARIMI, MY ARM HURTS ...
むっか〜
ANGER

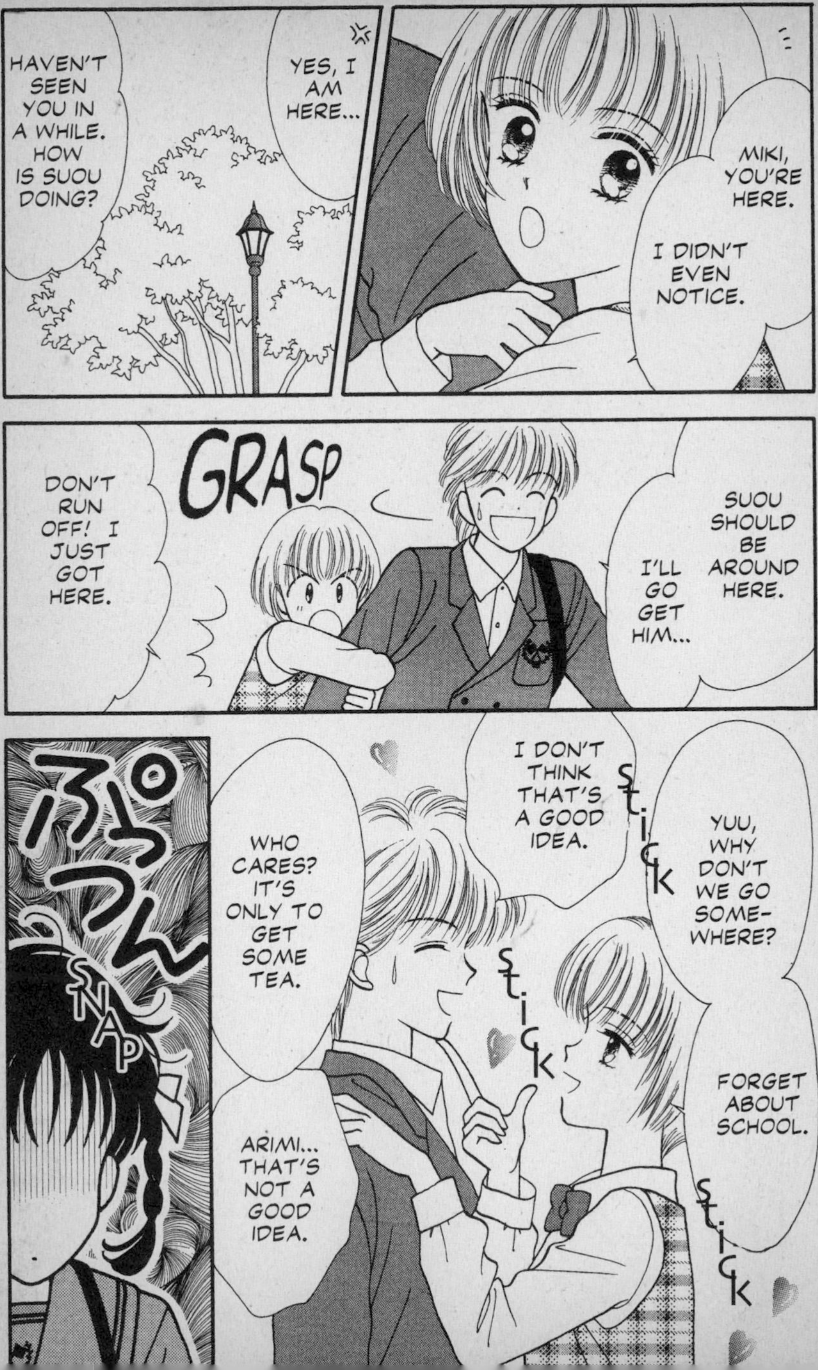
MIKI, YOU'RE HERE.
I DIDN'T EVEN NOTICE.
YES, I AM HERE...
HAVEN'T SEEN YOU IN A WHILE. HOW IS SUOU DOING?
SUOU SHOULD BE AROUND HERE.
I'LL GO GET HIM...
GRASP
DON'T RUN OFF! I JUST GOT HERE.
YUU, WHY DON'T WE GO SOME-WHERE?
STICK
I DON'T THINK THAT'S A GOOD IDEA.
FORGET ABOUT SCHOOL.
STICK
WHO CARES? IT'S ONLY TO GET SOME TEA.
STICK
ARIMI... THAT'S NOT A GOOD IDEA.
ぷつん
SNAP

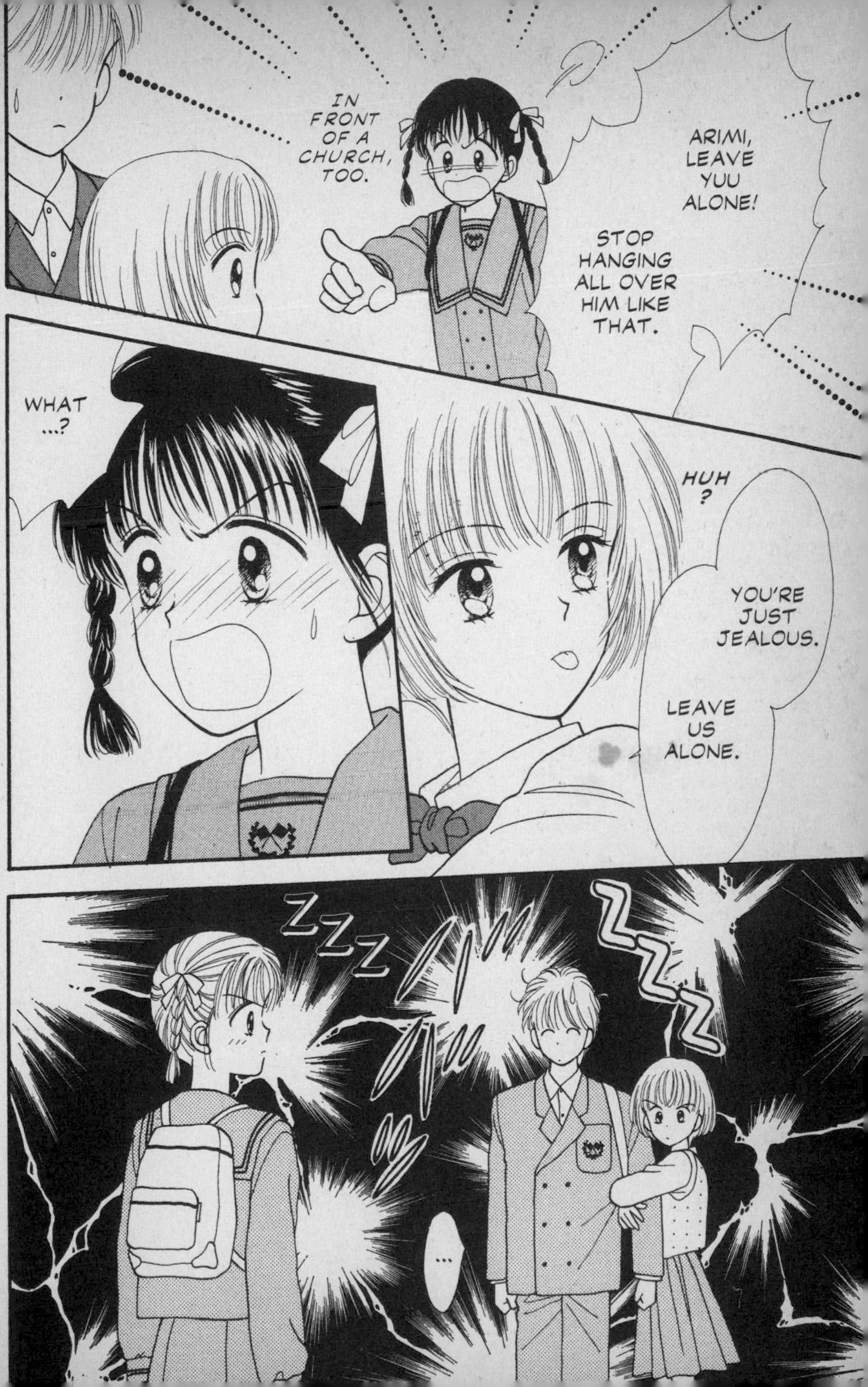
ARIMI, LEAVE YUU ALONE!
STOP HANGING ALL OVER HIM LIKE THAT.
IN FRONT OF A CHURCH, TOO.
HUH?
YOU'RE JUST JEALOUS.
LEAVE US ALONE.
WHAT ...?
ZZZ
ZZZ
...

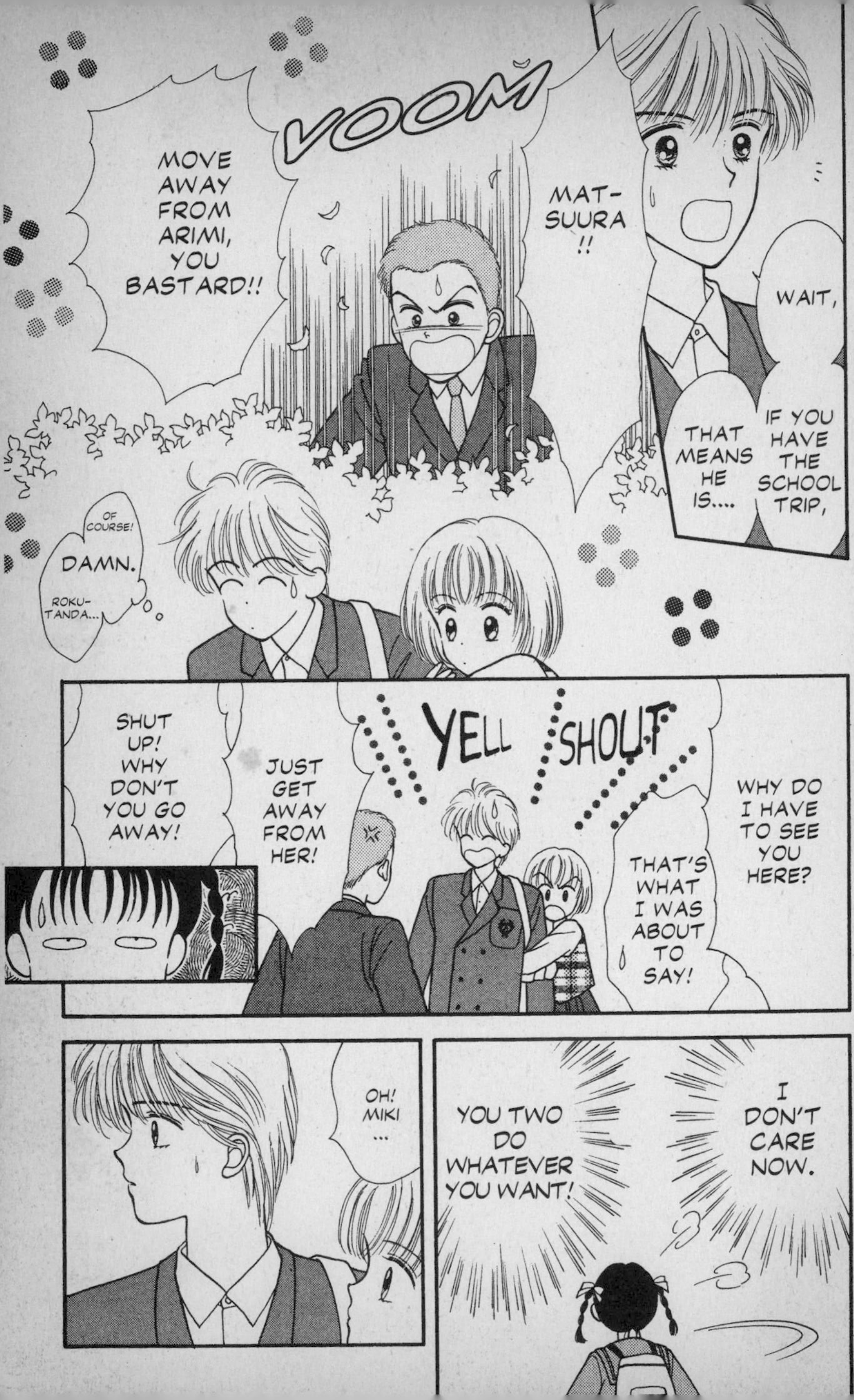
MAT-SUURA!!
WAIT,
IF YOU HAVE THE SCHOOL TRIP,
THAT MEANS HE IS....
VOOM
MOVE AWAY FROM ARIMI, YOU BASTARD!!
OF COURSE! DAMN. ROKU-TANDA...
YELL SHOUT
WHY DO I HAVE TO SEE YOU HERE?
THAT'S WHAT I WAS ABOUT TO SAY!
JUST GET AWAY FROM HER!
SHUT UP! WHY DON'T YOU GO AWAY!
I DON'T CARE NOW.
YOU TWO DO WHATEVER YOU WANT!
OH! MIKI ...

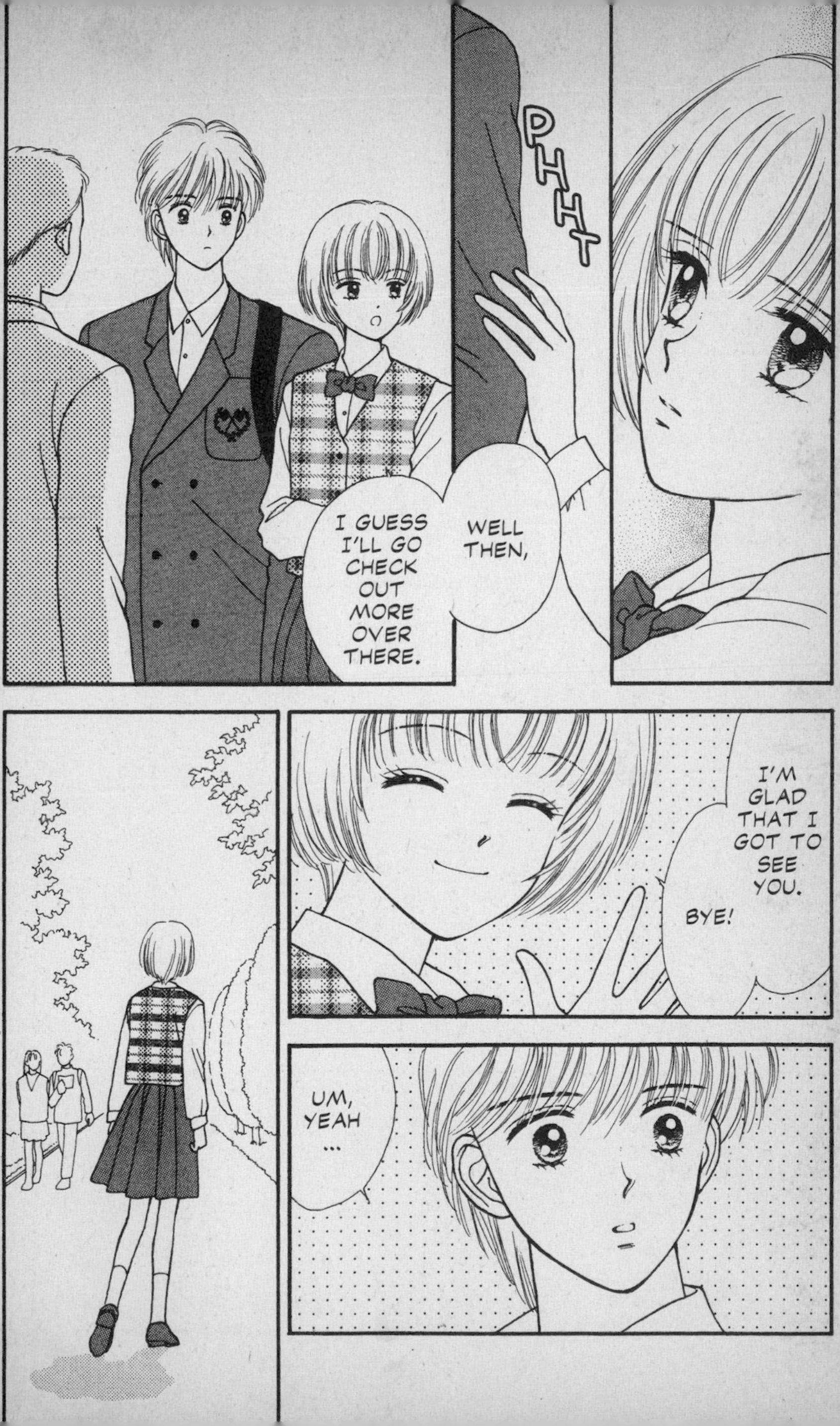
PHHT
WELL THEN, I GUESS I'LL GO CHECK OUT MORE OVER THERE.
I'M GLAD THAT I GOT TO SEE YOU. BYE!
UM, YEAH ...

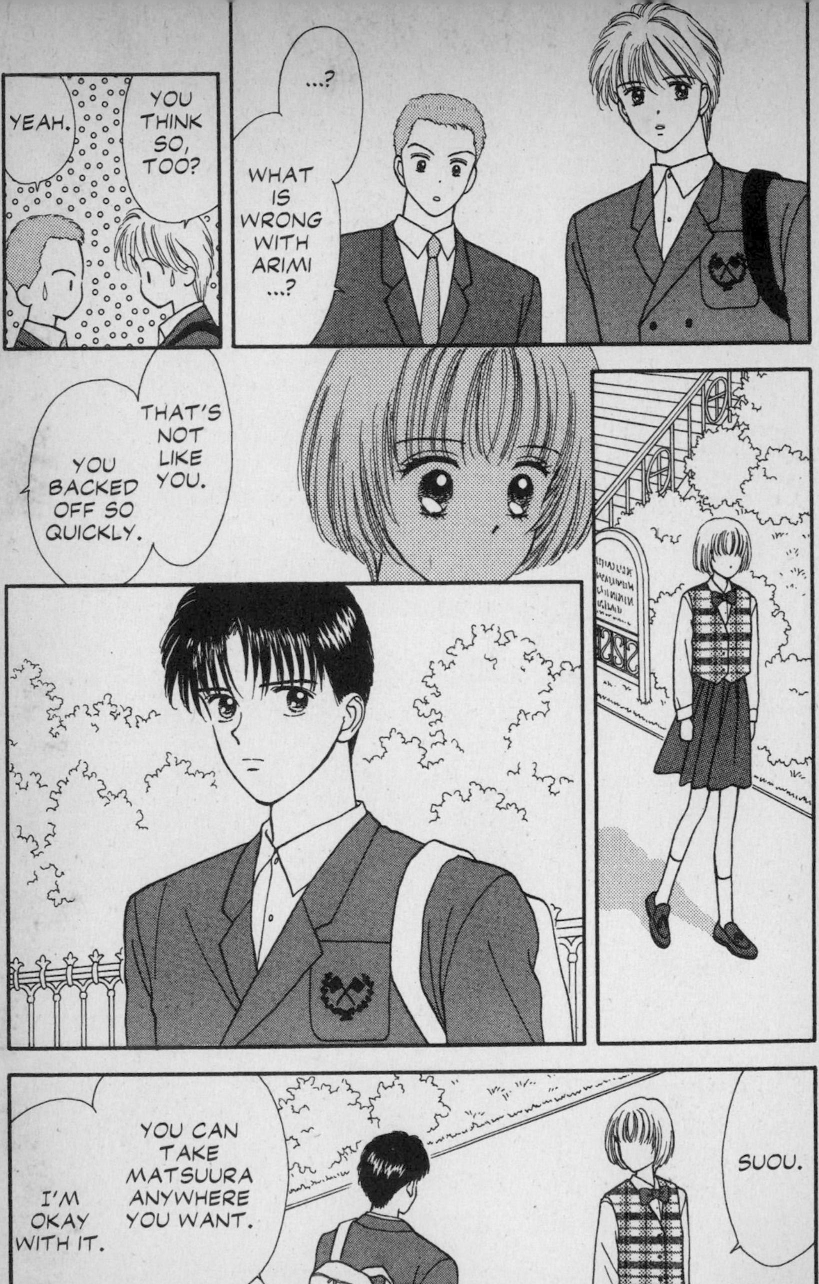
...?
WHAT IS WRONG WITH ARIMI ...?
YOU THINK SO, TOO?
YEAH.
THAT'S NOT LIKE YOU.
YOU BACKED OFF SO QUICKLY.
SUOU.
YOU CAN TAKE MATSUURA ANYWHERE YOU WANT.
I'M OKAY WITH IT.

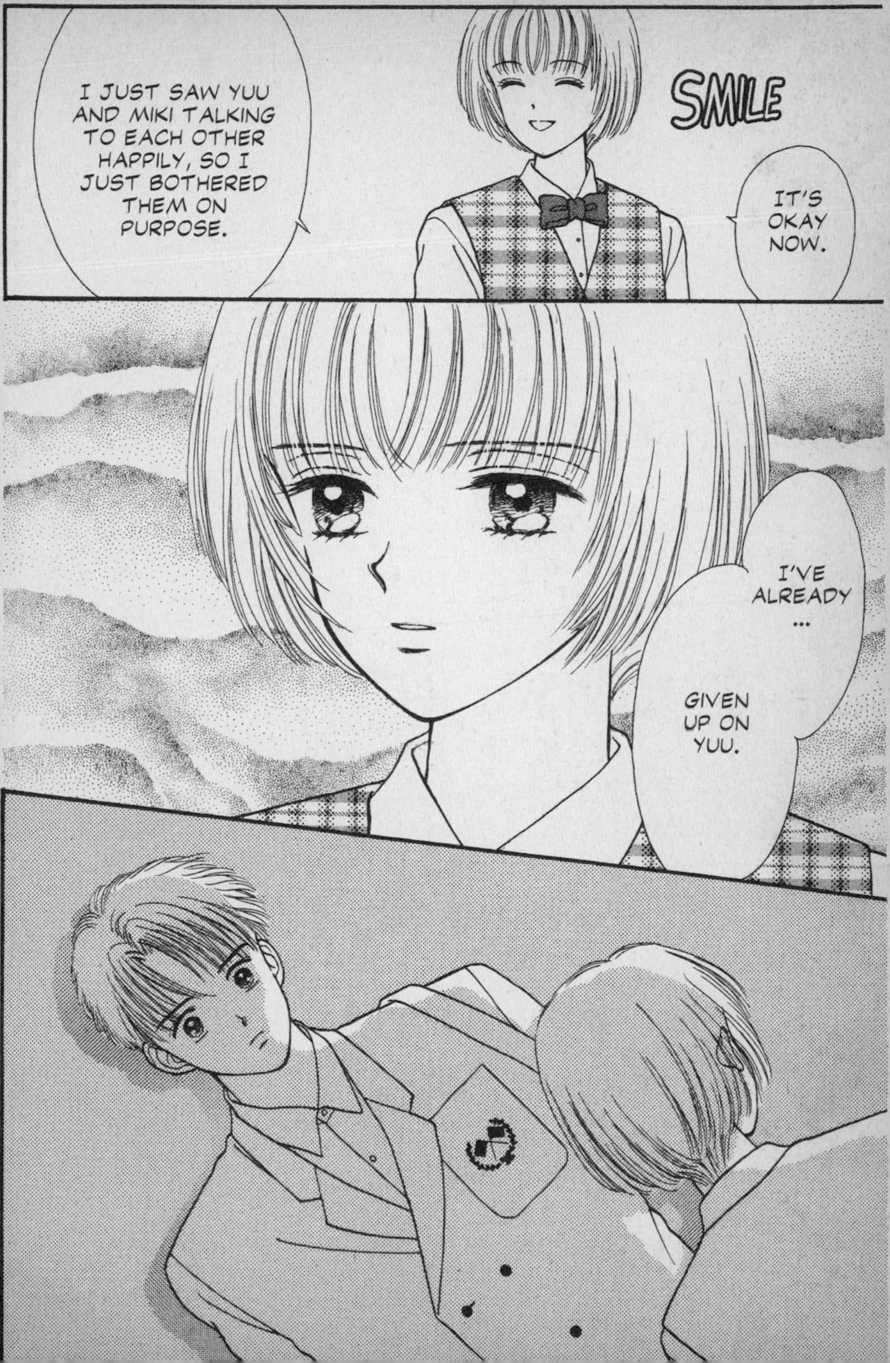
I JUST SAW YUU AND MIKI TALKING TO EACH OTHER HAPPILY, SO I JUST BOTHERED THEM ON PURPOSE.
SMILE
IT'S OKAY NOW.
I'VE ALREADY ...
GIVEN UP ON YUU.

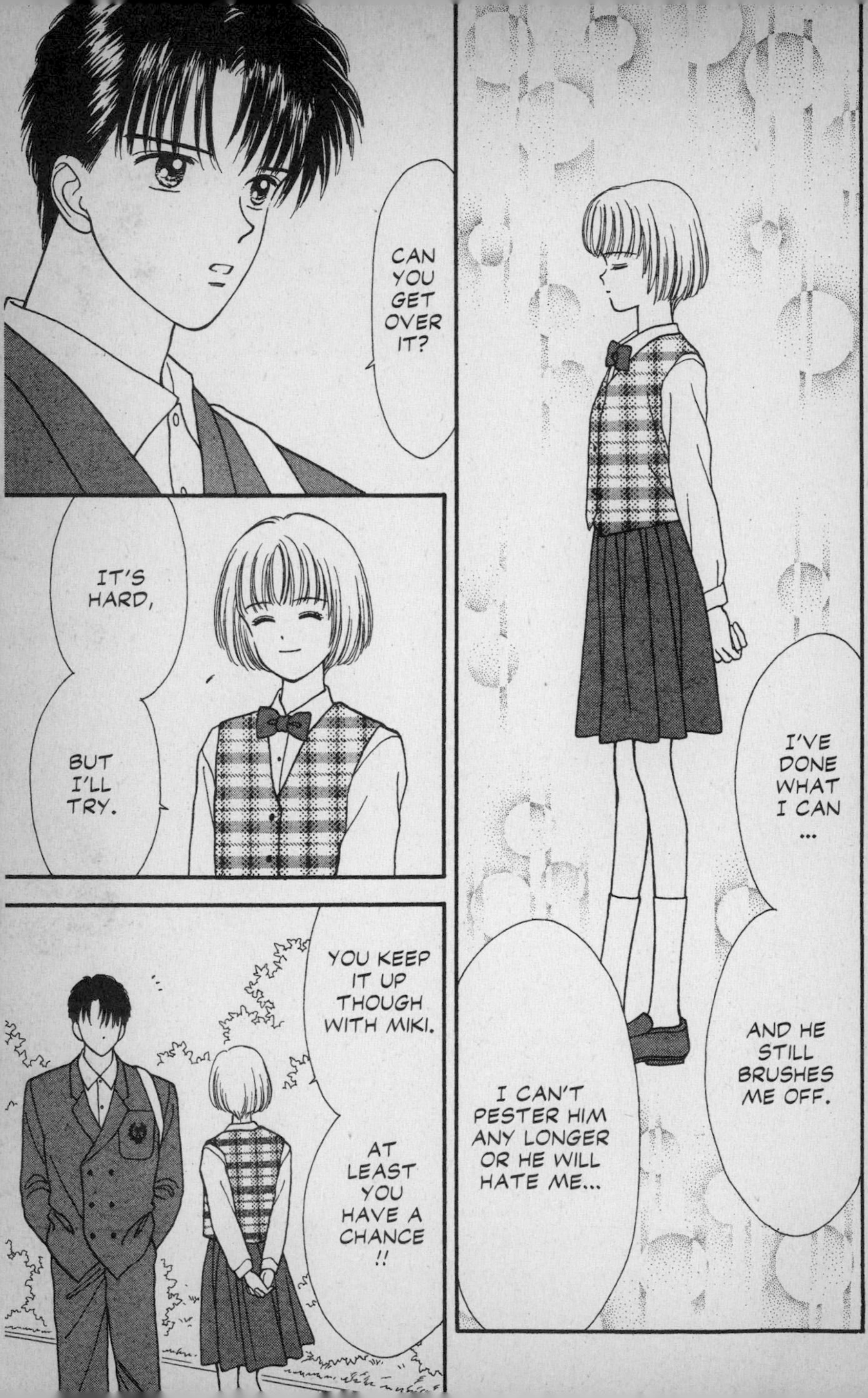
I'VE DONE WHAT I CAN ...
AND HE STILL BRUSHES ME OFF.
I CAN'T PESTER HIM ANY LONGER OR HE WILL HATE ME...
CAN YOU GET OVER IT?
IT'S HARD,
BUT I'LL TRY.
YOU KEEP IT UP THOUGH WITH MIKI.
AT LEAST YOU HAVE A CHANCE !!

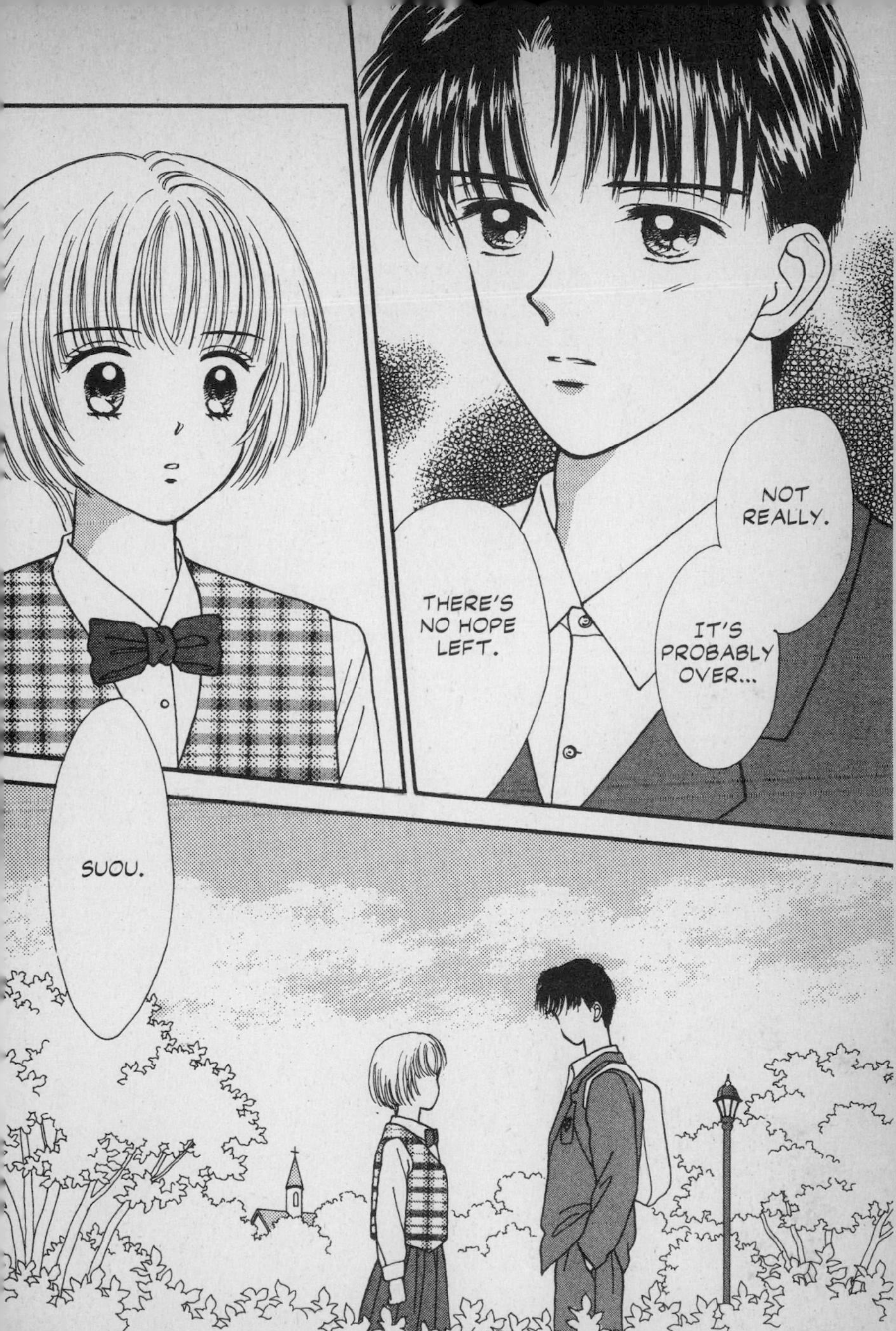
NOT REALLY.
IT'S PROBABLY OVER...
THERE'S NO HOPE LEFT.
SUOU.

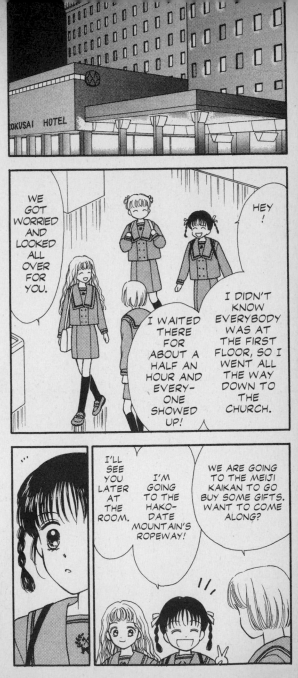

KOKUSAI HOTEL
HEY!
I DIDN'T KNOW EVERYBODY WAS AT THE FIRST FLOOR, SO I WENT ALL THE WAY DOWN TO THE CHURCH.
I WAITED THERE FOR ABOUT A HALF AN HOUR AND EVERY-ONE SHOWED UP!
WE GOT WORRIED AND LOOKED ALL OVER FOR YOU.
WE ARE GOING TO THE MEIJI KAIKAN TO GO BUY SOME GIFTS. WANT TO COME ALONG?
I'M GOING TO THE HAKO-DATE MOUNTAIN'S ROPEWAY!
I'LL SEE YOU LATER AT THE ROOM.
...

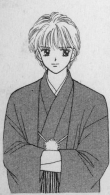

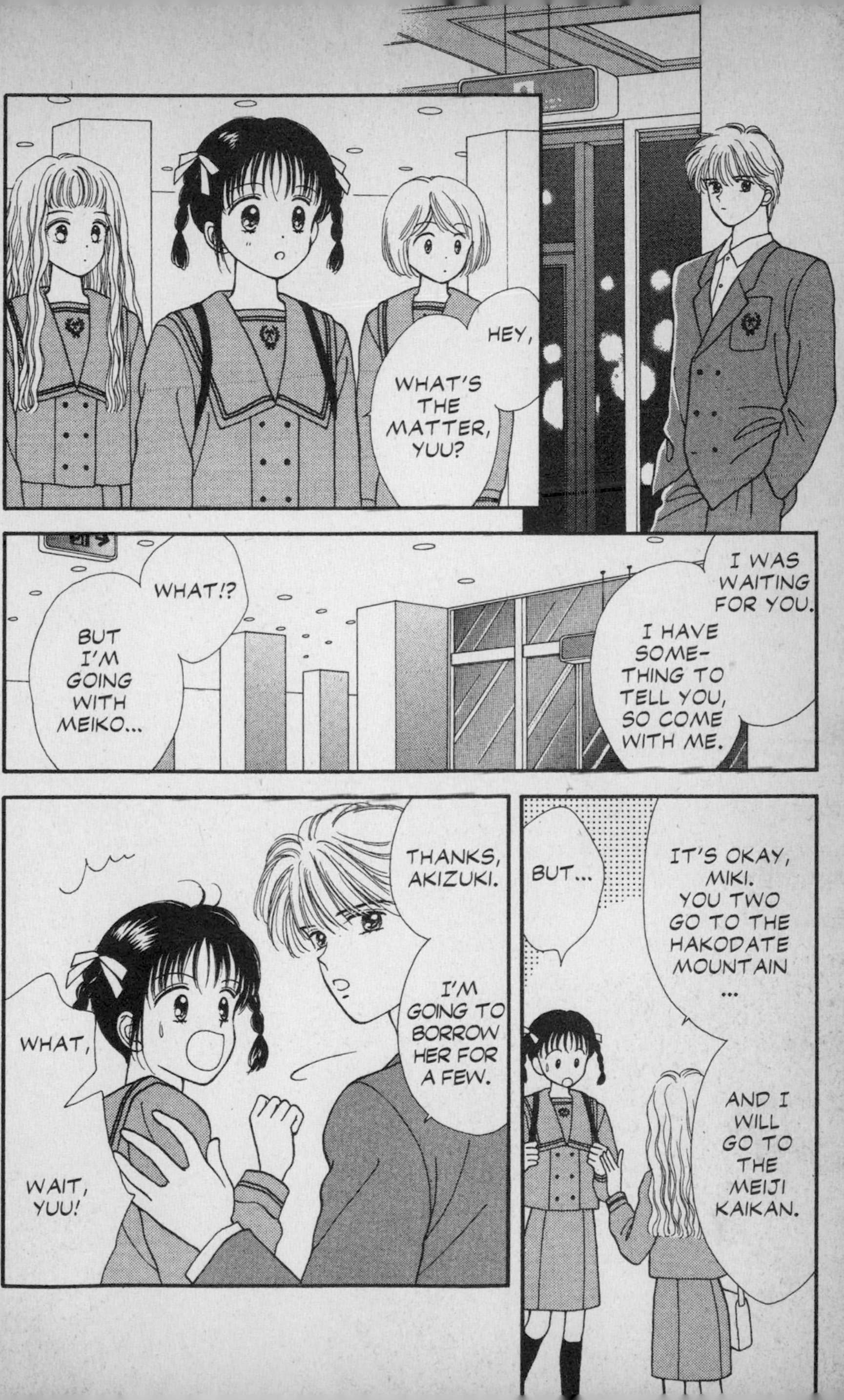
HEY,
WHAT'S THE MATTER, YUU?
I WAS WAITING FOR YOU.
I HAVE SOME-THING TO TELL YOU, SO COME WITH ME.
WHAT!?
BUT I'M GOING WITH MEIKO...
IT'S OKAY, MIKI. YOU TWO GO TO THE HAKODATE MOUNTAIN ...
BUT...
AND I WILL GO TO THE MEIJI KAIKAN.
THANKS, AKIZUKI.
I'M GOING TO BORROW HER FOR A FEW.
WHAT,
WAIT, YUU!

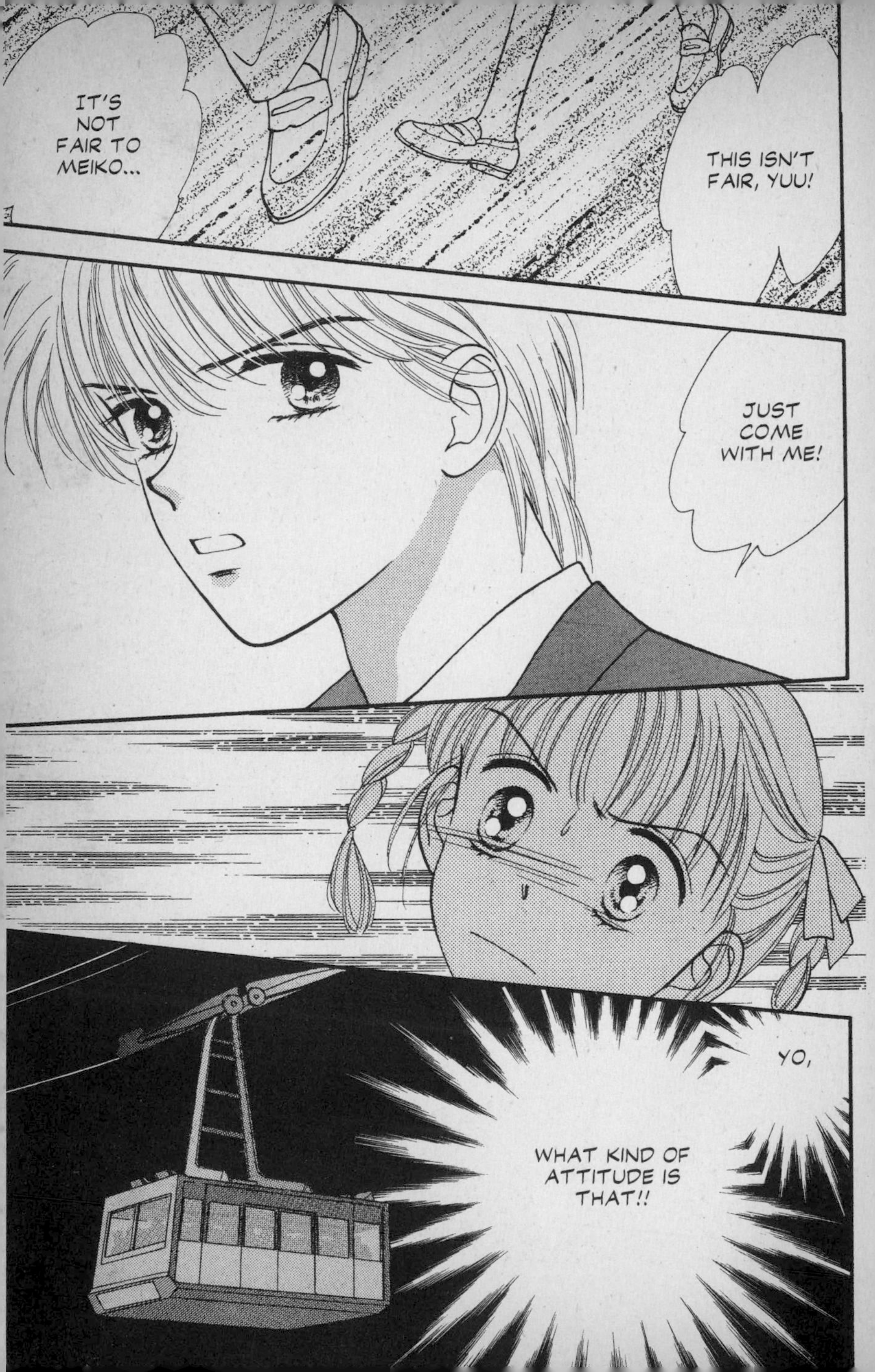
THIS ISN'T FAIR, YUU!
IT'S NOT FAIR TO MEIKO...
JUST COME WITH ME!
YO,
WHAT KIND OF ATTITUDE IS THAT!!

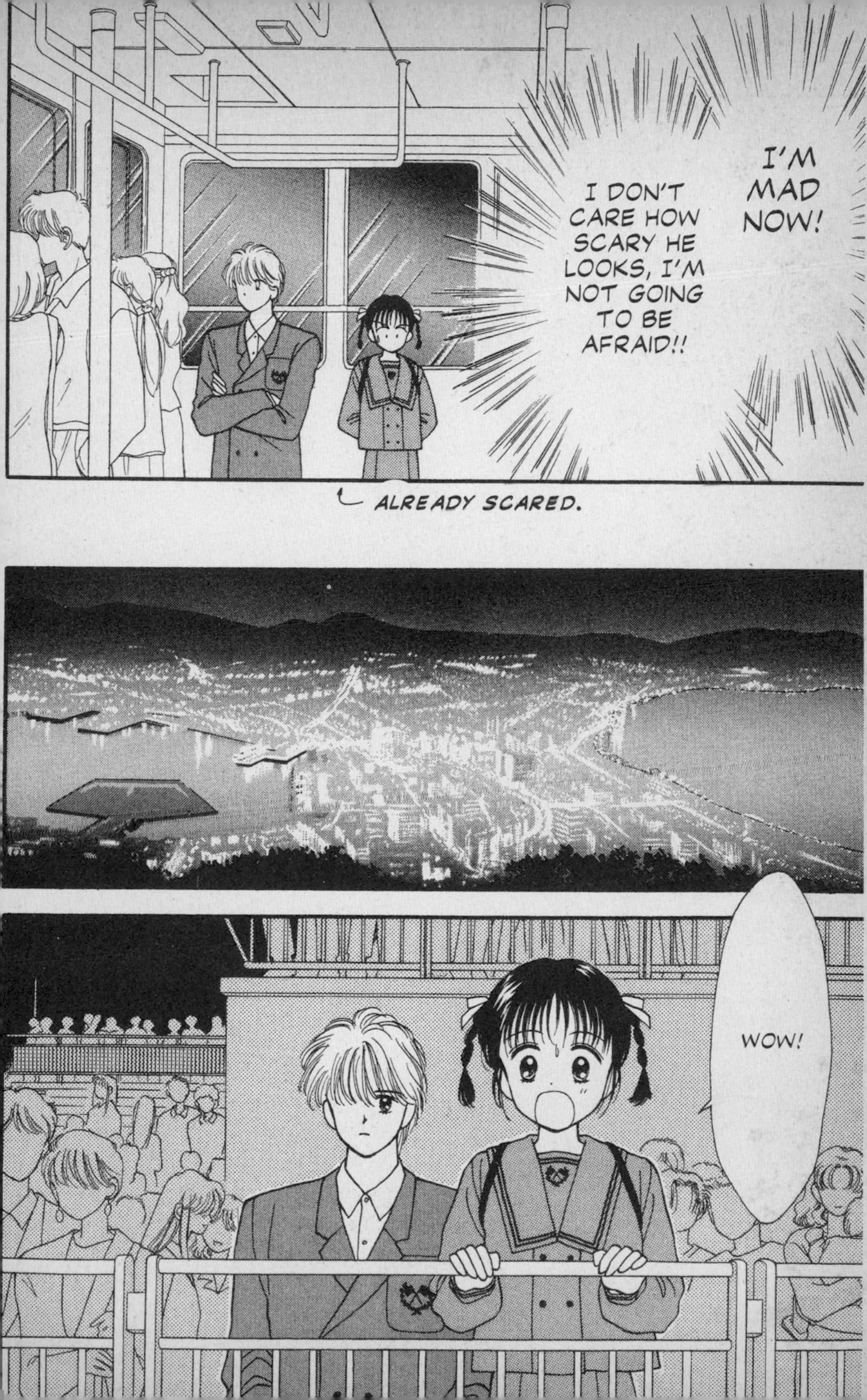
I'M MAD NOW!
I DON'T CARE HOW SCARY HE LOOKS, I'M NOT GOING TO BE AFRAID!!
ALREADY SCARED.
WOW!

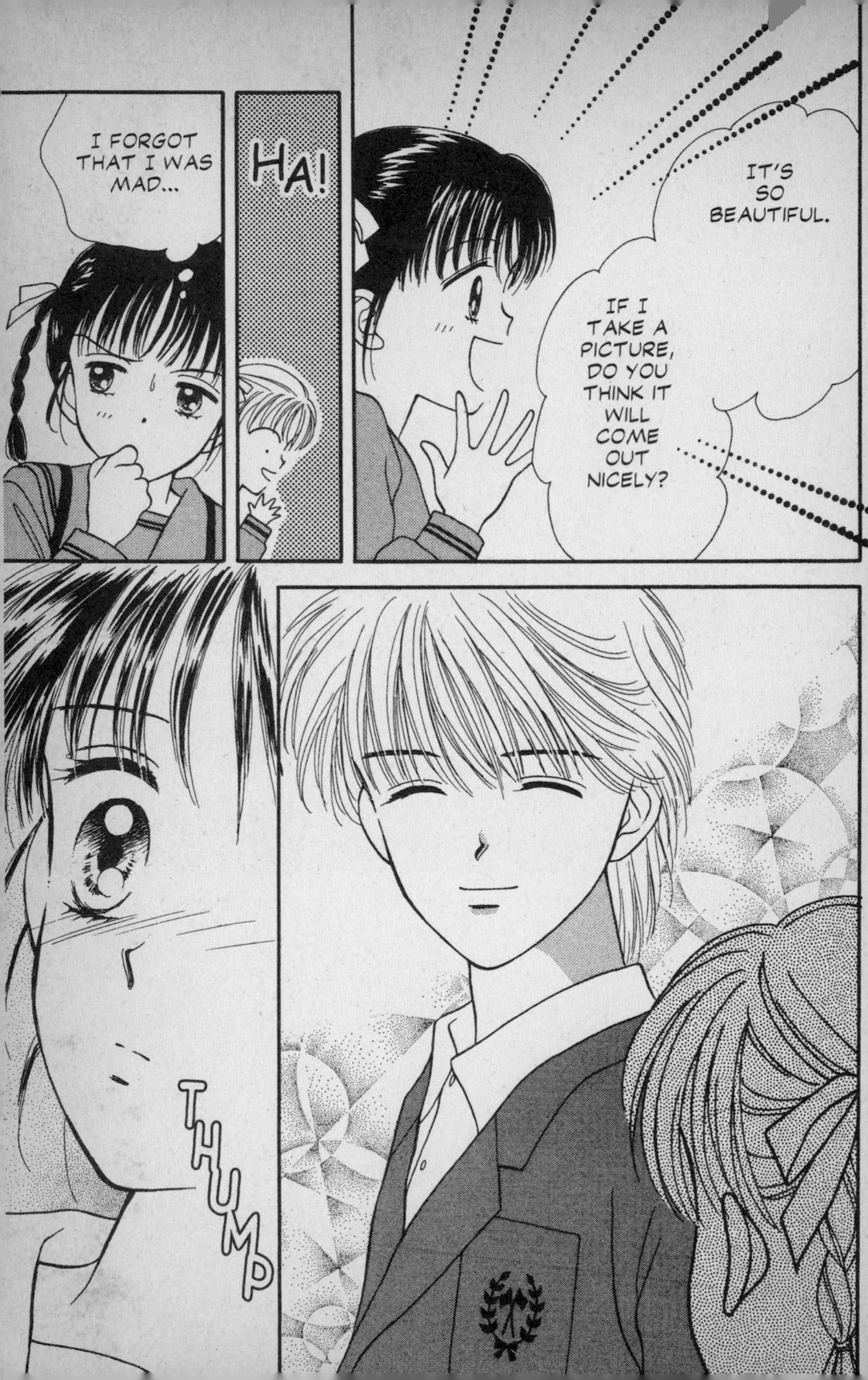
IT'S SO BEAUTIFUL.
IF I TAKE A PICTURE, DO YOU THINK IT WILL COME OUT NICELY?
HA!
I FORGOT THAT I WAS MAD...
THUMP

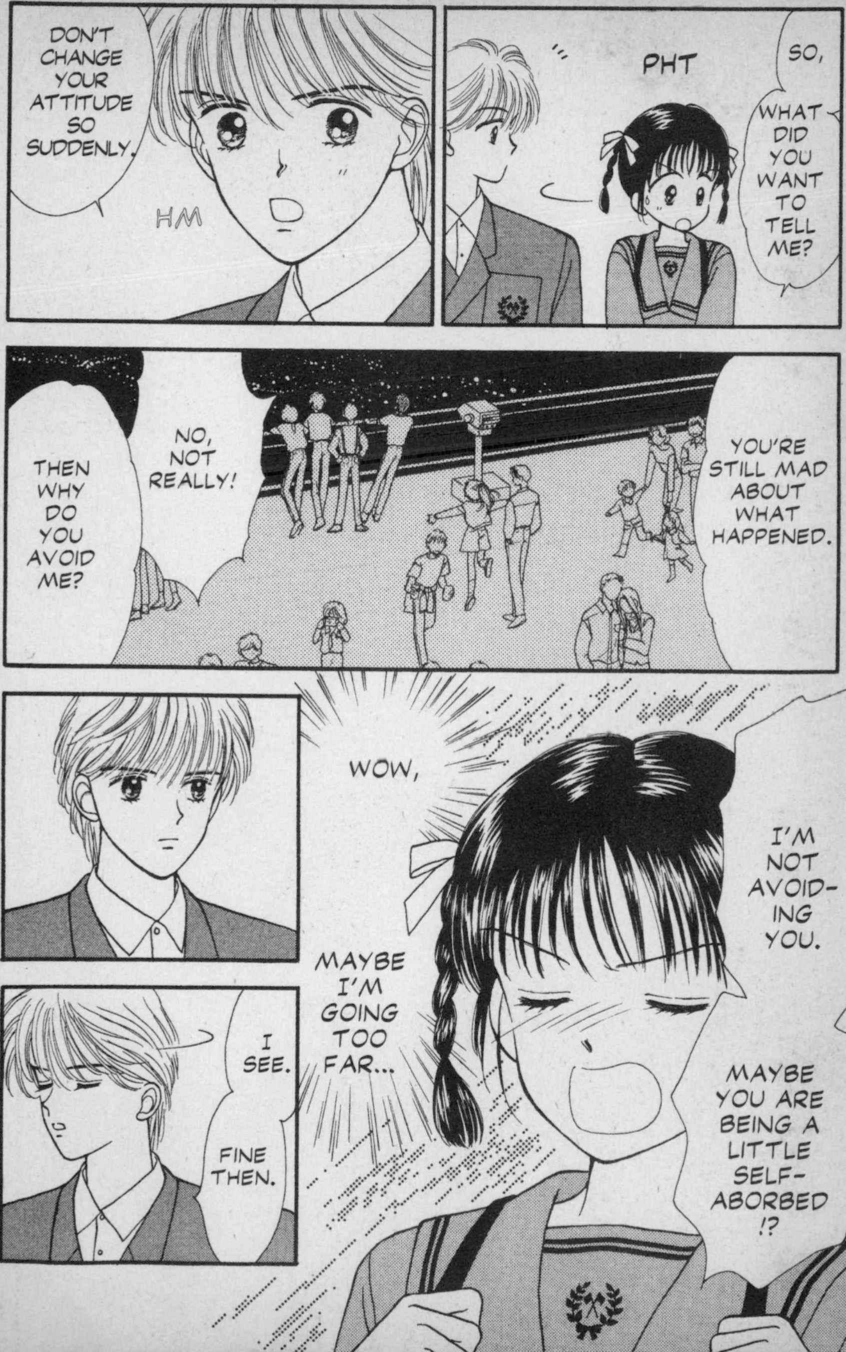
SO, WHAT DID YOU WANT TO TELL ME?
PHT
DON'T CHANGE YOUR ATTITUDE SO SUDDENLY.
HM
YOU'RE STILL MAD ABOUT WHAT HAPPENED.
NO, NOT REALLY!
THEN WHY DO YOU AVOID ME?
I'M NOT AVOID-ING YOU.
WOW,
MAYBE YOU ARE BEING A LITTLE SELF-ABORBED!?
MAYBE I'M GOING TOO FAR...
I SEE.
FINE THEN.

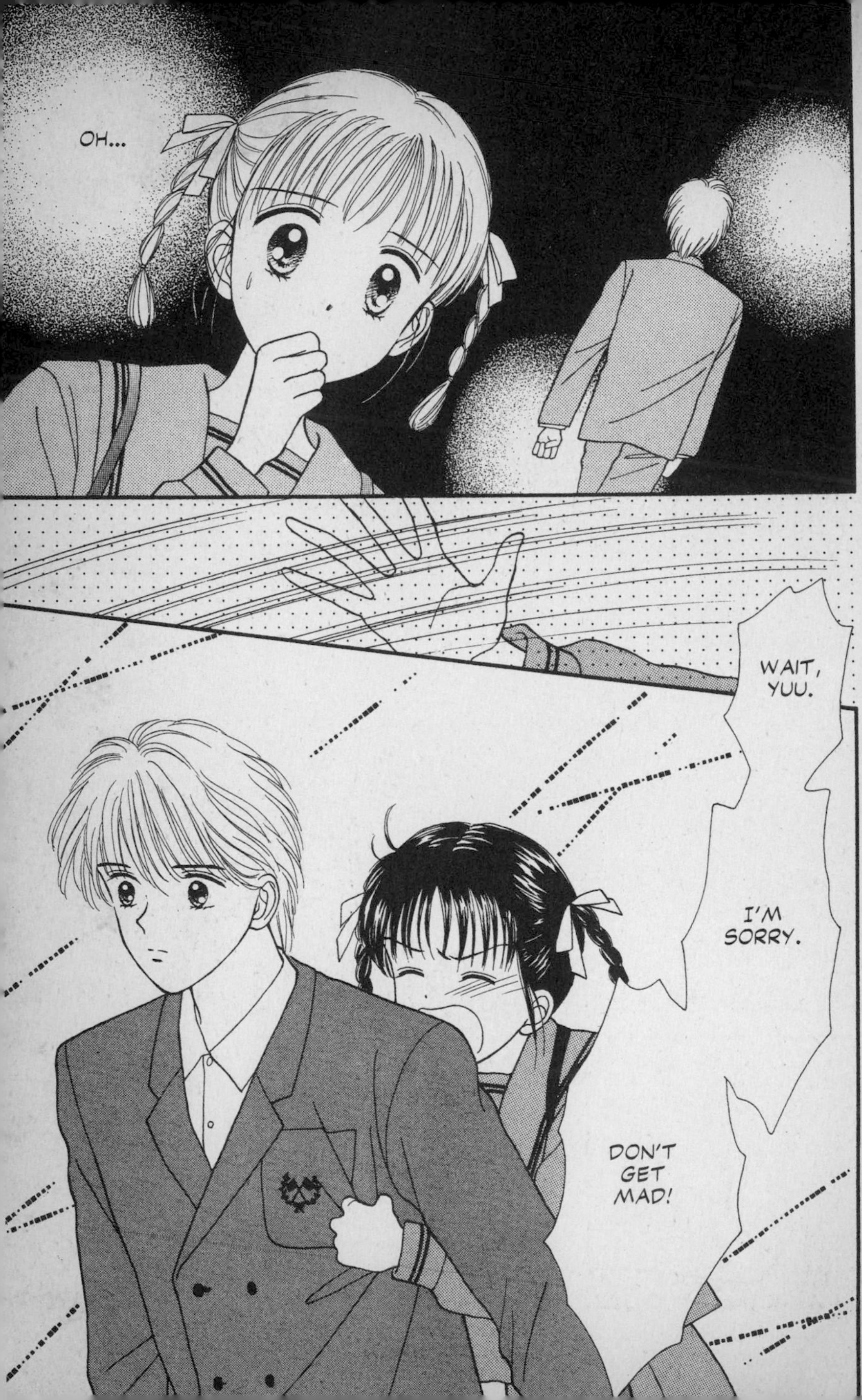
OH...
WAIT, YUU.
I'M SORRY.
DON'T GET MAD!

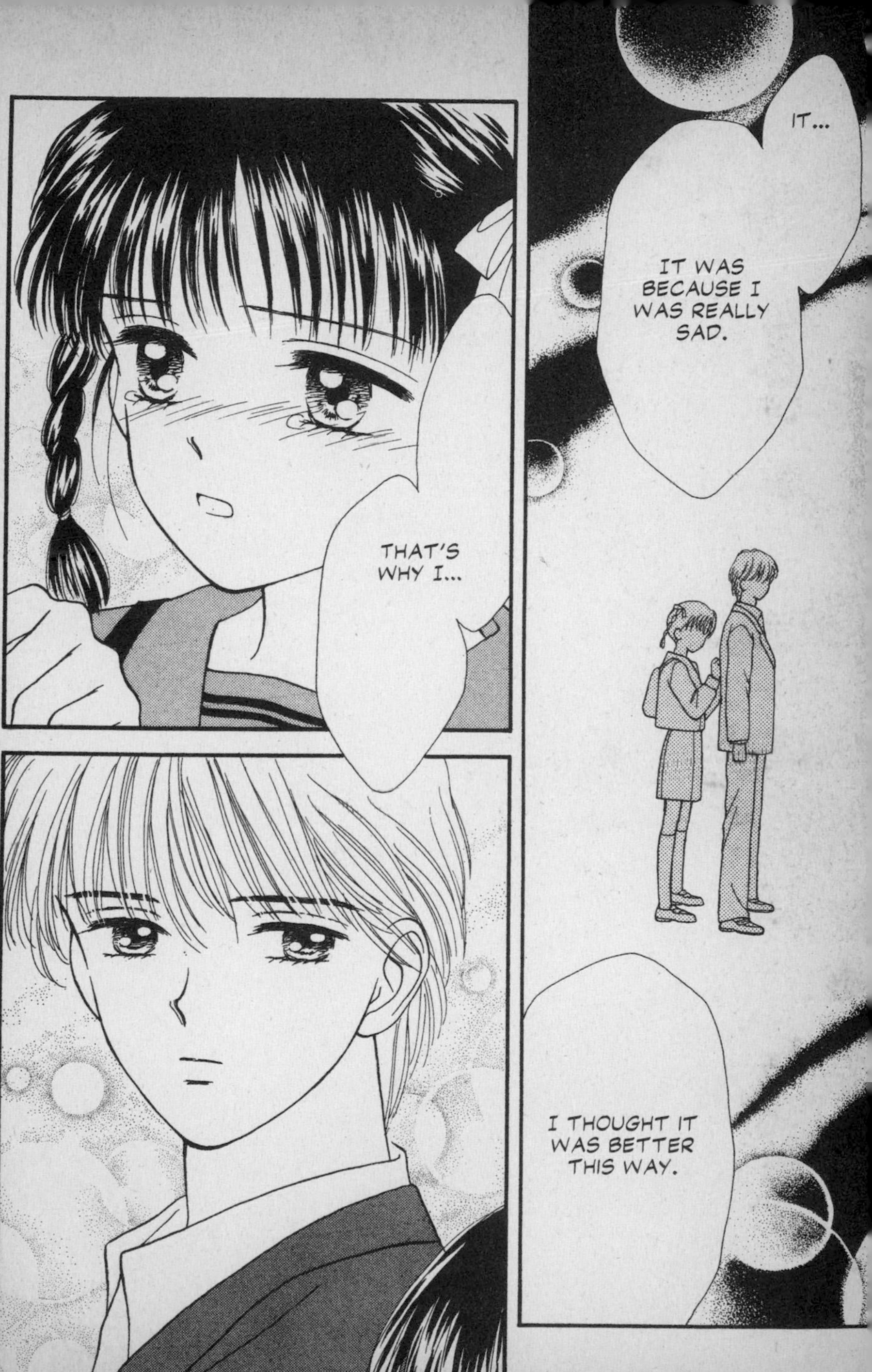
IT...
IT WAS BECAUSE I WAS REALLY SAD.
I THOUGHT IT WAS BETTER THIS WAY.
THAT'S WHY I...

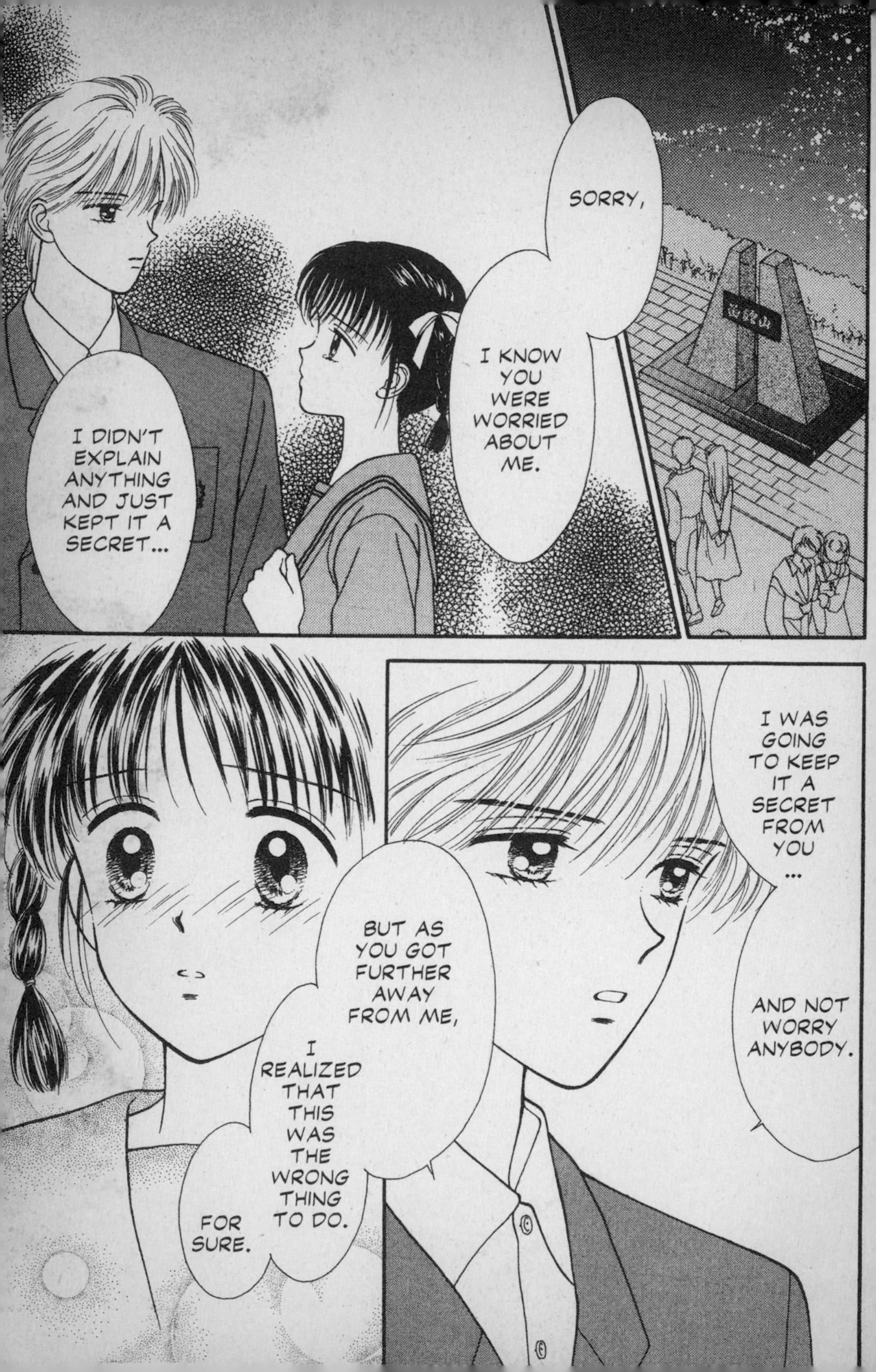
SORRY,
I KNOW YOU WERE WORRIED ABOUT ME.
I DIDN'T EXPLAIN ANYTHING AND JUST KEPT IT A SECRET...
I WAS GOING TO KEEP IT A SECRET FROM YOU ...
AND NOT WORRY ANYBODY.
BUT AS YOU GOT FURTHER AWAY FROM ME,
I REALIZED THAT THIS WAS THE WRONG THING TO DO.
FOR SURE.

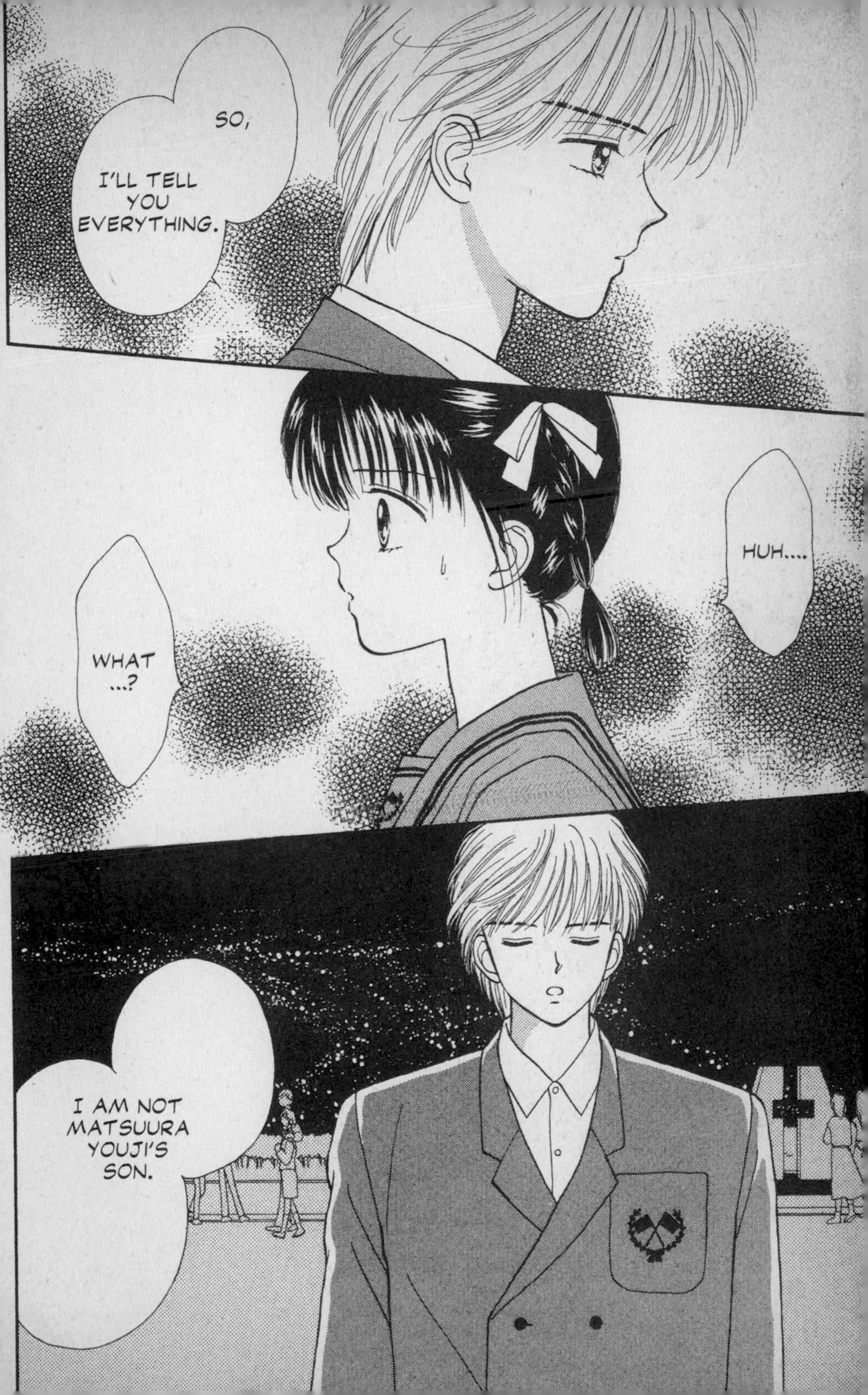
SO,
I'LL TELL YOU EVERYTHING.
HUH....
WHAT ...?
I AM NOT MATSUURA YOUJI'S SON.

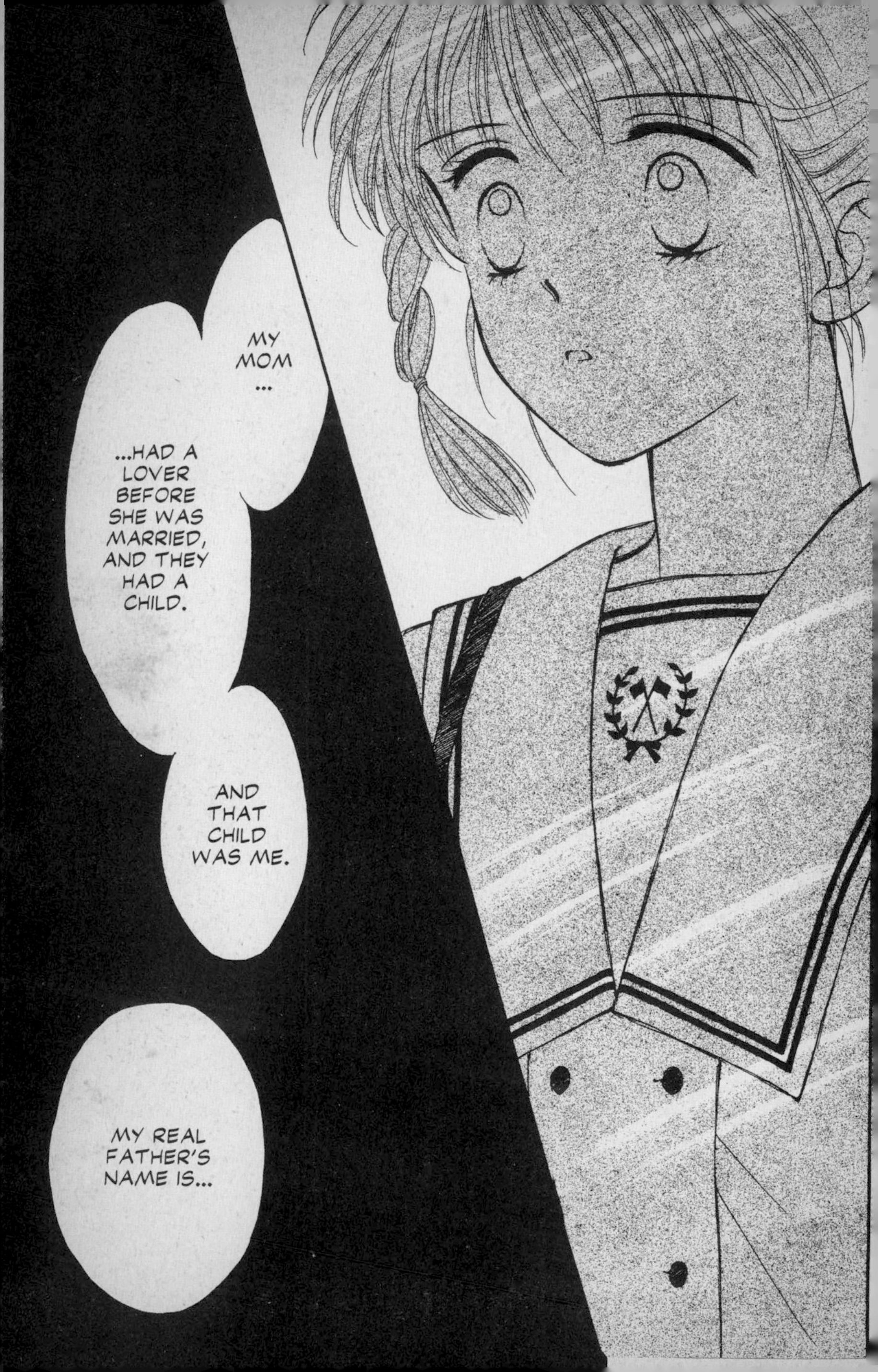
MY MOM ...
...HAD A LOVER BEFORE SHE WAS MARRIED, AND THEY HAD A CHILD.
AND THAT CHILD WAS ME.
MY REAL FATHER'S NAME IS...

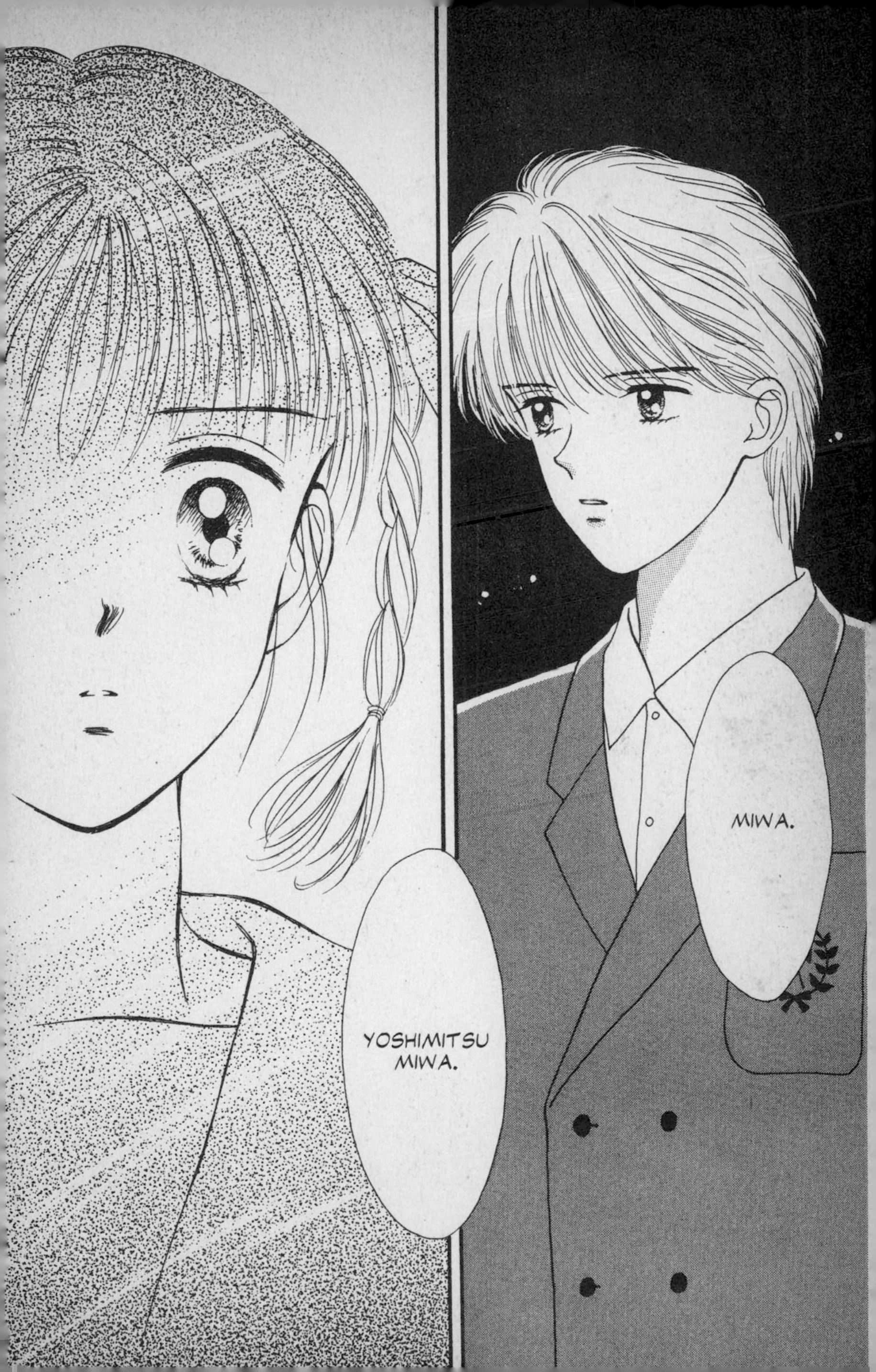
MIWA.
YOSHIMITSU MIWA.

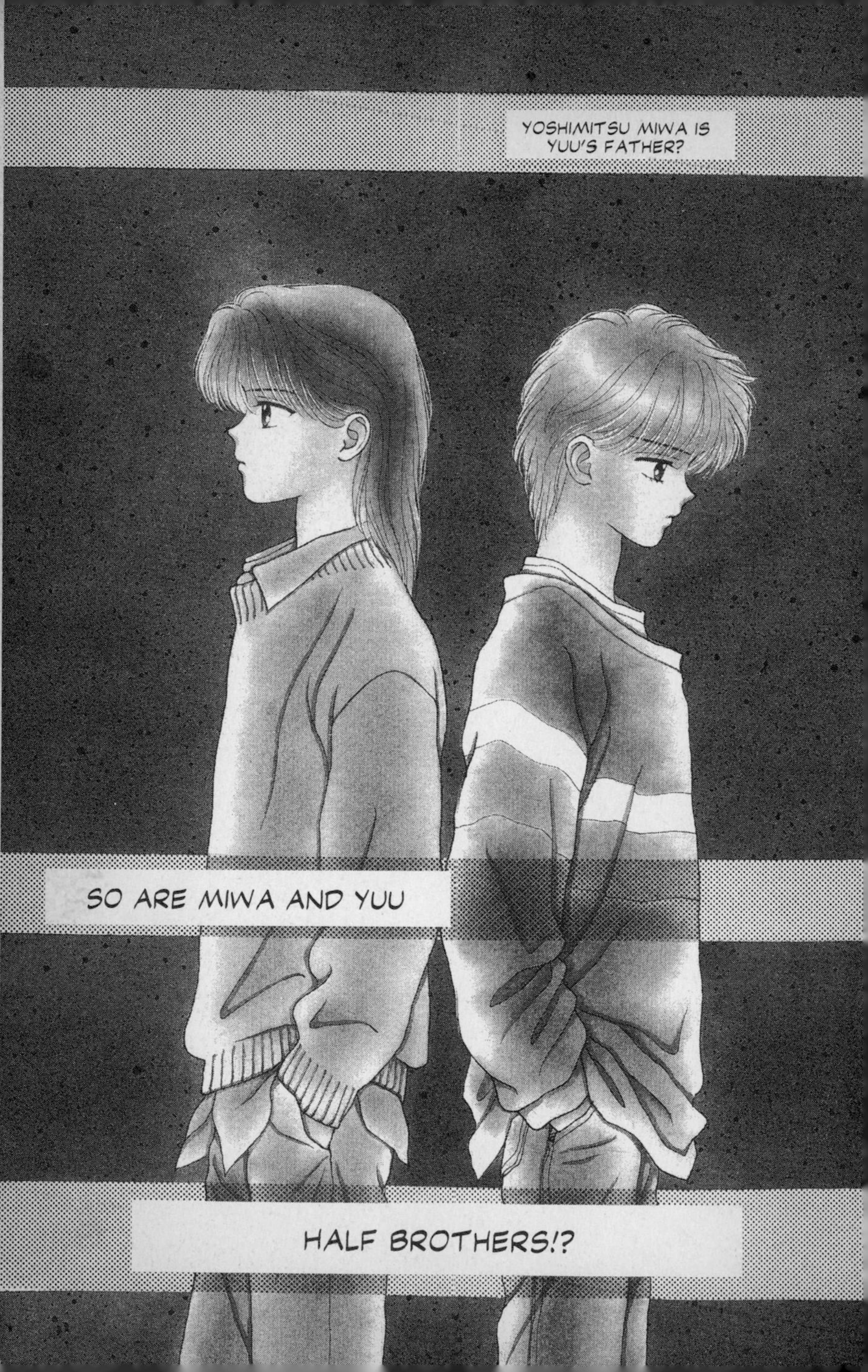
YOSHIMITSU MIWA IS YUU'S FATHER?
SO ARE MIWA AND YUU
HALF BROTHERS!?

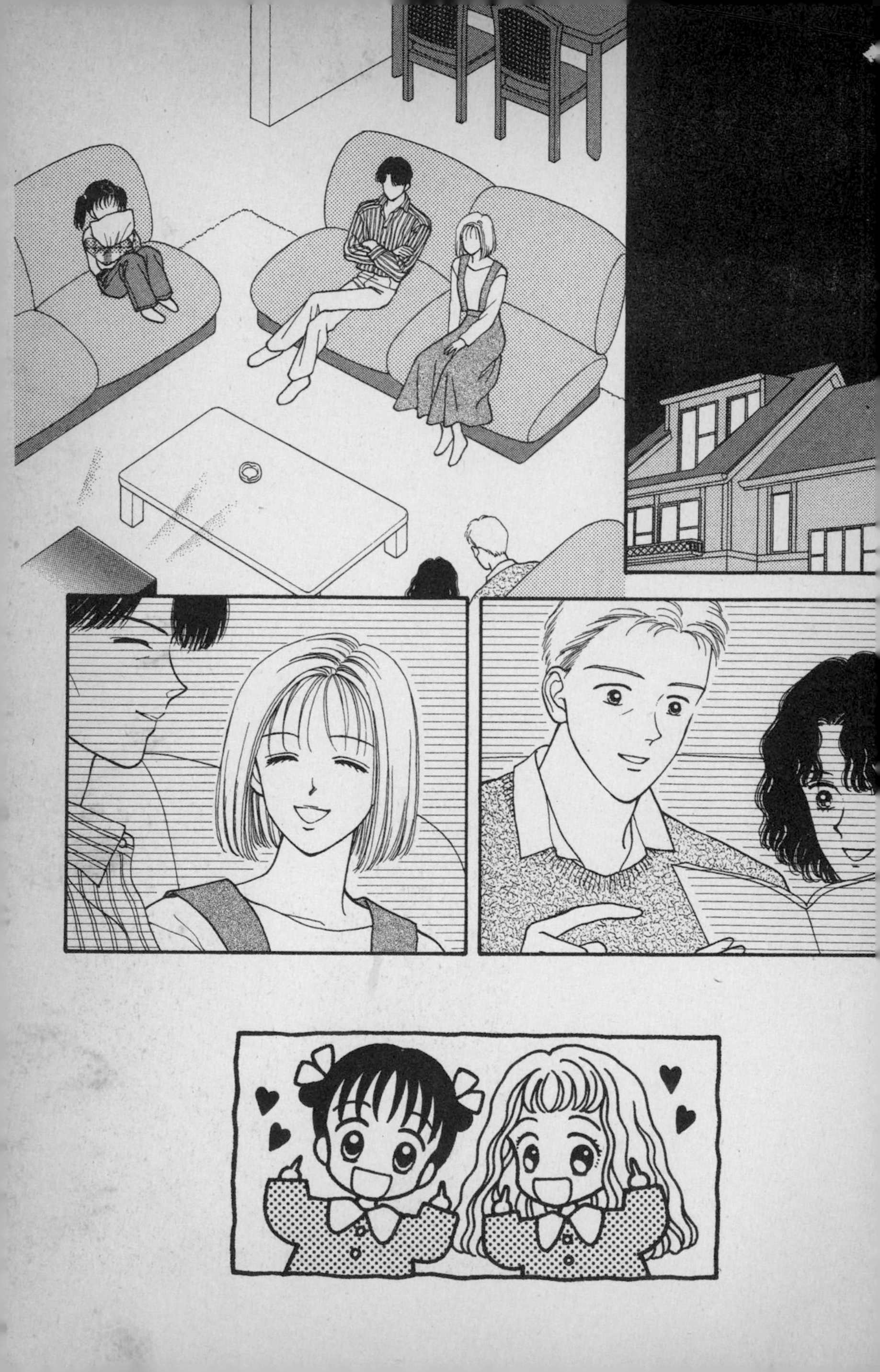

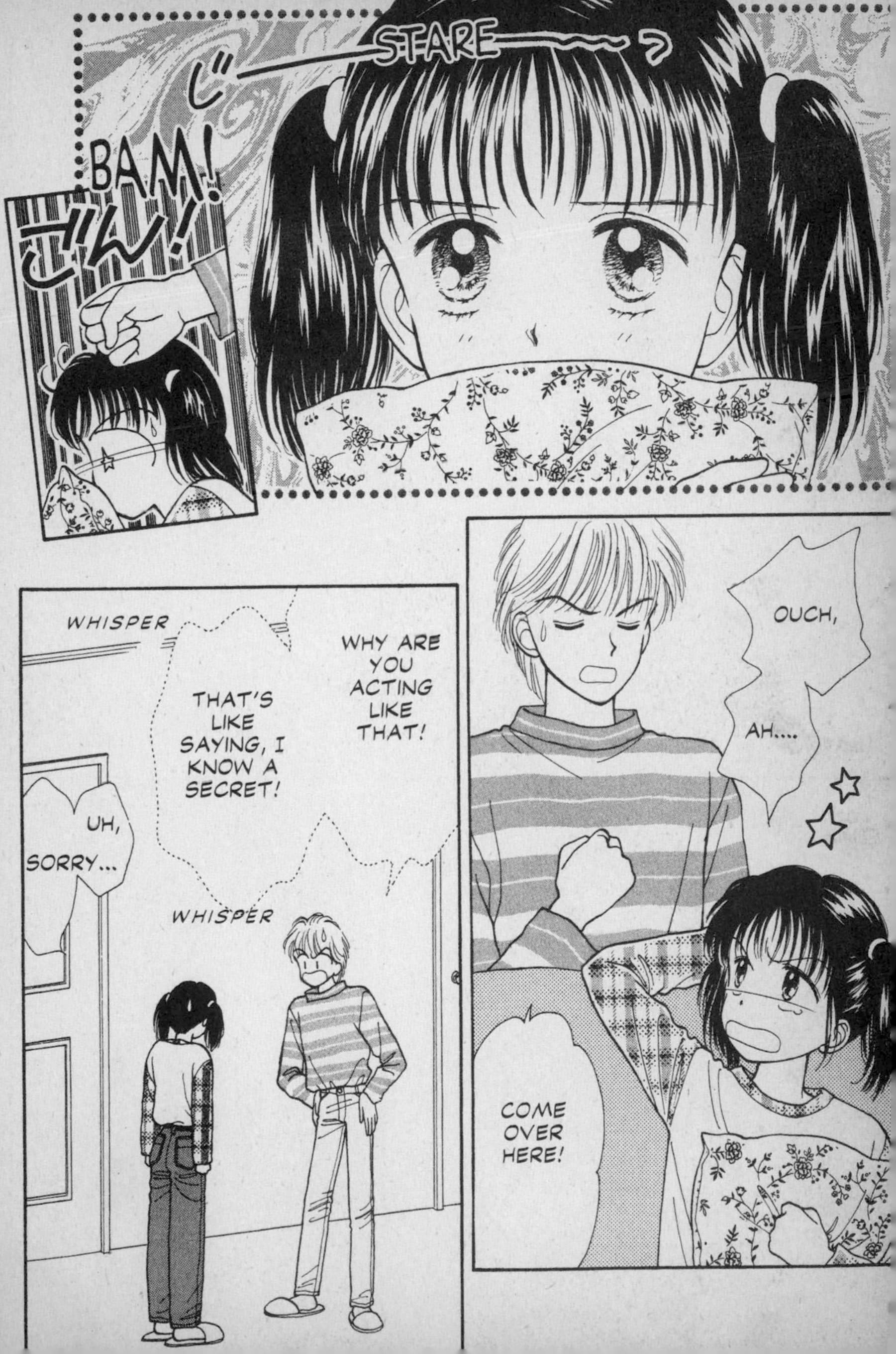
じ——STARE——っ
BAM!
ごん!
OUCH,
AH....
COME OVER HERE!
WHY ARE YOU ACTING LIKE THAT!
THAT'S LIKE SAYING, I KNOW A SECRET!
WHISPER
WHISPER
UH, SORRY...

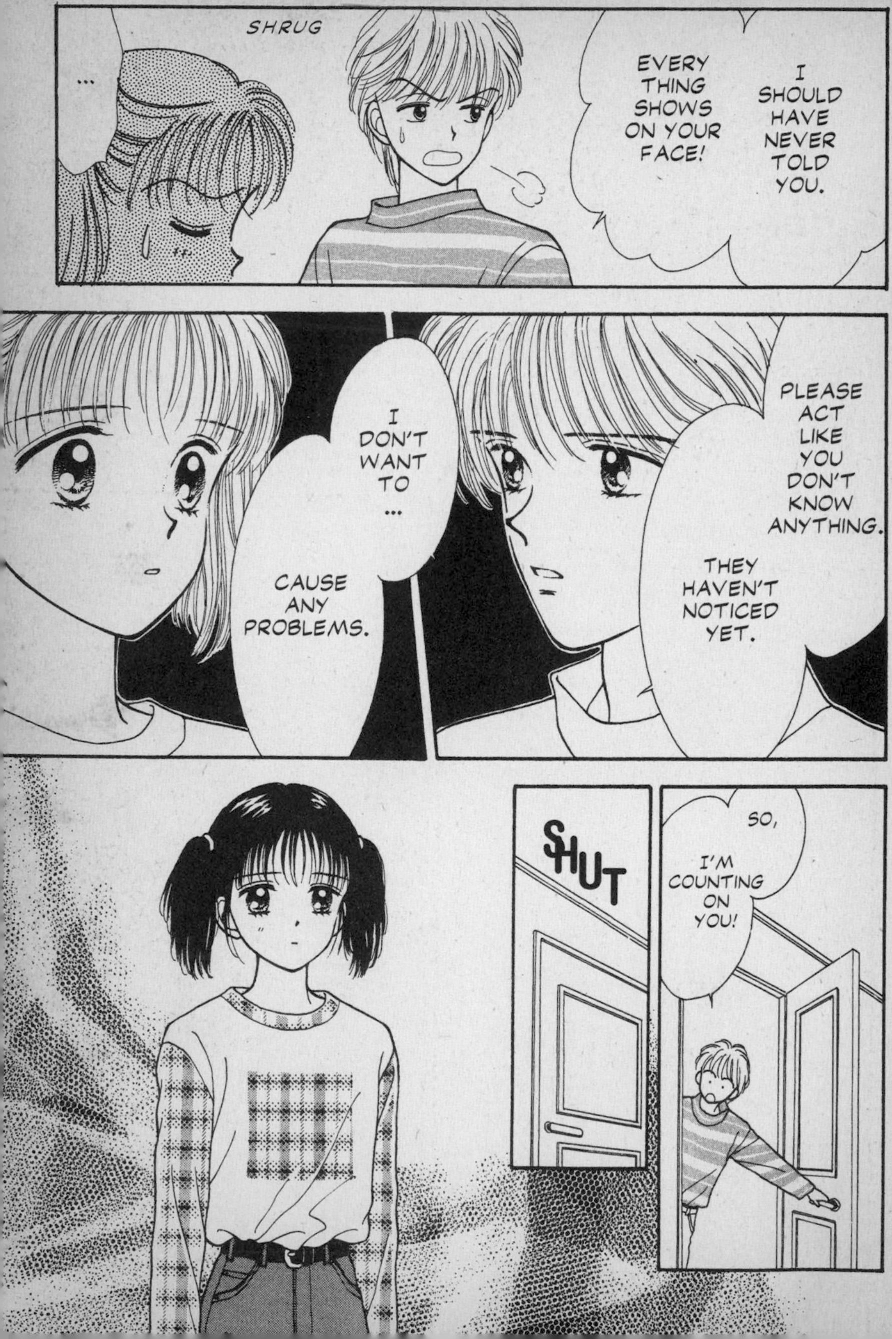
I SHOULD HAVE NEVER TOLD YOU.
EVERY THING SHOWS ON YOUR FACE!
SHRUG
...
PLEASE ACT LIKE YOU DON'T KNOW ANYTHING.
THEY HAVEN'T NOTICED YET.
I DON'T WANT TO ...
CAUSE ANY PROBLEMS.
SO,
I'M COUNTING ON YOU!
SHUT

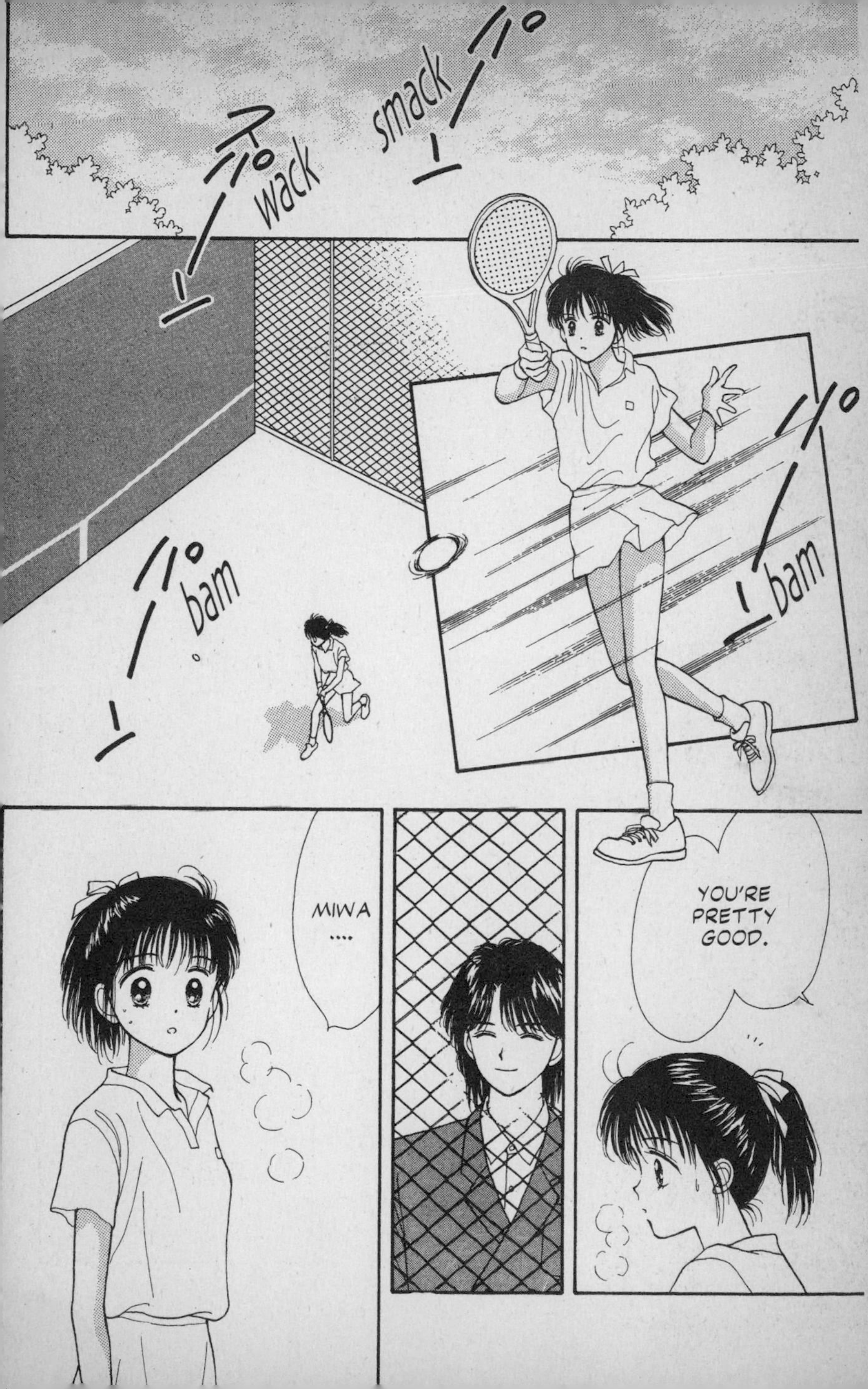
smack
wack
bam
bam
YOU'RE PRETTY GOOD.
MIWA ....

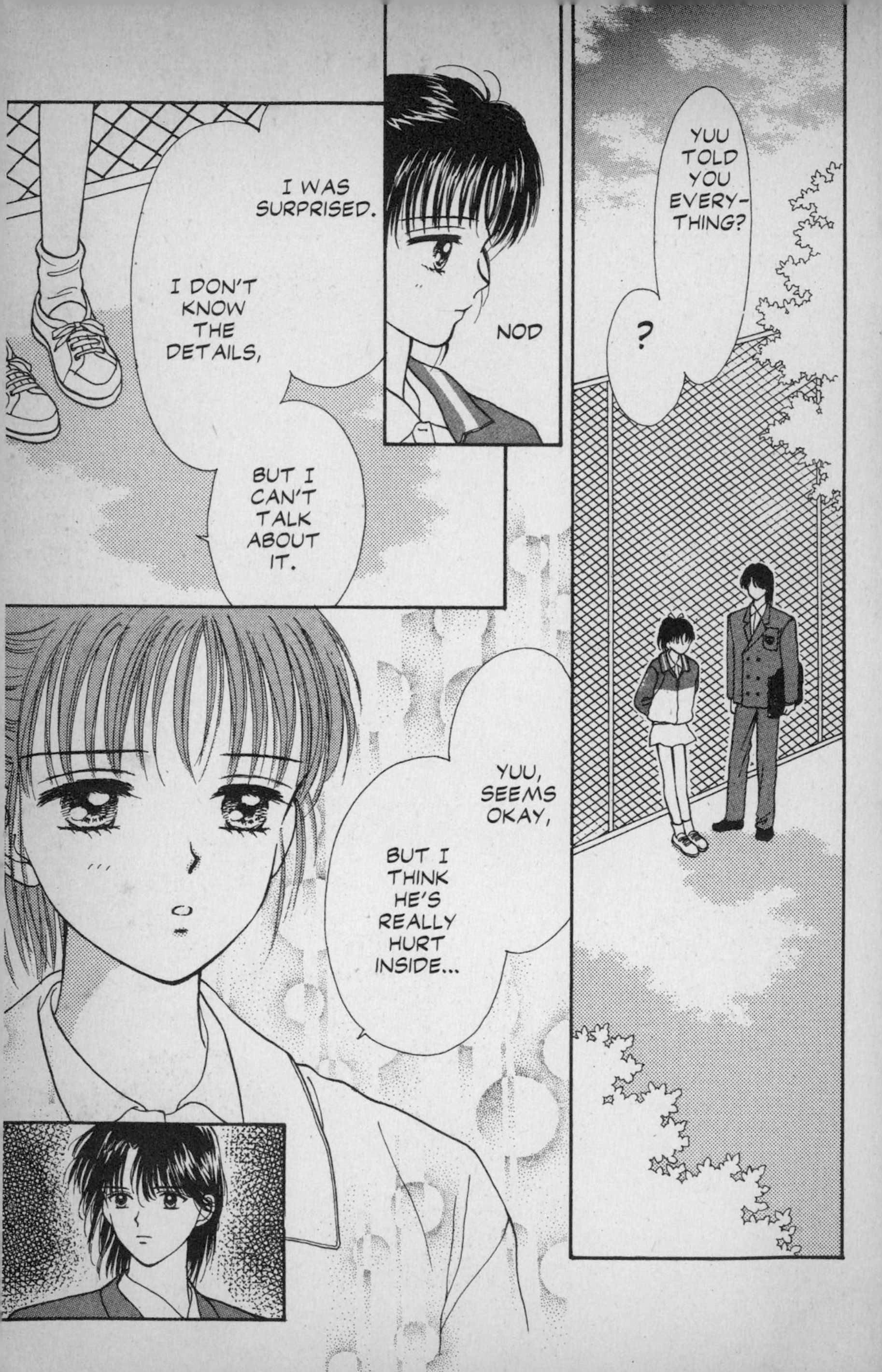
YUU TOLD YOU EVERY-THING?
?
NOD
I WAS SURPRISED.
I DON'T KNOW THE DETAILS,
BUT I CAN'T TALK ABOUT IT.
YUU, SEEMS OKAY,
BUT I THINK HE'S REALLY HURT INSIDE...

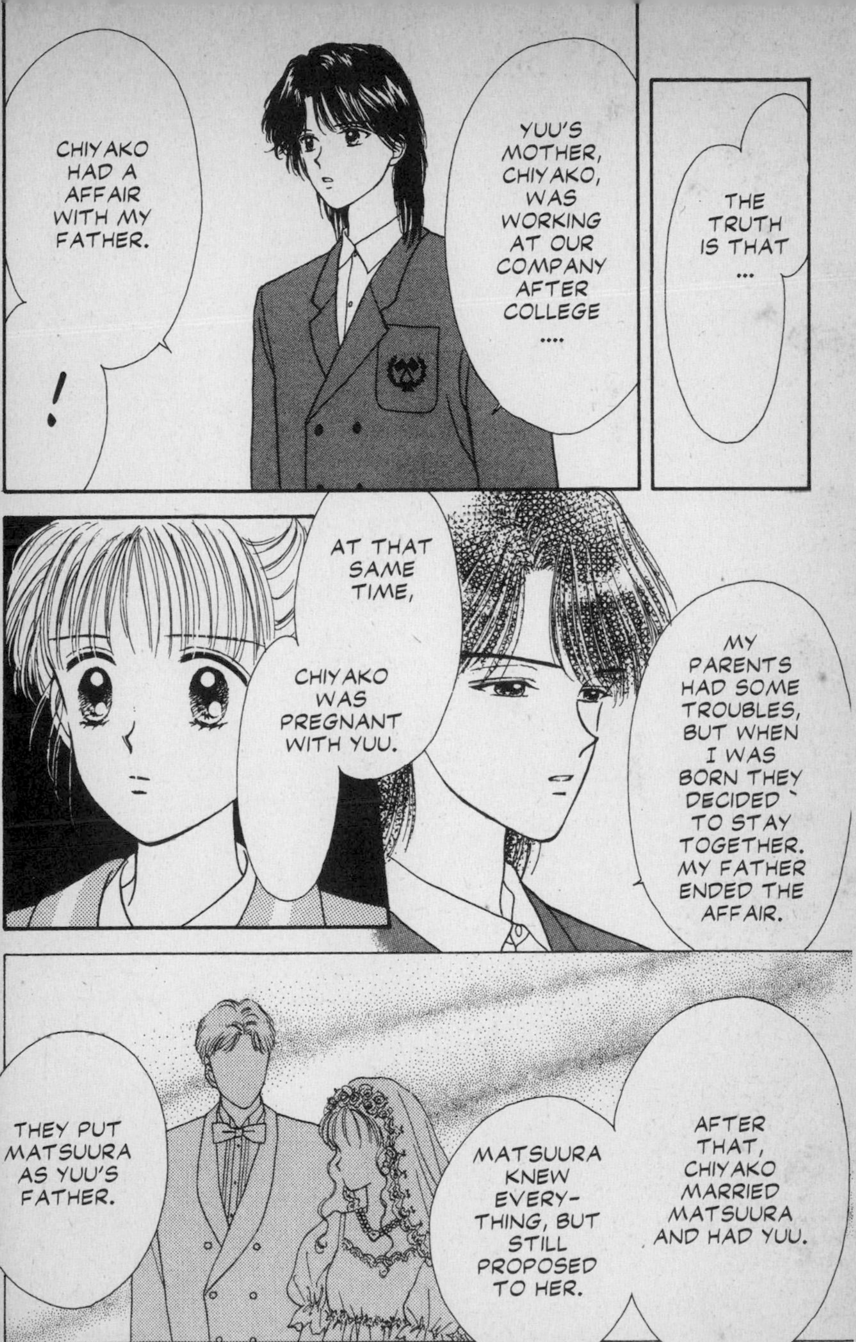
THE TRUTH IS THAT ...
YUU'S MOTHER, CHIYAKO, WAS WORKING AT OUR COMPANY AFTER COLLEGE ....
CHIYAKO HAD A AFFAIR WITH MY FATHER.
!
MY PARENTS HAD SOME TROUBLES, BUT WHEN I WAS BORN THEY DECIDED TO STAY TOGETHER. MY FATHER ENDED THE AFFAIR.
AT THAT SAME TIME,
CHIYAKO WAS PREGNANT WITH YUU.
AFTER THAT, CHIYAKO MARRIED MATSUURA AND HAD YUU.
MATSUURA KNEW EVERY-THING, BUT STILL PROPOSED TO HER.
THEY PUT MATSUURA AS YUU'S FATHER.

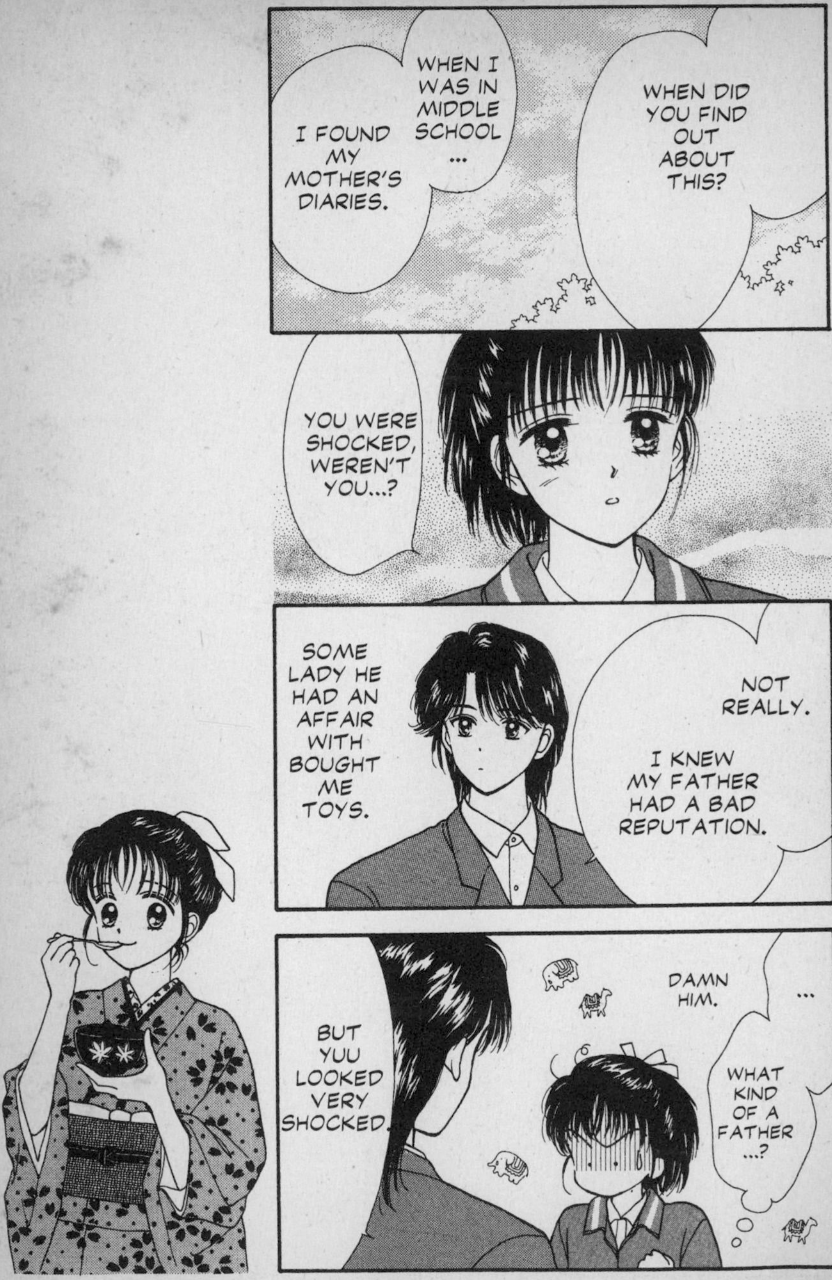
WHEN DID YOU FIND OUT ABOUT THIS?
WHEN I WAS IN MIDDLE SCHOOL ...
I FOUND MY MOTHER'S DIARIES.
YOU WERE SHOCKED, WEREN'T YOU...?
NOT REALLY.
I KNEW MY FATHER HAD A BAD REPUTATION.
SOME LADY HE HAD AN AFFAIR WITH BOUGHT ME TOYS.
...
DAMN HIM.
WHAT KIND OF A FATHER ...?
BUT YUU LOOKED VERY SHOCKED.

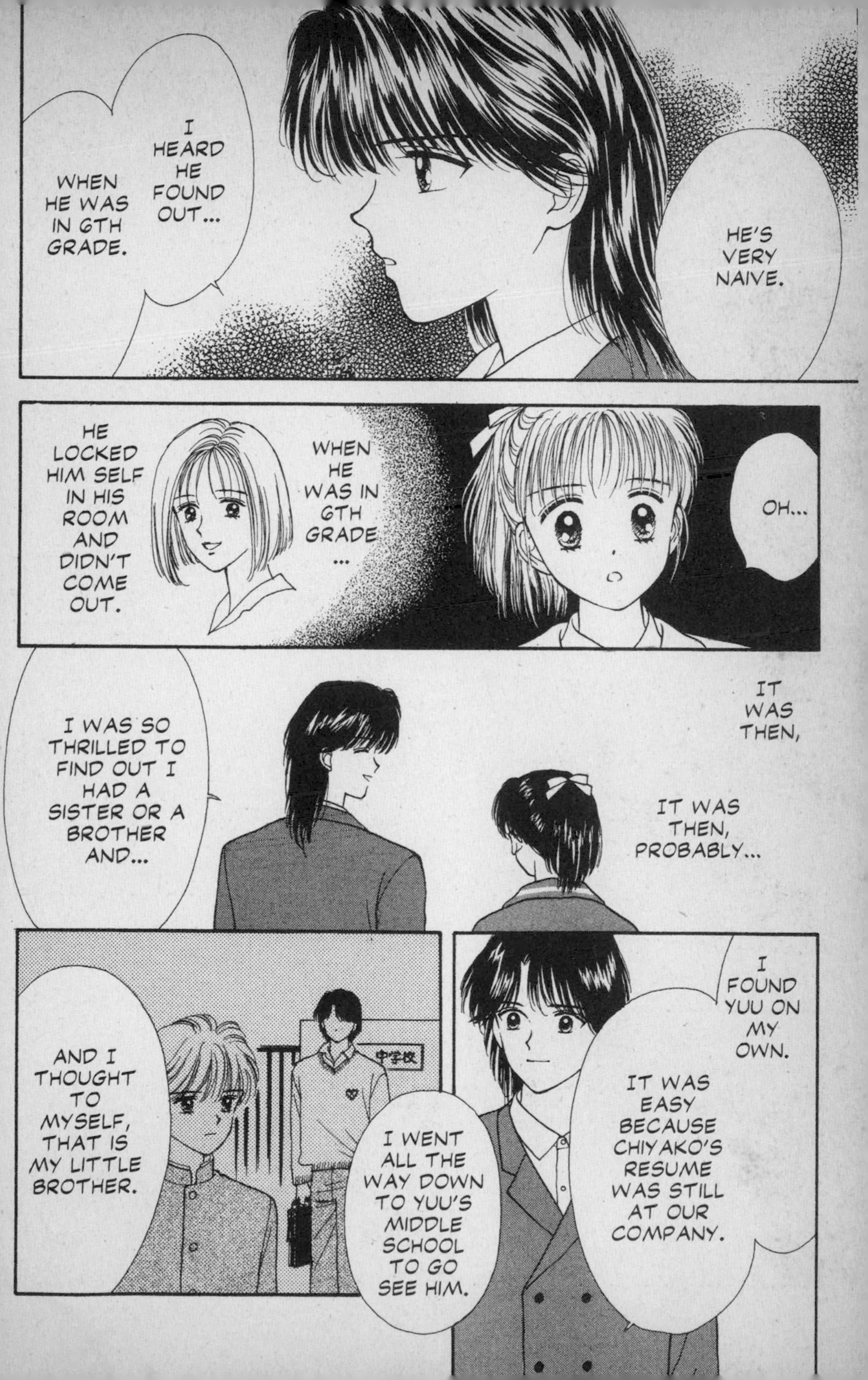
HE'S VERY NAIVE.
I HEARD HE FOUND OUT...
WHEN HE WAS IN 6TH GRADE.
OH...
WHEN HE WAS IN 6TH GRADE...
HE LOCKED HIM SELF IN HIS ROOM AND DIDN'T COME OUT.
IT WAS THEN,
IT WAS THEN, PROBABLY...
I WAS SO THRILLED TO FIND OUT I HAD A SISTER OR A BROTHER AND...
I FOUND YUU ON MY OWN.
IT WAS EASY BECAUSE CHIYAKO'S RESUME WAS STILL AT OUR COMPANY.
I WENT ALL THE WAY DOWN TO YUU'S MIDDLE SCHOOL TO GO SEE HIM.
中学校
AND I THOUGHT TO MYSELF, THAT IS MY LITTLE BROTHER.

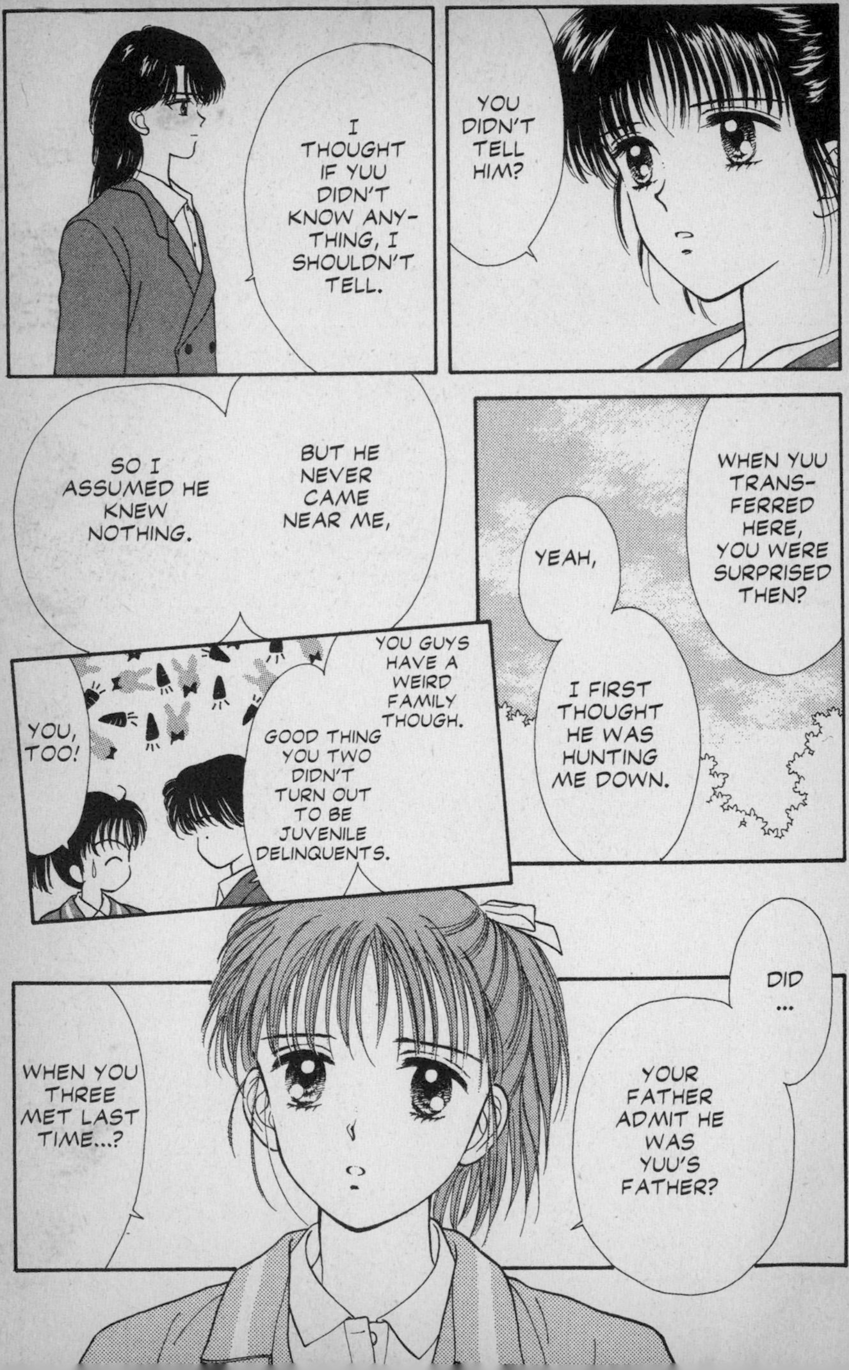
YOU DIDN'T TELL HIM?
I THOUGHT IF YUU DIDN'T KNOW ANYTHING, I SHOULDN'T TELL.
WHEN YUU TRANSFERRED HERE, YOU WERE SURPRISED THEN?
YEAH,
I FIRST THOUGHT HE WAS HUNTING ME DOWN.
BUT HE NEVER CAME NEAR ME,
SO I ASSUMED HE KNEW NOTHING.
YOU GUYS HAVE A WEIRD FAMILY THOUGH.
GOOD THING YOU TWO DIDN'T TURN OUT TO BE JUVENILE DELINQUENTS.
YOU, TOO!
DID ...
YOUR FATHER ADMIT HE WAS YUU'S FATHER?
WHEN YOU THREE MET LAST TIME...?

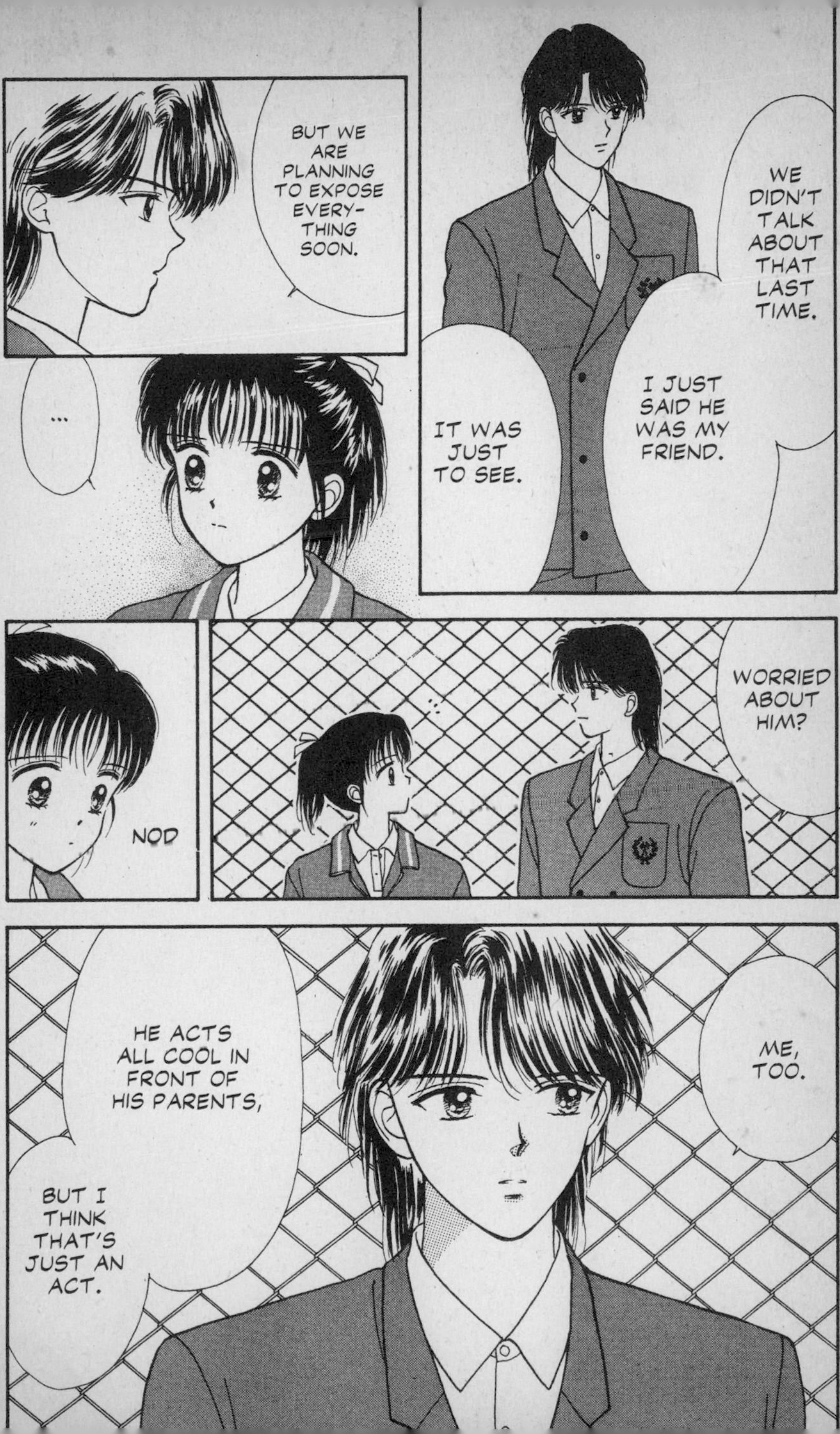
WE DIDN'T TALK ABOUT THAT LAST TIME.
I JUST SAID HE WAS MY FRIEND.
IT WAS JUST TO SEE.
BUT WE ARE PLANNING TO EXPOSE EVERY-THING SOON.
...
WORRIED ABOUT HIM?
NOD
ME, TOO.
HE ACTS ALL COOL IN FRONT OF HIS PARENTS,
BUT I THINK THAT'S JUST AN ACT.

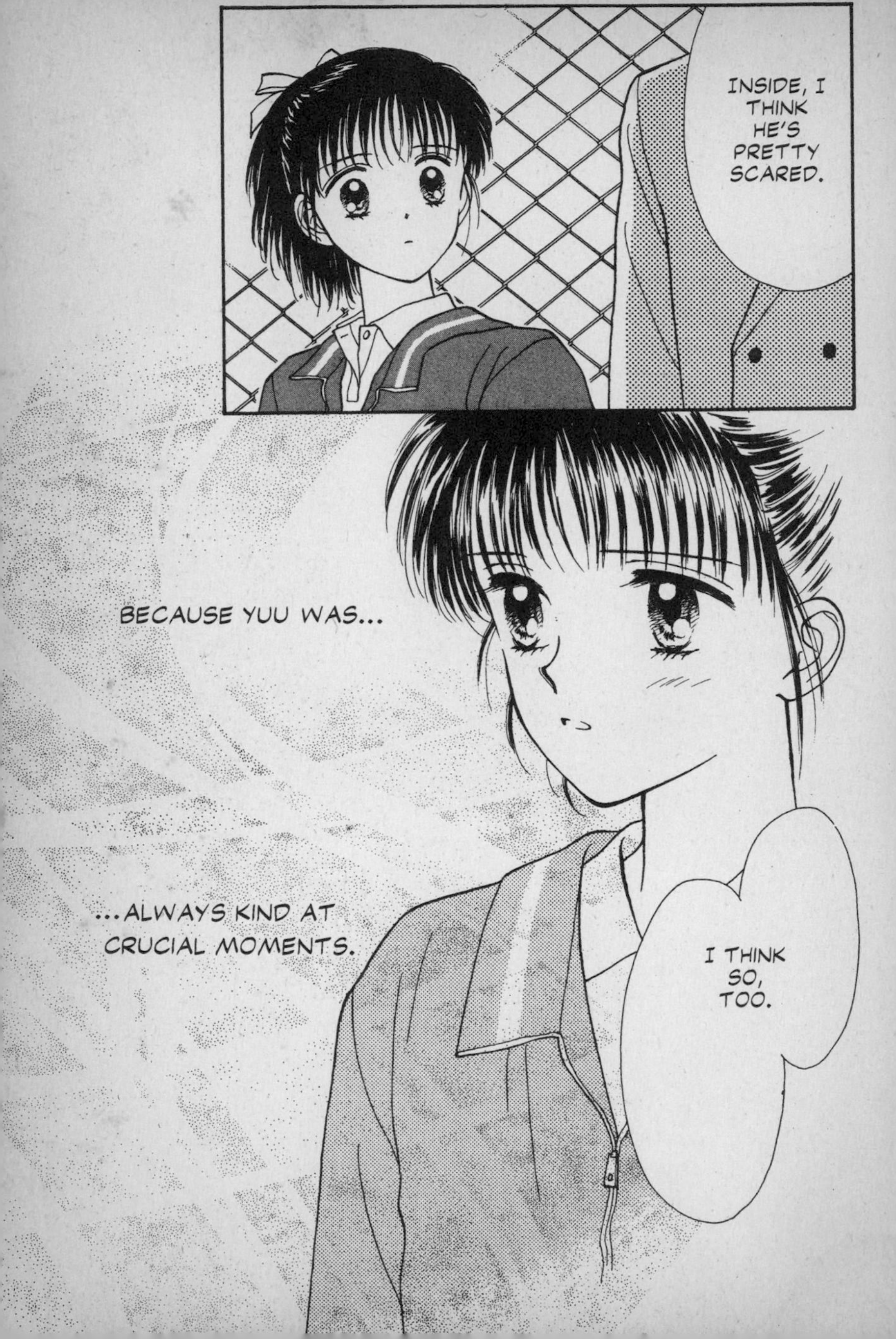
INSIDE, I THINK HE'S PRETTY SCARED.
BECAUSE YUU WAS...
...ALWAYS KIND AT CRUCIAL MOMENTS.
I THINK SO, TOO.

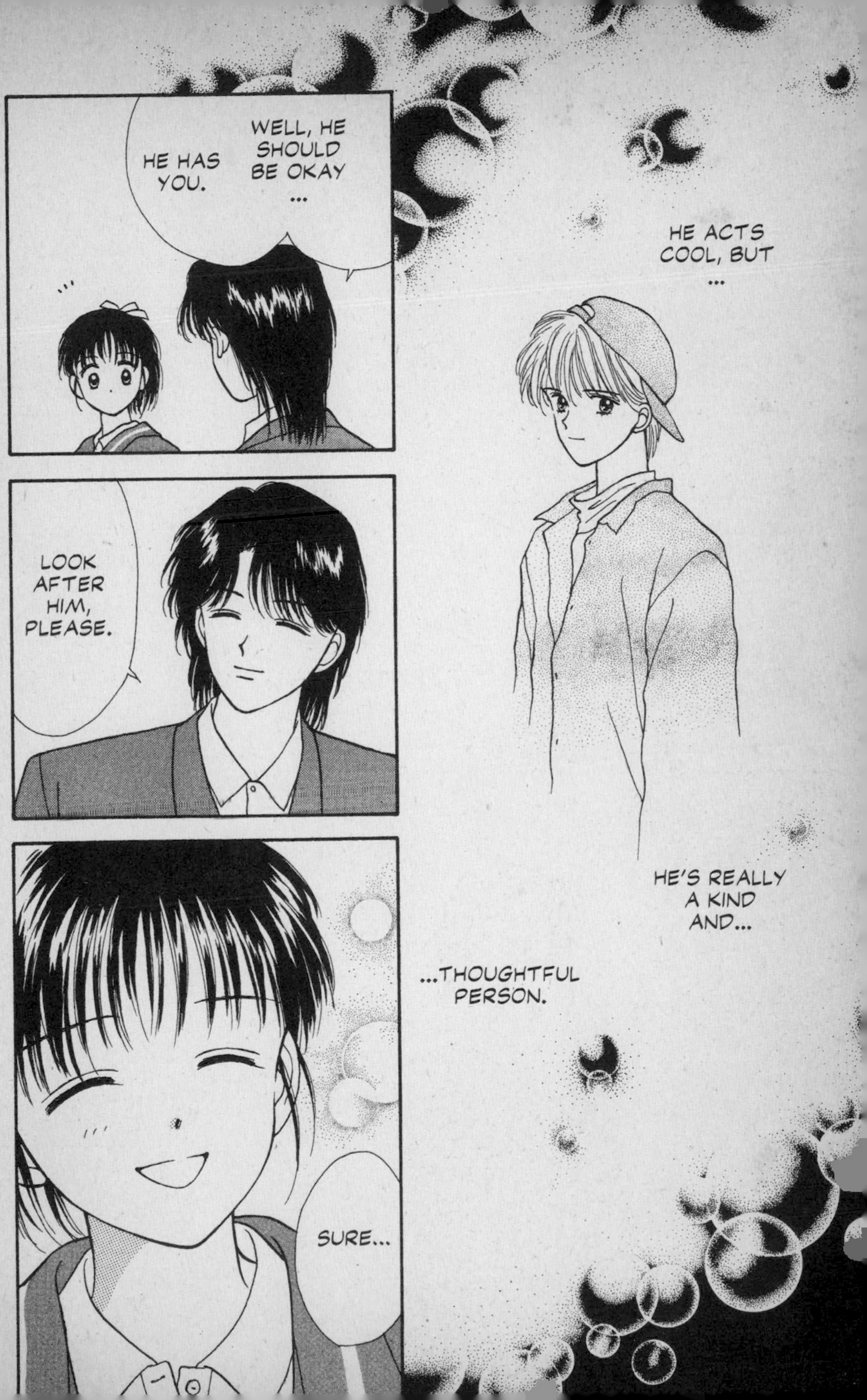
HE ACTS COOL, BUT ...
HE'S REALLY A KIND AND...
...THOUGHTFUL PERSON.
WELL, HE SHOULD BE OKAY ...
HE HAS YOU.
LOOK AFTER HIM, PLEASE.
SURE...

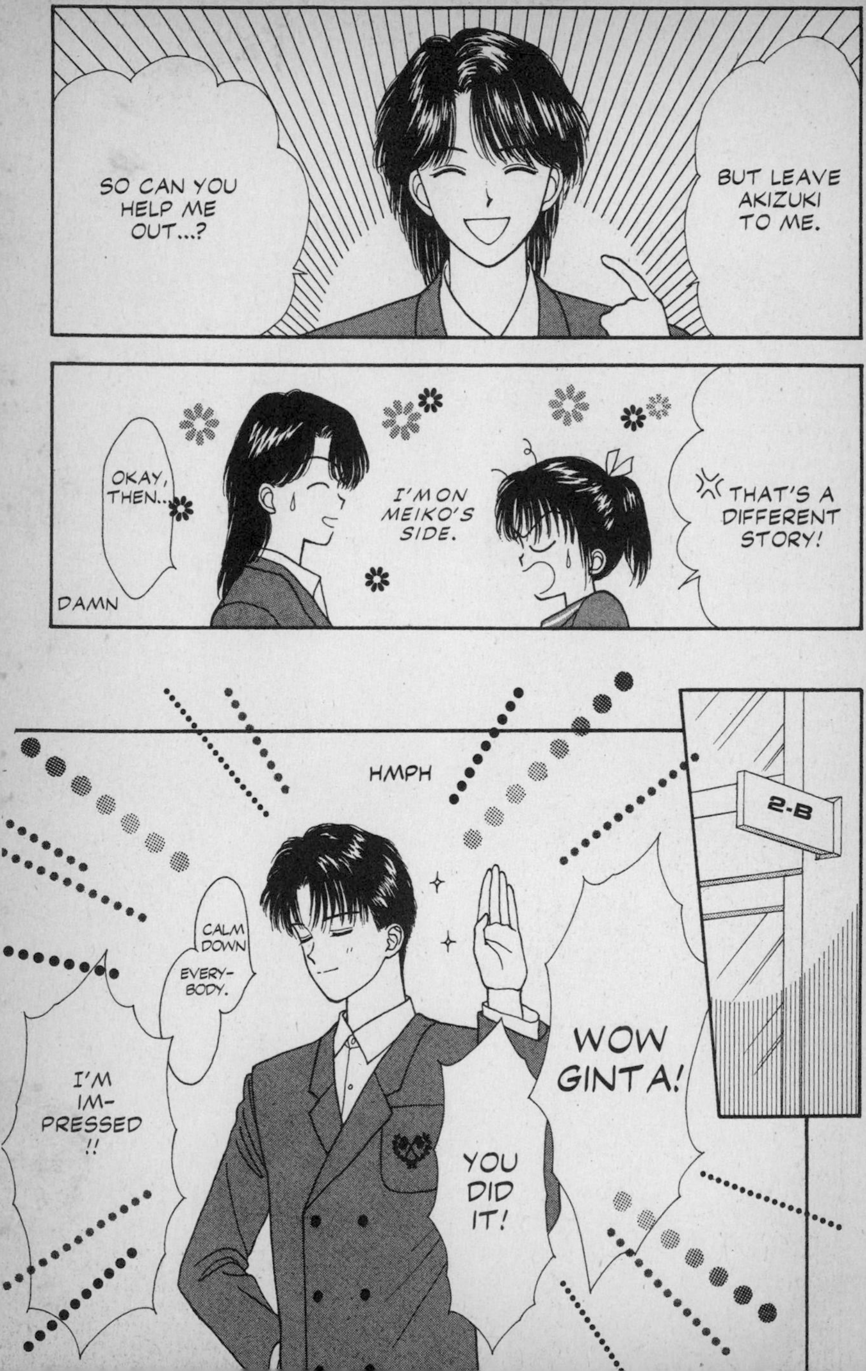
BUT LEAVE AKIZUKI TO ME.
SO CAN YOU HELP ME OUT...?
THAT'S A DIFFERENT STORY!
I'M ON MEIKO'S SIDE.
OKAY, THEN...
DAMN
HMPH
WOW GINTA!
CALM DOWN EVERY-BODY.
I'M IM-PRESSED!!
YOU DID IT!

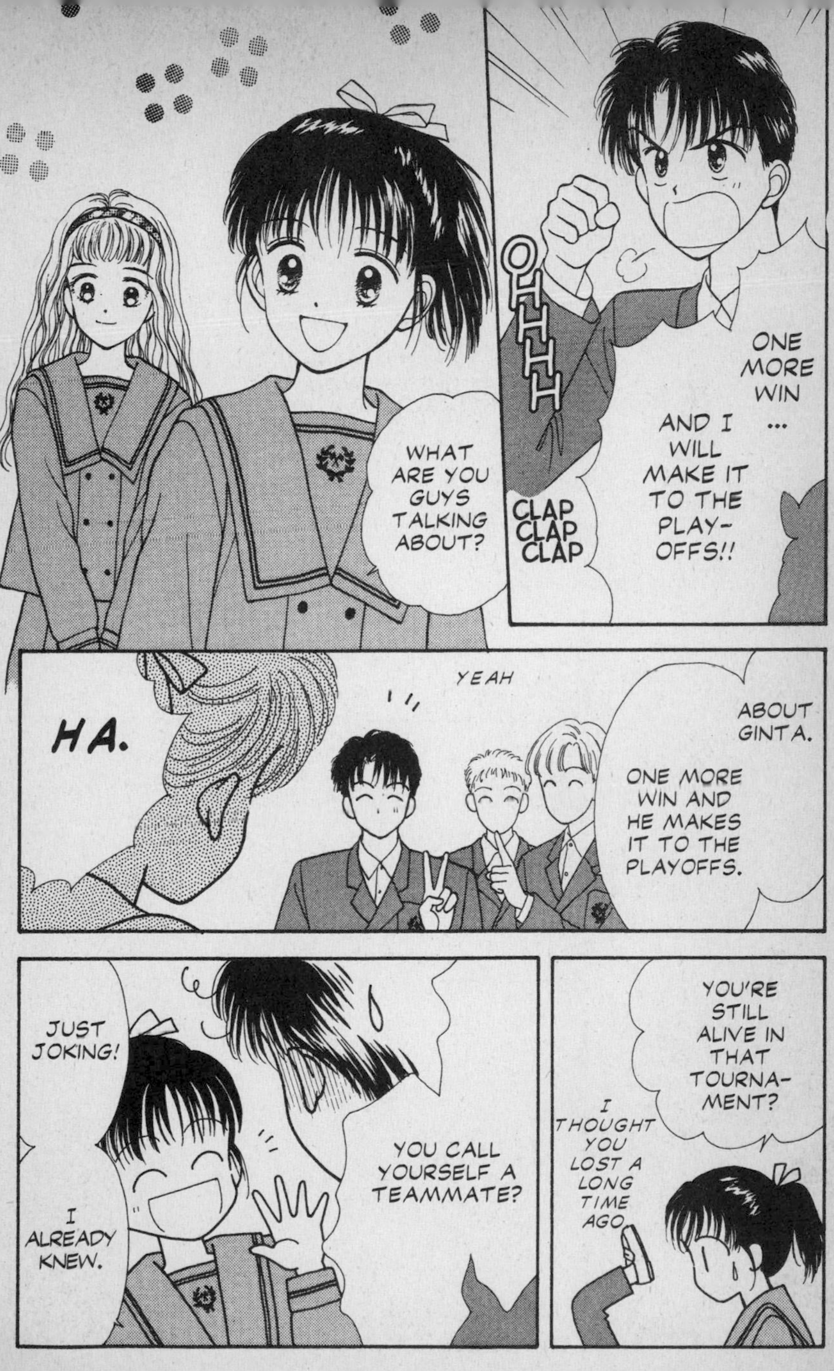
OHHHH
ONE MORE WIN ...
AND I WILL MAKE IT TO THE PLAY-OFFS!!
CLAP CLAP CLAP
WHAT ARE YOU GUYS TALKING ABOUT?
ABOUT GINTA.
ONE MORE WIN AND HE MAKES IT TO THE PLAYOFFS.
YEAH
HA.
YOU'RE STILL ALIVE IN THAT TOURNAMENT?
I THOUGHT YOU LOST A LONG TIME AGO.
YOU CALL YOURSELF A TEAMMATE?
JUST JOKING!
I ALREADY KNEW.

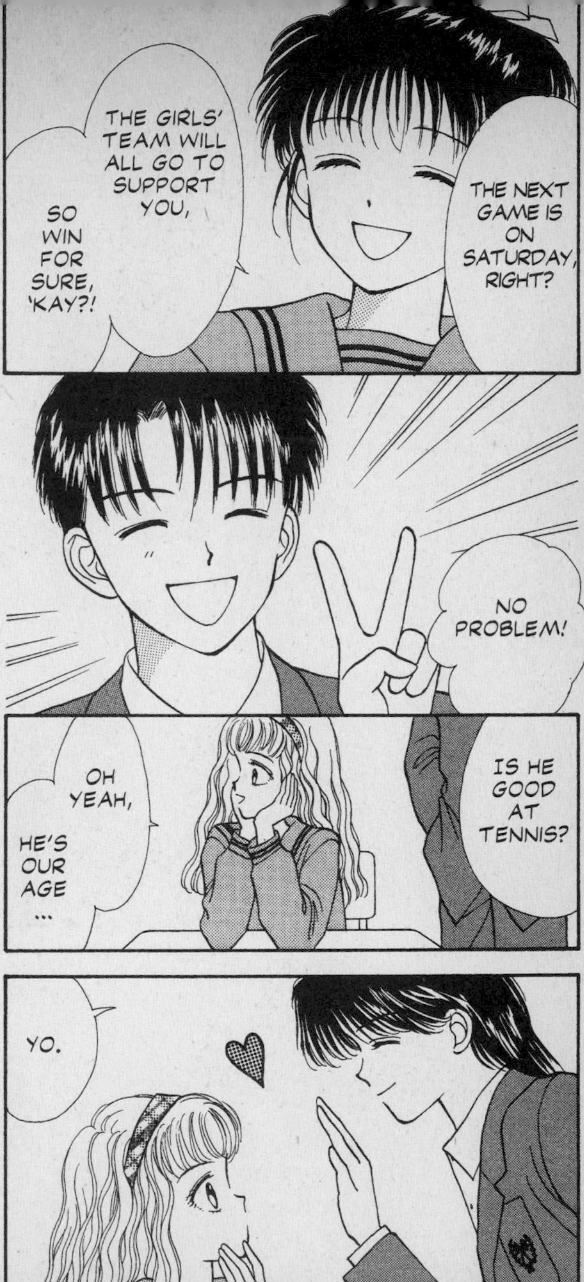
THE NEXT GAME IS ON SATURDAY, RIGHT?
THE GIRLS' TEAM WILL ALL GO TO SUPPORT YOU,
SO WIN FOR SURE, 'KAY?!
NO PROBLEM!
IS HE GOOD AT TENNIS?
OH YEAH,
HE'S OUR AGE ...
YO.

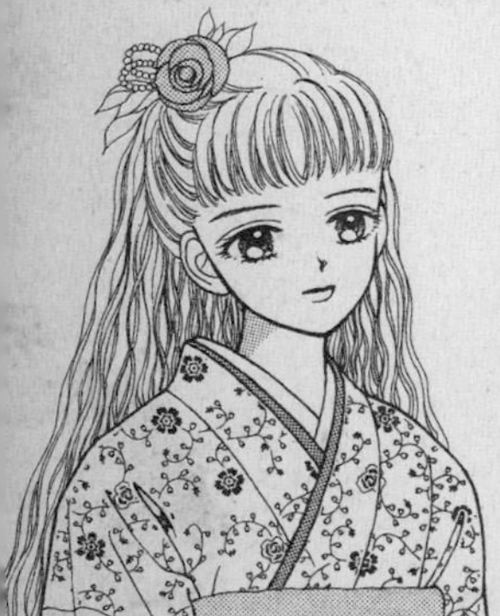

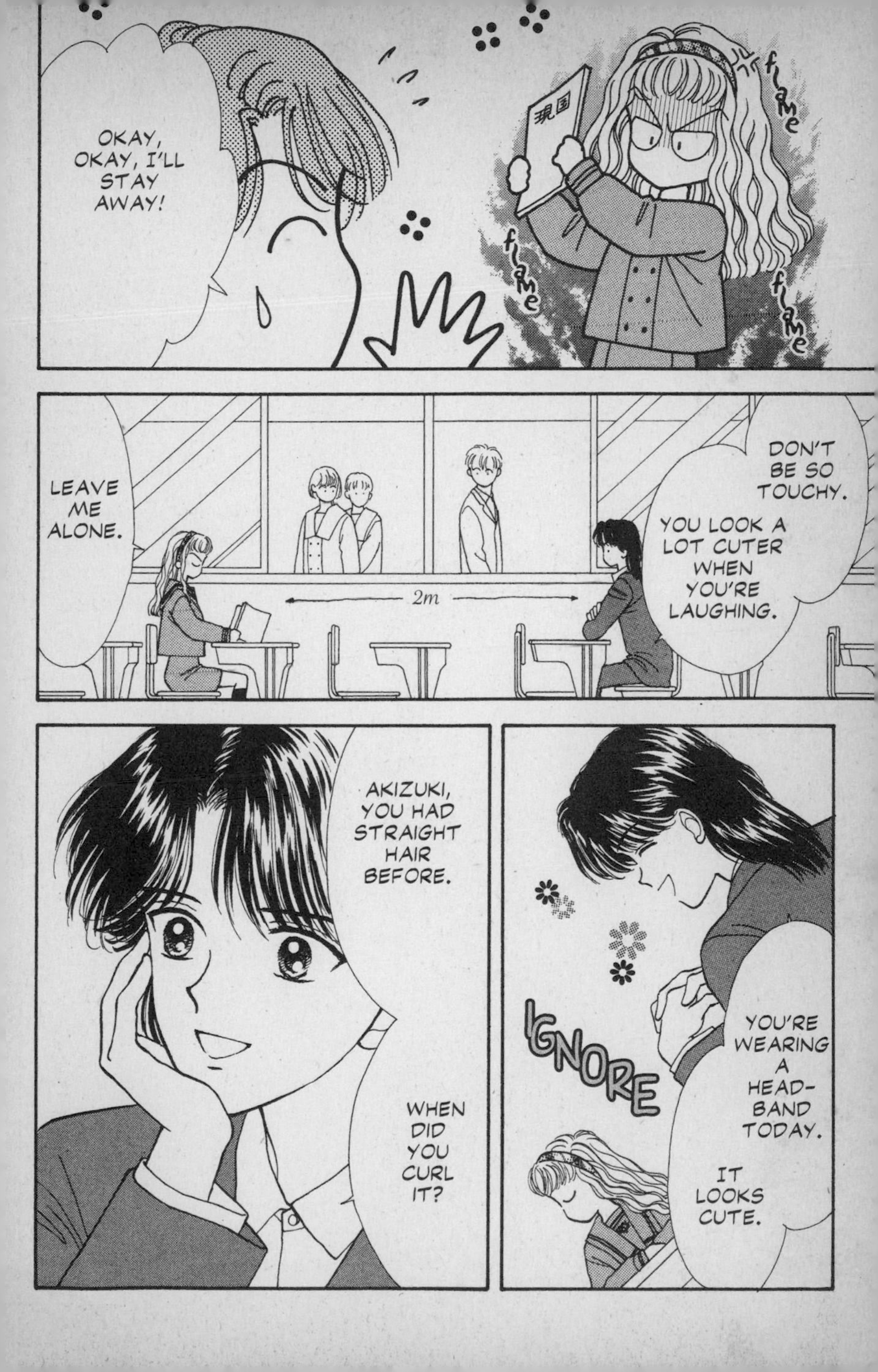
flame
flame
flame
現国
OKAY, OKAY, I'LL STAY AWAY!
DON'T BE SO TOUCHY.
YOU LOOK A LOT CUTER WHEN YOU'RE LAUGHING.
2m
LEAVE ME ALONE.
YOU'RE WEARING A HEAD-BAND TODAY.
IGNORE
IT LOOKS CUTE.
AKIZUKI, YOU HAD STRAIGHT HAIR BEFORE.
WHEN DID YOU CURL IT?

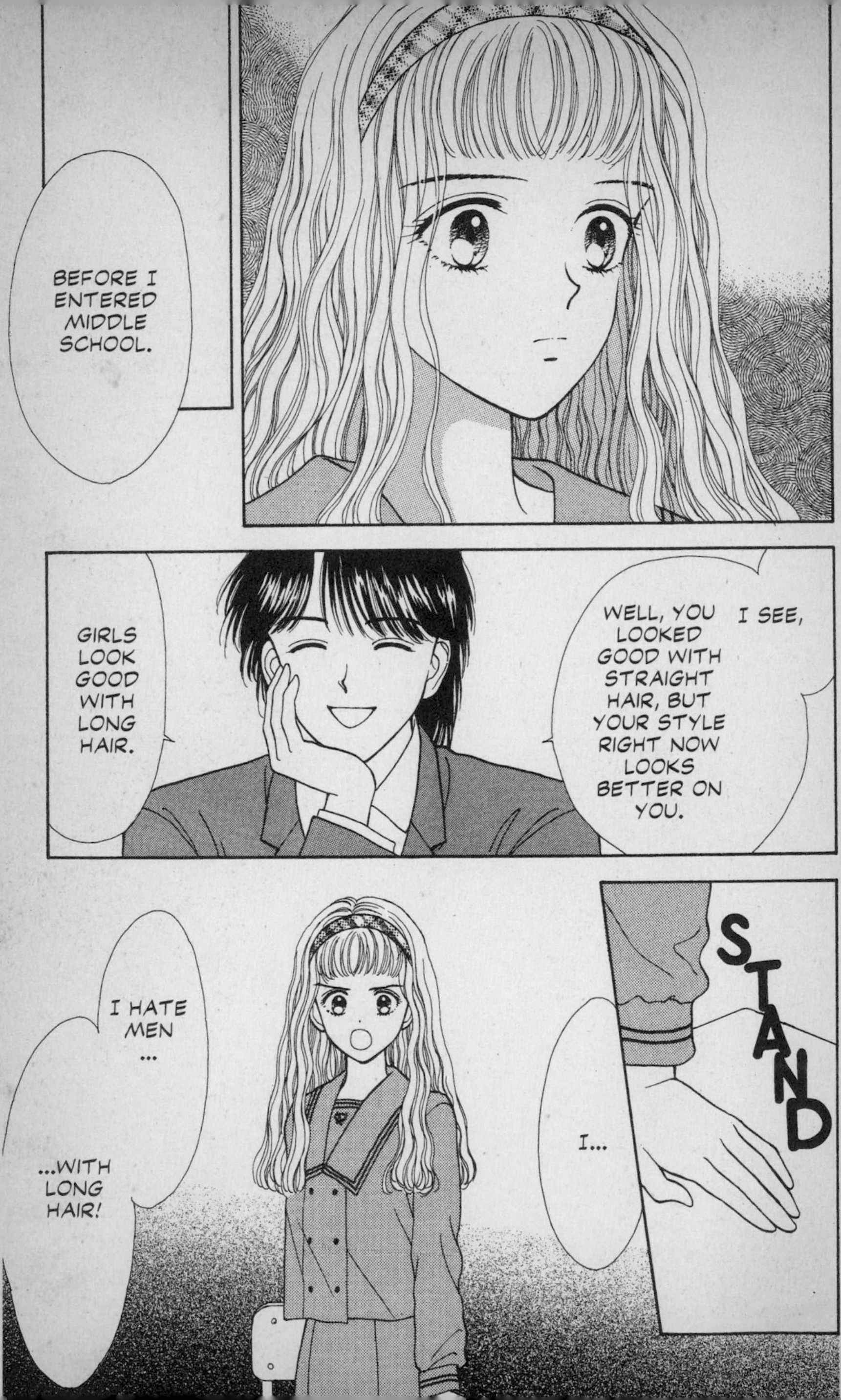
BEFORE I ENTERED MIDDLE SCHOOL.
I SEE,
WELL, YOU LOOKED GOOD WITH STRAIGHT HAIR, BUT YOUR STYLE RIGHT NOW LOOKS BETTER ON YOU.
GIRLS LOOK GOOD WITH LONG HAIR.
STAND
I...
I HATE MEN ...
...WITH LONG HAIR!

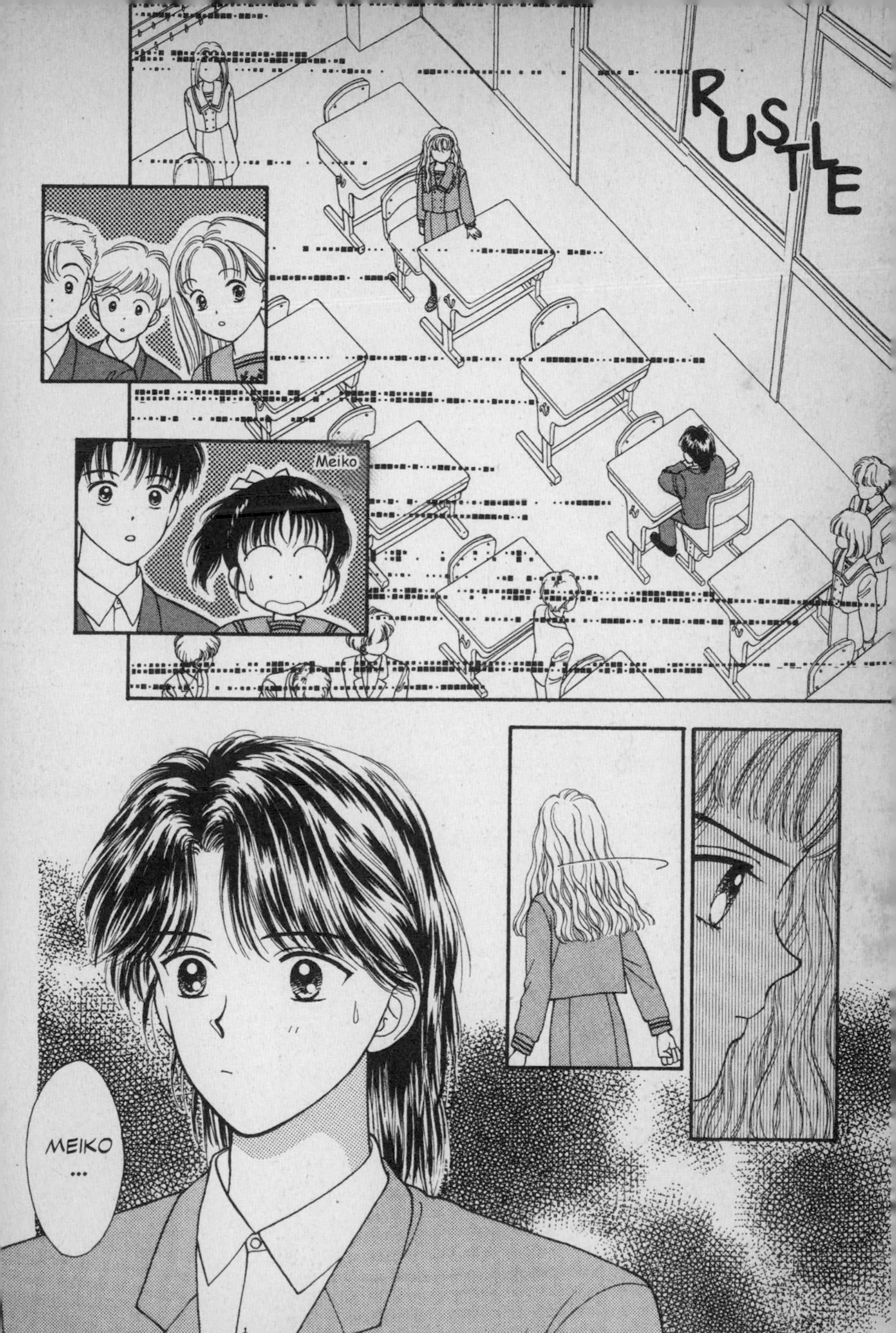
RUSTLE
Meiko
MEIKO ...

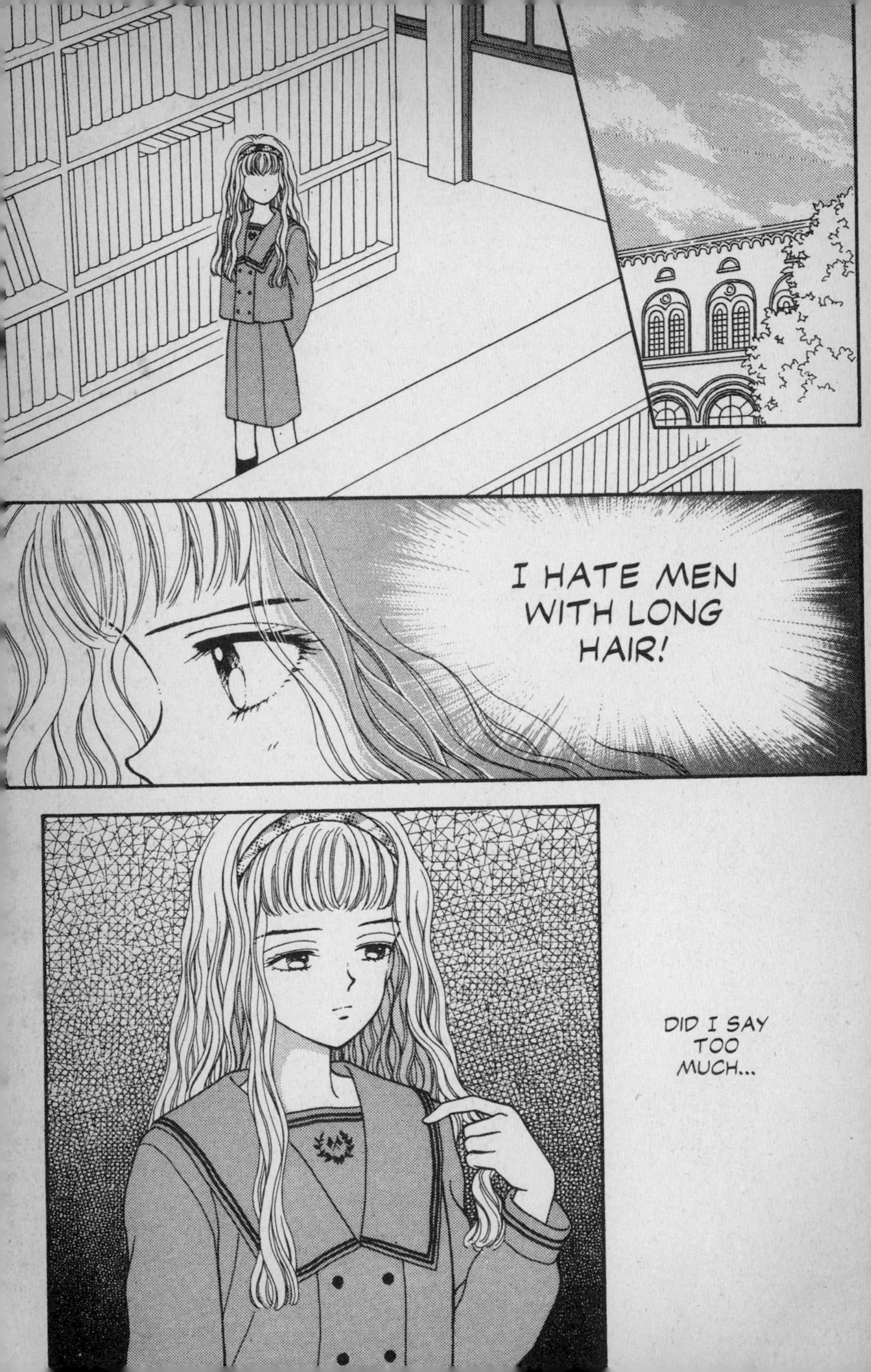
I HATE MEN WITH LONG HAIR!
DID I SAY TOO MUCH...

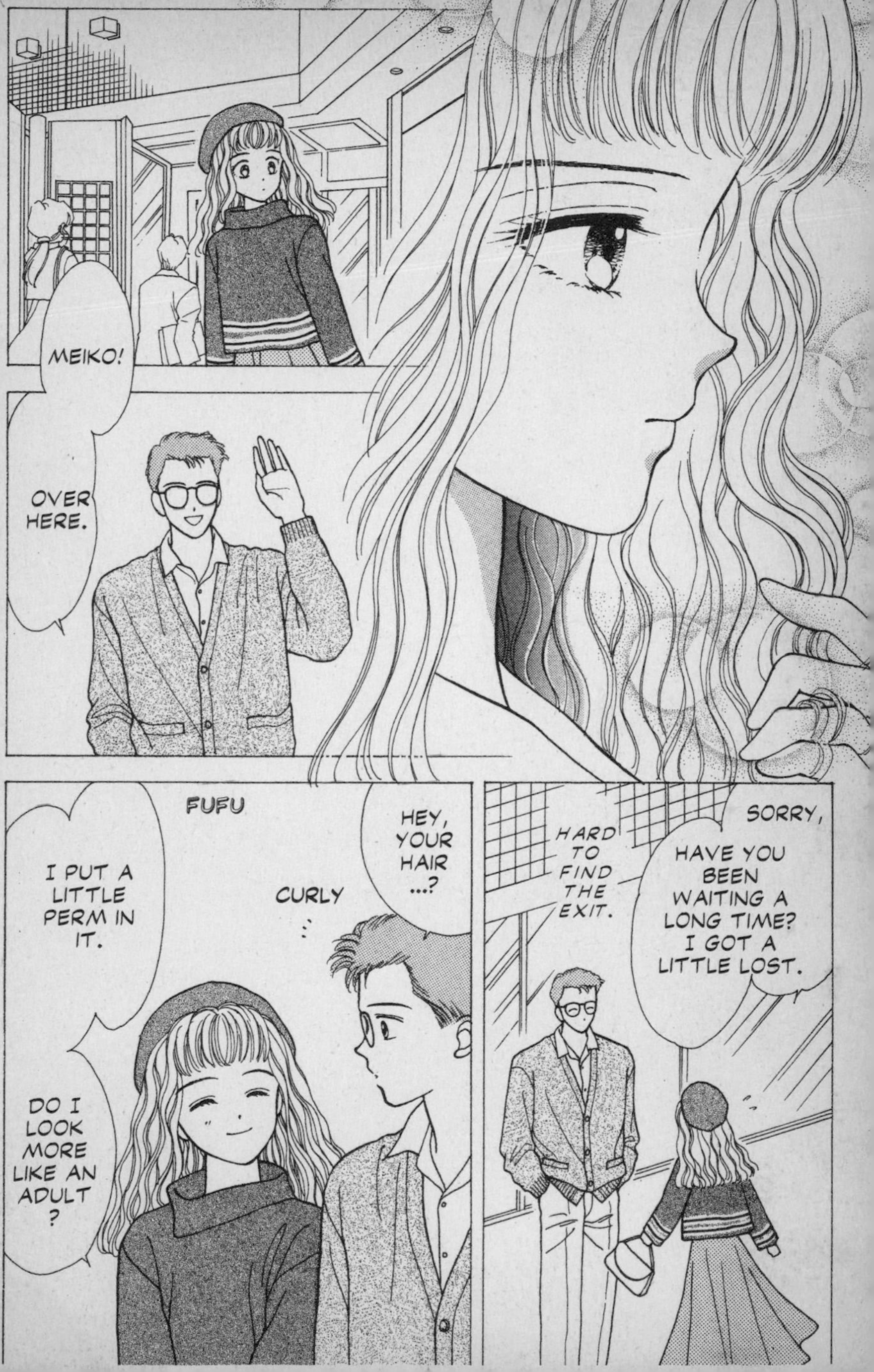
MEIKO!
OVER HERE.
SORRY, HAVE YOU BEEN WAITING A LONG TIME? I GOT A LITTLE LOST.
HARD TO FIND THE EXIT.
HEY, YOUR HAIR ...?
CURLY
FUFU
I PUT A LITTLE PERM IN IT.
DO I LOOK MORE LIKE AN ADULT?

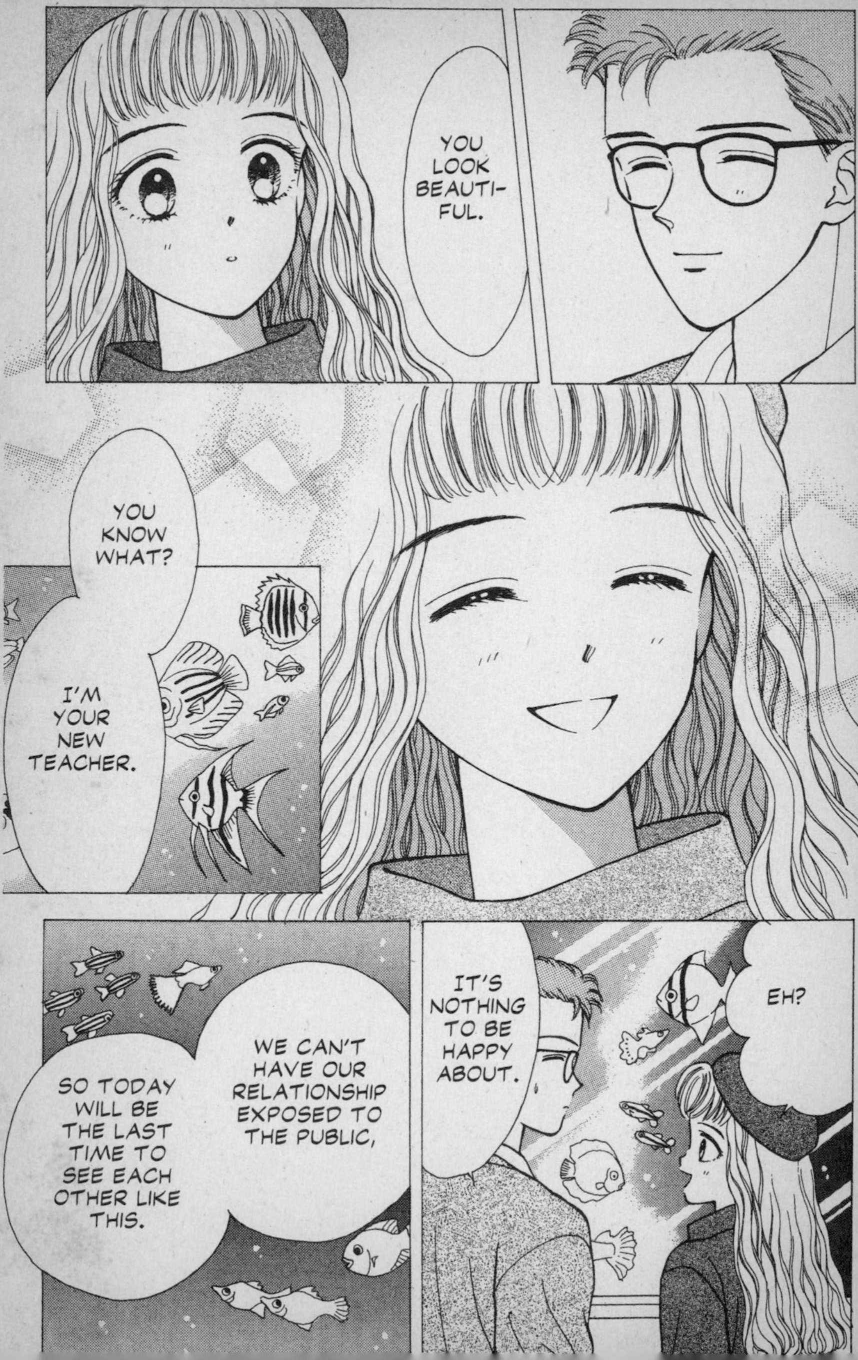
YOU LOOK BEAUTI-FUL.
YOU KNOW WHAT?
I'M YOUR NEW TEACHER.
EH?
IT'S NOTHING TO BE HAPPY ABOUT.
WE CAN'T HAVE OUR RELATIONSHIP EXPOSED TO THE PUBLIC,
SO TODAY WILL BE THE LAST TIME TO SEE EACH OTHER LIKE THIS.

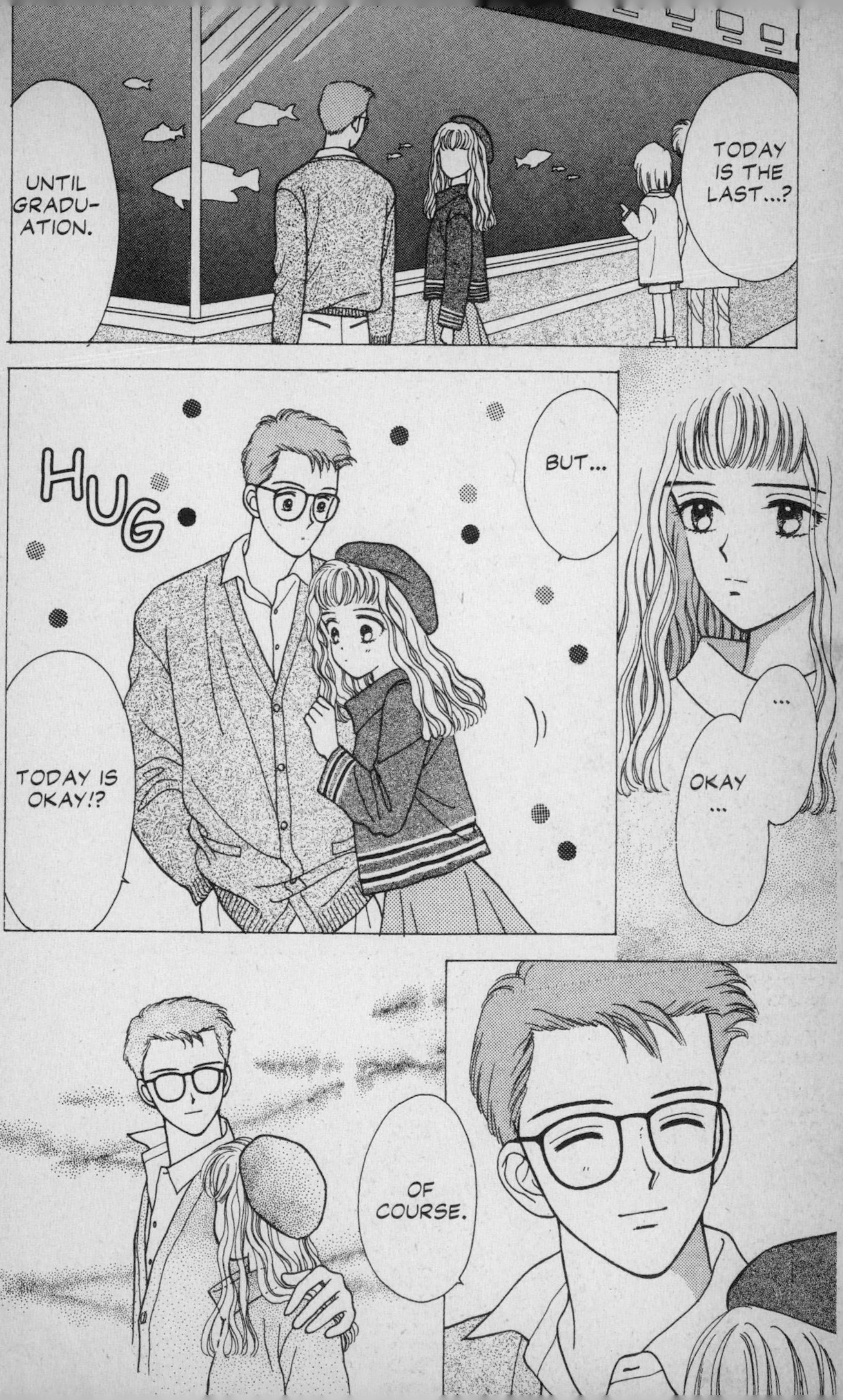
TODAY IS THE LAST...?
UNTIL GRADUATION.
...
OKAY ...
BUT...
HUG
TODAY IS OKAY!?
OF COURSE.

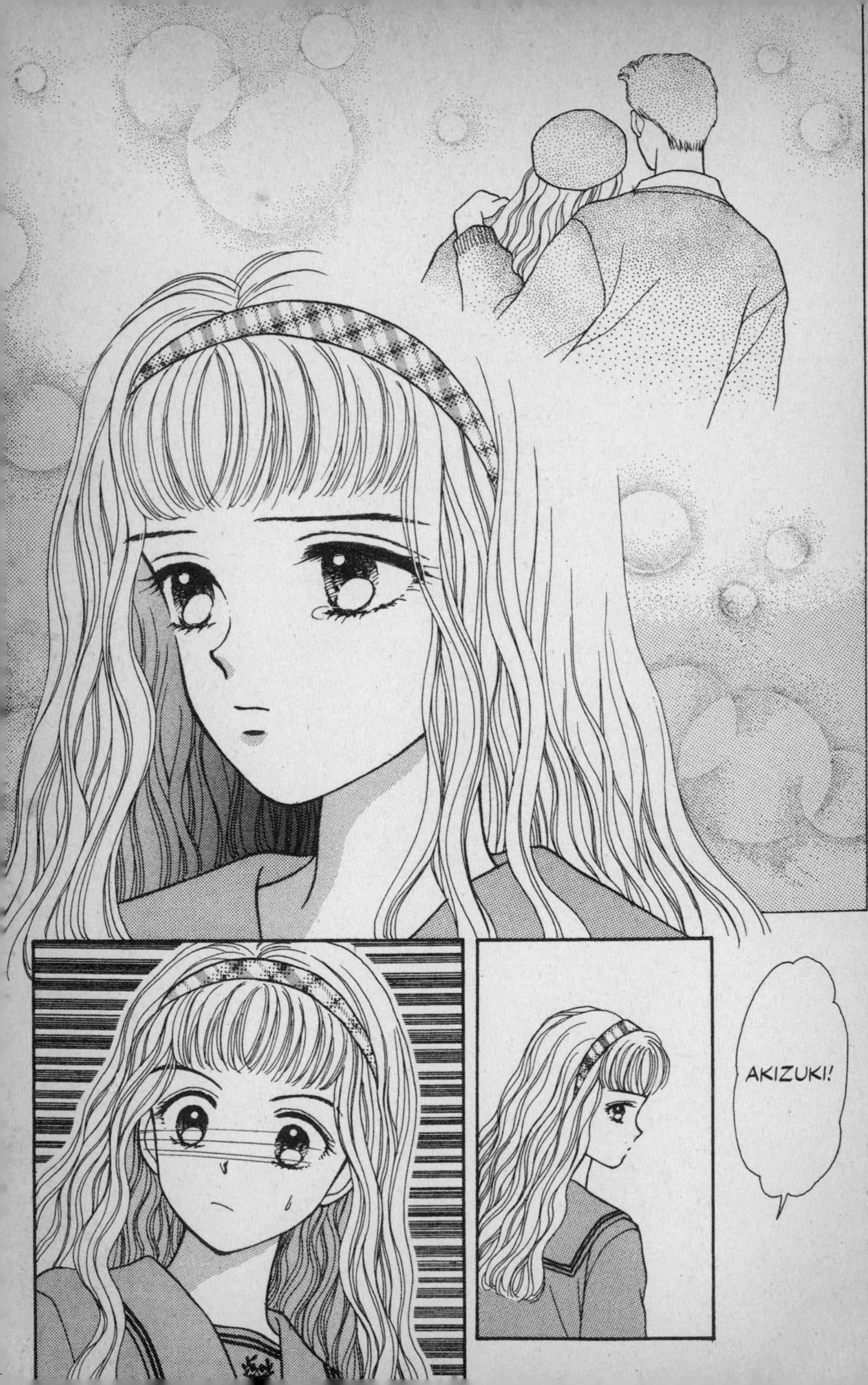
AKIZUKI!

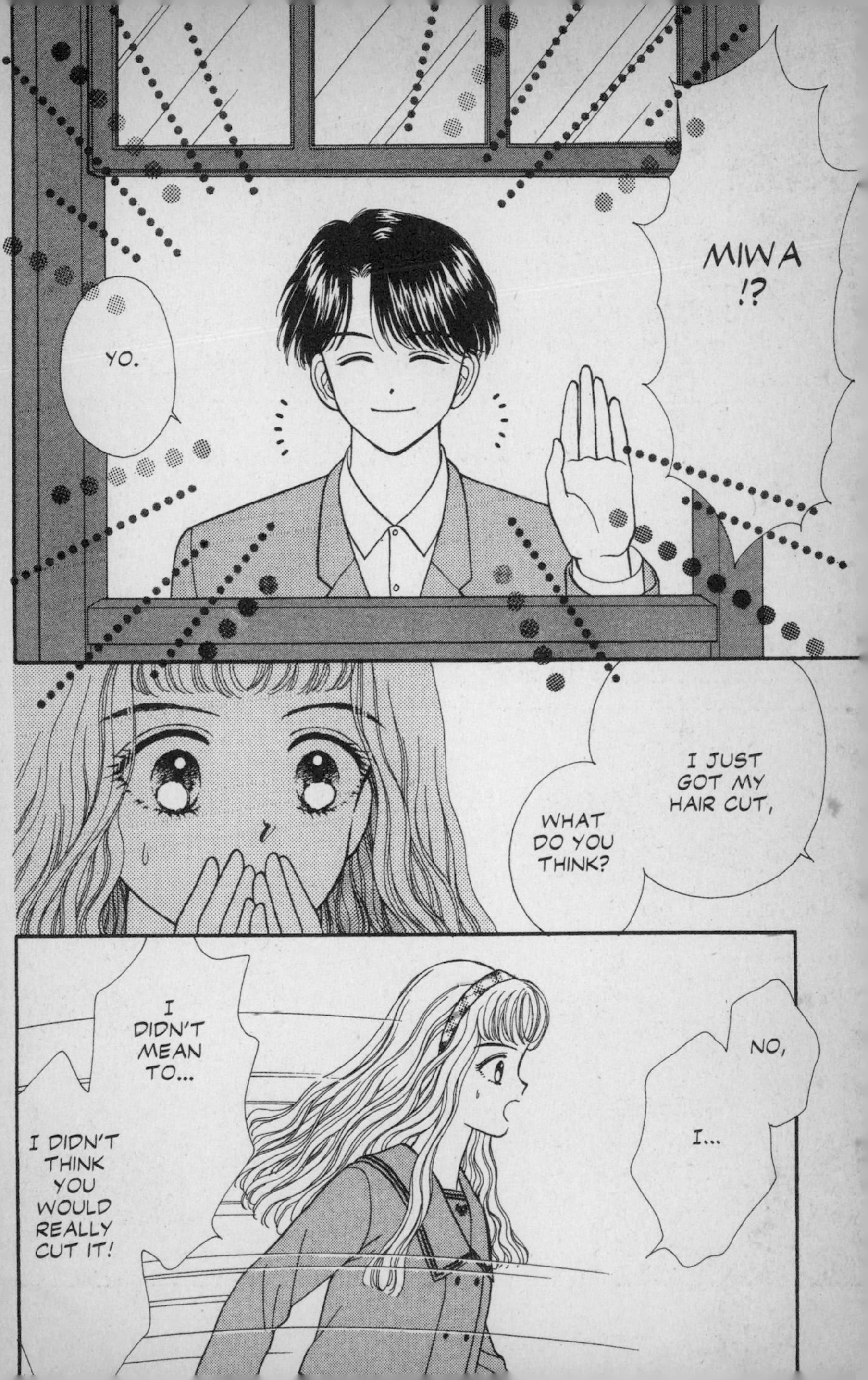
MIWA !?
YO.
I JUST GOT MY HAIR CUT,
WHAT DO YOU THINK?
NO,
I...
I DIDN'T MEAN TO...
I DIDN'T THINK YOU WOULD REALLY CUT IT!

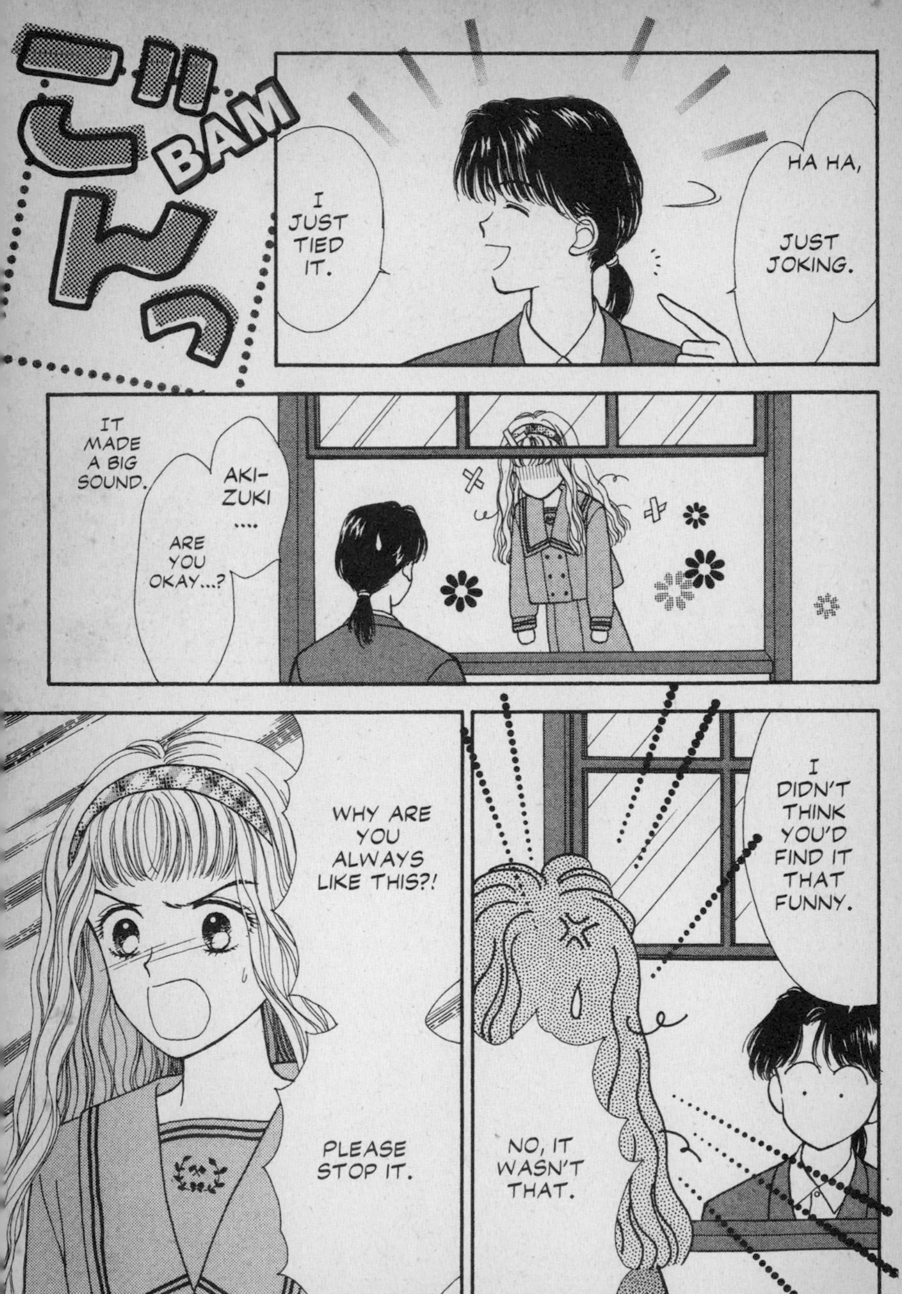
HA HA, JUST JOKING.
I JUST TIED IT.
BAM
AKI-ZUKI .... ARE YOU OKAY...?
IT MADE A BIG SOUND.
I DIDN'T THINK YOU'D FIND IT THAT FUNNY.
NO, IT WASN'T THAT.
WHY ARE YOU ALWAYS LIKE THIS?!
PLEASE STOP IT.

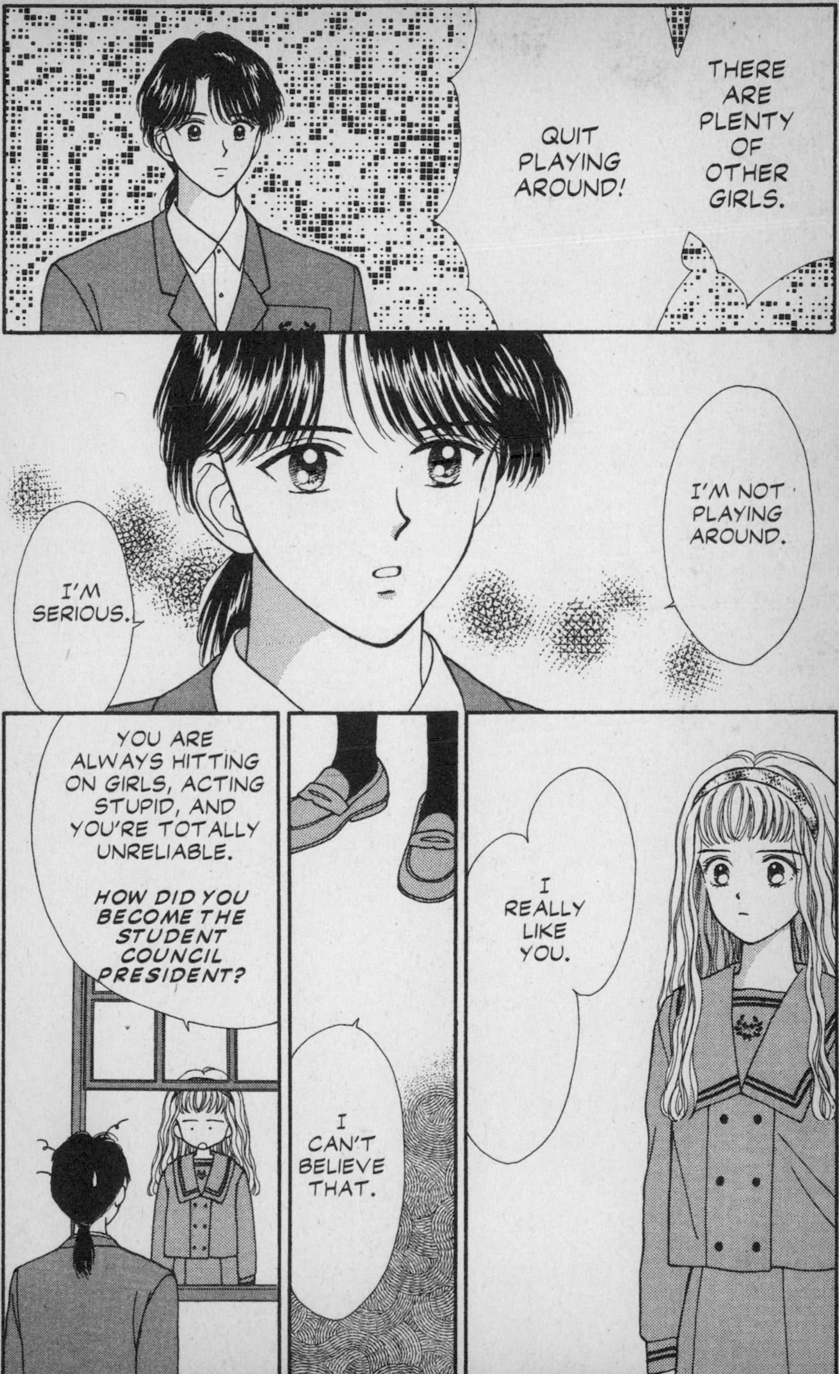
THERE ARE PLENTY OF OTHER GIRLS.
QUIT PLAYING AROUND!
I'M NOT PLAYING AROUND.
I'M SERIOUS.
I REALLY LIKE YOU.
I CAN'T BELIEVE THAT.
YOU ARE ALWAYS HITTING ON GIRLS, ACTING STUPID, AND YOU'RE TOTALLY UNRELIABLE.
HOW DID YOU BECOME THE STUDENT COUNCIL PRESIDENT?

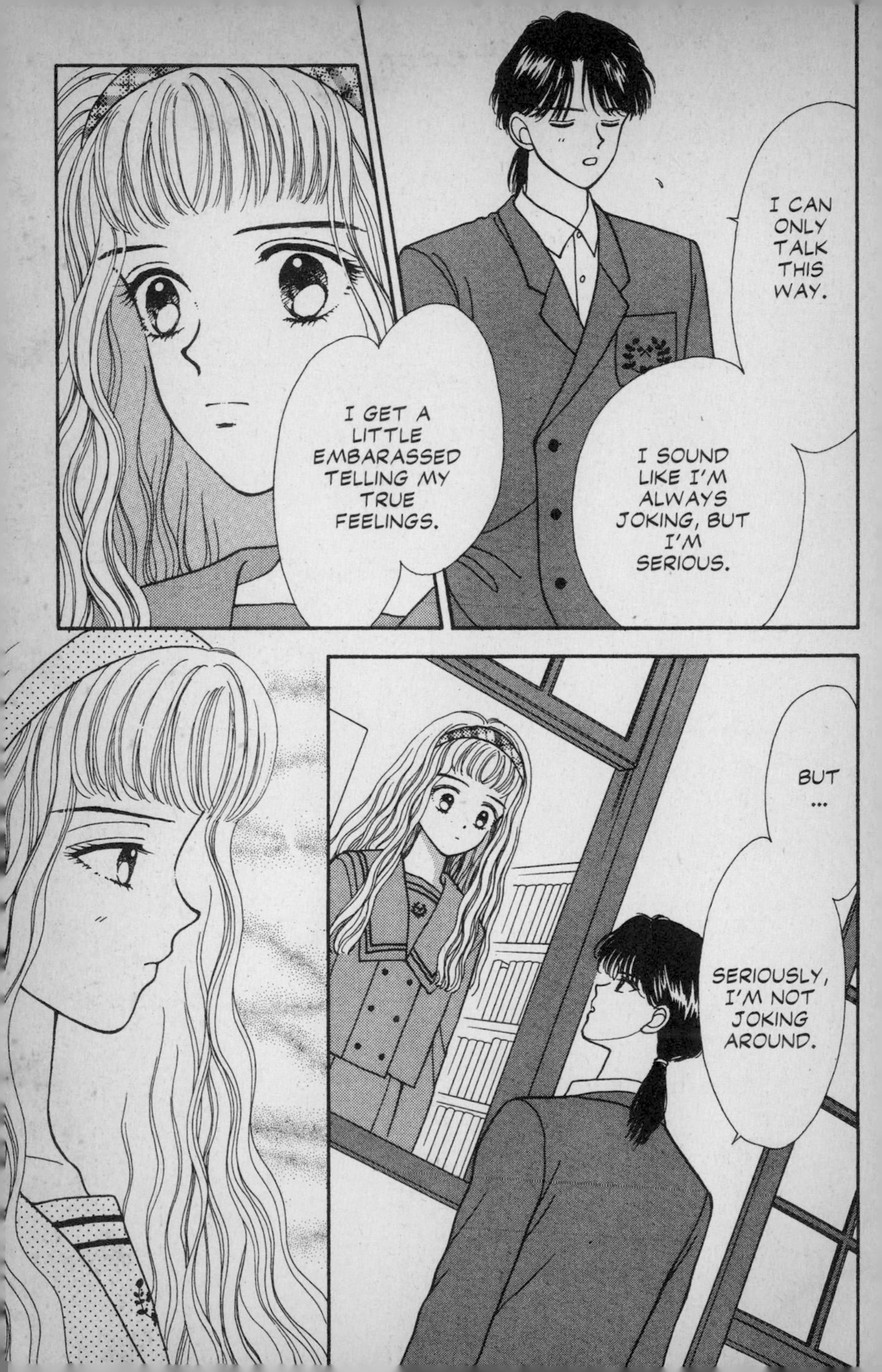
I CAN ONLY TALK THIS WAY.
I SOUND LIKE I'M ALWAYS JOKING, BUT I'M SERIOUS.
I GET A LITTLE EMBARASSED TELLING MY TRUE FEELINGS.
BUT ...
SERIOUSLY, I'M NOT JOKING AROUND.

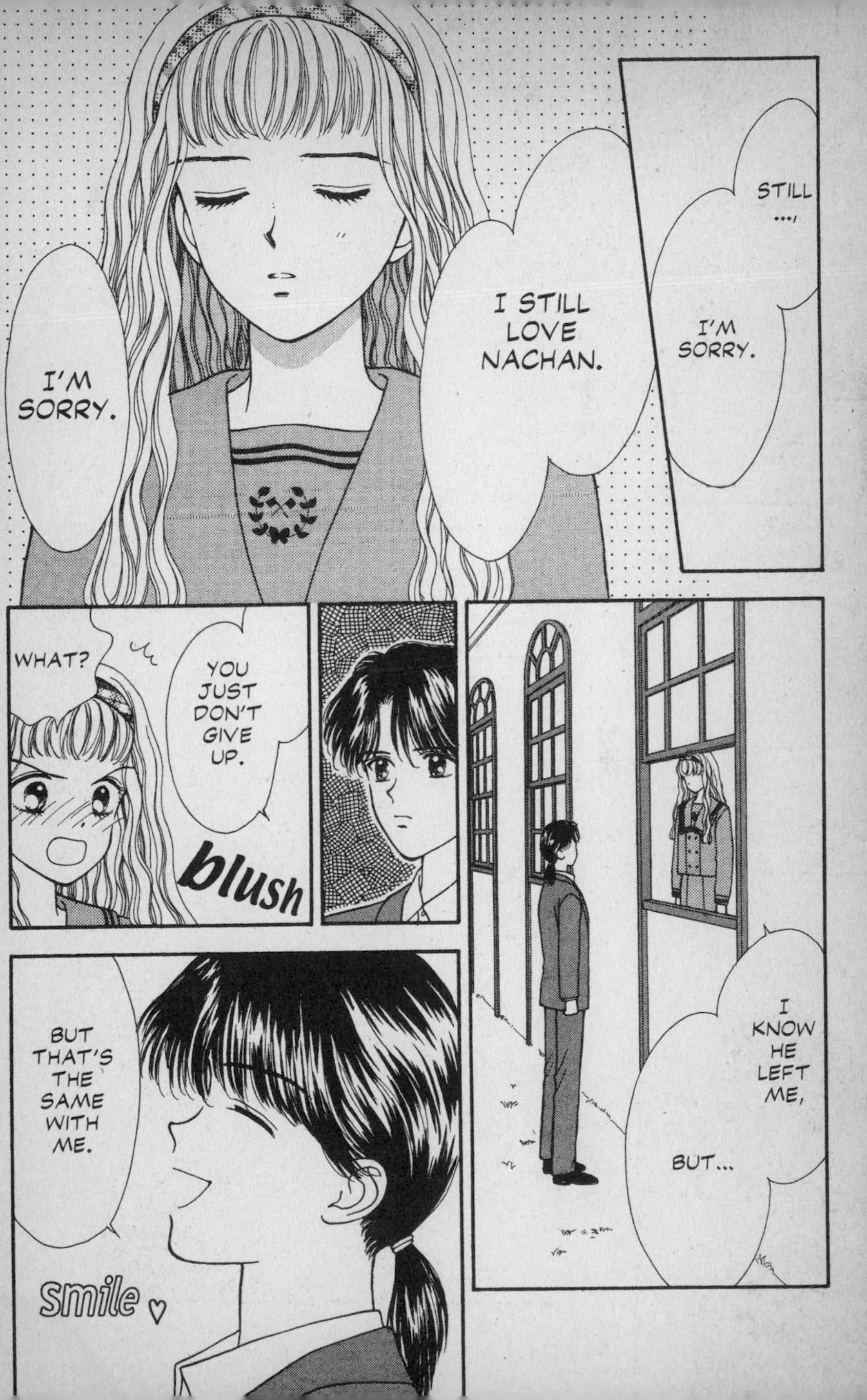
STILL ...,
I'M SORRY.
I STILL LOVE NACHAN.
I'M SORRY.
I KNOW HE LEFT ME,
BUT...
YOU JUST DON'T GIVE UP.
WHAT?
blush
BUT THAT'S THE SAME WITH ME.
smile ♡

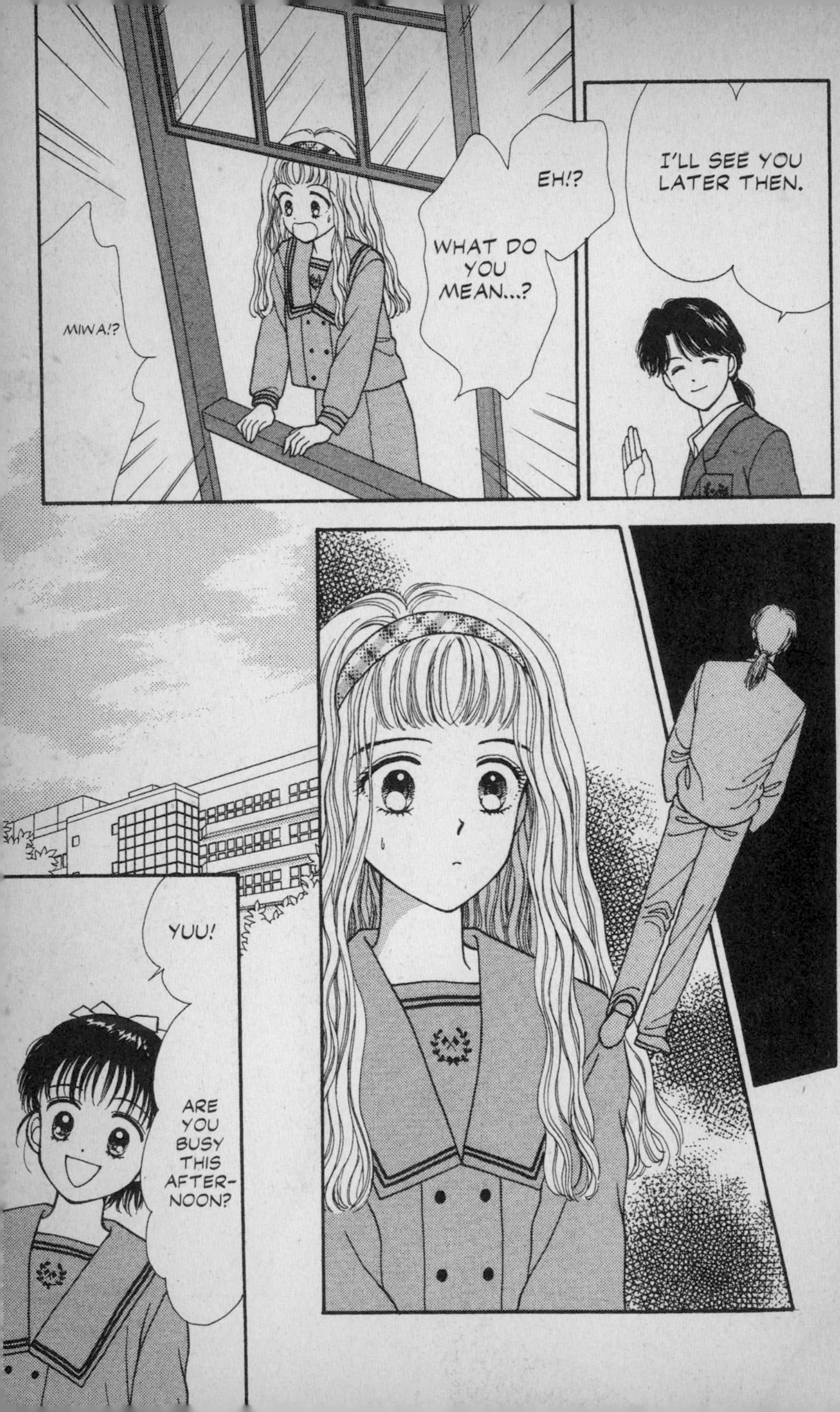
I'LL SEE YOU LATER THEN.
EH!?
WHAT DO YOU MEAN...?
MIWA!?
YUU!
ARE YOU BUSY THIS AFTER-NOON?

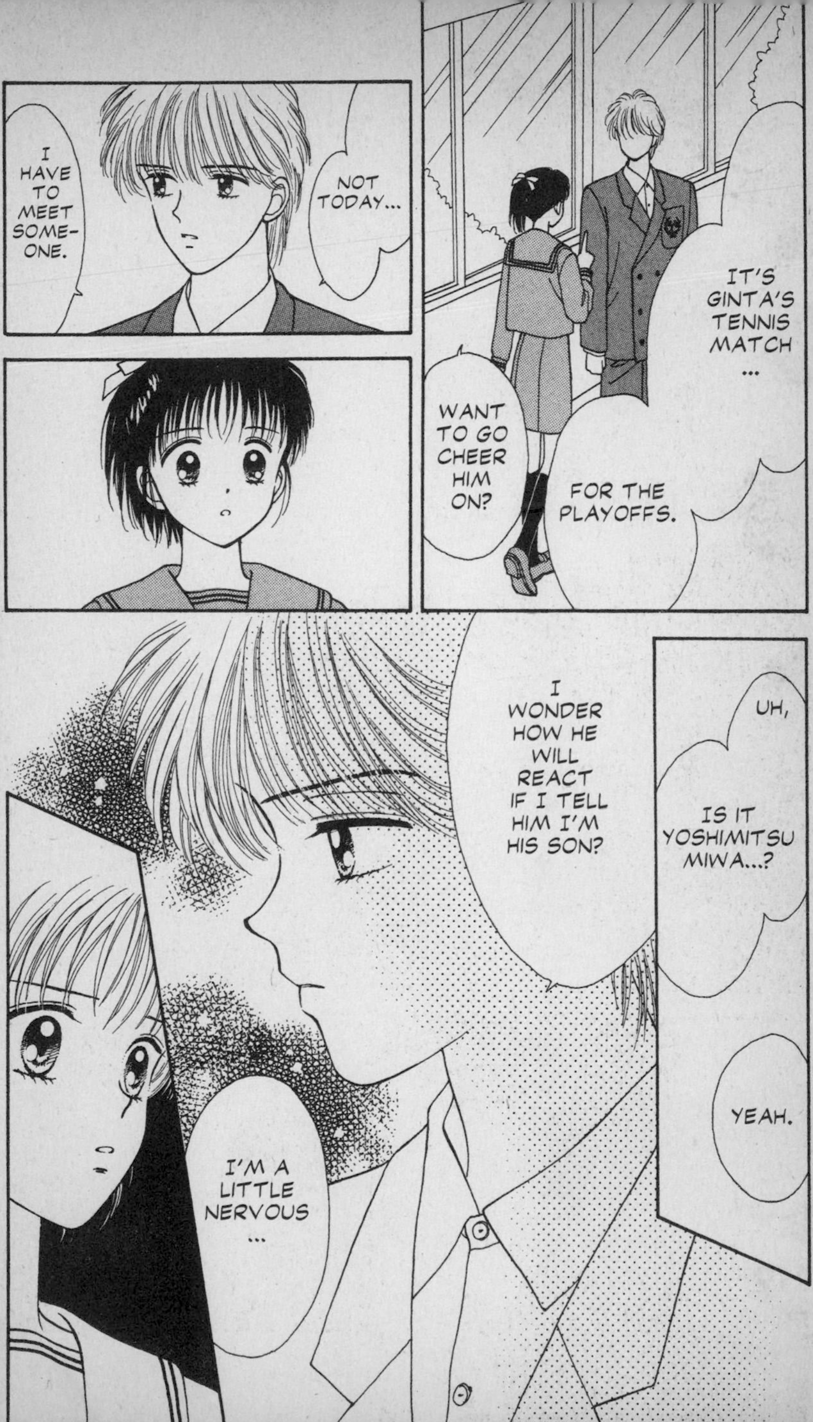
IT'S GINTA'S TENNIS MATCH ...
FOR THE PLAYOFFS.
WANT TO GO CHEER HIM ON?
NOT TODAY...
I HAVE TO MEET SOME-ONE.
UH,
IS IT YOSHIMITSU MIWA...?
YEAH.
I WONDER HOW HE WILL REACT IF I TELL HIM I'M HIS SON?
I'M A LITTLE NERVOUS ...

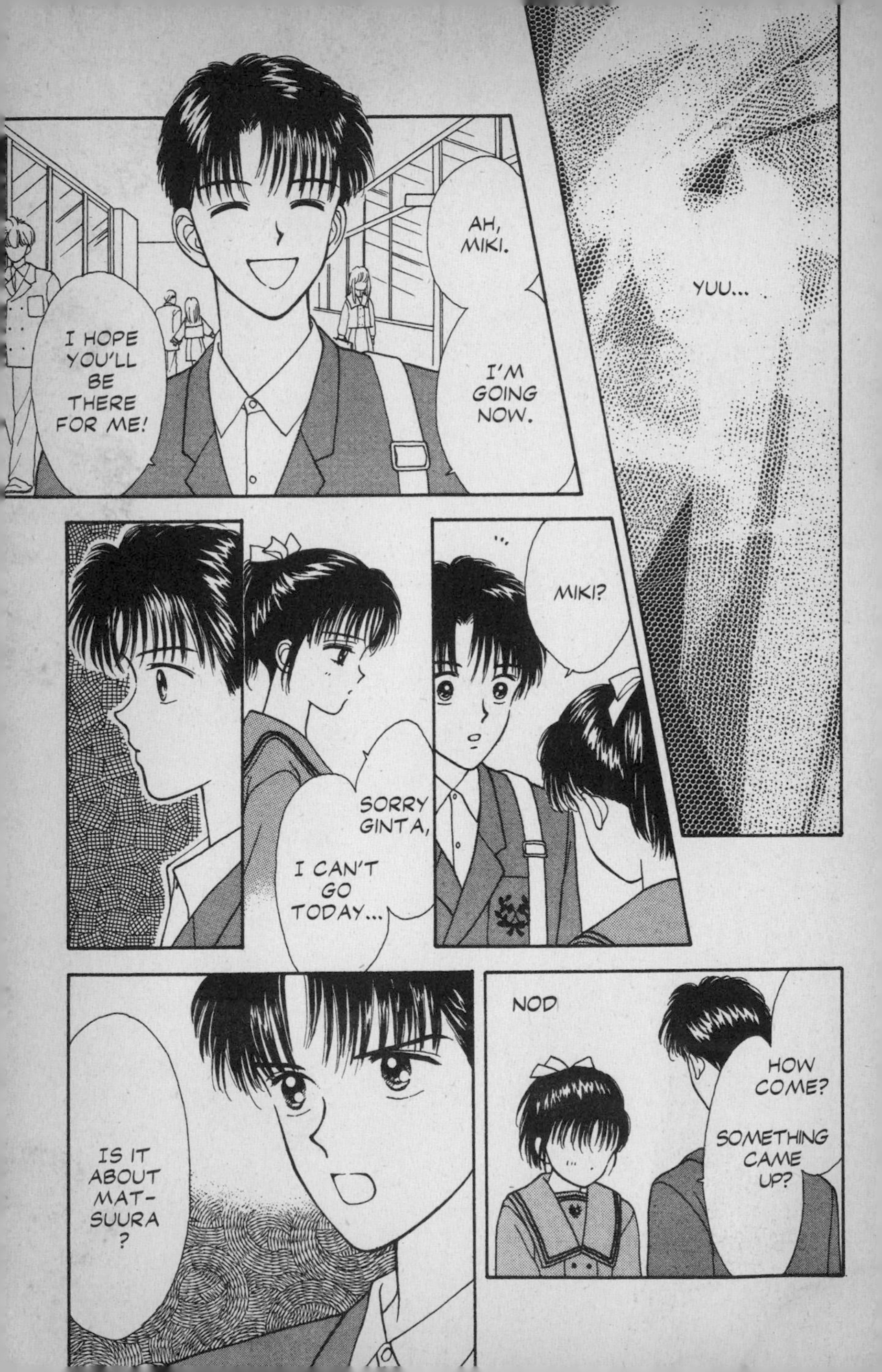
YUU...
AH, MIKI.
I'M GOING NOW.
I HOPE YOU'LL BE THERE FOR ME!
..
MIKI?
SORRY GINTA,
I CAN'T GO TODAY...
NOD
HOW COME?
SOMETHING CAME UP?
IS IT ABOUT MAT-SUURA?

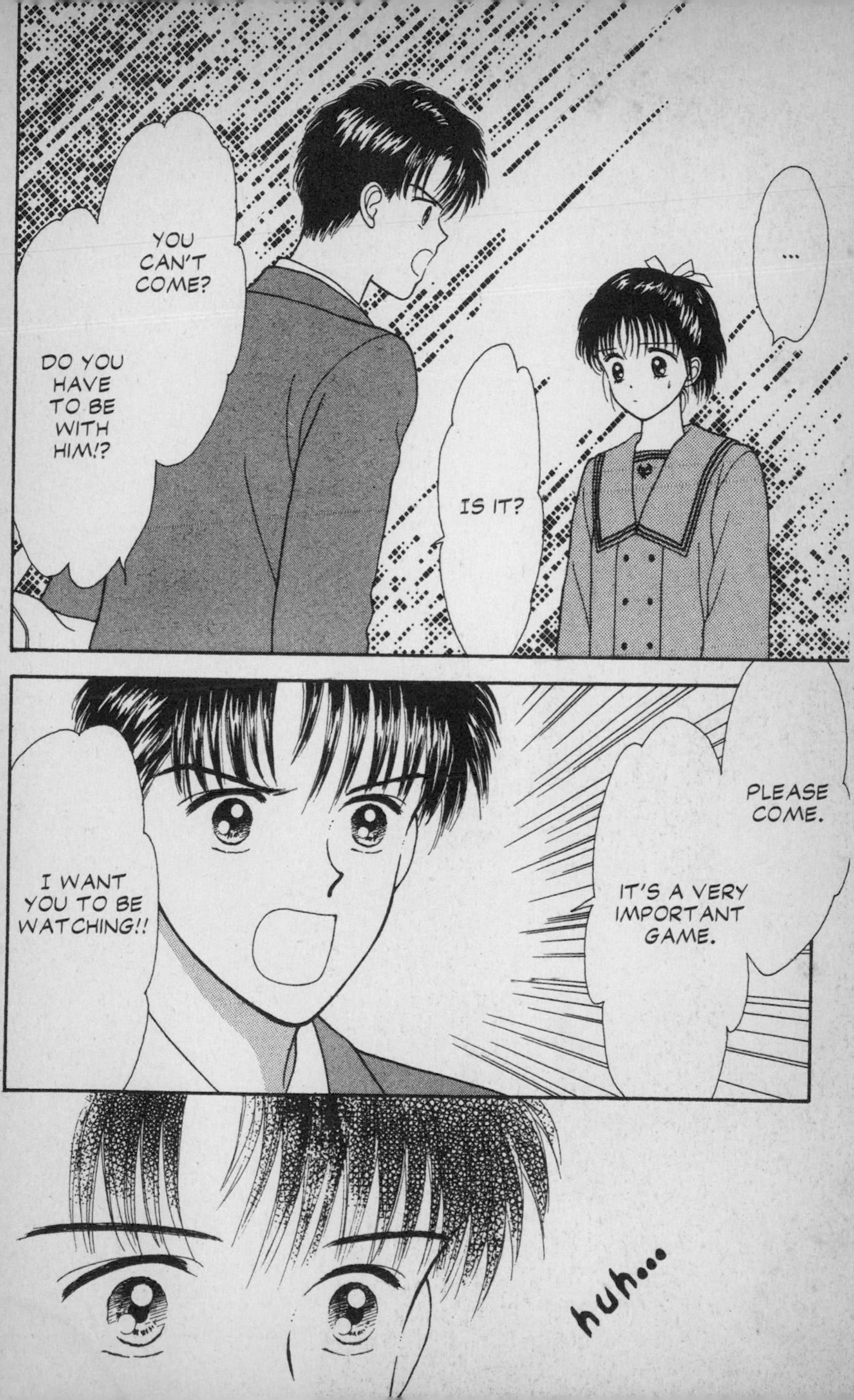
...
IS IT?
YOU CAN'T COME?
DO YOU HAVE TO BE WITH HIM!?
PLEASE COME.
IT'S A VERY IMPORTANT GAME.
I WANT YOU TO BE WATCHING!!
huh...

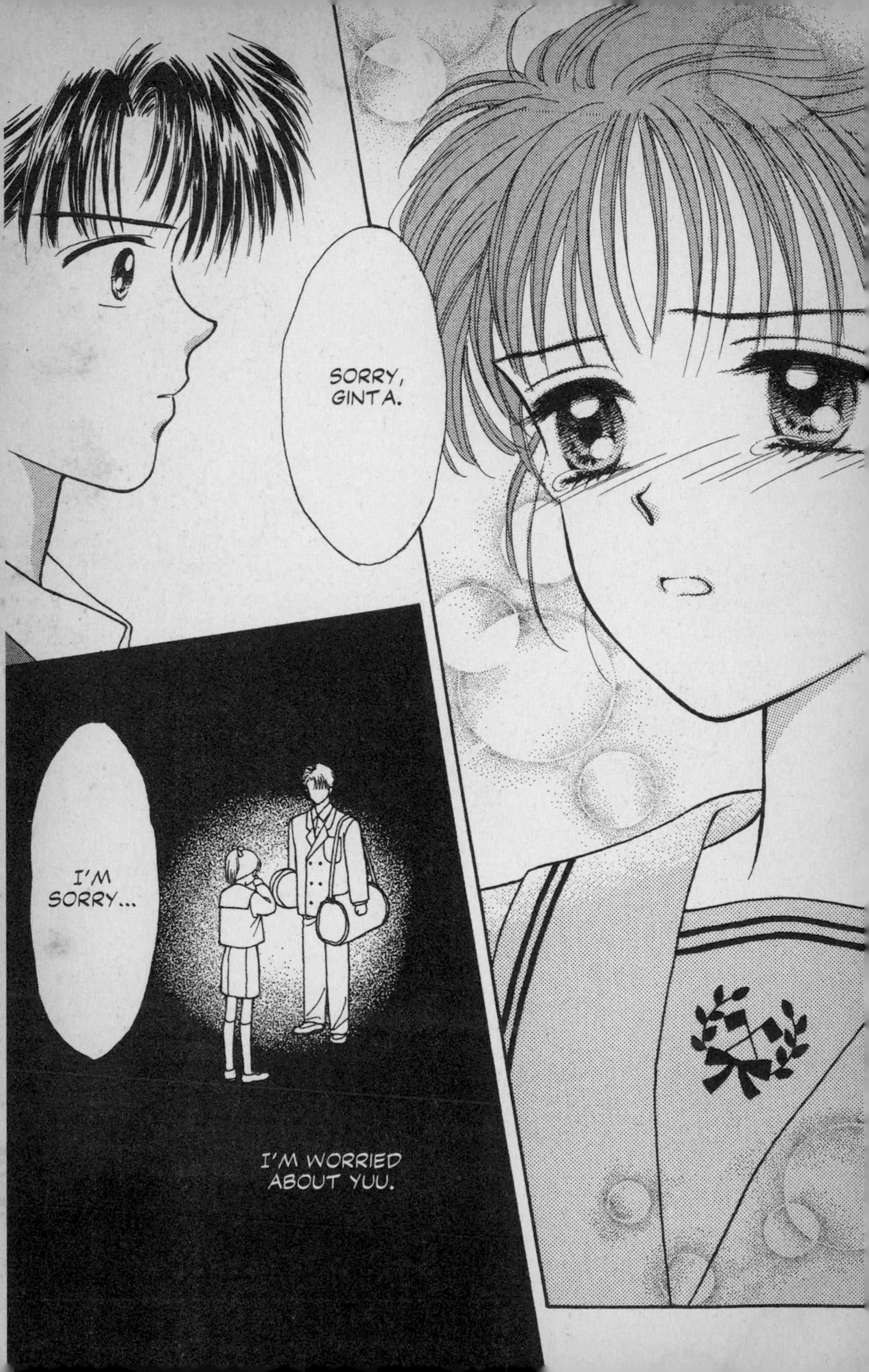
SORRY, GINTA.
I'M SORRY...
I'M WORRIED ABOUT YUU.

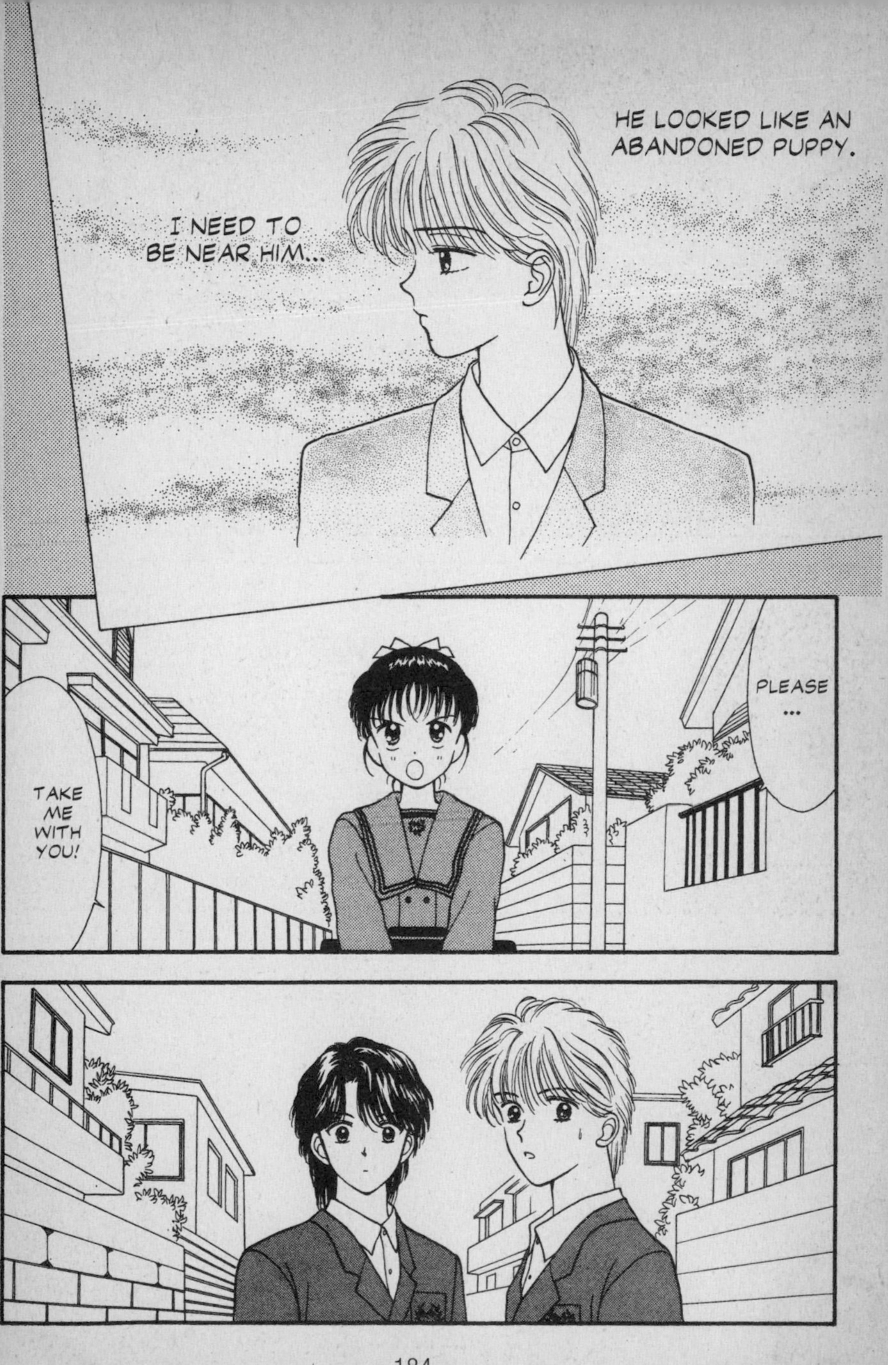
HE LOOKED LIKE AN ABANDONED PUPPY.
I NEED TO BE NEAR HIM...
PLEASE ...
TAKE ME WITH YOU!

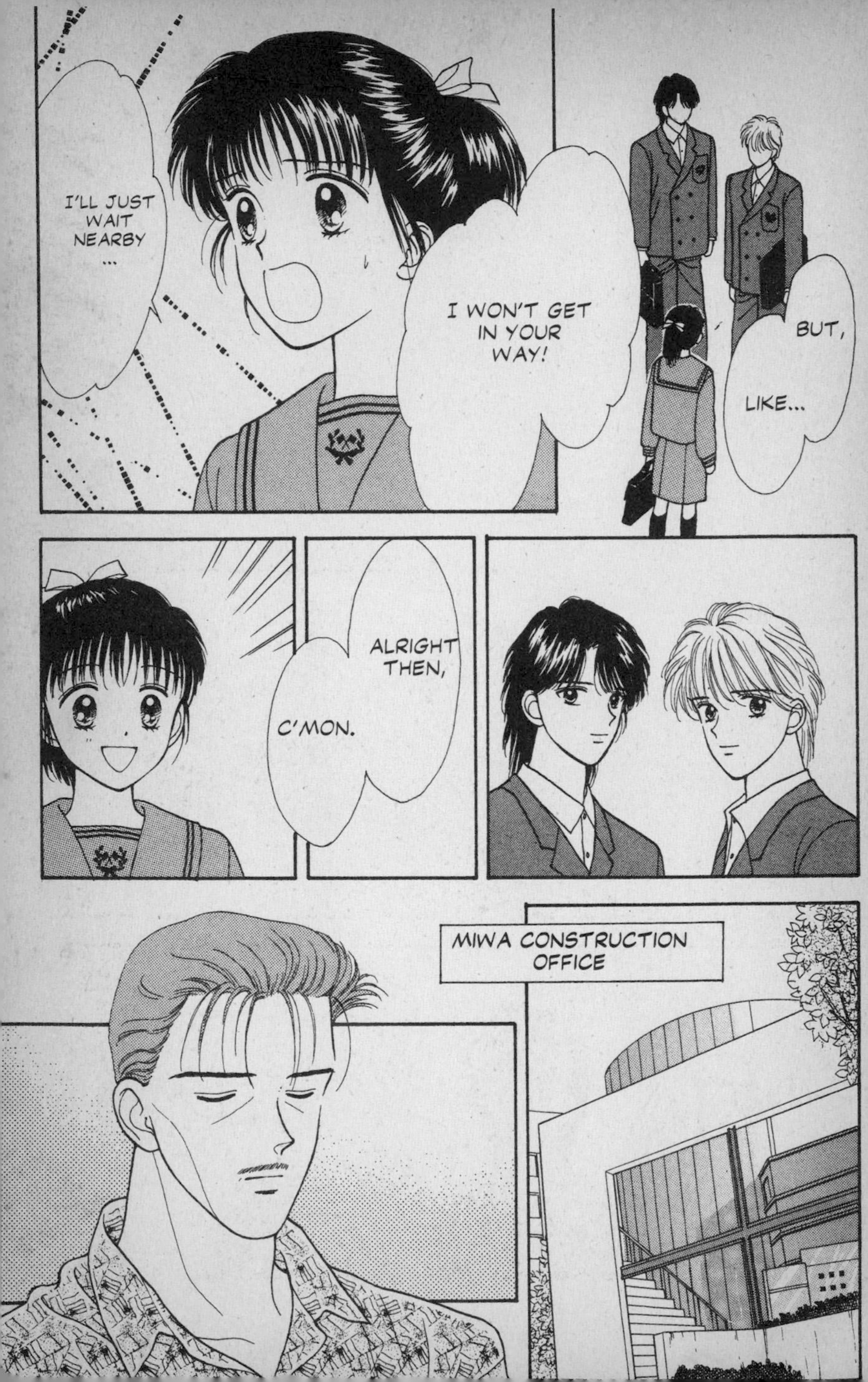
BUT, LIKE...
I'LL JUST WAIT NEARBY ...
I WON'T GET IN YOUR WAY!
ALRIGHT THEN, C'MON.
MIWA CONSTRUCTION OFFICE

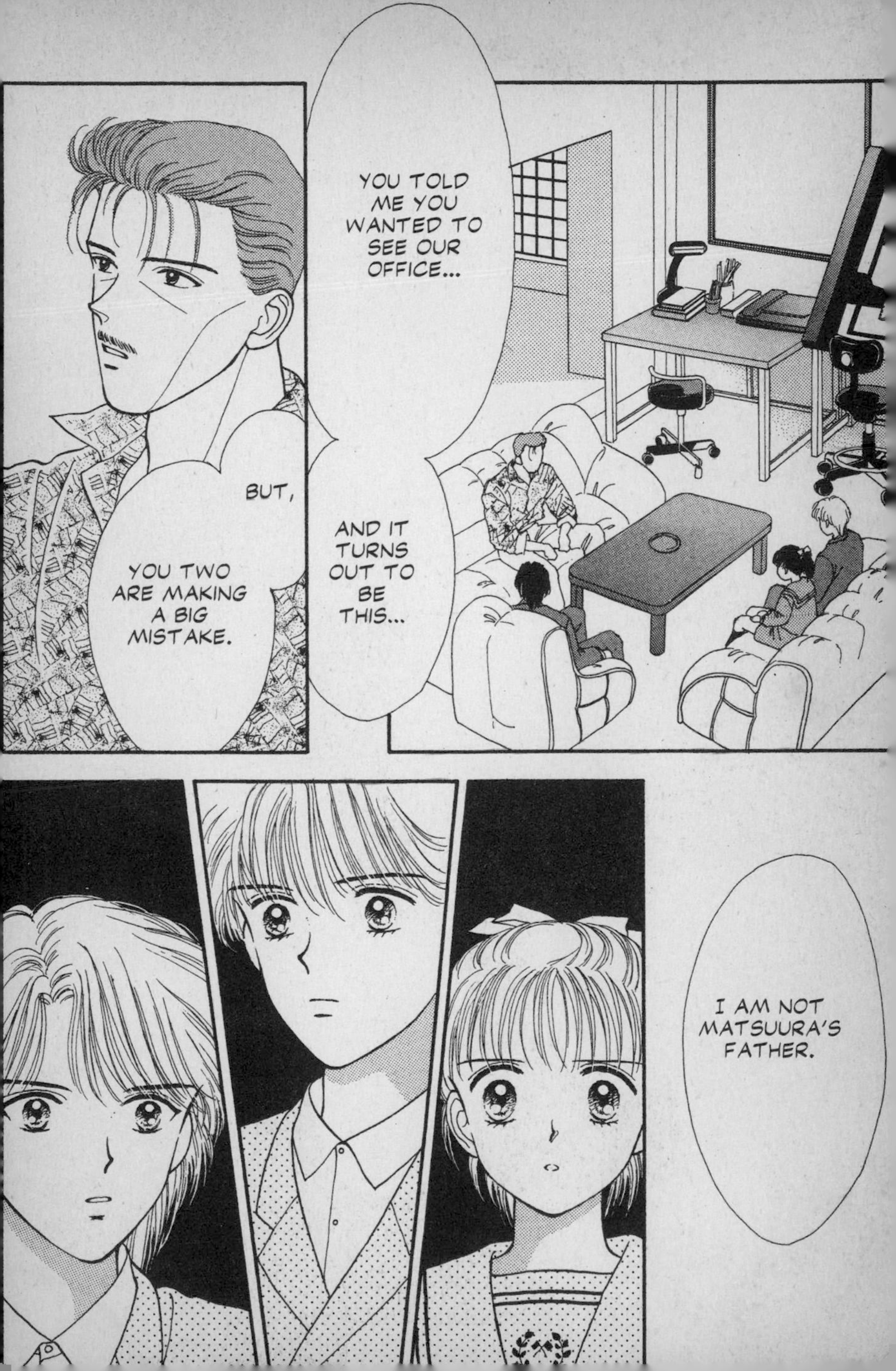
YOU TOLD ME YOU WANTED TO SEE OUR OFFICE...
AND IT TURNS OUT TO BE THIS...
BUT,
YOU TWO ARE MAKING A BIG MISTAKE.
I AM NOT MATSUURA'S FATHER.

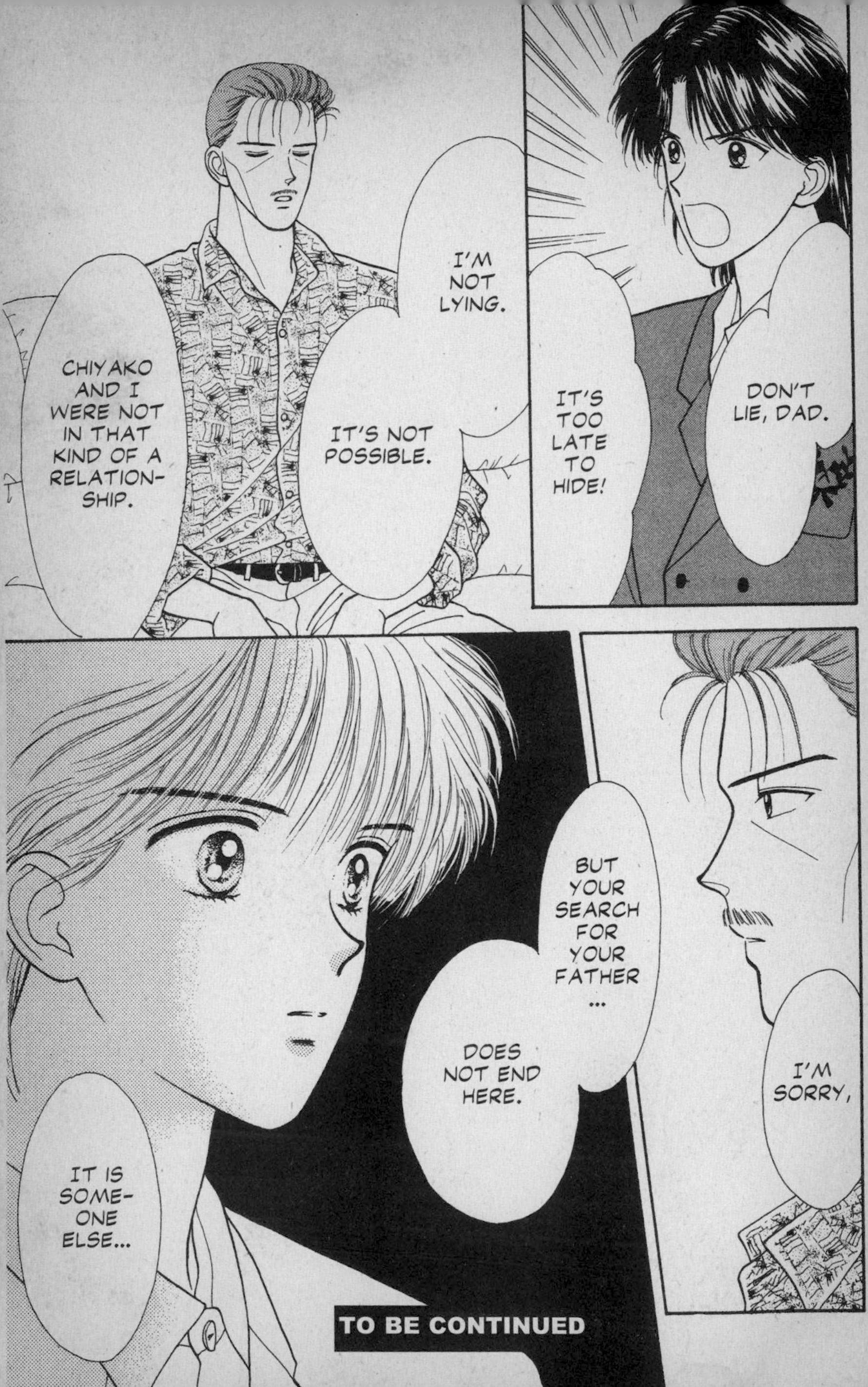
DON'T LIE, DAD.
IT'S TOO LATE TO HIDE!
I'M NOT LYING.
IT'S NOT POSSIBLE.
CHIYAKO AND I WERE NOT IN THAT KIND OF A RELATION-SHIP.
I'M SORRY,
BUT YOUR SEARCH FOR YOUR FATHER ...
DOES NOT END HERE.
IT IS SOME-ONE ELSE...
TO BE CONTINUED

COMING IN 2003

Marmalade Boy

VOLUME 5

JAPAN'S MOST FAMOUS DYSFUNCTIONAL FAMILY GETS EVEN MORE WHACKED WHEN YUU SUSPECTS HIS FATHER IS NOT HIS REAL DAD. AFTER HE CONFRONTS MIWA'S FATHER, HE'S EVEN MORE CONFUSED. HEARTBROKEN AND DESPERATE FOR THE TRUTH, YUU SEEKS SOLACE IN MIKI'S ARMS AND FINALLY PROFESSES HIS LOVE FOR HER. BUT AS MIKI AND YUU TAKE THEIR RELATIONSHIP TO A NEW LEVEL, TEMPTATIONS SEEM TO SPROUT UP EVERYWHERE THEY TURN. A HOT YOUNG MODEL DEVELOPS A MAJOR CRUSH ON YUU, AND A MYSTERIOUS STRANGER TRIES HIS BEST TO WIN MIKI'S DEVOTION. WITH SO MANY RELATIONSHIP ROADBLOCKS IN THEIR PATH, WILL THEIR BUDDING ROMANCE SIZZLE OR FIZZLE? FIND OUT IN THIS DRAMATIC VOLUME OF MARMALADE BOY, COMING IN 2003!